Cambridge Studies in Modern Political Economies

Editors
SUZANNE BERGER, ALBERT O. HIRSCHMAN, AND CHARLES MAIER

Patronage, power, and poverty in southern Italy

T0370681

Patronage, power, and poverty in southern Italy

A tale of two cities

JUDITH CHUBB

College of the Holy Cross

CAMBRIDGE UNIVERSITY PRESS

Cambridge
London   New York   New Rochelle
Melbourne   Sydney

CAMBRIDGE UNIVERSITY PRESS
Cambridge, New York, Melbourne, Madrid, Cape Town, Singapore,
São Paulo, Delhi, Dubai, Tokyo

Cambridge University Press
The Edinburgh Building, Cambridge CB2 8RU, UK

Published in the United States of America by Cambridge University Press, New York

www.cambridge.org
Information on this title: www.cambridge.org/9780521126793

First published 1982
This digitally printed version 2009

A catalogue record for this publication is available from the British Library

Library of Congress Cataloguing in Publication data
Chubb, Judith, 1947–

Patronage, power, and poverty in southern
Italy.

(Cambridge studies in modern political
economies)

Bibliography: p.

Includes index.

1. Italy, Southern – Politics and government – 1945– – Case studies.   2. Italy,
Southern – Economic conditions – 1945– – Case
studies.   3. Naples (Italy) – Politics and
government – 1945– – Case studies.
4. Naples (Italy) – Economic conditions – Case
studies.   5. Palermo (Sicily) – Politics and
government – Case studies.   6. Palermo (Sicily) –
Economic conditions – Case studies.
7. Patronage, Political – Italy, Southern – Case
studies.   I. Title.   II. Series.
DG829.C49   306′.2′09457   82–1325

ISBN 978-0-521-23637-9 Hardback
ISBN 978-0-521-12679-3 Paperback

Contents

v

Part II: The social bases of the machine

Part III: The prospects and the limits of change

Tables and Figures

Tables

vii

Figures

Acknowledgments

This study of urban politics in southern Italy grew out of dissertation research on the bases of local power in Palermo and was subsequently expanded in an attempt to take into account the fascinating sequence of events that began with the left-wing electoral victory in Naples in 1975. The original fieldwork in Rome and Palermo extended over the period from November 1975 to February 1977 and was supported by grants from the Fulbright Commission and the Foreign Area Fellowship Program of the Social Science Research Council. Subsequent research trips to Palermo and Naples in the summers of 1978 and 1980 were funded by the Agnelli Foundation and by a Batchelor (Ford) Summer Faculty Fellowship from the College of the Holy Cross.

My interest in Italy, stimulated during the year I spent at the Bologna Center of the Johns Hopkins School of Advanced International Studies, was deepened by my association with Donald Blackmer and Suzanne Berger. Having first given me the opportunity to work with them as a research assistant and having subsequently encouraged me to pursue graduate study in the Department of Political Science at M.I.T., their contribution to all phases of this project, not to speak of my general intellectual development, has been invaluable. Their example as scholars, as writers, and as teachers remains a standard to which I can only aspire. My intellectual and personal debt to both of them goes far deeper than these few words of thanks can convey. As for the other face of the research – its focus on urban politics and poverty – I am indebted to Michael Lipsky, who stimulated a lasting interest in these issues and in addition provided an essential non-Italianist perspective on the study in its original dissertation form. For much the same reasons, I want to thank Wayne Cornelius, who was generous with his time and comments in the early phases of the research.

x   *Acknowledgments*

In Italy, the staff of the Commission for Cultural Exchange between Italy and the United States, in particular Cipriana Scelba and Luigi Filadoro, were especially helpful and encouraging during the year I spent in Palermo, in terms both of interest in my research and material support in moments of need. I am equally indebted to the staff of ISVI in Catania, especially Professors Alberto Spreafico, Raimondo Catanzaro, and Franco Cazzola, and the members of the research group on the DC in Catania, for their material assistance, their insights into the bases of DC power and, above all, their personal hospitality. Professor Luigi Graziano of the University of Turin gave me invaluable assistance in clarifying the direction of the research in midstream, as well as by inviting me to present my preliminary results to his seminar in Turin; the exposure to Turin and the opportunity to discuss the South with northern students was an important cultural and intellectual experience for one who had been so deeply immersed in the South. In Palermo, Professor Gabriele Morello and the staff of ISIDA provided me with a place to work and with other greatly appreciated material support; their generosity made a difficult research situation somewhat easier.

My greatest debt, of course, is to all the people – in Rome, Palermo, and Naples – who consented to be interviewed and who tolerated my incessant questions. I owe a special thanks to Rosario Nicoletti, the regional secretary of the DC in Sicily, who let me follow his electoral campaign in June 1976, an experience that provided an otherwise impossible exposure to DC politics at the grass roots. With regard to the Neapolitan research, I can never repay the cordiality of the functionaries of the Provincial Federation of the PCI, without whose assistance Chapter 10 would never have been possible. Above all, I want to thank the people of the *quartieri popolari* of Palermo, whose hospitality to a foreigner in their midst sustained me through the long months of research.

Some of the material contained in this book has previously appeared in various forms: "The Social Bases of an Urban Political Machine: The Christian Democratic Party in Palermo," *Political Science Quarterly*, 96 (Spring 1981); and "Naples Under the Left: The Limits of Local Change," *Comparative Politics*, 13 (October 1980). Both of these articles also appear in slightly revised form in S. Eisenstadt and R. Lemarchand, eds., *Political Clientelism, Patronage and Development* (Beverly Hills, Calif.: Sage, 1981).

JUDITH CHUBB

Cambridge, Mass.
May 1982

Abbreviations

ACLI	Associazione Cristiana dei Lavoratori Italiani
AMNU	Azienda Municipalizzata Nettezza Urbana
CGIL	Confederazione Generale Italiana del Lavoro
CISL	Confederazione Italiana Sindacati Lavoratori
DC	Democrazia Cristiana
ESPI	Ente Siciliano per la Promozione Industriale
IACP	Istituto Autonomo Case Popolari
INPS	Istituto Nazionale Previdenza Sociale
MSI	Movimento Sociale Italiano
PCI	Partito Comunista Italiano
PLI	Partito Liberale Italiano
PRG	Piano Regolatore Generale
PRI	Partito Repubblicano Italiano
PSDI	Partito Socialista Democratico Italiano
PSI	Partito Socialista Italiano
UIL	Unione Italiana del Lavoro

Introduction

Palermo, exalted for its beauty by the Arabs 1,000 years ago, in the thirteenth-century site of the court of Frederick II, Holy Roman Emperor, and one of the major cultural centers of Europe, today enjoys quite a different fame. Capital of the mafia, a national symbol of venality and corruption in local government, Palermo, Italy's sixth largest city, is balanced precariously between Europe and Africa. Behind the façade of a prosperous modern metropolis, the crumbling slums, narrow twisting alleyways, and dank courtyards of the old city harbor conditions of housing, health, and sanitation more reminiscent of a Cairo or a Calcutta than of a major European city. Life in Palermo is a perpetual drama, from the daily torment of the city's chaotic traffic to the routine collapse of yet another *palazzo* in the old city to the periodic breakdown of basic services like garbage collection or public transportation to not infrequent outbursts of mafia warfare, which leave the city's streets strewn with bullet-ridden corpses.

In the face of all this, local government looks on in total impotence, more concerned with factional struggles over the distribution of key patronage positions than with the increasingly dramatic conditions of life in the city. Probably the major policy issue confronting local government in Palermo is the *risanamento* ("urban renewal") of the old city, devastated by the Allied bombing raids of 1943 and dealt a further blow by the earthquake of 1968. Until 1976 the progressive disintegration of the old city proceeded, despite endless electoral promises, undisturbed by any attempts at public intervention, with countless historical and architectural monuments allowed to deteriorate beyond hope of restoration. Crumbling buildings were propped up precariously by long iron bars installed across narrow alleyways, and entire streets were walled off to prevent the evicted inhabitants from reentering condemned dwellings or children from playing in the heaps of rubble from the *crolli* ("collapses") that have become an

1

everyday fact of life in the city. In 1976–77 national and regional funds totaling over U.S. $740 million were allocated to Palermo for the *risanamento* of the old city and related public-works projects, and the city was caught up in a heated political debate over how the money should be spent. Five years later, nothing had changed except that the old city had deteriorated still further, and the value of the original funds had been decimated by inflation. Not a lira had yet been spent; only at the end of 1980 were the initial technical proposals for the first phase of the *risanamento* even presented to the City Council.

Related to the failure of local administrations over the past thirty years to deal with the restoration of the old city is the desperate shortage of low-income housing in Palermo. Although several large public-housing projects have in fact been built since the mid-1960s, their allocation has traditionally been reserved for electoral purposes. Thus, in 1975–76 it required a mass protest movement on the part of residents of the old city to compel the city's administrators to assign several blocs of apartments that had been standing empty for months. Even where low-income residents have succeeded in obtaining public housing, they often find themselves banished to concrete deserts without basic infrastructures like water, electricity, and sewage lines or social services like schools, clinics, pharmacies, and the like.

Although the failure of public policy in Palermo is most evident in low-income neighborhoods, the quality of service delivery throughout the city is abysmally low. Public-service agencies have tended to function more to mobilize votes for local politicians than to maintain acceptable conditions of urban existence. The most glaring example is the city's garbage collection agency Azienda Municipalizzata Nettezza Urbana (AMNU). By the end of 1976 the sanitary conditions of the city had deteriorated to such a level – with garbage often lying uncollected for weeks or even months at a time in some of the poorer neighborhoods – that the local magistrate initiated an official investigation of AMNU, threatening its administrators with charges of criminal negligence, and of having exposed the city to the risk of a major epidemic. Not only do public services function sporadically and inefficiently at best but at times factional struggle within and among the governing parties becomes so intense that elective bodies and other public agencies are reduced to total immobility for extended periods of time. Thus, for example, the administration of the Province of Palermo virtually ceased to function from June 1975 until the end of 1976, and the Banco di Sicilia, the island's major credit institution, remained without a regularly elected president and *consig-*

lio d'amministrazione for a decade from 1969 until 1979 – both because of a bitter internal power struggle within the major governing party. Finally, the most telling indictment of local government in Palermo came in the mid-1960s, when, after a series of scandals related to the building boom sweeping the city and the simultaneous outbreak of a full-scale mafia war for control of the construction industry, the Italian Parliament created the so-called Antimafia Commission, which undertook an in-depth investigation of the activities of the municipal administration, revealing far-reaching collusion between city administrators and powerful mafia interests.

Yet, despite scandals, administrative paralysis, and the progressive degradation of the conditions of urban life resulting from them, the residents of Palermo have since 1952 regularly elected city governments controlled by the Christian Democratic Party (DC). In 1975, when virtually every other major Italian city turned to the left, electing local governments controlled by Communist-Socialist coalitions, and again in 1980, Palermo not only returned the Christian Democrats to power, but gave the party ever larger electoral margins. Given the undisputed failure of local government not only to provide essential public services but even to guarantee the functioning of normal administrative activities, how can the unbroken electoral success of the DC over the past thirty years be explained? By what means, despite its dismal record of performance, has the DC succeeded in generating and sustaining a solid electoral base in almost every sector of the urban population? Why have opposition groups critical of the DC's thirty-year record of misgovernment proven unable to mobilize mass support for an alternative? This last question assumes even greater relevance in a country like Italy, which boasts the world's largest nonruling Communist Party (30% of the vote in 1979), a party with formidable organizational and mobilizational resources. How can one explain the failure of the Communist Party in Palermo to attract a mass following, especially among the urban poor, who have paid the highest price for the catastrophic conditions of urban life that successive Christian Democratic administrations have bequeathed the city?

At the most general level, political scientists and others have sought explanations for political behavior like that observed in Palermo in the phenomenon of "clientelism." Until recently the bulk of the literature on clientelism consisted of anthropological studies of patron–client relationships in small rural villages.[1] From the anthropological perspective, clientelism refers to a particular kind of interpersonal relationship, based on the direct exchange of favors between two actors:

[It is] a special case of dyadic (two-person) ties involving a largely instrumental friendship in which an individual of higher socio-economic status (patron) uses his own influence and resources to provide protection or benefits,
or both, for a person of lower status (client) who, for his part, reciprocates by
offering general support and assistance, including personal services, to the
patron.[2]

The defining characteristics of the patron–client relationship are rec-
iprocity, inequality of status, and the personal, enduring nature of
the relationship, a kind of lopsided friendship. What distinguishes
clientelism from other forms of exchange relationship is its asymmet-
rical nature. In a patron–client relationship power is unidirectional,
the creation of a bond of personal obligation being used by the patron to subordinate the client to his will.[3] The key to such a relationship is the concentration of critical resources in the hands of a few, so
that the client, in order to enjoy access to the protection and material
resources controlled by the powerful, has no alternative but to return
loyally the benefits received.

Given this general definition of clientelism as a direct exchange relationship between two actors of unequal status and power, it is necessary to distinguish between the traditional patron–client bond
based on the economic position and personal prestige of the individual notable and clientelism as a system of gaining and managing political power on the part of a mass-based political party. Political science research has focused on the latter phenomenon, the political
machine, both in its classic form in American big-city politics of the
nineteenth and early twentieth centuries and as a major instrument
of mass mobilization in the present-day politics of many developing
nations.[4] In countries where patron–client ties were already deeply
rooted in traditional social structure, the introduction of universal
suffrage and competitive party politics transformed these preexisting
influence hierarchies into effective channels for the delivery of votes
from the newly enfranchised lower classes. In its early stages political
clientelism takes the form of competing cliques of traditional notables, each with his own personal following and personal ties to those
in positions of political power. The machine as a political institution
comes into being only when the organizational superstructure of a
modern mass-based political party is substituted for the personal influence networks of the notables. At this point the party organization
itself assumes the role of patron and the resources of the state take the
place of the personal economic and social power of the notable. Although with the emergence of the machine the forms of political organization undergo a radical transformation, the nature of political
support remains unchanged. The role of the traditional notable is

now performed by the party secretary, mayor, or parliamentary deputy, but politics continues to be rooted in the exchange of the vote for short-term individual benefits rather than in broader appeals of program or ideology. (This process of transformation of the clientelism of the notables into the mass patronage of the party machine in the specific case of southern Italy will be described in detail in Chapter 3.)

One of the central concerns of much of the literature on clientelism has been to identify the conditions under which clientelistic systems of power are likely to emerge and to perpetuate themselves, or, from the opposite perspective, the circumstances under which the mass support for political machines might be expected to break down. Political scientists and other students of clientelism have explained the maintenance of political machines primarily in terms of a constantly expanding flow of resources over time.[5] The assumption has been that any political system relying predominantly on short-term material incentives for popular support is by definition engaged in the wholesale squandering of public resources. It follows, then, that clientelism carries with it the seeds of its eventual demise; either the exhaustion of the available resource base through patronage spending or the onset of economic crisis for reasons external to the system itself will irrevocably undermine the popular base of the machine.

Palermo constitutes an ideal test case for theories of clientelism focusing on the need for a constantly expanding resource base. For thirty years the DC has maintained power in Palermo in a situation of chronic resource shortage. Not only is the local economy characterized by severe resource constraints (see Chapter 2) but the flow of resources from the center, which many observers[6] have seen as the key to the enduring strength of clientelism in southern Italy, has been very limited in Palermo. Furthermore, in 1975 and 1980, in the midst of the most severe economic crisis of the postwar period, the Christian Democrats in Palermo actually increased their share of the vote.

Why do people continue to support the machine in a situation of economic crisis when, given the shrinking resource base, the prospect of personal benefit from the patron–client bond is greatly reduced? The case of the Christian Democratic machine in Palermo clearly demonstrates that the essence of clientelism lies less in the distribution of plenty than in the skillful manipulation of scarcity. The key to understanding the patron–client bond is that it depends not on a continuous stream of benefits, but rather on sustaining the expectation of rewards in the maximum number of people with the minimum payoff in concrete benefits. In a situation of resource scarcity like that of southern Italy and in the absence of a competing political force that can offer concrete resources to replace those controlled by the machine, most people will continue to support the possibility, however slim, of immediate gain from the machine as opposed to abstract promises of long-term change. This reconsideration of the resource base necessary to sustain the machine is reinforced by detailed examination of the nature of the patronage resources upon which the DC in Palermo has depended. Although large-scale patronage hiring for local government jobs has, in Palermo as elsewhere, played an important role in the politics of the machine, this is not necessarily – as has been often assumed in other studies – the key to explaining mass support for clientelistic parties. On the contrary, as the research on Palermo demonstrates, a large proportion of DC patronage and, I would argue, that part which is most significant for understanding the nature of clientelistic power, is based on the discretionary implementation of the bureaucratic and regulatory functions of local government and implies no financial drain whatsoever on the public treasury.

It is thus not the quantity of available resources that is the determining factor for the survival of the machine, but rather the ability of the machine to control the channels of access to critical resources of all kinds, political and bureaucratic as well as strictly economic. Such concentration of power in the hands of a single party is particularly accentuated in a country like Italy, with its highly centralized administrative structure, extensive state intervention in the economy, unbroken domination of the central state by a single party since 1947, and intense politicization of the administrative apparatus. In a situation like that of southern Italy, where one-party domination is combined with public control of almost all relevant resources, there is no reason why economic crisis need necessarily spell the demise of the machine. Far from undermining mass support for the machine, economic crisis may, in fact, as in the case of Palermo, actually strengthen it, because, as the supply of available resources shrinks, the role of the dominant party as an obligatory intermediary between the individual citizen and the resources of the state is further accentuated.

Another major issue in the literature on clientelism is the question of who supports political machines and what kinds of benefits they receive in exchange for their support. The issue of the social bases of the machine has been addressed primarily from the perspective of the political participation of the urban poor. In works on both the big-city American machines of the nineteenth and early twentieth centuries and contemporary Third World (for the most part Latin-American) cities, the dominant assumption has been that the poor constitute the principal basis of mass support for political machines.[7]

The case of Palermo unequivocally refutes that assumption. Although a significant proportion of the urban poor in Palermo do support the machine, the electoral base of the DC extends beyond them to embrace almost every sector of the city's population, with the middle classes constituting as important a source of machine strength as do the poor.

The question of the class basis of clientelistic power in Palermo is explored in detail in Part II of this book, which provides an in-depth analysis of the concrete patronage mechanisms linking the DC to each of the major social groups in the city – white-collar employees, the local entrepreneurial elite (including the mafia), the traditional middle classes (shopkeepers and artisans), and the urban poor. In addition to revising earlier notions as to the class basis of clientelistic appeals, this investigation of the social bases of the machine demonstrates that general terms like "clientelism" and "patronage" tell us very little about the actual mechanisms linking the machine to distinct social groups. The research on the DC machine in Palermo reveals the existence of a range of patronage resources much broader and more diverse than has been depicted in most studies of political machines, as well as a clear distinction in the forms of patronage the party employs in its relationship with each social group. Not only does patronage mean something very different for the city employee or building contractor than it does for the street-vendor or slum family, but, more importantly, as has been indicated above, the diversity of patronage resources available to local governments means that, with the exception of the white-collar middle class (predominantly public employees), support for the machine on the part of other social groups depends primarily on benefits that require no direct expenditure of public funds.

Chapters 7 and 8 of this study will, however, be devoted entirely to the question of the relationship between the machine and the urban poor, looking not only at the mechanisms by which the DC maintains support in low-income neighborhoods but also at attempts to mobilize the poor on an alternative basis. Cross-national research has recognized clientelism as one of the predominant forms of political integration of the urban poor, especially in developing countries. At the same time, clientelism has been widely regarded as a backward or aberrant form of political participation, in contrast to the "norm" of interest groups and political parties based on programmatic or ideological ties. Until recently support for political machines on the part of the poor was seen to a large extent as a reflection of the backwardness of the poor themselves – their "nonpoliticization," their social and economic marginality, their lack of integration into the dominant culture.[8] It has been argued, for example, in the American context, that the poor, especially those from Catholic or peasant-based cultures, are more likely to hold a "political ethos" that is "private-regarding," in contrast to the middle class, particularly those of Anglo-Saxon Protestant origin, whose political ethos is founded on the idea that "politics should be based on public rather than private motives and, accordingly, should stress the virtues of honesty, impartiality, and efficiency."[9]

This kind of explanation of support for the machine, focusing on the distinctive characteristics of a presumed "culture of poverty" or on the "marginality" of the poor, was challenged during the 1970s by a number of new studies of the political behavior of the urban poor in several Latin American cities.[10] In contrast to the earlier literature, these studies emphasize the relationship between the poor and the larger political and socioeconomic context. In this view, the cultural values of the poor are no longer seen as the independent variable producing distinctively "backward" forms of political behavior. Instead, both the values of the poor and their political expression are explained as rational adaptations to external structural constraints, both economic and political. In those cases where clientelism constitutes the dominant form of political behavior among the urban poor, it is thus understood not in terms of the characteristics and values of those who support the machine, but rather in terms of the organizational choices of elites and of the presence or absence of alternative channels of demand making for the poor. As Martin Shefter put it in his study of the emergence of the Tammany Hall machine:

> Political machines did not simply reflect an underlying (and unambiguous) set of popular loyalties and preferences. Rather, dominant machines were *political institutions:* they succeeded in institutionalizing a particular pattern of such preferences, and in the process, other equally plausible lines of cleavage were organized out of politics . . . As a ruling *institution,* the survival of the machine . . . was contingent upon its capacity to channel and control the political behavior of its supporters, as much as to represent their preferences, and upon its capacity to engender an autonomous set of loyalties – loyalty to the institution itself – among its supporters.[11]

Although written with reference to the American experience of the nineteenth century, the above citation applies equally well to contemporary machines in southern Italy and other developing countries. In attempting to understand the political behavior of the urban poor, the critical question is not whether the poor are marginal or integrated, but on what terms their integration takes place. In contrast to cultural explanations of political behavior, an emphasis on elite organizational choice directs attention to the ways in which a political system is structured and how it distributes rewards as the critical factors in determining the responses of subordinate groups. What is seen by the poor as the proper scope of political activity, what alternative channels of political participation are available, and how these alternatives are evaluated in terms of potential costs and benefits, are not autonomous products of political culture. Demand making by the poor is strongly conditioned by the power of elites to set the parameters of legitimate political behavior. From this perspective, which the present study shares, the machine can best be understood as an effective and low-cost instrument for the preservation of the social, economic, and political status quo. By integrating the poor into the existing system with short-term individualistic rewards and the illusion of participation, the machine mitigates social and political conflict and impedes the organization of the poor along alternative lines. At the same time, the longer-term needs of the poor are not met, as the machine serves established economic interests at the expense of investment in substantive social policy.

The attempt to explain political participation in terms of the structural constraints, as well as opportunities, operating upon various social groups requires analysis not only of the linkages between specific social groups and the local political and economic context but also of the relationship between local power and the national political and economic system. One of the shortcomings of much research on local politics has been the assumption that either specific social groups or the local community as a whole can be studied in isolation. This study takes as its point of departure the opposite assumption: it is impossible to understand either the local economy or local politics outside the broader context of national politics and policy. In no case, and least of all in a highly centralized political system like that of Italy, is the local community a self-contained and self-sufficient entity; its behavior is shaped in innumerable ways by decisions made outside its boundaries and by the structural context within which it is embedded. The nature of these linkages in the southern Italian case is set out most explicitly in Part I of this book, which deals with the evolution of the "Southern Question," in both its political and economic manifestations, from 1860 to the present, with the economic structure of the southern Italian city, and with the development of Christian Democratic power, in Palermo and in the South more generally, during the postwar period. In Part II, devoted to the social bases of Christian Democratic power in Palermo, this theme is less evident, yet the dependency relationship binding the South to centers of national power looms in the background as a constant conditioning factor.

The linking of political behavior at the local level to broader struc-

tural variables raises a more general theoretical issue of major importance for underdeveloped areas like southern Italy and those parts of
the Third World where clientelism has become a leading form of political mobilization. Is there a distinctive political economy of clientelism? That is, is the emergence of clientelism as the dominant form
of political organization linked to an underlying structural context of
resource scarcity and economic dependency? If it can be ascertained
that clientelism tends to thrive in a particular socioeconomic context,
it must next be asked what relationship exists between political
power and economic structure once the machine is firmly established. Some scholars have argued that the machine is a transitional
form of political organization, rooted in the early stages of capitalist
development, and that it will inevitably give way to more modern
forms of politics as economic development proceeds.[12] Is politics a
relatively passive reflection of economic structure, as this argument
suggests, or, once in place, can a given political structure assume an
active role in shaping economic variables in such a way as to perpetuate the bases of its own power? More concretely, must clientelistic
regimes submit to the inevitable verdict of autonomous processes of
economic development, or can such a regime, through its control of
key levers of power, impede those processes of development that
would eventually undermine the bases of its support?

Southern Italy provides an ideal terrain for investigation of the relationship between clientelism and economic development.[13] Not
only has clientelism dominated local politics in southern Italy since
Italian unification in 1860 but the national government as well has
been controlled since 1947 by a party that has transformed the Italian
state into a huge patronage machine.[14] At the same time, the Italian
government has since 1950 promoted a massive developmental effort
in the South, which was and remains one of the most backward regions of Western Europe. The intimate interpenetration of politics
and economics in southern Italy – and the ways in which it shapes
future prospects for both economic and political change – is one of
the major themes of this book. The failure of development in the
South and the persistence of clientelistic power are two faces of the
same coin.

The research on the bases of Christian Democratic power in Palermo, which constitutes the bulk of this study, provides substantial
evidence in favor of the hypothesis that clientelistic politics may be
most firmly rooted precisely in situations of resource scarcity and
that, once installed, political machines may be able to secure such a
monopoly over the channels of access to critical resources as to become almost immune to political challenge from within. Yet the case

of another southern Italian city, Naples, seems directly to contradict this pessimistic assessment of the likelihood of change in clientelistic regimes. The cases of Palermo and Naples make for an intriguing comparison. The two cities share a similar history as royal capitals of the Kingdom of the Two Sicilies prior to 1860, a similar cultural tradition resulting from this shared history, and a distinctive socioeconomic structure closer to that of the contemporary Third World metropolis than to that of other major European cities (see Chapter 2). Until 1975 they also shared a long tradition of clientelistic power that appeared virtually immutable. Yet, from 1975 on, the political experiences of the two cities diverge radically. While in Palermo the local elections of 1975 further reinforced the domination of the ruling DC, in Naples the same elections produced a political earthquake – the DC machine was defeated and local power passed into the hands of a left-wing coalition led by the Communist Party.

In turning to Naples, Part III of the book explores the central question of the strengths and weaknesses of clientelistic regimes from the perspective of change rather than that of continuity. Taking as a point of departure the governance of Naples prior to 1975 by a powerful DC machine identical in its essentials to the one in Palermo, the analysis will focus first on the question of why the Naples machine suddenly lost its mass support. Why, in contrast to Palermo, was the DC monopoly over key centers of political and economic power in Naples no longer sufficient to guarantee electoral success? What alternative benefits could the Left offer to offset the DC control over key resources that has proven so vital in perpetuating the power of the machine in Palermo? Can any more general lessons be drawn from the Neapolitan experience as to the conditions under which support for even the most powerful political machine may crumble?

The Neapolitan case is important not only for the insights it can provide into the causes of change in clientelistic systems of power but also for the opportunity it presents to assess the impact of left-wing rule in a socioeconomic context like that of southern Italy. While the victory of the Left in 1975 and its reconfirmation in 1980 point to the potential for change in even the most deeply rooted clientelistic regime, the actual experience of left-wing local government in Naples underlines, as in the case of Palermo, the weight of external structural constraints in shaping political behavior at the local level. The linkages between economic structure and political structure at the local level and between local and national power have set severe limits on the extent of social and political change that can be achieved through control of local government alone. Although the DC machine has for the moment suffered political defeat, clientelism is far from dead in Naples, and the city's political future remains in the balance. In the analysis of the limits of change in Naples and of the dilemmas confronting the city's would-be reformers, the conclusions of the Palermo research take on renewed significance. Paradoxically, it is the precariousness of change and the resiliency of clientelistic appeals that emerge as major themes in a case study which begins as an inquiry into the demise of the machine.

What follows is a tale of two cities, once centers of the Mediterranean world and glittering capitals of Spanish viceroys and Bourbon kings, now examples of urban degradation and human misery unparalleled in the rest of Europe. Since World War II, Palermo and Naples have become symbols of political squalor as well. This study attempts to understand the causes of that squalor and to assess the dynamics of continuity and change in political systems like those of Palermo and Naples. It is hoped that the experience of these two cities, in both the despair and the hope they inspire, can not only yield new insights into the strengths and weaknesses of two alternative models of political mobilization and control but can shed some light on their human consequences as well.

Part I

The roots of clientelistic power

The old is dying and the new cannot be born; in this interregnum
there arises a great diversity of morbid symptoms.

Antonio Gramsci, *Prison Notebooks*

1

Politics in the South, 1860–1943: regime change and political immobility

The "Southern Question"

Politics and economics in cities like Palermo and Naples are indissolubly linked to the more general problem of the Italian South, the *questione meridionale*, which has plagued Italian politics since unification in 1860. Until 1950 the essence of the "Southern Question" lay in the contrast between a modern industrial society in the North and a traditional agrarian society in the South.[1] The bases of this disparity existed already at the time of unification, although in a much more attenuated form. Despite incipient industrial ventures in cities like Naples and Palermo, the South in general in 1860 found itself in a relatively disadvantaged economic position vis-à-vis the North, because of three important factors: (1) the harsh climate and topography and the objective resource poverty of the South; (2) its distance from central European markets; and (3) the survival under the Bourbon rulers of the Kingdom of the Two Sicilies of a social and economic structure still organized on a predominantly feudal basis.[2] The problem of the Mezzogiorno, however, cannot be understood simply as the encapsulation within a modern state of an underdeveloped society, traditional and stagnant. It is not that the South failed to develop, but rather that it developed in a certain way, in a tight and symbiotic relationship with the North. Though the relative backwardness of the South in 1860 cannot be denied, the persistence and indeed widening of the gap between North and South in the century following unification cannot be ascribed to natural forces alone. From 1860 until the present the nature of the Southern Question cannot be understood outside the context of political and economic decisions made at the national level.

The postunification relationship between North and South has its roots in the Risorgimento, the social and political movement that cul-

15

minated in the unification of the Italian states under the Piedmontese monarchy. Despite its representation in official Italian history as a movement of popular revolution against the Bourbon regime, the Risorgimento was in reality a combination of external military conquest and political alliances from above, effectively stifling the genuine pressures for radical social change that exploded throughout the South in response to Garibaldi's initial revolutionary rhetoric. The political foundation of the new Italian state was an alliance between the northern industrial bourgeoisie and the southern landed aristocracy. The response of the latter to the specter of revolution that swept the South in 1860 is brilliantly depicted in Lampedusa's *The Leopard*. In order to avert social upheaval, the aristocracy was willing to abandon the Bourbon monarchy and join forces with the Piedmontese, the condition for their support being the preservation of the social and economic status quo in the South, with regard to both the feudal organization of the agricultural economy and the existing structure of class privilege. The impact of the Risorgimento in the South has nowhere been described better than in the classic epigram of Lampedusa's hero: "If we want everything to remain as it is, everything must change."[3]

Although the social and political structure of the South remained virtually unchanged, the impact of unification upon the southern economy was immediate and disastrous. One of the first acts of the new national government was to impose a uniform tax and tariff policy upon the entire country. In the South this meant a sudden and drastic increase in taxes which, coupled with very limited public investment in the South, drained southern resources to finance northern industry. In addition, it meant the abolition of the high protective tariffs established by the Bourbon regime. Thanks to these tariffs, a substantial manufacturing industry, especially in textiles, had begun to develop in major southern cities like Naples and Palermo in the last years of the Bourbons; the sudden elimination of such protection decimated firms unprepared for the onslaught of northern competition, while opening southern markets to commercial penetration by the products of northern industry. The economic situation of the South was further aggravated by the protectionist swing in Italian economic policy in 1887 (part of a more general shift in tariff policy throughout Western Europe). The imposition of high external tariffs struck at the southern economy from both sides – the loss of traditional international export markets provoked a severe agricultural crisis, while at the same time the South was compelled to pay higher prices for manufactured products purchased from the North.

The postunification development of the South has been described by Sidney Tarrow as a process of "commercialization without industrialization."[4] While the penetration of the South as a market for externally produced goods had begun even before 1860, this process was accelerated by the economic policies of the new regime at the same time as the incipient industrialization of the South was reversed. In terms of southern society, unification reinforced the disintegration of traditional social roles and relationships provoked by the introduction of the market into the old feudal system, while rendering ever more improbable the development of an industrial structure that could create an alternative framework of stable social relationships.

With the progressive breakdown of the feudal system, then, southern society came to be characterized, in Antonio Gramsci's words, as a *grande disgregazione sociale* ("an immense social disaggregation").[5] Unlike the rest of Western Europe, the disintegration of feudalism in southern Italy failed to produce an independent entrepreneurial middle class; instead the social structure of the South remained polarized in two antagonistic blocs – the propertied elite and the mass of the landless peasantry. With the division and sale of the communal lands following the abolition of feudalism and that of Church properties after 1860,[6] a bourgeois landholding class came rapidly into existence;[7] rather than affirming itself as an autonomous and dynamic economic force, however, the nascent bourgeoisie focused its aspirations exclusively upon the land, and then primarily in terms of social prestige rather than productive investment. The landed aristocracy rather than the industrial or commercial middle classes constituted its model of social values and behavior.

Despite the predominantly agricultural character of the southern economy, life on the land has always been regarded with disdain by the propertied classes (and for that matter by the peasantry as well, who crowd into densely populated "agro-towns"[8] separated by miles of otherwise deserted countryside); large southern landowners have traditionally constituted an essentially urban elite, abandoning their estates to overseers in order to dedicate themselves to the more civilized pleasures of life in Naples or Palermo. Thus, while monopolizing the central resource of the southern economy, the landed aristocracy (and later bourgeoisie) constituted an absentee, rentier elite rather than a productive entrepreneurial class. Removed from any direct relationship with production, the landowners lacked the homogeneity and solidarity of a modern social class, being united only in defense of a social position based upon parasitic privilege.

An analogous process of social fragmentation occurred among the peasantry following the abolition of feudalism. Deprived of his feudal rights upon the land (the division of the communal and Church lands having benefited not the peasantry but the rising bourgeoisie), the peasant found his plight under freedom, if anything, more desperate. Projected without other resources than his labor into a market economy (in this case grounded in the fundamental fact of severe overpopulation), the peasant became bound in even more abject subordination to those who exercised absolute control over the one resource crucial to his survival: the land. Although, in the words of a contemporary observer, society was polarized into "oppressors and oppressed,"[9] this polarization produced surprisingly low levels of manifest social conflict. This apparent paradox can be explained by the extreme pulverization and diversification in patterns of land tenure resulting from the liquidation of feudalism. The typical peasant became a mixed figure, combining ownership of a few fragmented "handkerchiefs" of land, a variety of sharecropping or rental arrangements on other scattered plots, and finally day labor – all of which enabled him just to eke out a bare subsistence. Severe population pressure and scarce resources, combined with the extreme fragmentation of landholding, the diversity of agrarian contracts, and the insecurity of land–tenure relationships effectively impeded the development of class solidarity among the peasants, pitting them instead one against the other in fierce competition for access to the land.[10]

In the South the modernizing processes of urbanization and commercialization were thus superimposed upon a traditional agrarian economic base. The failure to stimulate not only industrialization but even a modernization and rationalization of agriculture prevented the formation of stable and homogeneous social classes, for example, on the model of the independent peasant proprietor in France or of a capitalist landholding bourgeoisie as in the case of the English gentry. With the advent of mass communications and models of mass consumption, the South provided an ever-expanding market for the products of northern industry, such demand being sustained by the rapid expansion of the tertiary sector in the cities and by income maintenance in the form of transfer payments and migrants' remittances in the countryside. Once the South was integrated into the national economic system on these terms, market mechanisms perpetuated and consolidated economic dualism, reinforcing the already substantial obstacles to autonomous industrialization of the South.

Politics in the South under Liberalism and Fascism

The Southern Question refers not only to the social and economic gap dividing northern and southern Italy but to distinctive patterns of political behavior as well. It is impossible to understand the evolu-

tion of postwar politics in the South without considering first the political climate in the eighty years between unification and the outbreak of World War II and thereby the types of political resources
upon which the postwar attempt to create a politics of mass participation in the South could draw. Italian political history after 1860
falls into two distinct periods, each of which shaped in critical ways
the political heritage with which the emerging mass parties would
have to come to terms in 1943: (1) the Liberal era, 1860–1922, and (2)
the Fascist experience, 1922–43.

Trasformismo, the politics of personality and patronage

Even before Italian unification in 1860, economic and social
relationships in southern Italy had been structured predominantly
on the basis of patron–client ties. Far from unique to southern Italy,
this phenomenon has been shown by anthropological research to be
characteristic of a wide range of traditional agrarian societies,[11] particularly those in which economic resources are scarce and access to
them concentrated in the hands of a restricted elite. What is particularly interesting about the Italian case is the politicization of these
relationships of traditional deference that came about with the introduction of parliamentary institutions and local self-government after
1860, and the process by which such a style of political behavior
came to shape the working of the entire Italian political system in the
decades that followed.

The political life of this period is best characterized by the Italian
term *trasformismo.*[12] In its strictest sense, *trasformismo* refers to a parliamentary strategy, initiated by Agostino De Pretis in 1876, by
which opposition deputies were induced to shift their votes to the
government majority in exchange for personal benefits and, above
all, access to state patronage. Parliamentary *trasformismo* had its roots
in an extremely restricted suffrage: less than 500,000 voters, or 1.9%
of the population in 1861, increased to 2 million voters, or 6.9% of
the population in 1882 (enfranchisement of the lower middle class
and the more highly skilled and educated artisans), with universal
male suffrage (8.5 million voters) being introduced only in 1913. The
Risorgimento, which might have mobilized the masses and brought
them into active participation in political life, had, as shown at the
beginning of this chapter, assumed instead the character of a military
conquest imposed from above upon a passive and largely indifferent
populace. With the masses effectively excluded from public life, politics revolved around competing cliques or factions built around the
figure of the "notable" and his personal following; the two major
parliamentary parties, the Destra and the Sinistra, in reality represented only loosely knit coalitions of such elite factions, without a

mass base or even an organizational existence outside the parliamentary group. Parliament was transformed into a bazaar, characterized not by political debate but by perpetual bargaining among government ministers, deputies, and their respective clienteles. Once such a system became entrenched, "neither ideas nor practical programs were used as weapons in the fight for national power, but became the instruments of transactions, jobs and influence, elections and positions."[13]

The central figure in the pyramid of *clientela* networks extending from the local notable to the government minister was the national deputy. The single deputy represented the interests and claims of his electors to those of his more powerful colleagues from whom ministers were chosen; the latter, in turn, would reward their supporters by providing them with particularistic benefits. The key to the successful functioning of this system was the discretionary power of the minister – free from bureaucratic norms of conduct – to dispose of highly individualistic rewards and sanctions. The deputy did not aggregate the demands of his constituents, but rather represented the individual claims of his *grandi elettori* ("great electors"), who for their part acknowledged only those benefits that could be directly attributed to the personal intervention of the deputy. Thus, in a system with a highly restricted suffrage and limited private resources, the mechanisms of political support transformed the state into an immense spoils system for the maintenance and enrichment of personal clienteles.

Southern deputies were the mainstay of *trasformismo*. Their behavior reflected the implicit alliance between the northern industrial bourgeoisie and the southern gentry by which national unification had been achieved. In return for access to government patronage and for complete freedom of action in local administrations, they were prepared to provide unquestioning support in Parliament to any government majority, regardless of its program. Gaetano Salvemini notes, for example, that between 1880 and 1900 the South regularly elected 200 deputies who were "eternally ministerial."[14] Further evidence of the strength of the ministerial bond in the South is provided by the following figures from the 1904 elections: in only 3 southern provinces were antigovernment candidates presented, as opposed to 7 in central Italy and 23 in the North.[15] The resulting political free-for-all in Parliament is depicted quite strikingly in the following accusation by Francesco Crispi in 1886, while he was still in the opposition:

You should see the pandemonium at Montecitorio when the moment approaches for an important vote. The agents of the government run through the rooms and corridors to gather votes. Subsidies, decorations, canals, bridges, roads, everything is promised; and sometimes an act of justice, long denied, is the price of a parliamentary vote.[16]

Upon acceding to the prime ministership the following year, however, he, too, would employ identical methods.

Until the emergence of Socialism and the Catholic Partito Popolare ("Popular Party") as mass political forces with the electoral reforms of 1912 and 1919, *trasformismo* successfully eliminated any effective opposition from the Italian Parliament. The Destra and the Sinistra, which had contested national power from 1860 until 1876, were molded into a single governmental majority by the "transformist" politics of successive prime ministers following the victory of the Sinistra in the elections of 1876. The organization of politics around personality and patronage rather than ideas and practical programs not only absorbed and neutralized the opposition but ultimately emptied the very concept of "party" of any meaning beyond that of a loose congeries of personal clienteles. The predominance of such individualistic and instrumental linkages among political elites had the long-term effect of inhibiting the development of a modern bourgeois party, a failure for which Italy would pay dearly in 1922.

In a broader context, *trasformismo* may be seen as an attempt on the part of ruling elites, particularly after the widening of the suffrage in 1882, to forestall the spread of radicalism among northern workers. The economic, social, and political dualism of Italian society provided successive governments with the means to achieve this end. Given the social and economic backwardness of the South (which discouraged the growth of organized political conflict) and the consequent dominance of personalistic politics (which facilitated governmental techniques of "electoral management"), the Mezzogiorno came to constitute a critical source of political stability for governments increasingly concerned with rising radical pressures in the North. Sustained by the unconditional parliamentary support of the mass of southern deputies, prime ministers like Giovanni Giolitti (1903–14) achieved sufficient maneuverability to successfully manage class conflict – through either cooptation or isolation of the opposition – up until the outbreak of World War I. For the South this meant a substantial increase in its political weight, but at a very high price – renunciation of an active voice in national policy and forfeiture of a serious national effort aimed at resolution of the *questione meridionale*. This was so because it was the very backwardness of the South that made it such an important political asset for national leaders. Southern elites welcomed *trasformismo* as a guarantee of the local status quo; for the masses, instead, it meant resignation to economic stagnation and feudalistic class dominance.

As we have seen, the keystone of this system of power was the

South; its critical links the local notable, the southern deputy, and the government minister. As electoral power remained firmly in the hands of the local notable, the success of parliamentary *trasformismo* clearly required a certain set of social, economic, and political conditions at the local level. Given the limitation of the suffrage, the introduction of democratic institutions into the Kingdom of the Two Sicilies, rather than promoting popular participation, had instead solidified and legitimized the absolute power of the landed aristocracy and the rising rural bourgeoisie.[17] In addition, the delegation by the state of substantial powers to the newly constituted municipal governments – responsibility for communal roads and lands, primary education, charitable institutions, certain forms of credit – meant control over sizable economic resources, thereby significantly raising the stakes in the struggle for local power. Local elites exercised this power exclusively in the pursuit of private interests, their own and those of their personal followings:

[In Sicily] the propertied class is small, and within it influence and authority are the exclusive monopoly of a very few. These men alone have a strong enough voice to make themselves feared by the Government. The election of deputies depends upon them, and they are the arbiters of what in other countries is rightly or wrongly considered the expression of public opinion. Furthermore, the interests of these few have nothing in common with those of the general population; they are the strictly personal interests of these elites and of the members of their clienteles . . . What matters to them is to maintain their own authority . . . which is based upon the power to assure to themselves, and even more so to their clients, the benefit, in one form or another, from public resources of every kind, as well as the power to impose, wherever necessary, to their own and their clients' advantage, their personal authority over that of the law.[18]

For every necessity of their lives – from birth to marriage, migration, and death – those sectors of the population excluded from power (the peasants and the urban poor) were wholly dependent upon the narrow circle of notables who controlled the *municipio* ("city hall"), in most cases also the arbiters of their economic survival through their ownership of the land.[19] In addition to their exclusive grip on the legitimate instruments of municipal power, many local notables sought to reinforce their position through alliances with criminal elements like the mafia. Against such a monopoly of power and of the means of violence, both public and private, the peasant or urban laborer had no legal recourse; the only alternatives were resignation or collective violence.[20]

This system of legalized *prepotenza* ("the rule of the strongest") was made possible by the tacit system of alliances linking local officials to the holders of national power. The principal intermediary at the local level was the Prefect, an agent of the central government, whose function was to oversee the activities of local administrative bodies, with the ultimate sanction of dissolution in the case of irregularities. In practice, however, the Prefect's main task was to insure the election of deputies loyal to the government even at the expense of the honesty and efficiency of local administrations. In return for the votes controlled by local notables, the Prefect often closed his eyes not only to all manner of administrative irregularities and corruption but even, particularly in the Sicilian case, to the outright collusion among local politicians, magistrates, and the mafia.[21] The climate of local politics in the South throughout this period is vividly evoked in the following passages from Guido Dorso and Giustino Fortunato, two of the most prominent Liberal exponents of the Southern Question:

Having become the dominant social force, the rural bourgeoisie adapted all political activity to its particularistic mentality. Everywhere the party of the local doctor was set against that of the pharmacist and that of the municipal secretary against that of the schoolmaster, in a feudalistic struggle to seize control of the city hall and from there to favor one's followers and oppress one's adversaries. All political struggle, then, was organized around the municipal treasury, the Prefect exploiting budget deficits to initiate a process of legal blackmail in favor of the government parties. For this reason, southern politicians always tended to be "ministerial." In fact, if they held power, they had to be "ministerial" to avoid the administrative inquests of the Prefect; if, instead, they were in the opposition, they sought the favor of the government in order to unseat their adversaries. Under such conditions, political organization in the South could not help but consist in a continual mediation between successive governments at the center and the passive southern masses, excluded from formal institutions. This mediation was performed by the deputies, who assured the government of the votes and the tranquility of the southern masses and received in return privileges and impunity for those under their protection.[22]

The small elector votes for the promise or threat of the great elector. The great elector is such by profession, since he receives either a contract or a concession or a similar favor. The city government is a crowd of people who, being paid with vanity, permit the support which the great electors bring them to be paid for out of public funds. It is a group of profiteers who corrupt and are corrupted in the fullest sense of the word. The city councillor, in order to receive favors from the *Giunta* [the executive body of local government], leaves its hands free; the *Giunta*, not to antagonize the Mayor on certain matters, closes its eyes to others. The party promises honors, protection and immunity to win the friendship of the most influential and hard-working electors, and these barter electoral agitation as a means of making money, getting jobs . . . or merely so as not to be imprisoned. The election becomes, therefore, an interest in itself, and the best candidate is not the most intelligent or the one with the greatest integrity, but rather the one from whom you can hope for the greatest advantage and protection in your private interests, whether legal or illegal.[23]

In such a political system, the individual was compelled to seek the protection of a more powerful patron: to remain outside a clientelistic network meant total powerlessness.

Local political bosses, especially in the larger cities, were often recruited from the professional middle classes. This was particularly true of lawyers, given the paucity of professional outlets relative to the number of lawyers turned out by the traditional educational system that prevailed in the South. With his special talents for brokerage and mediation, the lawyer thus frequently looked to politics as a logical professional alternative. The political vocation of the rising professional middle classes is even more comprehensible if viewed in the light of the economic and social bases of southern society:

It was natural that in a society characterized by poverty this ascending class should turn to politics and the economic resources of the state. In a largely immobile agrarian society, politics was the most important, if not the only, channel of social mobility and the resources of the state, the only source of income independent of land.[24]

This passage points to the critical factor in explaining the role of the South in national politics as well as the predominant model of political behavior at the local level – the limited indigenous resources of the South and its consequent economic dependence upon the state. It was the economic resources of the state, however limited with respect to the postwar expansion of state responsibility for welfare and economic development, that formed the cement holding together the clientele networks stretching from local notables to government ministers. The same economic backwardness that impeded the emergence of organized political parties on a class or interest-group basis inexorably pressed people into the vertical networks that constituted the only channel for extracting resources from the sole available source, the state.

The Fascist interlude[25]

To all appearances the advent of Fascism should have ushered the South into the era of mass politics and accomplished, where the Risorgimento had failed, its political integration with the rest of the nation. Indeed, the mass party, with its centralized bureaucratic organization reaching into the smallest rural village, and the network of para-political secondary associations linked to it formed the very basis of the Fascist regime. As with the Risorgimento, however, the new political structures, rather than revolutionizing the South, soon found themselves instead progressively infused with the traditional values and methods of southern politics. Prior to the March on Rome in 1922, Fascism as a mass movement had existed only in the North, where it had arisen in reaction to the organized strength of the Socialists and the Partito Popolare. In the South, on the contrary, given the weakness of organized parties, Fascism as an "anti-Bolshevik" movement simply had no raison d'être. Given the limited effectiveness of the ideological appeals by means of which he had achieved power in the North, Mussolini, like the Liberals before him, came quickly to the realization that he could win the necessary support in the South only by striking an agreement with the *grandi elettori*, the leaders of the traditional clienteles. So long as Mussolini required electoral support, as well as the votes of southern deputies for critical measures like his Electoral Reform Bill, the few "ideological" Fascists in the South, whose goal was to eliminate the old clienteles and mobilize the masses directly, found themselves powerless to prevent the infiltration of the *fasci* by the local bosses. In fact, the old politics of *trasformismo* continued unabated under the new regime. Once it became clear that the Fascists would obtain a major share in national power, the entire South became Fascist almost overnight, with local cliques competing to jump on the bandwagon before their opponents, in the hope thereby of reinforcing their claim to municipal power. Fascism's success was insured when the most prestigious southern politicians – De Nicola, Orlando, Salandra (the latter two former prime ministers) – led a group of nearly eighty Liberal ministers and deputies who agreed to join Mussolini's slate for the 1924 elections. In contrast to its revolutionary fervor in the North, Fascism in the South for the most part merely absorbed the old leadership class – and with it the old style of politics – under a new name.

Fascism in the South thus came to rely for support on the most conservative sectors of society, and in western Sicily this meant an alliance with the mafia. So long as elections continued, the support of the mafia was essential to mobilize votes for the Fascist-Nationalist list; from the viewpoint of the mafioso, this was the ideal situation, for his control over such a sought-after commodity provided him with an efficient instrument of control over the politicians upon whose protection he depended. Once the Fascist dictatorship was established, however, and elections abolished, the relationship between Fascism and the mafia underwent a transformation of great interest as an indication of the social bases and functions of the new regime in the South. Originally emerging as the agents of the landowning classes and guarantors of social peace in the countryside, the mafia bosses had, by the end of World War I, "extended their high-handed and oppressive treatment even to landowners . . . They started by systematically withholding payment of their rent either in money or in kind and they often finished by forcing landowners to sell off their land at ridiculously low prices."[26] Under these conditions it is not surprising that many large landowners, once they recognized in Fascism an equally effective and less burdensome means of defending their estates against the peasants, did not hesitate to sacrifice their erstwhile allies to the new regime:

The aristocratic members of the landowning class welcomed Fascism with open arms – not so much because they shared the Duce's ideology but because they recognized his dictatorship as decidedly conservative and as a means to the restoration of the good old days with all their privileges preserved. But above all they hoped that the establishment of a strong police regime would enable them to free themselves from their by now inconvenient alliance with the mafia.[27]

With the consolidation of the Fascist regime, involving the abolition of the electoral system and the nationalization of the Fascist militia, mafiosi as local strongmen were deprived of their raison d'être . . . Where the Fascist State guaranteed vested landed interests and established effective security in the countryside, mafiosi were rendered obsolete.[28]

Having once lost the protection of their patrons, individual mafiosi became easy targets for the fierce campaign of repression unleashed by Mussolini under the direction of the Prefect Cesare Mori, for, once its dominance was secured, Fascism tolerated no rival power structures. Despite claims to the total elimination of the mafia, however, only minor and middle-level mafiosi – those most directly compromised by outright criminal activities – fell into Mori's net. The most influential mafia leaders – the *mandanti*[29] of the acts for which their subordinates were rounded up – had themselves by this time become quite respectable; many were in fact noted politicians or members of the Palermo aristocracy. When Mori in his enthusiasm became so imprudent as to denounce such figures for their mafia connections, thereby threatening the very political class upon which Fascism depended, he was soon transferred, and the much-hailed war on the mafia abruptly petered out.

Thus, while the more obviously criminal elements of the mafia were arrested and exiled, the top-level mafia bosses assumed positions of power and prestige within the regime itself. Fascism succeeded in stamping out the mafia as a criminal organization by providing a more efficient substitute; it succeeded in monopolizing the use of violence without, however, transforming the social and economic conditions in which the mafia had flourished. It was thus no surprise that the mafia rapidly reemerged as soon as Fascism fell, and the state once again proved unable, without the aid of private violence, to guarantee landed property against the onslaught of the peasant masses.

Despite the organizational structures of a modern mass party, Fascism as a political movement never really penetrated the South. In the South, in fact, the prefect, as representative of the state, maintained the upper hand over the party, prefiguring the eventual transformation throughout Italy of Fascism from an aggressive ideological movement to a bureaucratized official cult, subordinated to a state administration itself increasingly infiltrated by southern intellectuals and southern styles of political behavior. It was in this governmental guise that Fascism had its greatest impact on the South. Combining grass-roots organizational penetration with control of the state apparatus, the Fascist Party can perhaps be seen as a precursor of the postwar party of mass patronage, so well exemplified, as we shall see, by the Christian Democratic Party. With the great expansion of state activities under Fascism, the party became the major dispenser of political patronage – jobs, public works, personal favors, and privileges – with the party functionary replacing the local notable (in title if not in person) as the key intermediary in the patronage chain. The use of the party to channel patronage resources helps explain the great expansion of party membership in the South after consolidation of the Fascist regime, when party membership became a major criterion for access to many jobs and indeed, in the 1930s, obligatory for all civil servants and teachers. Despite the suppression of democratic institutions, then, the extreme politicization of the state under Fascism encouraged the perpetuation of an essentially "transformist" model of politics – only by now *trasformismo* had entered the age of mass politics.

2

The southern economy: modernization without development

Twenty-five years of state intervention in the South

By the end of World War II, the abyss dividing North from South had become so profound that the only possibility of resolving the Southern Question seemed to lie in a policy of direct intervention by the state to promote and sustain economic development in the South. Such a policy was initiated in 1950 with the establishment of the Cassa per il Mezzogiorno, set up as a special arm of the government, independent of the regular ministries, in order to facilitate rapid and effective action in the South. The balance sheet of the first twenty-five years of special intervention in the South is a mixed one and has been the object of bitter political debate in Italy.[1] On the one hand, the face of the South has changed dramatically since 1950. Indicators of economic performance (see column 5 of Table 2.1) show impressive increases in per capita income and in industrial output. Employment in agriculture has declined sharply, while significant gains have been made in both industry and services. Important advances have been made in the struggle against illiteracy and infant mortality, two of the primary indices of social backwardness.

Yet, despite these objective gains and the massive amounts of public investment needed to produce them,[2] the Cassa has failed to achieve one of its primary objectives: between 1950 and 1975 the gap between North and South widened rather than narrowed. The limits of development in the South emerge most clearly from an examination of the labor market. The most glaring failure of the Cassa's development policies is the fact that total employment in the South in 1975 was actually lower than in 1950. Despite the dramatic increase in industrial investment, the creation of new jobs in the industrial and service sectors was insufficient to absorb the massive outflow of manpower from agriculture (Table 2.2). This is reflected in extremely

Table 2.1. *Indicators of regional differences, 1951–71*

	South[a]		Center-North[a]		South[b] (1971)	Center-North[b] (1971)
	1951	1971	1951	1971		
Per capita income	67.9	64.3	119.0	119.6	253.7	270.4
GDP at factor cost	24.5	22.9	75.5	77.1	272.2	298.5
Agriculture	38.6	42.6	61.4	57.4	174.8	148.1
Industry	17.0	16.6	83.0	83.4	380.7	391.9
Services	22.7	23.5	77.3	76.5	299.1	285.2
Employment	33.0	34.3	66.7	65.7	91.8	101.8
Agriculture	42.6	50.4	57.4	49.6	50.0	36.5
Industry	22.5	23.2	77.5	76.8	145.2	139.3
Manufacturing	19.5	17.6	80.5	89.4	122.0	138.0
Construction	32.3	40.0	67.7	60.0	209.5	149.7
Services	27.4	27.8	72.6	72.2	142.2	138.8
Public administration	33.3	34.3	66.7	65.7	163.4	156.3
Industrial investment outlays	15.1	35.4	84.9	64.6	732.3	239.2

[a] All Italy = 100.   [b] 1951 = 100.
Source: Data from Comitato dei Ministri per il Mezzogiorno; table reproduced from Gisele Podbielski, *Italy: Development and Crisis in the Post-War Economy* (Oxford: Clarendon Press, 1974), p. 137.

low rates of labor-force participation[3] and in the migration between 1950 and 1975 of over 4 million persons from the South to the industrial centers of northern Italy and central Europe.[4] In addition to the persistence of chronic unemployment, the standard of living in the South continues to lag far behind that of the rest of the country: although in absolute terms per capita income in the South increased almost three times between 1950 and 1975, it has actually declined relative to per capita income in the North (Table 2.1).

Above all, the Cassa has not succeeded in stimulating an autonomous, self-sustaining process of industrialization in the South. Not only did the South at the end of the 1970s remain to a large extent dependent upon resource transfers from the center but the type of industrialization that has occurred has created a series of new imbalances and distortions. These include polarization of the industrial structure between a handful of publicly financed giants and thousands of traditional artisanal shops, a widening of regional disparities *within* the South, and a rapid urbanization of southern society, which has transferred the overpopulation problem from the countryside to the cities, leading to a serious degradation of urban infrastructures and to the emergence of growing social and political tensions.

Table 2.2. *Occupational structure of the labor force, 1951–71*

	1951	1961	1971
South			
Agriculture	3,627,151 (55.3%)	2,789,972 (43.2%)	1,696,678 (30.2%)
Industry	1,492,947 (22.7%)	2,003,887 (31.1%)	1,995,335 (35.6%)
Tertiary	1,442,902 (22.0%)	1,657,169 (25.7%)	1,919,276 (34.2%)
Total	6,563,000 (100%)	6,451,694 (100%)	5,611,289 (100%)
North			
Agriculture	2,246,711 (29.0%)	1,385,385 (17.5%)	752,581 (9.4%)
Industry	3,371,905 (43.5%)	4,052,119 (51.1%)	4,263,482 (53.3%)
Tertiary	2,137,750 (27.6%)	2,487,764 (31.4%)	2,976,341 (37.2%)
Total	7,756,366 (100%)	7,925,268 (100%)	7,992,404 (100%)

Note: In order to simplify comparison, this table reports figures only for the North and South, excluding the Center.
Sources: ISTAT, *9°, 10°, 11° Censimento generalo della popolazione* (1951, 1961, 1971).

How can the limits of the development process in the Mezzogiorno be explained? While the poverty and backwardness of the South may initially have been due to objective natural factors and subsequently to the workings of the market in a unified economy, the failure of two and a half decades of deliberate state intervention to narrow, if not eliminate, the North–South gap cannot be understood without looking in greater detail at the strategy guiding public investment in the South. From its establishment in 1950 until 1957, the Cassa concentrated its activity upon the creation of infrastructures (61.5% of investment from 1950 to 1960),[5] with the majority of funds allocated to agriculture. While the official justification for such massive public investment in infrastructures was that it would pave the way for future investments by private industry, this was also part of a broader "welfare" policy – together with agrarian reform – aimed at mitigating social tensions in the South while maintaining the bulk of the peasantry upon the land. In 1957, the orientation of the Cassa changed radically, reflecting a new strategy of providing direct incentives to public and private industrial investment in the South. Such a policy shift implied abandoning the agricultural interior and concentrating future interventions in *poli di sviluppo* ("development poles"), the majority of which were located in the vicinity of the large coastal cities. This change in investment strategy signified an end to efforts to restrain the agricultural exodus and opened the way to the massive out-migration of the 1960s, as well as stimulating a growing differentiation between zones of development and zones of marginality within the South itself.

While originally intended to favor small- and medium-scale, relatively labor-intensive industries, incentives were increasingly granted to large public and private firms in precisely those sectors – steel, chemicals, and petrochemicals – in which the ratio of labor to capital is lowest.[6] Despite the magnitude of the investment in these sectors, however, they made only a very limited contribution to industrial takeoff. First, because of high levels of capital intensity, these investments led to only minimal increases in industrial employment; in addition, most of the managerial and technical personnel and the skilled workers were brought in from outside. Second, most of these firms had little propulsive impact on the local economy in terms of stimulating the creation of a supportive network of small and medium-sized firms; in fact, in many areas, industrial employment actually fell as the new industries undermined the traditional fabric of artisanal firms without creating sufficient new jobs to absorb the labor thereby displaced. Finally, most of these industries, both public and private, were subsidiaries of northern companies artificially implanted in the South to take advantage of the generous state subsidies, but without any real linkages to the local economy: not only did control remain firmly in the hands of outsiders but production was almost entirely oriented to external markets. Although not all industrial investment has been of this type, these highly visible "cathedrals in the desert" have become a symbol of all the limits and contradictions of the postwar development effort in the South.[7]

Another explanation of the failure of the Cassa to promote a self-sustaining process of development in the South focuses on the lack of clearcut priorities and of coordination among projects, which is attributed above all to the absence of any coherent national industrial policy.[8] Without such a frame of reference, not only have the initiatives of the Cassa often been unplanned and at times even contradictory but, given the total lack of coordination between the Cassa and the ordinary activities of the public administration, economic measures have at times been adopted which, at best, did not take into account the special problems of the South and, at worst, deliberately favored the interests of other regions.

Taking this argument one step further, the absence of clearcut policy guidelines for the Cassa's investments in the South has produced a series of ad hoc, haphazard interventions often determined more by political pressures than by criteria of economic rationality. Conceived as a special streamlined instrument to channel state funds into carefully chosen development projects, the Cassa was soon transformed into a political bandwagon for the maintenance of local clienteles. The primacy of political considerations in the distribution of funds has been such that the Cassa has been described as "the most formidable instrument of bureaucratic clientelism with which the country is endowed," and "the most hallucinatory example of state parasitism and organized waste,"[9] perpetrating a massive dissipation of public resources for the purpose of maintaining intact the vast clientelistic networks that constitute the foundations of political power in much of the South.

The linkages between the management of the Cassa and the exigencies of local clientelistic politics, however, may have implications going beyond the particularistic distribution of state funds to sustain local party bosses. An argument has been made that the fundamental choices concerning the strategy of public intervention in the South have been conditioned from the outset by the necessity for the dominant Christian Democratic Party to maintain a certain type of power base in the South.[10] Local party leaders, it is held, coming for the most part from the nonproductive middle classes described above, saw industrialization as a long-term threat to their power and therefore, often in alliance with the leaders of the Cassa itself, exercised a continual rearguard action against the concrete realization of such initiatives. That such pressures could achieve even partial success, in contradiction to the stated policy of a government led by their own party, can be understood only in terms of the logic of internal factional politics in the DC and of the weight that southern politicians carry in these factional struggles, issues that will be more fully explored in Chapter 3. At a certain point, however, outright local resistance to industrialization became incompatible with increasing national pressures, both economic and political (e.g., the formation of a Center-Left government in the mid-1960s), to avoid total stagnation of the southern economy, so that a compromise solution was reached:

The compromise solution . . . was to direct to the South industrial complexes not likely, because of their organizational characteristics, to promote integration with the pre-existing economic base. In this way clientelistic con-

trol . . . remained substantially guaranteed, and the new industrial investments served only in a very indirect and marginal way to promote the further
development of the areas in which they were located.[11]

We return, therefore, to the theme of "industrialization without development." A development strategy based upon "development
poles" and "cathedrals in the desert" may in this view be seen as
perfectly functional to the needs of the national political leadership:
on the one hand it undermined the opposition through a massive
program of industrial investment in the South, while on the other it
preserved in large part the traditional economic and social structure
of the South upon which the DC's clientelistic local power bases depended, as well as – at least throughout the 1960s – sustaining a flow
of low-cost migrant labor to northern factories.

Thus, while the South has seen far-reaching transformations since
1950, the crux of the *questione meridionale* – the disparity between
North and South – remains unchanged. During the 1970s the Southern Question once again became a central issue of national politics.
The rhetoric failed to disguise, however, the steady deterioration of
the already fragile socioeconomic fabric of the South, from the mid-
1970s on, under the impact of the economic crisis. Not only have
bankruptcies and layoffs increased at alarming rates but the closing
off of the traditional safety valve of emigration has rendered rapidly
rising unemployment ever more explosive. In 1977, the South, with
35% of the Italian population, accounted for 24% of national income
and 44% of unemployment. The official unemployment rate (which
seriously undercounts true unemployment) was 10.1% in the South
as opposed to a national average of 7.2%. Given the need to make
difficult choices in the allocation of increasingly scarce resources, national economic policy in recent years has consistently favored the
industrialized North. Top priority has been accorded to safeguarding
production and employment in the most advanced regions of the
country, making the diversion of resources for new investment in the
South increasingly unlikely. Between 1976 and 1977, for example, the
investments of the Partecipazioni Statali ("state holding sector"),
which accounts for over 40% of industrial development in the South,
declined by 35%.[12] In addition, many of the existing state-controlled
firms have, with the government no longer able to sustain their
chronic deficits, come under growing pressure for cutbacks. Thus,
the prospects for the South at the beginning of the 1980s appear
grimmer than ever. Despite the rhetoric of the "centrality" of the
Southern Question, the needs of the South have once again, as
throughout Italian history, been subordinated to the interests of the
more advanced regions of the country.

The city in southern Italy

Within the overall context of the *questione meridionale,* the cities present a dimension of the problem quite distinct from that of the peasant world upon which most studies of the South have concentrated. As indicated in the previous section, one of the most far-reaching corollaries of the type of development that has taken place in the South has been the transformation of the Mezzogiorno from a rural to an urban society. Despite massive out-migration, the rate of postwar urbanization has been dramatic. In 1951 only eight southern cities had more than 100,000 inhabitants, and these accounted for only 16% of the southern population; by 1971 the number of such cities had risen to fourteen and their share of the total population to 23.4%. As of the 1971 census, Naples, with over 1,200,000 inhabitants, was Italy's third largest city, while of the seven Italian cities with between 300,000 and 1,000,000 inhabitants, three (Palermo, Catania, Bari) were located in the South.[13] As a result of this process of rapid urban expansion without concomitant development of the productive capabilities of the city and of basic urban infrastructures, the cities have increasingly become a focal point for the strains and contradictions produced by the model of development pursued in the South over the past thirty years: superimposition of the image and aspirations of an affluent consumer society upon a precarious and largely unproductive economic base has created a permanent breeding ground for potentially explosive social tensions.

The preindustrial city

Analysis of the demographic and economic structure of major southern cities like Palermo and Naples is an essential precondition for understanding the functioning of their political systems. The southern Italian city is quite distinct from its northern counterpart, in many ways resembling more closely the large "tertiary" cities of the Third World. The origins of this distinctiveness lie in their very different patterns of historical development. While northern cities grew up as commercial and later industrial centers, Naples and Palermo have traditionally been the administrative centers of the Italian South, serving over the centuries as the seats of successive royal and vice-royal courts and of the bureaucratic apparatus. required to extract an agricultural surplus from the surrounding countryside. Until 1860 these two cities represented the prototype of "the classical preindustrial metropolis – normally a capital – living on a resident court, state, church, or aristocracy."[14] A "monumental parasite," in Fernand Braudel's words, Naples was the largest city in Europe at the end of the sixteenth century, with a population of

280,000.[15] As in the countryside, the urban social structure was highly polarized. In addition to the resident court and the bureaucracy, both Naples and Palermo exerted an irresistible attraction to the landed elite of the agricultural interior; the other face of the city was that of the tradesmen, artisans and the mass of the *sottoproletariato* ("the urban poor"), all of whom were dependent for survival upon either the consumption or the largesse of the dominant classes.

The lower classes of the preindustrial city formed the basis of what Eric Hobsbawm calls the "city mob," which periodically shook the foundations of social and political order in pretwentieth-century Europe.[16] In the "classical preindustrial metropolis" the *sottoproletariato* or *popolino* maintained a symbiotic relationship, both economic and political, with the resident court and nobility, a relationship brilliantly evoked in the following paragraphs from Hobsbawm's *Primitive Rebels:*

In such cities the *popolino* lived in an odd relationship with its rulers, equally compounded of parasitism and riot. Its views – if that is the right word – may be set out fairly lucidly. It is the business of the ruler and his aristocracy to provide a livelihood for his people . . . This is all the more necessary since such princely centers are not normally industrial towns . . . If for one reason or another the usual livelihood of the people was jeopardized or broke down, it was the duty of the prince and his aristocracy to provide relief and to keep the cost-of-living low.

Providing he and they did their duty, they received active and enthusiastic support. Indeed, ragged and miserable as it was, the populace identified itself with the splendour and greatness of the city, which it naturally often – but not necessarily – identified with the ruler . . . It was not directly exploited by the Bourbon or Papal court, but was on the contrary its parasite, sharing, however modestly, in the city's general exploitation of the provinces and the peasants – the root of all Mediterranean pre-industrial city economy . . . The rulers and the parasitic poor thus lived in a sort of symbiosis. There was not even much need to keep the two classes apart, as in the modern cities. The traditional medieval or absolutist metropolis has no *beaux quartiers:* slums and street markets adjoined the palaces as we may still see them doing in parts of Rome or Palermo . . .

Provided the ruler did his duty, the populace was prepared to defend him with enthusiasm. But if he did not, it rioted until he did. This mechanism was perfectly understood by both sides, and caused no political problems beyond a little occasional destruction of property, so long as the normal attachment of the *menu peuple* to its city and rulers was not replaced by some other political ideal or so long as the rulers' failure to do their duty was no more than temporary. The threat of perennial rioting kept rulers ready to control prices and to distribute work or largesses . . . Since the riots were not directed against the social system, public order could remain surprisingly lax by modern standards. Conversely, the populace was quite satisfied with the effectiveness of this mechanism for expressing its political demands, and required no other, since these demands were for little more than a bare subsistence and a little entertainment and vicarious glory.[17]

Unlike most large European cities where, beginning in the nineteenth century, large-scale urban renewal projects progressively removed the poor from the central business and administrative quarters of the city, Naples and Palermo have to a large extent retained the urban structure of the preindustrial city: in the center of the old city, just a few feet behind the busy shops and government offices that line the major thoroughfares, one steps directly into a world of decaying slums, tortuously winding alleyways, and chaotic street markets where the *sottoproletariato* continues to reign supreme. In Hobsbawm's words, it is "only when one walks through, say, Palermo, where the Quattro Canti are still the nerve-center of the city, within rifle-shot of the palaces, the government offices, the slums and the markets, will he feel in his bones what the call 'the populace has risen' meant in the days of the classic 'mob.'"[18]

The contemporary southern metropolis

The status of Naples and Palermo as capital cities ended abruptly with Italian unification in 1860, provoking severe malaise in these cities whose economies had been so dependent upon court and bureaucracy. The population of both cities has in many ways, however, maintained a "capital" psychology; in the case of Palermo the establishment of an autonomous regional government in Sicily in 1946 provided the city with the excuse to resurrect with renewed pomp and pretense its past role as vice-royal capital, a role that has continued to have a determining influence on the city's socioeconomic structure (in most of the rest of Italy, regional governments were introduced only in 1970, and with greatly restricted powers and personnel compared to the Sicilian case).

Cities like Palermo and Naples are emblematic of the phenomenon of "urbanization without industrialization" that has characterized postwar development in southern Italy. Herein lies one of the major differences in the nature and role of the city in northern and southern Italy. In contrast to the North, where urban expansion took place in response to an expanding demand for industrial labor, rural–urban migration in the South only aggravated a chronic disequilibrium between urban population growth and employment possibilities. Although both Palermo and Naples exercise an attractive function vis-à-vis their hinterlands, these cities form part of a larger peripheral area exporting labor to external industrial centers. As a result, the overall migratory balance of both cities has been consistently negative, with population growth due exclusively to natural increase.[19]

The most important factor for understanding the seemingly contradictory migratory flows to and from the city is their distinction along class lines. In-migration from the interior has been of two types: (1) a massive influx of the provincial middle classes, swelling the ranks of the newly created regional bureaucracy in Palermo and setting off an intense process of frenetic land speculation in both cities from the late-1950s until the early 1970s; and (2) peasants, small shopkeepers, artisans, laborers, and *ambulanti* ("street-vendors") attracted by the mirage of the city, the majority of whom, in the absence of stable employment possibilities, soon join their urban-born counterparts in yet another wave of migration, this time toward the industrial centers of northern Italy and central Europe. This distinction reflects the structure of the local economy, an economy with extremely limited productive capabilities, in which the primary source of stable employment is the public administration. Under these circumstances the only alternative for thousands among the urban poor, the petty artisans and shopkeepers, and increasing numbers of young people with high-school and university degrees has been and remains migration.

Probably the most outstanding characteristic of the urban economy is its inability to provide stable employment for a large proportion of the city's population. The first indicator of the gravity of the situation is the extremely low rate of formal labor-force participation. In 1971 the "active population" was only 25.8% in Naples and 26.2% in Palermo, compared to a national average of 34.8% and a figure of 40.5% for a northern industrial city like Milan; in both southern cities these figures have decreased since 1951 (Table 2.3).[20] Similar declines in the percentage of the active population throughout the country were initially attributed to rising levels of affluence, which stimulated increased scolarity and the voluntary exiting from the labor force of women and older workers, but such an interpretation proved difficult to reconcile with data showing a greater decline in the South than in the North.[21] Later studies explain the decline instead in terms of an accelerating process of productive decentralization taking place within the Italian industrial structure since about 1969.[22] According to this interpretation, large numbers of workers, particularly in the sectors of textiles, clothing, and metalworking, have been laid off from regular factory jobs and reabsorbed into a variety of forms of "precarious" employment that do not appear in official labor-force statistics. The strategy on the part of the large firm is to reduce labor costs and increase flexibility in the use of the work force by reducing factory employment to a minimum and subcontracting substantial portions of the productive process to small artisan shops or women working at home. In this way the firm avoids both the observance of national contracts in terms of wages, hours,

Table 2.3. *Labor force by economic sector, 1951–71*

	1951	1961	1971
Palermo			
Total population[a]	490,692	587,985	642,814
Active population[b]	136,165	152,645	168,319
Active as % of total population	27.7	26.0	26.2
Active population by sector			
Agriculture	16,208	15,430	9,756
	(11.9%)	(10.1%)	(5.8%)
Industry	45,880	56,673	58,972
	(33.7%)	(37.1%)	(35.0%)
Tertiary	74,077	80,542	99,591
	(54.4%)	(52.8%)	(59.2%)
Naples			
Total population[a]	789,436	941,590	1,226,594
Active population[b]	300,431	333,054	316,001
Active as % of total population	38.1	35.4	25.8
Active population by sector			
Agriculture	11,991	10,046	5,787
	(4.0%)	(3.0%)	(1.8%)
Industry	118,061	134,177	123,598
	(39.3%)	(40.3%)	(39.1%)
Tertiary	170,379	188,831	186,616
	(56.7%)	(56.7%)	(59.1%)

[a] These figures refer to the "resident" population.
[b] This refers to the active population *in condizione professionale*.
Source: ISTAT, 9°, 10°, 11° *Censimento generalo della popolazione* (1951, 1961, 1971).

and employee benefits (up to 40% of labor costs in Italy) and the severe limitations on the ability to fire workers imposed by Italy's powerful unions.

In the South, however, the decline in the rate of labor-force participation and an increase in the number of very small firms reflect the dynamics of a very different economic structure. Although research in certain areas, particularly Naples, has revealed high levels of subcontracting and work at home, in Palermo and many other parts of the South there are no large industrial firms present locally to subcontract work out to small shops, while northern firms have no reason to search so far afield for cheap labor when there seems to be, at least for the moment, an abundant supply closer to home. In these areas the declining level of labor-force participation can more readily be explained by other factors: (1) the impact of the massive exodus from agriculture and the crisis of traditional artisanal activities which, in the absence of industrial expansion, have provoked large-scale out-migration among the most productive age groups of the population; (2) with the progressive deterioration of the urban economy, particularly severe in moments of economic crisis like the present, there is, as in the North, a process of expulsion of workers from the limited factory jobs that exist and a further pulverization of an already fragmented industrial and commercial structure as people struggle to get along by setting up independent shops. What one is confronted with here, however, is not a resurgence of small shops surviving and at times prospering because of a subcontracting relationship with large, modern firms, but rather a situation of desperate competition among thousands of independent marginal producers, struggling to survive in a market already dominated by their northern counterparts.

The problem of unemployment is overwhelming in cities like Naples and Palermo, but one for which it is difficult to give more than a very impressionistic analysis, because available data present serious problems with regard to completeness and reliability.[23] Official figures (those people registered at local unemployment offices) seriously understate the extent of actual unemployment, for they exclude all those who would be willing to work if employment were available, but who have withdrawn in discouragement from the official labor market. The official unemployment rate in Palermo in June 1979 was about 12%, while Naples showed a level of almost 25%, or 126,000 persons at the beginning of 1981; in both cities unofficial estimates of unemployment run double the official figures.[24] Even without reliable statistics, however, one conclusion is inescapable: urban unemployment in the South has reached levels that seriously threaten social and political stability (see Chapter 10 for discussion of the political role of the unemployed in Naples).

With regard to the occupational structure of the southern city, the data from the 1971 census (the latest available as of this writing) provide, despite their limitations, a general picture of the distribution of the labor force among economic sectors.[25] Comparison of the figures for Palermo and Naples with those for the rest of Italy, and in particular for a northern industrial city like Milan, demonstrates the disparity in the structure of the urban economy between North and South (Table 2.4). Not only is industrial employment much lower in the southern cities but construction accounts for a significantly higher proportion of such employment (this is especially true for Palermo, where construction absorbs almost one-third of all industrial employment). While northern cities average 12 manufacturing jobs

Table 2.4. *Occupational distribution of the labor force by sector, 1971 (in percentages)*

	Palermo	Naples	Milan	Italy
Rate of labor force participation	26.2	25.8	40.5	34.8
Agriculture	5.8	1.8	0.3	17.2
Industry	35.0	39.0	47.0	44.3
Construction (as % of industry)	31.9	17.9	9.8	24.3
Tertiary	59.2	59.1	52.7	38.4
Commerce and services	34.7	37.2	37.2	25.2
Public administration"	13.0	10.0	4.9	6.5

" The true weight of the public sector is understated by Italian census figures, which include only administrative personnel of various levels of government. All other public employees are recorded under the specific sector in which they work.
Source: ISTAT, *11° Censimento generale della popolazione* (1971).

per 100 inhabitants (as high as 20 in Milan and Turin), the average for southern cities is only 5 (even Taranto, the most industrialized southern city, having only 9 manufacturing jobs per 100 inhabitants).[26] Even worse, the census data show that, while in both Naples and Palermo industrial employment rose significantly between 1951 and 1961, it had fallen again by 1971 to levels only slightly above those of 1951 (Table 2.3).

Another indication of the structural weakness of industry in the southern city is the average number of employees per firm – 6.5 in Palermo and 7.8 in Naples compared to 13.2 in Milan. In both Palermo and Naples about 90% of all industrial firms and 26% of industrial employment are accounted for by firms with fewer than 10 employees, in contrast to 83.5% and 16.3% respectively in Milan (Table 2.5). During the 1960s, the decade of the Italian "economic miracle," the industrial structure of the two southern cities actually deteriorated. The census data show a sharp decrease in employment levels and average firm size at the same time as the total number of firms increased (Table 2.6). This apparent contradiction points to the process of increasing pulverization of the industrial structure discussed above: both those workers laid off from regular factory jobs and new workers entering the labor market find employment prospects only in an expanding "precarious" sector (including large numbers of women working at home in Naples), which tends to elude both the census and official regulation.

This hypothesis is reinforced by data on marginal employment (Table 2.7), showing an overall increase between 1961 and 1971 of about 10,000 in Palermo and 18,000 in Naples, with the most substantial gains, after services, in construction and manufacturing.[27]

The mass of marginal workers concentrated in the service sector (and in commerce as well, although they are camouflaged in the census data by the large number of merchants who work in the city while residing in nearby communities) points to a final critical aspect of the urban economy – the impressive swelling of the tertiary sector, in both absolute and relative terms, between 1951 and 1971. Although the 1971 census shows relatively similar levels of tertiarization in northern and southern cities, the meaning of this phenomenon, given the disparity in levels of industrialization, is radically different in the two cases. (For a more detailed analysis of the nature and functions of the tertiary sector in the southern Italian city, see the section dealing specifically with it later in this chapter.)

The remainder of this chapter will examine in greater depth the four key sectors of the urban economy: manufacturing, construction, the tertiary sector, and the activities of the urban *sottoproletariato*.

Manufacturing. Manufacturing is usually considered the basic indicator of the degree of industrial development of an economy. In Naples and Palermo not only is the percentage of the labor force employed in manufacturing much lower than in an industrial city like Milan (22% in Palermo and 31% in Naples, as opposed to 41.6% in Milan) but the structure of the sector discourages any but the most generic use of the term "industrial." Average firm size is only 5.3 employees in Palermo and 6.7 in Naples, as opposed to 13.4 in Milan. In Palermo, of the 4,834 manufacturing firms registered by the 1971 census, only about 80 have over 50 employees and only 4 over 500 employees. The only two firms in the city that resemble modern industrial complexes are the Cantieri Navali (shipbuilding) with 3,700 employees (down from 5,000 a few years ago) and the Sit-Siemens (electronic components) with about 2,000 employees in two plants. Both these firms, as well as about 20 medium-sized firms (50– 250 employees) are sustained by public capital, the first two by a state holding company (IRI) and the others by the Ente Siciliana per la Promozione Industriale (ESPI), the regional equivalent of IRI. Manufacturing in Palermo is thus polarized between a handful of large and medium firms maintained by public, or at any rate nonlocal, capital and a myriad of traditional artisanal shops, the successful medium-scale local entrepreneur being almost nonexistent.

This proliferation of tiny "marginal" firms operates for the most part in such traditional sectors as food processing, clothing and shoe manufacture, furniture building, and auto repair (classified under industry rather than services in the Italian census). As we have seen, the economic position of the majority of these firms is quite different

Table 2.5. *Distribution of industrial and commercial firms by size, 1971*

Size of firm	No. of industrial firms			Total industrial employees		
	Palermo	Naples	Milan	Palermo	Naples	Milan
0–9 employees	4,935 (91.8%)	10,683 (90.5%)	25,579 (83.5%)	10,122 (26.8%)	23,836 (26.0%)	65,876 (16.3%)
10–49 employees	356 (6.6%)	884 (7.5%)	3,964 (12.9%)	7,364 (19.5%)	17,312 (18.9%)	79,720 (19.7%)
50 employees and over	83 (1.5%)	235 (2.0%)	1,076 (3.5%)	20,290 (53.7%)	50,564 (55.1%)	258,411 (64.0%)

Source: ISTAT, *5° Censimento dell'industria e del commercio* (1971).

from that of their counterparts in the North, where many small-scale firms are functionally linked through arrangements like subcontracting to large firms in the modern sector. In the South, on the contrary, such firms are experiencing an ever-deepening crisis precisely because they have lost their economic raison d'être: on the one hand, because of the type of industrial development pursued in the South ("the cathedrals in the desert"), they lack the type of symbiotic relationship with the modern sector that has given a renewed stimulus to small firms in the North; on the other hand, even their traditional function of producing for local markets has been seriously undermined by northern competition. These firms have managed to survive thus far for two basic reasons: (1) their miniscule size and almost total nonunionization, which enable them to avoid the high labor costs and rigidities in the use of the work force that afflict larger firms; and (2) the availability, because of the dearth of alternative sources of employment, of a sizable work force willing to accept employment under such conditions.

In general terms, the Neapolitan economy is essentially similar to that of Palermo and most other southern cities – if anything, because of its size and importance, the distortions provoked by the process of "urbanization without industrialization" are even more accentuated in Naples. What makes Naples unique, however, is that, backward as its economy appears when compared with that of a modern industrial city, what limited industrial investment *has* occurred in the South has been concentrated disproportionately in the Neapolitan area. Some 60%–70% of the entire industrial apparatus of the South is located in the region of Campania (the majority within the metropolitan area of Naples); of this industry, approximately 70% is accounted for by public enterprise, primarily in the sectors of metal-

Table 2.5. (cont.)

No. of commercial firms			Total commercial employees		
Palermo	Naples	Milan	Palermo	Naples	Milan
10,897	23,687	41,350	21,168	47,264	95,296
(97.6%)	(97.5%)	(93.8%)	(73.9%)	(75.9%)	(52.3%)
232	545	2,398	4,213	9,688	45,612
(2.1%)	(2.2%)	(5.4%)	(14.7%)	(15.6%)	(25.1%)
35	54	340	3,267	5,317	41,114
(0.3%)	(0.2%)	(0.8%)	(11.4%)	(8.5%)	(22.6%)

working and steel. As a result, by comparison with other southern cities, Naples can boast a substantial industrial base, dominated by huge publicly sustained firms like the Italsider steelworks (8,000 workers) and the Alfa Sud automobile factory (15,000 workers). Although they remain isolated islands in the vast sea of artisan workshops and the seemingly endless waves of the unemployed, these large, highly unionized complexes have provided Naples with a compact and combative working-class nucleus that is missing in a more purely tertiary city like Palermo. For discussion of the political impact of this working-class presence in Naples, see Chapter 10.

In both Naples and Palermo, the already fragile manufacturing base has been further eroded since the onset of the current economic crisis in 1973–4. The rates of bankruptcy among small and medium-sized firms – especially in the sectors of textiles, clothing, shoes, and food processing – have been frighteningly high.[28] Those medium-sized firms that remain have resorted to massive use of the Cassa Integrazione in order to avoid large-scale layoffs.[29] As the crisis has deepened, even the large firms of the state-holding sector, whose chronic deficits had heretofore been sustained by public funds, have begun to join in the trend first toward use of the Cassa Integrazione and eventually the threat of actual layoffs.

Construction. As indicated above, construction accounts for a disproportionate share of industrial employment in southern cities. The role of the construction industry has been especially pronounced in Palermo, where a large proportion of manufacturing firms produce supplies for the construction industry and are thus dependent for survival upon the health of this sector. The weight of the construction industry in the local economy (about 33% of the industrial work

Table 2.6. *Regular employment in industry, 1961–71*

	Palermo			Naples		
	1961	1971	Change in employment, 1961–71	1961	1971	Change in employment, 1961–71
All industry						
No. of firms[a]	5,069	5,314		10,528	11,792	
No. of employees	36,780	34,790	−5.4%	103,677	91,104	−12.1%
Average no. of employees/ firm	7.3	6.5		9.8	7.7	
Manufacturing						
No. of firms[a]	4,779	4,834		9,948	10,952	
No. of employees	28,017	25,538	−8.8%	81,534	73,408	−10.0%
Average no. of employees/ firm	5.9	5.3		8.2	6.7	
Construction						
No. of firms[a]	232	248		774	765	
No. of employees	6,304	5,808	−7.9%	17,348	12,318	−29.0%
Average no. of employees/ firm	27.2	23.4		22.4	16.1	

[a] These figures refer to the census category *unità locali*.
Note: Because of the nature of the census-taking process, these figures exclude most "marginal" employment.
Source: ISTAT, 4° *and* 5° *Censimento dell'industria e del commercio* (1961 and 1971).

force in Palermo and 18% in Naples compared to only about 10% in Milan) is important as an indicator not only of the lack of true industrial development but also of the nature of much of so-called industrial employment in the South. The construction industry in general tends to be highly sensitive to swings in the business cycle and therefore to offer unstable employment prospects. This cyclical vulnerability is aggravated in southern Italy by the structure of the industry itself: like manufacturing, it is composed primarily of a myriad of small firms (of about 300 construction sites in Palermo in 1976, only 15 employed over 100 workers, with average size being 25–30

Table 2.7. *Marginal employment by sector, 1961–71*

	Palermo		Naples	
	1961	1971	1961	1971
Agriculture	14,794	8,987	9,049	5,179
Manufacturing	4,924	11,427	16,385	24,613
Construction	15,426	12,979	14,499	9,091
Services	13,228	24,938	29,269	48,570
Total	48,372	58,331	69,202	87,453

Source: Comparison of figures from the *Censimento generale della popolazione* and the *Censimento dell'industria e del commercio*. For an explanation of the method, see footnote 27.

workers)[30] employing traditional labor-intensive techniques and offering extremely precarious working conditions – without contractual guarantees for minimum wages, social security benefits, enforcement of safety standards and, most of all, job security. The core of what can be considered true industrial workers in this sector is quite limited: in Palermo only about one-third of construction workers are specialized, the remainder being recruited from the masses of unemployed *sottoproletari*.[31] The bulk of the work force thus constitutes an unstable and fluctuating labor reserve that can easily be taken on or laid off in response to cyclical conditions.

The size and nature of the work force employed in construction have important implications not only for the local economy but for local politics as well. Given the fragmented and precarious structure of the sector, unionization has until recently been limited to those few large firms (mostly nonlocal) operating on public-works contracts; as one union leader put it, "Union organization in this sector is extremely difficult, because it means trying to organize the unemployed."[32] The plethora of small-scale – and frequently illegal (i.e., without necessary licenses and authorizations) – construction sites that continue to spring up like mushrooms on the periphery of the city remain, for the most part, dominated by the logic of paternalism and personalism, aided by the almost complete nonfunctioning of the state employment office (Ufficio di Collocamento), whose purpose it is to guarantee impartiality in hiring and firing. As a result these firms form an important link in the chain of clientelistic politics on which local power is based.

The tertiary sector. As shown above, the economy of the southern city is heavily weighted toward the tertiary sector. The two major components of the tertiary sector, and the city's principal sources of income are: (1) the public administration, and (2) commerce and services. Given the importance of external public intervention in sustaining the local economy in the South, the vast array of activities and services that in one way or another come under the heading of "public administration" constitute the heart of the urban economy. The true weight of the public sector is much greater than the official census figures indicate (13% in Palermo, 10% in Naples, 4.9% in Milan). The official figures include only the administrative personnel of the national, regional, provincial, and municipal governments as well as the employees of the public school system and the state social-security and health-insurance systems. They exclude the workers in the *aziende municipalizzate* ("city-run firms") providing garbage collection, transportation, gas, and water (about 5,000 in Palermo and 10,000 in Naples), in hospitals and banks (a large percentage of which are public in Italy), and in a myriad of public and semipublic agencies (*enti*) and state-controlled enterprises (which are counted in the census under the industrial sector to which they belong). A quasi-official estimate (based on contributions to state health-insurance programs) placed the total number of public employees in Palermo (still excluding workers in publicly owned industries) at about 35.6% of the labor force.[33]

Census data on the structure of the commercial and service sectors underline the abyss between the role of such sectors in Naples or Palermo as opposed to a city where these activities increase in a complementary relationship with an expanding productive base. In the southern city, where the traditional economic structure was already skewed toward tertiary at the expense of productive activities, two decades of "industrial development," rather than readjusting the occupational distribution of the urban population, produced instead an even further increase in the weight of the tertiary sector at the expense of industry (see Table 2.3). As in the case of industry, commerce is polarized between a handful of large supermarkets and department stores and thousands of family-run shops (Table 2.5). In both Palermo and Naples, the average commercial firm has only 2.6 employees, with over 70% of all shops employing only 1 or 2 persons, usually family members; in addition, about 20% of all commercial licenses (plus a very large number of unlicensed sellers) are represented by *ambulanti*.[34] Including estimates of unlicensed sellers, there is about one shop or vendor for every 40 inhabitants in Naples and for every 50 in Palermo.[35] As one observer in Palermo put it, "This is not a city, but a huge bazaar."[36]

The role of commerce and services in the urban economy, closely linked to the concept of "urbanization without industrialization," is more similar to the situation in Third World cities than to that of urban centers in the rest of Western Europe or the United States. Like most Third World cities, the southern Italian city exerts a strong migratory pull upon its hinterland, an attraction far in excess of the limited "formal sector" employment it can offer ("formal sector" referring to regularized employment in firms that pay minimum wages and normal benefits, while the "informal sector" includes both a wide range of independent activities in petty commerce and services and wage labor in tiny shops where minimum wage and other labor regulations cannot be enforced). Very often, as indicated above, low-income residents of the city, migrants as well as natives, find employment in the construction industry. By its very nature, however, construction activity is subject to extreme seasonal and cyclical swings, so that employment in this sector – especially for unskilled laborers – is particularly unstable.

Given the severe shortage of regular employment possibilities in the formal sector in proportion to the labor supply, people turn to a wide range of informal activities, primarily in the tertiary sector, in order to make ends meet in the absence of, or in the intervals between, more stable jobs. The most common of these activities are the manifold forms of petty commerce and services, as well as some forms of neighborhood-based manufacturing (e.g., shoes, clothing, certain kinds of foodstuffs) – activities generally characterized by easy entry and exit and relatively low capital and skill requirements. Definition of such pursuits as "refuge" activities is in no way intended as pejorative or as a denial of the very real functions they may serve within the overall urban economy. Such functions include: (1) serving as necessary links between wholesale outlets and the individual consumer in the absence of large supermarkets and department stores; (2) adapting production and distribution to the particular needs of low-income neighborhoods – for example, provision of lower-quality, cheaper goods (especially in the case of shoes, clothing, and household needs), extension of credit, making goods easily accessible on a day-to-day basis; (3) in the absence of adequate social welfare programs, providing a cushion against total loss of income through unemployment and, from the point of view of elites, providing a buffer against potential social explosions; (4) maintaining, at no cost either to the industry or the state, a substantial labor reserve to meet the fluctuating needs of industries like construction. The recognition of the importance of such functions by government elites is shown – in the case of Italy at least – by the effort throughout the postwar period, at the level of both national legislation and local government licensing activities, to sustain small shopkeepers and businessmen. In the case of commerce, this has promoted an extreme fragmentation of the distributive network and impeded the entry of large supermarkets and department stores.

Some scholars have argued, on the basis of research in Third World cities, that it is a mistake, rooted in Western preconceptions, to define employment in the informal sector as a refuge activity.[37] They show instead that many participants in such activities consciously choose them over regular factory or office jobs because they prefer the personal autonomy inherent in such work to the fixed hours, work pressures, and subordination to superiors that come with formal sector employment. Such an argument may certainly have some validity in developing countries where, even in regular factory jobs, workers have little union protection and are subject to harsh working conditions and low wages, or, in a country like Italy, for a minority of highly skilled craftsmen or well-established shopkeepers. In general, however, the strength of the labor movement in Italy is such that it really does make a qualitative difference – in terms not only of wages but above all of health and pension benefits and job security – whether one works in the formal or informal sector. In southern Italy, the precariousness of economic survival in general is such that the primary aspiration of every worker is a guarantee of stable employment – and this means either the public sector (doormen, garbage men, bus drivers, etc.) or a regular factory job. Given the limited employment possibilities in these two categories, many people spend a lifetime making ends meet in a variety of informal sector activities (see the next section). In the Italian case, I think it is fair to say that, not only in the eyes of outside observers but in the perceptions of participants themselves, such means of earning a living are seen precisely as refuge activities, not a free choice but a necessity to be endured in the eternal hope of finding something better.

The northern industrial city also boasts a large tertiary sector, but it is one much less marked by the day-to-day struggles for survival of the very poor and one that has developed in concomitance with, rather than in the absence of, a productive economic base. In advanced industrial nations, the increasing tertiarization of the urban economy has been seen as an index of the approach of "postindustrial" society. In southern Italian cities, on the contrary, a quantitatively similar phenomenon has a radically different significance; here it reflects not rising levels of affluence and leisure, but rather the expedients of the poor in a society that offers them few other alternatives.

The urban *sottoproletariato*. To a large degree cities like Naples and Palermo still retain the bipolar class structure of the preindustrial city: on the one hand, the middle classes – of whom the vast majority are either professionals or civil servants – who have taken over the role traditionally played by the court and the land-owning aristocracy, and on the other, the urban *sottoproletariato*. In a city like Palermo (and in Naples only to a slightly lesser degree), with only a minimal proportion of the population represented by a stable industrial working class, the term *sottoproletariato* describes almost everyone who is neither a landowner, a professional, or a member of the bureaucratic and commercial middle classes. Hobs-bawm's description of the nineteenth-century "city mob" continues to apply quite well to the present-day urban *sottoproletariato* in Naples or Palermo: petty artisans, marginal wage earners, and finally the mass of street-vendors, small dealers of various kinds, and all those who survive by making ends meet on a day-to-day basis.[38]

Despite the importance of the *sottoproletariato* in the economy of the southern city, concrete data on the numbers of people in ques-tion and the types of work performed simply do not exist. Because of the precarious ways in which these people make a living, they are for the most part excluded from official labor-force statistics, and no in-dependent studies have as yet concerned themselves in any system-atic way with this sector of the urban economy. A first approxima-tion of the numbers of people classifiable as *sottoproletariato* may be obtained from the figures on the marginal work force (Table 2.7), al-though even these figures almost certainly err substantially by omis-sion, as many members of the marginal labor force do not appear even in calculations of the active population. Taking family members into consideration, unofficial estimates of the size of the *sottoprole-tariato* in major cities like Naples and Palermo run as high as one-third to one-half of the total urban population.[39]

Attempting to gain a precise idea of the distribution of various trades within such an amorphous category as *sottoproletariato* is a thankless task. In the absence of any sort of systematic survey of the social and economic reality of the urban slums, the best available sources of information are two partial, but extremely vivid and inci-sive, studies on Palermo carried out in the late 1950s,[40] and two re-cent investigations, one socioeconomic and one ethnographic, of life in the Neapolitan slums.[41] The concept of industrial worker as gen-erally understood in the West is virtually an unknown quantity among the residents of the crumbling alleyways and dank courtyards of the old city in Naples or Palermo. For these slum dwellers an *indus-triale* ("industrialist") is one who keeps busy (*si industria*):

The term "industrial worker" is a meaningless expression in southern Italy. Anyone who does not work plowing the soil considers himself an "industrial worker." One might be employed as a *spicciafaccende* (one who assists others

– usually the poor and illiterate – in procuring documents from public offices), an *accuogliapanni* (hawker of used clothing), an *arriffatori* (seller of chances for a neighborhood lottery), a *petrusinari* (seller of parsley and basil), or a *borsaiolo* (purse snatcher), the most "industrious" of all.[42]

The primary fact of life for the *sottoproletario,* in contrast to the industrial worker, is the constant uncertainty of economic survival, not only in terms of the duration of work over time but even in the very trade one exercises:

The rhythms of work appear even more characteristic than its forms. Just as the normal state of a river in North Africa is to be without water, the almost normal condition here is to be without work. In the course of a day as in the course of a year or a lifetime, work lasts much less than unemployment . . . Furthermore, professional mobility is extreme. Not only is the rate of change rapid, but the successive transformations may appear surprising to one who comes from an industrialized country. The bricklayer becomes a shoemaker, the hairdresser a bricklayer, the blacksmith a tripeseller. The original trade, if it ever existed, in the end counts much less than the succession of substitutions: porter, bootblack, vendor of parsley or prickly pears, stevedore, car-washer. There is neither specialization nor fragmentation of tasks . . . The artisan sells, the vendor manufactures, the herb-gatherer then cooks his herbs, the candy-seller makes up his own product for the next day, and the exploited attempt to exploit in turn.[43]

What emerges vividly from these accounts is the classical figure of the *mille mestieri* (literally "a thousand professions"), that is, a person who changes his trade from day to day.[44] Given the paucity of alternative sources of employment, the economy of the center-city slums revolves about the manifold forms of petty commerce and services whose success is facilitated by the continuing physical proximity of the urban poor to the major business and administrative centers of the city:

In this jungle of great and small powers, everyone tries to sell to everyone else. An economy of recuperation dominates the city. It is the sordid recuperation of the city's waste, the gathering up of the meager offerings of nature: gatherers of snails, pickers of lavender, young collectors of cigarette butts or orange peels, collectors of garbage who spend half the night filling their baskets, stealing wastes from the city government in order to sell them directly to the peasants of the Conca d'Oro . . . The tripe seller passes and the soup-woman sets up a table in the middle of the street, for those, as she puts it, who don't have enough money to eat at home. When all of this is sold, there remain pumpkin seeds, sawdust, brooms. Above all, there remains the lottery . . . Two hundred *arriffatori* walk through the streets selling tickets whose color changes every day, in order to prevent fraud; for thirty lire one can win bread, pies or coal. Is the beggar offering his holy images a seller of chances as well? For him his activity is a job: he follows his itinerary with the regularity of a bureaucrat.[45]

A rare objective mirror of conditions of life and work in the Palermo slums is offered by the data from Danilo Dolci's 1956 survey of the residents of two center-city neighborhoods, the Capo and the Cortile Cascino, the results of which can be extended in their general outlines to the mass of the urban *sottoproletariato*. Among male heads of family Dolci found the following occupational distribution:[46]

Capo

32	street-vendors
9	laborers
8	shoemakers
4	bricklayers and carpenters
3	streetcleaners
1	stevedore
1	tailor
1	plasterer
1	house painter
1	cart decorator
1	driver
1	wood-inlayer
1	lathe operator
1	poolroom attendant
1	barber's assistant
1	mailman
1	sawdust seller
1	grocery clerk
1	money changer
1	seller of black-market cigarettes
10	no trade reported
4	disabled
13	welfare recipients

Cortile Cascino

39	collectors of junk metal
18	gatherers of old rags and cardboard
4	laborers
2	stevedores
2	street cleaners
2	shoemakers
1	military draftee
1	street-vendor of fruit and vegetables
1	parsley-seller
1	blacksmith's assistant
1	doorman
1	house painter
1	stonemason
14	welfare recipients

The majority of women in these neighborhoods, in contrast to the general Sicilian tendency for women to remain in the home, work either as laundresses or domestic servants. In Naples, on the other hand, *lavoro a domicilio* ("work at home") plays a central role in the economy of the center-city slums; it has been estimated that within the city of Naples alone 40,000–50,000 people, primarily women and children, work at home on a subcontracting basis, especially in the clothing and shoe industries.[47]

The struggle for survival in the slums of Naples and Palermo is dominated not only by the continual uncertainty of work but also by its constant overlap with various forms of more or less illegal activity. Two of the major economic pursuits in slum neighborhoods are the sale of contraband cigarettes and theft (from endemic purse snatching by young boys to much more sophisticated and well-organized operations linked to the petty "mafia" or "camorra" bosses who still hold sway in the underworld organization of the slums). In Naples an estimated 50,000 contrabandeers provide a major source of income for the slum economy. Apart from contrabandeers, thieves, and prostitutes, even the ordinary man-in-the-street, trying desperately to make ends meet with a small shop or a pushcart of fruit and vegetables, finds it almost impossible to live in a state of perfect legality: those who operate without the full array of required licenses and authorizations run into the thousands, and fines and prison sentences are accepted as a regular and inevitable part of life.

One of the most characteristic aspects of life in the slums of Naples or Palermo is the widespread dependence, of the individual family as well as of the local economy, on child labor (see Figure 2.1). Both cities boast a vast army of child workers, compelled by sheer necessity to begin working part-time at the age of 7 or 8, and then to leave school altogether at 11 or 12, upon completion of the 5th grade (the last year of elementary school in Italy):[48]

They are the errand boys of the coffee bars, grocery stores, delicatessans, bakeries and barbers; the workers in citrus-fruit warehouses and small shoe and textile factories, the umbrella and hat makers; the young carpenters, mechanics, typesetters and apprentices in artisan shops; the young girls who do domestic labor, sew trousers, and clerk in shops; the street-vendors. There is not a single sector of the economy, apart from the industrial and public sectors, in which minors between the ages of 7 and 18 are not employed.[49]

Given the clandestine nature of such activity, there are of course no exact data on the numbers of children involved; unofficial surveys, however, have produced estimates of a minimum of 8,000 working children in Palermo and an incredible figure of 100,000 in Naples.[50]

These children work 10–12 hours per day, earning an average of 3,500 lire (about U.S. $4) per week; they are totally deprived of social-security and health-insurance coverage, and are frequently exposed to serious health and safety hazards. Despite stringent laws prohibiting child labor, local officials of the State Labor Office are powerless to enforce compliance in the face of the complicity of the child and his family. In one recent case in Palermo a 10-year-old boy working in a butcher shop lost his arm in a meat-grinding machine, but the courts were unable to bring charges against the employer, because the boy and his family obstinately insisted that the child was merely "playing" in the shop when the accident occurred. Episodes such as this are a horrifying index of the stark poverty that haunts the slums of cities like Naples and Palermo, where a child can find work more easily than an adult and where, as a result, whole families eke out a bare subsistence on the meager wages of several children. Worst of all, poverty and child labor, provoking as they do substandard scho-

Figure 2.1. Child labor in Palermo. *Source:* Nicola Scafidi (Palermo).

lastic performance and early abandonment of school for full-time work, are part of a vicious circle for these children, condemning them to a hopeless future in which they in turn will be forced to send their children out to work in order to survive.

3

Christian Democracy in the postwar South: clientelism and the failure of reform

With the fall of Fascism and the establishment of the Republic, Italian politics, in the South as in the North, was dominated by the competition among the three mass parties – the Communists (PCI), the Socialists (PSI), and the Christian Democrats (DC). The traditional notables and local cliques that had dominated southern politics since 1860, even under the guise of Fascism, inexorably gave way before the grass-roots organizational penetration of modern ideologically based political parties. Yet, in spite of a radical transformation of the outward forms of politics, the clientelistic bases of political behavior inherited from the pre-Fascist period have remained remarkably resilient – if anything, given the greatly increased role of the state, they have been reinforced. The apparent paradox of the coexistence of the organizational structures of a modern mass party with a highly personalistic model of political behavior is best epitomized by the evolution of the Christian Democratic Party in the postwar period, although it permeates to a greater or lesser degree all political parties in the South. The purpose of this chapter is to analyze the development of mass politics in the postwar South through a detailed account of the transformation of the dominant party, the DC, both in its internal structure and in its relationship with its electorate and with the state.[1] Observers of the DC in the South over the past three decades have debated at length the issue of the party's true nature: is the DC to be considered a modern mass party or is it instead merely a recreation of the traditional clientele system? This chapter will attempt to provide an answer.

As shown in Chapter 1, Fascism, despite the introduction of the organizational structures of the mass party and a significant expansion in the scope of state intervention, failed to alter seriously either the dominant modes of political behavior or the basic socioeconomic structure inherited from the era of *trasformismo*. While the basic con-

55

text of southern politics thus remained remarkably unchanged from unification until the fall of Fascism in 1943, the Fascist regime did in one way fundamentally shape the course of postwar politics – this decisive act was the reconciliation of the Catholic Church and the Italian state. The Lateran Pacts of 1929, ending over half a century of mutual hostility, institutionalized the role of the Church within the Italian state, granting it wide powers in the sphere of education and family law. The most important provisions in terms of future political development, however, were those permitting the maintenance and organizational autonomy of Catholic religious and lay institutions at a time when all other forms of organized public life had been either suppressed or brought under direct Fascist control. These Church-related groups, in particular Catholic Action, succeeded in keeping alive the germ of Catholic political activism begun by the Partito Popolare and in laying the bases for an independent leadership class behind the monolithic façade of the Fascist regime. Given the elimination of all other competing groups, the Lateran Pacts clearly placed Catholics in a privileged position to assume power when Fascism fell.

The early postwar years: the dominance of the notables

In 1943 the Christian Democratic Party was constituted on the foundations of the pre-Fascist Partito Popolare. Founded in 1918 by Don Luigi Sturzo, a Sicilian priest, the Partito Popolare was conceived as a mass-based Catholic party and rapidly came to rival the Socialists in its organization of peasant cooperatives and its radical program for land redistribution. Like all other parties, the Partito Popolare was outlawed under Fascism, but many of its leaders, reinforced by the new generation brought up in the ranks of Catholic Action, reemerged after the Liberation intent upon reconstituting a popular Catholic party. In the initial postwar years, the DC harked faithfully back to the radical heritage of the Partito Popolare, presenting itself as a progressive, mass-based party in active competition with the Left. Particularly with regard to the critical problems of the South and the peasantry (these were the years of massive, and often violent, land occupations throughout the South), the DC's programs differed little from those of the Communists – bread and work for all, a radical agrarian reform, and a series of structural reforms identical in substance to those demanded by the Left.

In practice, however, implementation of the party's progressive programs in the South ran up against formidable obstacles. Organizational zeal and radical rhetoric were insufficient to overcome the vast economic, social, and political abyss between the North and the South where, except for short-lived peasant outbursts, politics had remained blocked in traditional clientelistic channels. In the North, the DC was truly a popular party, with a broad and politically conscious mass base, particularly among Catholic workers, a deeply rooted network of secondary associations linking the party to key sectors of society (workers, women, youth, etc.), and a coherent ideology combining Catholic idealism with a concrete program of structural reforms. The South, on the contrary, lacked not only the articulated class and interest structure of the North but was without even a tradition of organized Catholicism, let alone of mass political participation.

Party organizers were confronted with a situation in which the arena of politics was monopolized by a restricted circle of local notables.[2] Lacking any independent means of organizational penetration, the Christian Democrats, like the Fascists before them, soon found themselves compelled to turn to the local *grandi elettori* in order to gain electoral support. In the absence of an organized mass base upon which to draw for cadres, many of the DC's local leaders in this early period were recruited from the ranks of the pre-Fascist Liberal notables, mostly landowners or professionals. In addition, as the DC consolidated its hold on power at the national level, increasing numbers of local notables who had initially adhered to right-wing parties and movements – for example, the Liberals, the Monarchists, the Uomo Qualunque (loosely translatable as "Everyman's Party"), the Sicilian Separatist movement – transferred their allegiance, in the best "transformist" tradition, to the DC, the party of government.

In Sicily, in the months immediately following the Allied landing, the Separatists were the dominant political force. Although the movement succeeded in arousing widespread mass support, its leadership remained firmly in the hands of the large landowners and their principal ally, the mafia; behind the rhetoric of colonial oppression by the mainland, the real concern of the Separatist leaders was the prospect of a Left-dominated government in Rome that might undermine their power and privileges. With the granting of Sicilian autonomy in 1946, however, and the progressive affirmation of the DC in national politics, the landowners and mafia bosses who had sustained the Separatist movement increasingly came to see in the DC the expression of those forces of social conservation in the name of which they had led the Separatist struggle. It would not be long before many of the most powerful mafia bosses of western Sicily, astutely perceiving where their best interests lay (the power of the mafia having always relied upon a symbiotic relationship with the holders of political power), would deploy their impressive vote-gathering capabilities under the banner of Christian Democracy.[3] Thus, while the DC spoke the language of a progressive mass party, its organizational structure increasingly came to depend upon traditional structures of political influence and control.

The progressive enrollment of right-wing forces in the ranks of the DC was especially marked in a city like Palermo. In the early postwar years both Palermo and Naples constituted major strongholds for parties like the Monarchists and the Uomo Qualunque. In the institutional referendum of 1946 the vote for the Monarchy was 84.2% in Palermo and 78.9% in Naples, compared to a national average of 45.7%. The Uomo Qualunque was a meteoric, but short-lived, phenomenon of right-wing populism, combining a vague nostalgia for Fascism with demagogic appeals to the lower-middle class and the urban poor. (See Tables A.2 and A.4 for postwar electoral results in Palermo and Naples.) The Monarchists, although led by prominent aristocrats and landowners, relied on substantially the same social base and electoral techniques – populist "antistate" appeals coupled with the traditional deference relationship between the aristocrat and the urban *sottoproletariato*, both reinforced by mass distribution of spaghetti just prior to election day.

In Palermo the process of alliance with, and eventual absorption of, the right-wing notables and their clienteles by the DC was already well under way by 1946 and climaxed, a decade and a half later (1963), with a full-scale shift of allegiance on the part of the city's most prominent Monarchist politicians, including the party's regional secretary and several members of its national parliamentary delegation; in Naples, the national stronghold of the Monarchist movement, this process of realignment took place only after 1958, when the Monarchist administrations that had governed the city since 1952 were dissolved by prefectural order.[4] In both cities each of these "conversions" involved a precise *quid pro quo:* in most cases an appointment to a position of power in one of the numerous agencies and institutions under the tutelage of local government, or a promise of election to a higher public office, in return either for critical votes in the City Council or, increasingly, outright adherence to the DC. The results of this operation were clearly advantageous to both sides: on the one hand, the ex-Monarchists, Liberals, and Qualunquisti gained access to positions of power attainable only through the ruling party, while, on the other, the DC secured control over the extensive electoral fiefdoms of the old right-wing notables – especially in the *quartieri popolari* of the old city and the outlying rural *borgate* ("townships") where the DC had few independent means with

Table 3.1. *Voting shifts between municipal elections of 1952 and 1956 in two types of* quartieri popolari

	1952	1956
Centro storico (Tribunali, Monte di Pietà, Palazzo Reale, Castellammare)		
Right (Monarchists, MSI)	28,772 (46.1%)	18,522 (31.9%)
DC	13,533 (21.7%)	19,092 (32.9%)
Left (PCI, PSI)	14,881 (23.8%)	15,476 (26.7%)
Total vote	62,438 (100%)	58,019 (100%)
Borgate (Brancaccio, Settecannoli, Villagrazia)		
Right	7,660 (44.5%)	5,332 (27.0%)
DC	3,777 (21.9%)	8,017 (40.7%)
Left	3,416 (19.9%)	4,257 (21.6%)
Total vote	17,209 (100%)	19,719 (100%)

Note: Turnout levels for these elections were 75.7% in 1952 and 80.9% in 1956. Data disaggregated at the level of *quartiere* are not available for earlier elections.
Source: Electoral statistics of the Comune di Palermo.

which to displace the deeply rooted right-wing clienteles. In the case of Palermo, the dynamics of this process at the neighborhood level can be seen from Table 3.1, which shows the change in the respective positions of the DC, the Right, and the Left in low-income areas of the city between the administrative elections of 1952 and 1956 (disaggregated data for earlier elections being unavailable). At a more general level, examination of the respective fortunes of the DC and the Right in each of the elections for City Council between 1946 and 1964 provides unambiguous testimony as to the direction in which the DC moved to establish its political hegemony (Table 3.2).

The tendency for the DC to fall back upon local notables in the absence of an articulated organizational structure at the local level was reinforced by the generally conservative electoral base of the party in the South. In contrast to the broad working-class and peasant base provided the party in the North through its linkages to a strong Cath-

Table 3.2. *Administrative elections in the city of Palermo, 1946–64 (percentages of vote and number of seats on City Council)*

	DC	Right[a]	PLI	PSDI	PRI	PSI	PCI	Other[b]	Turnout
1946 (60 seats)	14.5 (9)	44.3 (27)	11.5 (7)	—	—	9.8 (6)	12.1 (7)	7.8 (4)	36.8
1952 (60 seats)	25.0 (16)	41.1 (25)	3.9 (2)	4.5 (2)	1.3 —	22.5[c] (14)		1.7 (1)	75.7
1956 (60 seats)	35.8 (23)	28.8 (17)	3.9 (2)	5.4 (3)	0.4 —	8.6 (5)	16.2 (10)	0.9 —	80.9
1960 (60 seats)	37.9 (24)	17.7 (10)	4.1 (2)	4.4 (2)	7.1[d] (4)		13.8 (9)	14.9 (9)	82.6
1964 (80 seats)	44.4 (37)	10.1 (7)	9.8 (8)	6.2 (5)	4.7 (4)	6.0 (5)	13.0 (11)	5.8 (3)	83.5

[a] "Right" includes the following parties: in 1946 the Monarchists and the Uomo Qualunque; in 1952 the Monarchists, the neo-Fascists (MSI), and the Sicilian Separatists; from 1956 to 1964 the Monarchists and the neo-Fascists.

[b] All local groups, of little political interest, except in 1960, when the entire "other" vote is represented by Unione Siciliana Cristiano Sociale (USCS), a group that split from the DC in 1958 to form a regional government (under Silvio Milazzo) stretching from the far Right to the far Left, but excluding the DC. USCS enjoyed widespread popular support in the regional elections of 1959 and the local elections of 1960 before being absorbed in part back into the DC, in part into the PRI.

[c] Joint list PSI-PCI.

[d] Joint list PSI, PRI, and Partito Radicale.

Note: Dash signifies no lists.

Source: Ministero dell'Interno.

olic subculture, a substantial part of the DC's electorate in the South was composed of moderate middle-class elements who had voted for the various Liberal factions prior to Fascism. These voters, along with a majority of the preexisting political elite in the South, supported the DC as a party capable of attracting and controlling the masses without the threat, thanks to the party's bond with the Catholic Church, of large-scale changes in social structure. The Church, through its grass-roots network of parishes, itself played an important role in mobilizing votes for the DC, especially in the countryside and in low-income urban neighborhoods (for further discussion of the changing role of the Church, see Chapter 7, "Patterns of political participation and political control"). As the DC consolidated its hold on power, it attracted as well many ex-Fascist functionaries and middle-class "intellectuals" seeking positions in the public offices and agencies controlled by the DC. This influx of opportunists seeking jobs and patronage, like that of the right-wing notables and the moderate bourgeoisie, was scarcely compatible with the national party's progressive ideology and programs. Such contradictions inexorably pushed the Christian Democrats to the right in order to maintain the party's electoral base. The DC thus found itself in a paradoxical position: "a party of the center inclined toward the left, it received almost half of its electoral support from a mass on the right."[5]

This policy of retrenchment on the right soon came to prevail at all levels of the DC. Beginning with the expulsion of the Left from the national government coalition in 1947 and reaching a peak first in the anti-Communist electoral crusade of 1948 and subsequently in response to the right-wing backlash triggered by the agrarian reform of 1950, it corresponded in the internal politics of the party with the ascendancy of the moderate faction led by Alcide De Gasperi (prime minister from 1945 to 1953) in Rome and at the local level by notables like Franco Restivo (president of the Sicilian Region) in Palermo.[6] This policy yielded the DC significant electoral gains, particularly in the South, as demonstrated by the following comparisons of DC and right-wing votes in national elections between 1946 and 1958 (Table 3.3).

The "rebirth of the DC": Fanfani's reforms and the rise of the "young Turks"

De Gasperi was opposed within the DC by the "leftist" followers of Giuseppe Dossetti. This group of young men, many of them veterans of the Resistance, had close ties with the Catholic trade unions and pushed for the realization of the program of structural reforms elabo-

Table 3.3. *Relative strength of the DC and the Right in national elections, 1946–58 (in percentages)*

	North[a]		South	
	Republic	Monarchy	Republic	Monarchy
Institutional referendum, 1946	66.2	33.8	36.2	63.8
	DC	Right[b]	DC	Right[b]
Constituent Assembly, 1946	35.5	5.9	35.0	33.8
Parliamentary elections, 1953	41.0	15.5	38.3	26.3
Parliamentary elections, 1958	41.3	10.4	44.4	18.8

[a] North here is intended as both northern and central Italy; Lazio I have included in the South.
[b] Right here includes the PLI as well as far-Right groups like the monarchists, the Uomo Qualunque, and the neo-Fascist MSI.
Note: The 1948 elections are excluded because, due to their plebiscitary nature as a choice between the DC and the Left, the results exaggerated the true strength of the DC with respect to the Right.
Sources: For the referendum and the Constituent Assembly, see ISTAT, *Elezioni per l'assemblea constituente e referendum istituzionale, 2 giugno 1946* (Rome, 1948); for the elections of 1946, 1953 and 1958, see Francesco Compagna and Vittorio de Caprariis, *Studi di geografia elettorale, 1946–1958* (Naples, 1959).

rated by the DC in 1945–6 but subsequently set aside in the quest for votes and allies on the Right. Upon Dossetti's retirement from political life in 1951, the leadership of the "left" passed to Amintore Fanfani, who proceeded to organize a new *corrente* ("faction"), Iniziativa Democratica, no longer directly challenging the leadership of De Gasperi, as had Dossetti, but rather attempting to establish himself as De Gasperi's natural successor. His chance came with the electoral setback of 1953 (when De Gasperi's attempt to secure the DC an absolute parliamentary majority through electoral reform – the so-called *legge truffa*, which awarded 65% of seats in Parliament to the party winning 50.1% of the vote – backfired at the polls) which, coupled with De Gasperi's illness, opened the way for a change of leadership and a "turn to the left" within the DC.

The Congress of Naples in 1954 formalized the conquest of the DC by Fanfani.[7] Fanfani's solution to the identity crisis of the party – the clash between a progressive ideology and a conservative electorate – was to sacrifice neither, but rather to undertake the transformation of the DC into a modern mass party. The goal of the new political secretary was to create a "party of active and responsible members,"[8] a party with an autonomous organizational structure, free from dependence on powerful external pressure groups like the Church and big business and, in the South, free from the grip of local notables. In the South, these proposed reforms implied a far-reaching program of *political* as well as economic development, complementing the already established agencies of state economic intervention (the Cassa per il Mezzogiorno and the agrarian reform agencies) with the organizational structures of a modern political party. Fanfani's design was to transform the population of southern Italy "from passive recipients of more-or-less appreciated favors into people who self-consciously seek projects that will lift them out of their extraordinary depression,"[9] "to create a politics of facts and ideas instead of a politics of agitation and macaroni."[10] In order to bypass the old notables and to mobilize directly the mass base of the party, Fanfani established the Office for the Political and Organizational Development of the Depressed Areas, sending party organizers throughout the South to set up party sections, to hold public assemblies to discuss the party's programs and its actions in the government, and to stimulate grass-roots participation in the life of the party.

To understand the outcome of these reforms in the South, it is necessary to look more closely at the means by which Fanfani's project for the rebirth of the DC as a modern, mass-based political organization was translated into practice at the local level. The case of Palermo is emblematic of what happened to a greater or lesser degree throughout the South.[11] In Palermo the conquest of the party by the "left" preceded Fanfani's victory at the Congress of Naples in 1954. By the early 1950s, in fact, the "old guard" of moderate notables, led by Restivo, had abandoned personal control of the Provincial Federation in order to assume more prestigious public offices, thereby leaving the door open to the "young Turks." The leader of the "new guard" of *fanfaniani* in Palermo was Giovanni Gioia, who in 1956 would become as well Fanfani's political secretary in Rome. Beginning his political career as representative of the party's youth organizations, by 1953, despite rearguard opposition from the moderates, Gioia was elected at the age of 28 to the position of provincial secretary, carrying with him a group of trusted friends whom he immediately placed in key posts in the party apparatus. Like his mentor Fanfani, Gioia's rise to power was accompanied by the slogans of "renewal, the struggle against clienteles and personalistic politics, and moralization of the party and of public life."[12]

Fanfani's campaign against the notables coincided perfectly with the rivalry between Gioia and Restivo in Palermo. At this time the DC in Palermo had neither an effective organizational structure nor a functioning electoral apparatus; DC politics was conducted from the offices of the individual notables rather than from that of the Provincial Secretary. In contrast to notables like Restivo, whose personal prestige and political influence were independent of the party apparatus, for which their interest and esteem were minimal, the "young Turks" carried out their assault on the party leadership through a single-minded concentration on the details of party organization, seeing in control of the apparatus the key to imposing the authority of the provincial secretary over that of the notables. The success of Gioia and his contemporaries throughout the South was rooted in domination of the party at the grass roots, and above all in control of the critical process of *tesseramento* ("recruitment of members") upon which all power within the DC ultimately rests.

In response to Fanfani's directives, hundreds of new party sections were established in the South, particularly in the larger cities; it was these new sections, apparently the instruments for making the DC a truly popular party, which would provide the foundation for a revolutionary transformation in the organization of power within the DC. The local sections (presently 59 in the city of Palermo alone) are the keystone for control of the party because it is there that *tesseramento* takes place. Within the DC, party offices at all levels are elective, with the electors the *tesserati* ("card-carrying members"). Thus, he who controls the process of recruitment to the party can wield substantial power over the selection of the party leadership, even at the national level. The size of the delegation that each section sends to the Provincial Congress, and which the Provincial Federation in turn sends to the National Congress are determined respectively by the number of *tesserati* in each local section and in the province as a whole. Control of the Provincial Congress means control over the composition of the Provincial Committee, the governing body of the party at the local level, which controls the formation of the party's electoral lists and, even more importantly, conditions the outcome of national leadership struggles through its selection of delegates to the National Congress. In a party like the DC, composed of several competing factions, a local leader who can guarantee a sizable bloc of congress votes to the national faction chief is an invaluable asset and in a position to demand substantial rewards in return for his services. The respective roles of national and local leadership are aptly delineated in the following description:

In Rome the power of the national faction chiefs is determined by the number of *tessere* (membership cards) which they control. But party members are recruited in the provinces, through the "vassals" or local faction chiefs. This sets off a mechanism which at the same time degrades and exalts the figure of the "vassal." It degrades him because it makes him an *ascaro*,[13] a proconsul, powerful not for his contribution to political debate but rather for the number of members which he adds to the faction's national strength. He is exalted because, in exchange, the "vassal" obtains from Rome concrete support for his own positions of local power; he receives an investiture which he uses in turn to fortify his "fiefdom."[14]

At first glance, the ascent to power of the "young Turks," focused as it was on laying the organizational bases of a mass party in the South, may seem to exemplify precisely the type of reform that Fanfani's project for the rebirth of the DC had envisaged. In reality, however, the outcome was quite different. The new generation of DC leaders in the South were not noted for their scruples in the pursuit of power; the ideological goals in the name of which they had taken over from the old guard were rapidly subordinated to the quest for power as an end in itself, for the conquest and maintenance of which any means were justified.[15] The strengthening of the party's organizational base meant in practice the creation of an exclusive weapon for consolidating the power position of a particular leader or faction. Given the importance of the *tessere* in the struggle for local and national power, it is hardly surprising that they became the object of unscrupulous political maneuvering: from 18,113 in 1952, party membership in the Province of Palermo jumped to 27,835 in 1953 (the year Gioia began his drive for control of the party) and then gradually climbed to 39,057 by 1959 (by which time the dominion of the *fanfaniani* within the party had become unchallengeable); from then on, party membership has remained substantially unchanged at between 40,000 and 45,000, reflecting a practical freeze on new members in order to maintain the existing balance of power.[16]

Once *tesseramento* became the decisive weapon in the struggle for internal party power, the concept of party membership underwent a drastic transformation. No longer did the *tessera* of the DC signify active participation in the life of the party, nor at times the very knowledge of being a party member: "The *tessera* of the DC is like a blank check: it can be given out to anyone – to relatives, to the deceased, to persons chosen at random from the telephone book or from health-insurance lists."[17] The life of the local party section became, and remains, a mere formality; those sections that have an actual locale (and many do not, existing only on paper) open their doors only during electoral campaigns – they perform no other function, either political or social. The sections thus exist solely to lend a semblance of legitimacy to an organizational hierarchy erected upon a membership base which – even in those cases where the *tessera* actually corresponds to a living person – remains completely excluded from participation and decision making. Elections for the leadership

organs of the party – from the section secretary to the critical delegates to the Provincial Congress – are orchestrated to correspond to
outcomes negotiated beforehand among the local faction chiefs; the
expected ratios are transmitted from above to the section secretary,
who tabulates the "electoral results" accordingly. In very few cases
do the sections even make a semblance of calling the members to
vote and, in those rare instances when they do, the outcome is
closely controlled. Serious debate or discussion of political, social, or
economic issues in local organs of the party, from the neighborhood
section to the Provincial Committee, is practically nonexistent; they
are called together only for the formal ratification of decisions already
taken elsewhere.

The nerve center of this system of power is the party's organizational office, the Ufficio di Organizzazione, which supervises the
process of *tesseramento,* thereby exerting effective control over the
membership of every party section. While the formal duties of this
office are purely bureaucratic, the faction that controls it holds the
ultimate weapon against its rivals – it can limit the number of *tessere*
available to those section secretaries loyal to an opposing faction.
The role of the Ufficio di Organizzazione and its municipal adjunct,
the Comitato Comunale, are so critical that, from 1953 until the realignment of party factions in Palermo in the spring of 1976, both offices were constantly under the direct control either of Gioia himself
(even after his election to Parliament in 1958) or of one of his closest
associates.

That such a degradation of the internal life of the party could per-
sist for over twenty years despite denunciations by the minority factions to the national control organs of the DC[18] is made possible by
the factional structure of the DC and the relationship between national and local faction chiefs outlined above. In terms of these linkages between local and national DC power, the Sicilian wing of the
party has always played a particularly important role:

Sicily weighs heavily and has always weighed heavily in the internal equilib-
ria of the DC, because of the chronic inflation of the number of *tessere* and the
particular ruthlessness (*spregiudicatezza*) of the island's faction chiefs. One
need only consider that the faction of Fanfani counts on Sicily for one-third of
its membership – that is to say, if Gioia fell from power in Palermo, Fanfani's
strength at the next party congress would be reduced to the proportions of a
Scelba [a minor party leader]. And the same goes for his competitors if Lima
should collapse instead.[19]

The same argument can be made, however, for all local party fiefdoms in the South (the Gavas in Naples, DeMita in Avellino, Drago
in Catania, etc.). In each case, unscrupulous manipulation of the in-

ternal life of the party in order to insure local positions of power has been tolerated by the DC leadership in Rome because of the critical votes that local bosses bring to the struggle for national power.

The drive for local hegemony

This section will focus exclusively on the consolidation of power by Gioia and the *fanfaniani* in Palermo. Although the names and factions may differ, the process described below corresponds in its essentials to that which occurred in Naples and virtually every other southern city during the 1960s.[20]

Side by side with his drive to achieve total mastery of the party, Gioia embarked upon a complementary strategy to extend his dominion from the party to the city as a whole. He began by using his control of the party apparatus to elect his followers to the city and provincial councils and to place his men in key positions both in local government offices and in the numerous *enti* ("semi-autonomous agencies") under the tutelage of the municipal, provincial, and regional administrations.[21] Even more than by the career of Gioia himself, who after 1958 spent most of his time in Rome, the conquest of local government and through it domination of virtually every aspect of the political, economic, and social life of the city by the "clan" of the *fanfaniani* is exemplified by the political ascent of Gioia's most trusted deputy and collaborator, Salvo Lima.[22] Lima was recruited in the early 1950s by Gioia, then responsible for the party's youth movement and sports activities, to preside over the DC's local soccer squad. He proved so adept at the art of turning sports to the purposes of political propaganda that, when Gioia assumed the post of Provincial Secretary in 1953, Lima was promoted to head the party's propaganda office, a power center in the apparatus second only to the Ufficio di Organizzazione, at that time in the hands of another Gioia faithful, Giuseppe Lo Forte. Although Gioia retained the title of Provincial Secretary even after joining Fanfani's secretariat in Rome, control of the party in Palermo was in effect delegated to Lima and Lo Forte. In charge of the distribution of propaganda materials and other party resources among the local sections during election campaigns, Lima proved a master at the wooing of section secretaries and *capi-elettori*,[23] weaving a dense fabric of personal loyalties at the base of the party, loyalties that he would eventually turn against Gioia and exploit to advance his own political career.

In 1956 Salvo Lima, still an obscure party functionary popular only among section secretaries, was elected to the City Council with 8,012 preference votes, in fourth place in a list of sixty DC candidates, most of whom were far better known than he. (In Italy one votes both for a party list and for a maximum of three individual candidates within that list. It is the latter, the personal preference vote, which is at the heart of clientelistic politics in the South.) As a result of a series of obscure behind-the-scenes maneuvers within both the DC and the City Council, this unknown young man was elected assessor of public works and deputy mayor in the new administration. Lima's election to these key positions in city government was the critical move in Gioia's drive for control of the city, for the Department of Public Works had jurisdiction not only over public works but over all aspects of urban planning and the licensing and regulation of construction activity; in the period of intense urban development just beginning in the mid-1950s, control of this key department meant control of the construction industry and thereby of virtually the entire urban economy. Lima spent only two years as assessor of public works before assuming the mayoralty upon the death of the incumbent in 1958, but in this short period he succeeded in laying the bases of a new system of alliances between the DC and the local entrepreneurial class, which would become one of the principal pillars of DC power in Palermo. (For a more detailed discussion of the process of urban expansion in Palermo and the relationship between the DC and the construction industry, see Chapter 6.)

Reelected in 1960 with 18,927 preference votes, Lima moved to reinforce his power as mayor by assuming direct control of the party apparatus. Exploiting a new national DC regulation which declared the positions of national deputy and provincial secretary to be incompatible, Lima forced Gioia to step down and in 1962 assumed the post of provincial secretary himself, thereby insuring the complete support of the party for the highly questionable real-estate operations which he was engineering through his control of the city government (see again Chapter 6). By the early 1960s, then, the hold of the *fanfaniani* on the levers of local power was complete. Within the party, opposition to the high-handed methods of Gioia and Lima had been stifled by the national DC leadership's recognition of Gioia as its privileged interlocutor in Palermo. Within the city government, Gioia not only controlled the mayoralty, the major assessorships, and an overwhelming majority of the DC city councillors, but succeeded, together with Lima, in putting together a far-reaching system of political alliances – involving primarily the smaller parties to the right of the DC, but at times capturing votes even within the opposition parties on the left – which made the will of the DC in local government practically unchallengeable.[24] This alliance strategy was based on the principle of "full employment," that is, securing the votes of individual politicians within other parties by guaranteeing them patronage positions within the vast array of public and semi-public *enti* controlled by local government or even, in some cases, election to the regional or national parliaments if they would formally transfer their allegiance to the DC. The culmination of this strategy was reached in 1963 with the wholesale absorption of the leadership of the Monarchist party into the DC. This success, combined with the total subordination of minor parties like the PRI and the PSDI to the DC, guaranteed the *fanfaniani* such a solid majority that the corruption of individual politicians on a vote-by-vote basis was no longer necessary.[25]

This capacity to push measures through the City Council by sheer force of numbers, however, would have been insufficient without concomitant control of the organs delegated by the state to oversee the legitimacy of the acts of local government. This function, exercised elsewhere in Italy by the prefect, an agent of the central government, has in Sicily been delegated by the special regional charter to two bodies that are in practice direct extensions of the dominant political forces at the regional and local levels. Overall supervision of local government – including the power to dissolve local elective bodies and nominate a special commissar to take over their functions – is the domain of the regional Assessorato agli Enti Locali. This key center of power has traditionally been held by someone close to the *fanfaniani*; since 1968 it has been controlled directly by Gioia through Giacomo Muratore, one of his closest deputies and himself Provincial Secretary of the DC in Palermo from 1968 until 1974. The direct scrutiny of the acts of the municipal and provincial administrations for legitimacy (i.e., conformity with existing laws) is the role of the Commissione Provinciale di Controllo ("Provincial Control Commission"), which is elected by the Provincial Council, one of the bodies it is supposed to control. Under these circumstances, the party or parties that control local elective bodies can in turn insure the tutelage of their own interests by those organs that are intended to exercise impartial supervision over the acts of local government. In the words of a parliamentary inquiry on the functioning of local government in Sicily, "the provincial control commissions . . . have proved inadequate to their assigned task, on the one hand because of objective operational difficulties, on the other because they have become too closely tied to existing centers of power to offer the necessary guarantees of independence and impartiality."[26]

Having thus established a solid power base through control of the city government, Gioia's circle of power rapidly expanded in a self-reinforcing upward spiral: power and patronage produced votes, which in turn brought with them access to new centers of power and patronage. From the key assessorships, the city bureaucracy, and the *aziende municipalizzate* (garbage collection, public transportation, gas and water) operating under the control of the *municipio*, the *fanfaniani* extended their reach to include the provincial administration and important sectors (e.g., the Assessorato agli Enti Locali) of the regional government, as well as their respective *enti*. Secure in his hold on local government, Gioia then moved to weld close relationships with the prefect, the police, the major centers of economic power, both public and private, and the Catholic trade union (CISL). In sum, he transformed the position of provincial secretary of the DC from a second-rate organizational post into an authoritative and often determining influence in local political and economic life: "with Gioia the provincial secretary of the DC became a public authority, possessing a power which extends far beyond the party itself."[27]

The *fanfaniani* thus succeeded in constructing a far-reaching system of power which permitted them, from the mid-1950s until the mid-1970s, to exert an unchallenged mastery – without any effective control from within the DC, from other political parties, or from the legal organs of control over local government – not only over the party apparatus but over all major centers of political, administrative, and economic power in the city (Table 3.4). In effect, the entire public sphere was transformed into a powerful political machine for the advancement of personal and party fortunes. This system of power, built up in the name of a regeneration of the DC, had, while publicly rejecting the notables and their traditional clienteles, reconstructed an organizational and political framework in which the mass base of the party remained equally isolated from active participation in political life.

The betrayal of the rhetoric of rebirth in the transformation of the party apparatus into a personal fiefdom contested by rival faction chiefs was matched by the external alliance strategy of the DC in its drive for local hegemony. Like the "old guard" before them, Gioia and company quickly came to realize that, once having forsaken a direct political relationship with the masses, electoral success required a *modus vivendi* with local notables. As we have seen earlier in this section, Gioia's lieutenants in the City Council soon forgot their recent appeals for the moralization of public and party life and outdid their predecessors in the active recruitment of right-wing votes. Confronted with the pressures of electoral competition and of political rivalries within local government bodies, the DC thus opted for the security of the old-style *clientela* networks rather than face the uncertainties of a program of economic and social reforms appealing

Table 3.4. *Principal centers of DC power in Palermo*

Regional government
President of the Region
Key assessors
Regional bureaucracy (6,500 employees)
Special economic agencies (7,000 employees)

Control organs
Assessorato Regionale agli Enti Locali
Commissione Provinciale di Controllo

City government	*Provincial government*
Mayor	President of the province
Key assessors	Key assessors
City bureaucracy (3,800 employees)	Provincial bureaucracy (850 employees)
Aziende municipalizzate (5,600 employees)	

*Major centers of power under direct or
indirect tutelage of local government[a]*

Banks
Hospitals
IACP (public housing authority)
ECA (Ente Comunale di Assistenza)
Ente Autonomo Porto di Palermo
Consorzio per lo Sviluppo Industriale

[a] For a more complete listing see Table 4.4.

directly to the masses. The much-heralded "struggle against the no-tables" ended with large-scale realignment of local politicians, both Christian Democrats and newly won converts from other parties, under the banner of the *fanfaniani,* and with the substitution of the new-style party boss, with his power in the party apparatus and in control of local government, for the old-style notable with his personal following based on traditional authority and prestige. The clientelistic basis of politics, however, remained unchanged; if anything, it was expanded and intensified, extending its sway into areas of social and economic life where it had heretofore been relatively unknown. The "politics of agitation and macaroni" had once again triumphed.

The party of mass patronage

The DC of 1958, when Gioia was elected to Parliament with 83,758 preference votes, was not, however, merely a refurbished edition of the notable-based party of 1950. Despite the apparent continuity in the type of relationship linking party elites to their electoral base, fundamental changes had indeed taken place in the structure and functioning of the DC. A highly articulated organizational hierarchy, linking the most remote southern village to the national leadership in Rome, had replaced the loose congeries of notables upon whom the party had formerly relied for access to the masses; in addition, an entirely new leadership class had been created from within the party by opening the road to parliamentary careers to those who worked their way up through the party apparatus. The formal structures of the DC had been radically transformed, and yet the creation of a direct ideological and/or programmatic bond between the party and its electorate was as far from realization as before.

Why had Fanfani's design for the transformation of the DC into a modern political organization gone awry in the South? The factors involved are dual, on the one hand political, on the other organizational. In order to succeed, Fanfani's reforms would have required a political as well as an organizational strategy for the South – that is, enactment of those fundamental structural reforms necessary to overcome the historical emargination of the southern working classes, in particular the peasants and the *braccianti* ("landless laborers"). The first "Popular Assembly" held in the South in 1954 under the aegis of the Office for Depressed Areas in fact stressed such a popular program, directing its appeal above all to the workers and peasants. By the following year, however, the focus of the party's strategy had already shifted to the middle classes. Fanfani urged the DC to consider the southern middle classes "the frames and hinges of the social system" and to give them the support necessary "to assume willingly the functions of the *pilot* of southern Italian society."[28] The so-called middle classes of the South, however, were in the vast majority precisely those groups against whom Fanfani's reforms had initially been directed – the absentee landowner, the parasitic intermediary, the local notable (doctor, lawyer, or pharmacist), the mafia boss. Once any project of social and economic transformation of the South had been abandoned, and the DC had shifted its attention to these social groups, the role of the party became increasingly one of mediation between such groups and the holders of local and national power. Such mediation was almost inevitably clientelistic, since "as political power shifts from prestigious individuals to party organizations without a corresponding rise in political ideology, patronage must take the place of personal loyalty as a basis of affiliation."[29]

Paradoxically, Fanfani's organizational reforms had quite the opposite effect from what he had intended. Conceived as a weapon to defeat the personal followings of the old notables within the party and to forge a direct political relationship with the masses, the newly created organizational structure of the DC served instead as a more viable and efficient foundation upon which to construct an even more far-reaching system of clientelistic politics. The product of Fanfani's reforms in the South was indeed a mass party, but of a new kind – a party of mass patronage. While the organizational structure of the "new DC" was clearly that of a modern mass-based political party, in the linkages between the party and its electoral base the personalistic tie continued to predominate over the ideological or programmatic bond. The effect of Fanfani's organizational revolution, with its enormous increase in the power of the party apparatus, was not to eliminate clientelism but rather to transform the individual patron–client tie based on the personal prestige of the traditional notable into the mass clientelism of the party bureaucracy.[30] In Sidney Tarrow's words, the DC gave birth to a new system of "horizontal clienteles,"[31] replacing as the critical link in the patronage chain the individual client with the secondary associations allied more or less closely with the DC (in particular, CISL, ACLI, Coldiretti, associations of shopkeepers, artisans, and industrialists).[32]

In the North, where a wide range of economic resources exists independent of the state, these secondary associations, despite their affiliation with the DC, have served a relatively autonomous function of aggregating group interests within society and representing these interests within the party; in fact, the factional structure of the party to a large extent reflects these competing interests, with the left-wing *corrente* of Forze Nuove, for example, drawing its strength primarily from working-class organizations like the CISL and the ACLI, while certain of the right-wing factions rely heavily for support on the Church and its more traditionalist lay associations. In the North, then, the political role of these secondary associations approximates a model of interest-group representation.

In the South, on the contrary, the relationship between the DC and its collateral organizations is a very different one, reflecting a structural context where virtually all relevant resources are channeled through the state. Rather than functioning as autonomous representatives of group interests vis-à-vis the party, organizations like the CISL and the Coldiretti (the two key associational arms of the DC in the South) have been relegated to an entirely subordinate, and essentially clientelistic, function. Their role is dual: assistance and vote gathering. Despite their formal function of organizing and representing group interests, these associations have acted for the most part as intermediaries for the satisfaction of the individual needs of their members – a job in a state-controlled factory, breaking through bureaucratic red tape to facilitate the granting of a health or pension benefit, obtaining subsidies or credits for small farmers and artisans, and the like. Whereas once the fulfillment of such requests depended on the individual power of the local notable, it is now the union leader or party functionary who, due to his organizational position rather than his personal prestige or economic power, can intervene – either directly or through local political leaders – with the DC-controlled public agencies or state-supported industries that control the requisite resources. As in the North, these secondary associations are frequently associated with particular DC factions, but the linkage is often a purely contingent one, reflecting less ideological affinity than the "capture" of a given organization by a particular faction chief. Like the traditional notable, these politicians, through their position in the party or the government, guarantee the external connections necessary to satisfy the individual needs of the group members, utilizing the organization in turn as a personal fiefdom for electoral purposes.

The material basis for the creation of such a system of power has been the tremendous expansion of state intervention in the South in the postwar period and the progressive interpenetration of the DC and the state administration.[33] The establishment of the Cassa per il Mezzogiorno as an instrument for channeling massive amounts of state funds into economic development of the South was a key factor in the transformation of patronage relationships in southern Italy. By liberating the DC from its initial dependence on external forces like the Church, big business, and local notables, it gave the party the means to construct a totally new *clientela* system, combining the paternalistic management of the new welfare state with direct party control over an unprecedented outpouring of public resources for public works and economic development projects. What has taken place in southern Italy since 1945 is a "statalization of society"[34] together with a "privatization of state power for personal political aims."[35] The former refers to the progressive widening of the sphere of public intervention into the areas of the economy and of civil society previously under private control – banks, hospitals, social security and health insurance programs, public-controlled or supported industries, job placement, etc. – in each case creating an independent bureaucratic structure tending to impede rather than facilitate the satisfaction of individual needs. This process of infiltration of the state, perceived in the South as an alien and unresponsive entity, into those areas of most immediate concern to the individual citizen has stimulated the second process: the privatization of state power for political ends. With the domination of ever wider spheres of social and economic life by impersonal bureaucratic structures, control of a public office or agency can – given the elephantine functioning of the Italian bureaucracy – prove highly profitable to a politician by transforming a citizen's right to service into a particularistic benefit to be obtained only through the personal intervention of the political intermediary.

Public power has been used to create and maintain personal political fiefdoms. This is true not only of the type of individual welfare benefits channeled through the DC's collateral associations in the South but, on a grander scale, of the entire state program of economic intervention. A common tactic is the ministerial telegram announcing the allocation of public funds for a local project, thanks to the intervention of such-and-such a deputy or party leader. As one observer has written:

It is never the State or the national community that appropriates sums for this or that project, for the construction of houses or schools, for the realization of public works or industrial programs: it is always thanks to the interest of this or that local deputy or the local secretary of the DC.[36]

The state has thus become an instrument for the maintenance of a given party regime, a reservoir of patronage resources with which to build political careers and party fortunes.

The accompanying chart sets out in schematic form the differences between the party of mass patronage and the two forms of political organization generally considered polar types along the spectrum of political development: the individual patron – client tie and the modern ideologically based mass party (Table 3.5). The combination of the organizational structure of the latter with the techniques of political mobilization and consensus building characteristic of the former has led most observers to view the party of mass patronage as a transitional form, linked to a situation of economic backwardness, and therefore destined to move inevitably toward the prototype of the ideological/interest-based party as economic development crystallizes the class and interest cleavages characteristic of modern industrial society.[37] Reflection on the political development of southern Italy over the last thirty years, however, gives rise to serious doubts regarding the universal validity of such a unidirectional model of political development. It is clear that the DC has adapted many of the traditional techniques of patronage politics to a political system characterized by high levels of mass political participation and by a greatly increased scope of state intervention in society and in the economy. It is less clear, however, that the politics of mass patronage perfected to such a high degree by the DC will necessarily be under-

Table 3.5. *A developmental model of political organization*

	Patron–client ties	Party of mass patronage	Ideological or interest-based party
Political context	Parliamentary democracy with limited suffrage. Limited role of the state, essentially regulatory; limited penetration of state and party apparatus at local level, thus critical role of mediation by local notables.	Parliamentary democracy with universal suffrage. Interventionist state, with active welfare and development functions; pervasive presence of state and party apparatus throughout society; one-party dominance and inter-penetration of party and state.	Parliamentary democracy with universal suffrage. Interventionist state; type of party system open.
Socioeconomic context	Traditional agrarian economy, poorly integrated with the nation as a whole. Feudal class relationships. Local resources extremely limited, thus reliance on state for resource flow.	Breakdown of traditional economic and social order, but incomplete capitalist development. Fragmented social classes. Limited local resources and reliance on state funds in terms of public bureaucracies, transfer payments, and development programs.	Advanced industrial society. Modern social classes. Sufficient private resources to free the economy from dependence on the state.
Organizational structure	"Parties" only loose coalitions of individual politicians and their personal followings. No grass-roots party presence nor any permanent organizational structure outside Parliament.	Centralized bureaucratic structure with local units throughout the national territory. Para-political secondary associations to maintain constant presence in civil society.	
Bases of support	No mass membership or political mobilization of the masses. Vertical ties based on relationship of personal deference between the individual and the notable. Support based on exchange of personalistic benefits.	Mass membership, but mobilization limited to elections. Basis of political mobilization remains individualistic, but the notable is replaced by an organized political party. Collateral associations function primarily to channel individualistic benefits.	Mass membership. Attempt to maintain high and constant levels of mass mobilization. Mobilization on the basis of collective interests, ideological or programmatic. Collateral associations organize and represent group interests.
Relationship to the state	Public sphere limited, thus substantial formal autonomy, but access to state resources important to maintain support.	Survival depends on control of public resources; interpenetration of party and state.	Relationship to the state one of ideological opposition, alternation of power, or interest-group bargaining.

mined and eventually transformed by the impact of economic development alone. The key to understanding the last thirty years of Italian political development is the almost absolute control by the DC over the state apparatus and over major sectors of the economy, either through outright state control or substantial public participation, not to mention the leverage exerted on private enterprise through governmental programs of incentives and subsidies and control of major banks. So long as it can maintain its hold on these key levers of power, the DC has the means to either prevent or at the very least control the very processes of economic development that are seen as undermining the bases of its power. The history of the Cassa per il Mezzogiorno provides eloquent testimony of the subordination of the goal of economic development to the demands of a given system of political power. The crucial determinants of the existing system of power in the South are political, not economic. Under these circumstances, the politics of mass patronage may well be merely a transitional phase, but the stimuli required to produce the transformation are nowhere to be seen.

The local sources of DC power

The party of mass patronage depends on linkages both from above and from below, to centers of both national and local power. Those who have viewed the party primarily from the perspective of its ties to national power have focused on its role as a mediator between the central state and a resource-scarce periphery. Best developed in the studies of Sidney Tarrow and Percy Allum,[38] this approach associates the shift in power within the DC from the notables to the party apparatus with a transformation of the underlying mechanisms of DC consensus in the South from the individual favors of the traditional notables to the mass favors of an organized political party and a modern welfare state. In this view the primary basis of DC power in the South is the manipulation of state resources (in the form of both economic development programs and subsidies for various social and economic groups) for clientelistic purposes, and the major instrument of that power the new "horizontal clienteles" that have replaced to a large extent the individual patron–client bond.

Looking at the overall postwar strategy of the DC in the South from the perspective of Rome, such an interpretation is entirely valid. Indeed, without the leverage wielded by local party leaders in national factional struggles and the access to state patronage resources guaranteed by the interpenetration of the DC and the state administration over thirty years of unbroken power, it is doubtful whether a political machine like that of Gioia in Palermo could have maintained its monopoly on local power for over twenty years. In the last analysis, one of the fundamental supports of Gioia's regime was his privileged relationship with the center, first as Fanfani's most trusted lieutenant and then, thanks to Fanfani's protection, as deputy and minister in his own right.

Yet, if one approaches the problem instead from the perspective of local politics, a very different picture emerges, one in which a decisive role continues to be played by the very techniques of traditional patronage politics that observers of the "modern" DC have regarded as at best marginal vestiges of a bygone era, and in any case largely ineffective when compared with control over the major centers of state economic power. Looking at DC politics from the bottom up, one is struck, at least in an economic setting like that of Palermo where state development funds have had a very limited impact, with the pervasiveness and apparent efficacy of a very different style of clientelistic politics from the one that emerges from the general analysis of DC politics in the South outlined in the preceding pages. Despite the vastly increased scope of public intervention in the postwar period and the centralized structure of the Italian state, substantial – and thus far largely unexplored – powers remain in the hands of local administrations. Even under the conditions of chronic deficit in which local governments struggle to survive, these powers can provide the basis for powerful local political machines, even in the absence of a conspicuous flow of resources from the center.

In brief, my argument is that, while resource flows from the center cannot be ignored, the key to DC power in the major southern cities has been less control of the Cassa per il Mezzogiorno than control of the *municipio* ("City Hall"). This is not at all to deny that local positions of power could not be maintained in the long run without external support, as the structure of internal DC politics makes abundantly clear. The real issue here is the interplay between power within the party and power within society. At the local level, each reflects the other, because control of the party organization produces electoral success (measured in terms of personal preference votes), which in turn reinforces one's position within the party as well as providing access to critical levers of power within the society at large. The central point to be made is that, despite the importance of national support to sustain and protect positions of local power once attained, the means by which that power is generated are predominantly local.

The preeminence of local levers of power can be illustrated by the outcome of the latent rivalry between Gioia and Lima in Palermo, which finally exploded publicly on the occasion of the parliamentary elections of 1968. After having dominated, and in a sense symbolized, Palermo politics for almost ten years, Salvo Lima gave up his official duties in 1966 in order to prepare his candidature for Parliament in 1968.[39] This move placed him in direct competition with Gioia, whose official spokesman and most loyal collaborator he had heretofore been considered. Although Gioia and Lima conducted the electoral campaign in tandem, the pressure for personal affirmation fostered intense competition for preference votes behind the façade of unity. The outcome was stunning. Lima, virtually unknown outside Palermo and with no independent contacts at the national level, came in first among all DC candidates in the constituency of western Sicily, outdistancing government ministers and undersecretaries, a former president of the Region, and, most unpardonably, Gioia himself. The rivalry born of this electoral showdown has since conditioned every facet of Palermo politics, Lima having broken with Gioia and set up an independent faction after the elections. After nearly a decade of bitter internecine struggle within the DC, which periodically paralyzed local administrations for months at a time, Lima finally succeeded, by the beginning of 1977, in consolidating a new coalition of factions around himself and in relegating Gioia and his supporters to the minority in both the party and the municipal and provincial administrations. Even before the victory of the new coalition was formalized, many of Gioia's supporters had rushed to join the Lima bandwagon. In a context where political loyalties are determined above all by power, Lima has, through his control of the party organization and local government, come to exercise a personal domination over the political life of the city equal to that of Gioia in his heyday. The faces and factions may have changed, but the methods of gaining and maintaining power have proved remarkably resilient.[40]

The moral of this story is the electoral and political triumph of the man who built up his political base first and foremost through manipulation of local levers of power. Both before and after 1968, Gioia's prestige and contacts in the national party organization and the state apparatus far surpassed those of Lima.[41] Yet, precisely because of his increasing preoccupation with national affairs, he was compelled to leave the critical details of the organization of power at the grass roots – the section secretaries, the *capi-elettori*, and the vast *clientela* network represented by control of local government – to his deputies in Palermo. This system functioned admirably, combining national and local levers of power to create an unchallengeable political monopoly, so long as Gioia's subordinates restrained their own ambitions. Once Lima decided to make the break, however, his strategic superiority, rooted in the labyrinthine networks of personal loyalty painstakingly built up over years of direct control of local power, ultimately prevailed. It is to these concrete mechanisms of power at the local level that we will now turn in Part II.

Part II

The social bases of the machine

4

The white-collar middle class

How has the Christian Democratic Party in Palermo succeeded, over a period of thirty years, in creating and sustaining a powerful political machine incorporating almost every sector of the urban population? Viewed from the grass roots, the mechanisms of power are both more simple and more complex than the channels of access to national power outlined in Chapter 3. The major social groups upon which DC power in Palermo rests – the middle classes (in particular public employees), the local entrepreneurial class, and the urban poor – roughly correspond to the key sectors of the urban economy as it has taken shape in the postwar period: public administration, the construction industry, and the vast array of "marginal" economic activities that characterize the urban *sottoproletariato*. In consolidating its relationship with each of these groups, and through them its domination of the city as a whole, the DC has, within the framework of a general clientelistic strategy, developed a highly articulated system of political consensus and control, employing clearly differentiated patronage techniques and types of resources with regard to each of the above social groups.

Because of the dependence of a clientelistic system of power on short-term material incentives, many studies of political machines have emphasized the need for a constantly expanding resource base in order to maintain electoral support, seeing an inherent limitation of the machine in its inevitably inflationary consequences; it is therefore argued that either resource scarcity or economic crisis is likely to spell the downfall of patronage-based parties or elites.[1] In the specific case of southern Italy, observers have emphasized the massive transfer of resources from the national government to the South; this influx of public resources from the center, it is held, has, by substituting for local resource scarcity, provided the economic underpinning for clientelistic power at the local level.[2] While not denying the importance of the resources of the state in sustaining positions of local power in the South, this study argues that such an explanation is not sufficient to explain the strength of the DC in southern cities where, despite external resource flows, severe resource constraints (and in recent years a shrinking economic base) have been the outstanding characteristic of the local economy. Although virtually total control over resources at the local level has been a crucial factor in the maintenance of DC power in Palermo, this tells us little about the nature and quantity of the resources in question, or about the distinctive ways in which these resources are utilized to mobilize support among different social groups. In this and the following chapters each of the key social groups listed above will be examined in turn, focusing on the specific patronage mechanisms that link them to the larger system of DC power. The purpose of the examination is twofold: first, to provide an illustration of the means by which a relatively autonomous political machine can be constructed and sustained at the local level in a situation of chronic resource shortage; and second, to suggest a more refined and differentiated view of the bases of political support among distinct client groups than has thus far emerged from the existing literature on clientelism and political machines.

The middle classes in Italian politics

Throughout the postwar period the *ceti medi* ("middle classes") have constituted the cornerstone of DC power in Italy. In the Italian context the term *ceti medi* is used to refer to two distinct sectors of the population: on the one hand, the traditional independent middle classes (small farmers, shopkeepers, and artisans); on the other, white-collar employees in both the private and public sectors. The importance attributed to these groups in the DC's political strategy is a product both of the party's recognition of the long-term trend toward increasing tertiarization of the economy common to all advanced industrial societies and of a political judgment as to the critical stabilizing role of the middle classes in a political system exposed to extremist threats on both the Right and the Left. This stabilization function attributed to the *ceti medi* by Italian political elites has two distinct components: (1) consciousness of the historical propensity of the Italian middle classes to support right-wing political movements in moments of social unrest, for example, Fascism in 1922, the Uomo Qualunque[3] in the immediate postwar period, and neo-Fascism in recent years; and (2) recognition of the critical role of the traditional middle classes in absorbing a substantial part of the "marginal"

Table 4.1. *Class structure over time in three industrialized nations (in percentages)*

	Italy		France		United States	
	1881	1971	1886	1968	1890	1969
I. Bourgeoisie[a]	1.9	2.6	3.1	3.2	5.8	6.0
II. Middle classes	45.9	49.5	47.5	52.1	49.8	54.0
IIa. White-collar workers	2.1	17.0	7.2	26.6	9.9	38.0
Private sector	0.6	8.9	5.5	19.3	7.7	24.1
Public sector	1.5	8.1	1.7	7.3	2.1	13.9
IIb. Independent middle classes	41.2	29.1	36.6	22.2	35.2	9.0
Small farmers	22.5	12.1	23.1	11.2	22.7	2.6
Shopkeepers	2.7	8.7	3.7	6.1	2.1	2.7
Artisans	16.1	8.3	9.8	4.9	10.4	4.0
IIc. Others[b]	2.6	3.4	3.7	3.3	5.0	7.0
III. Working class	52.2	47.8	49.4	44.7	47.2	40.0

[a] "Bourgeoisie" includes landowners, entrepreneurs, managers, and professionals.
[b] "Others" includes groups like the clergy and the military.
Source: Paolo Sylos-Labini, *Saggio sulle classi sociali* (1975), p. 164.

labor force, thereby reducing unemployment and lessening the potential for social explosions.[4] Throughout the postwar period, the threat of social instability has been a constant preoccupation of the Italian ruling class; as a result, especially in moments of social or political crisis, the government has dispensed a flow of special benefits to placate any potential stirrings of discontent among the *ceti medi*.

The importance of the *ceti medi* in Italian society today is only in part a reflection of social changes resulting from economic modernization. In most advanced industrial societies, within the framework of an overall increase in the weight of the middle classes, the relative positions over time of the traditional middle classes on the one hand and of white-collar employees on the other have tended to reflect a process of economic development that has all but eliminated the former while producing a tremendous expansion in the ranks of the latter. In Italy, however, the traditional middle classes continue to constitute over one-quarter of the labor force while, among white-collar employees, public servants assume a disproportionate weight (Table 4.1). This preponderance of the self-employed and of public employees within the *ceti medi* reflects a deliberate political strategy aimed at protecting and maintaining substantial sectors of the traditional middle classes, as well as creating a vast public bureaucracy that has come to represent a key force in Italian society. As can be

Table 4.2. Class structure in Italy, 1951–71 (in percentages)

	1951			1961			1971		
	North	Center[a]	South	North	Center[a]	South	North	Center[a]	South
I. Bourgeoisie	2.1	2.0	1.7	2.0	2.0	1.9	2.5	2.9	2.4
II. Middle classes	53.3	63.5	58.4	48.9	61.1	55.4	45.8	55.6	51.6
IIa. White-collar workers	10.4	12.1	7.5	13.2	17.0	10.2	16.8	23.4	13.3
Private sector	6.3	6.5	3.0	8.1	8.5	3.9	10.2	11.7	5.2
Public sector	4.1	5.6	4.5	5.1	8.5	6.3	6.6	11.7	8.1
IIb. Independent middle classes	40.4	47.7	48.5	32.8	40.2	42.2	26.0	27.8	34.7
Small farmers	25.1	33.5	35.9	17.8	24.3	26.0	9.7	10.4	17.0
Shopkeepers	7.6	6.2	5.7	8.1	7.3	7.1	8.8	8.3	8.6
Artisans	7.7	8.0	6.9	6.9	8.6	9.1	7.5	9.1	9.1
IIc. Others	2.5	3.6	2.4	2.9	3.9	3.0	3.8	4.4	3.5
III. Working class	44.6	34.5	39.9	49.1	36.9	42.7	51.7	41.5	46.0

[a] The figures for the Center are skewed, especially with regard to public employees, because of the presence of the city of Rome.
Source: Sylos-Labini (1975), p. 157.

Table 4.3. *Estimate of the distribution by party of the votes of various social classes (in percentages)*

	I	IIa	IIb	IIc	III	Total
PCI/PSIUP	—	12.1	25.3	2.0	60.6	100
PSI	—	21.9	18.7	—	59.4	100
PSDI	7.1	14.3	28.6	—	50.0	100
PRI	14.3	14.3	42.8	—	28.6	100
DC	1.6	14.4	36.0	3.2	44.8	100
PLI	10.5	15.8	42.1	10.5	21.1	100
MSI-Monarchists	5.6	38.8	22.2	11.2	22.2	100
Others	—	25.0	25.0	—	50.0	100

Note: The numerical headings used in this table refer to the class categories set out in Tables 4.1 and 4.2. The calculations are based on the results of the 1968 parliamentary elections. Dashes signify zero.
Source: Sylos-Labini (1975), p. 192.

seen from Table 4.2, the pivotal role of the *ceti medi* – and within them of these two privileged sectors – is particularly accentuated in the South, where the limits of economic development, coupled with the constant threat of social unrest due to mass unemployment, have maximized the social and political functions of the middle classes.

Recent studies of the functions of the *ceti medi* have gained broader public attention in the context of political debate over the eventual role of the middle classes in a strategy of left-wing hegemony.[5] Thus far, as shown in Table 4.3, the middle classes have formed the back-bone of electoral support for the DC and, even more overwhelmingly, for its minor coalition partners, the PRI and the PLI, not to mention the neo-Fascist MSI. To understand the conditions under which the *ceti medi* might be won over by a left-wing coalition (or at the very least neutralized), it is essential first to analyze the bases of their present integration into the existing system of power. Pizzorno has outlined two opposing strategies of consensus: one based on "individualistic attraction," the other on the "institutionalization of collective demands," essentially interest-group politics.[6] Politics in postwar Italy has been characterized by the predominance of the former strategy, a strategy defined by Pizzorno as one of "utilizing the very inequalities which should give rise to dissent and rejection of the system and making them serve instead as an incentive to participation in the benefits which the system can distribute."[7] Because of their propensity to prefer individual over collective advancement, Pizzorno sees the middle classes as central to the success of such a strategy, constituting a reservoir upon which political elites can draw to enlarge the area of individualistic attraction.

The means used by the DC in pursuit of this strategy of individualistic attraction have been more a policy of consensus through mediation than direct emanation of legislative or administrative measures favoring specific categories within the middle classes. The intermediary role of the DC has been dual, both economic and political. On the one hand, it has intervened to protect and sustain the traditional middle classes in their function of controlling the marginal labor force; on the other, it has moved to create a new, politically dependent middle class, particularly in the South. The exercise of this intermediary function by the DC has been made possible by the party's uninterrupted monopoly of state power and in many areas, especially in the South, of local power as well. This power has been used to create a substantial subsector of the middle classes, in the private as well as the public sector, dependent for survival upon the political choices of the dominant party rather than upon market forces, thus creating a clear bond of both individual and class interest between these sectors of the *ceti medi* and the ruling parties. The concrete mechanisms by which this system of individualistic consensus has been maintained – the allocation of public spending, control of access to credit, and what Pizzorno calls "the power of licensing and interdiction"[8]– vary substantially among different groups within the middle classes. This chapter will deal with the principal component of the *ceti medi* in Palermo, the *impiegati pubblici* ("public employees"), and the use of the public payroll as an instrument of political patronage, while Chapter 5 will examine the special relationship between the DC and the local entrepreneurial elite as well as the party's ties to the traditional middle classes.

The DC and public employees in Palermo

The case of public employees conforms most closely to the "resource theory" of clientelism, which sees the key to the success of the machine in its control of the public treasury and its large-scale distribution of public resources, primarily in the form of job patronage, for political ends. In Palermo, as in other southern cities, job patronage has played a fundamental role in the system of power built up by the DC over the past thirty years, although its significance goes far beyond the simple exchange of a job for a vote.

In order to understand the importance of public employees within the overall DC strategy of consensus, it is necessary first to examine in greater detail the scope and powers of the public sector in Pa-

Table 4.4. *Public sector employment in Palermo, 1976*

National government	2,000
Regional government	6,500
Special economic agencies of the regional government	7,000
Provincial government	850
Municipal government	3,850
Aziende municipalizzate (garbage collection, public transport, gas, and water)	5,600
State railroad system	4,000
Other public transport	2,000
Post office	2,000
Banks	3,000
Hospitals and state social-security and health-insurance systems	8,000
Total	44,750

Source: "Inchiesta sugli impiegati," *L'Ora* (July 2 and 7, 1976).

lermo. As in all major urban centers in the South, public employees in Palermo have come to constitute the single most important component of the city's social and occupational structure, not only forming the core of the urban middle class but also to a large extent shaping the aspirations of the masses of the urban poor who form the base of the social pyramid. The *impiegato*, in sum, has set the social tone of the city and in large part determined the directions of urban expansion, investment and consumption over the past twenty years. Although the 1971 census registers the number of public employees in Palermo as 21,935, or about 13% of the labor force, this figure is far too low, because it includes only those persons employed in the administrative functions of government, in the public schools, and in the national social-security and health-insurance systems. It excludes workers in city services like garbage collection and public transport, in hospitals, banks, and numerous other semipublic agencies and organizations, all of whom, given the tremendous expansion of public intervention in postwar Italy, are clearly to be understood for the purposes of this study as public employees. Although exact figures for certain categories are difficult to come by, Table 4.4 provides a minimum estimate of the actual dimensions of public sector employment in Palermo in 1976. This total of almost 45,000 public employees, over double the official figure, still excludes many of the autonomous *enti* that operate under the tutelage of the various organs of local government. An overall estimate prepared on the basis of social-security contributions in fact places the number of public employees in the city as high as 60,000 or 35.6% of the labor force.[9]

This mass of public employees has constituted one of the principal

pillars of DC power in Palermo. The decision of the local DC to channel a substantial part of its political energies into the creation of a
huge, politically dependent class of public employees stems on the
one hand from the limited resource base of the local economy, and on
the other from the perceptions of the rising DC leadership in the
early 1950s as to which political instruments were most readily available and in which direction they could be most efficaciously employed to establish a stable base of support for the party. In a city in
which the local economy is overwhelmingly dependent upon the
public sector, a political strategy centered on the control and manipulation of the resources of local government seems a logical choice.
Through conquest of the elective bodies of local government (the
Commune, Province, and Region), the DC gained the means by
which to extend its control not only into every sector of a powerful
public bureaucracy, but also, thanks to the appointive powers of
local government, into the administrative organs of a far-reaching
network of semipublic *enti* whose influence extends into every sector
of the city's economic, social and cultural life. To give some idea of
the scope of such power, Table 4.5 lists the sectors of competence of
the three levels of local government (in terms of their departments or
assessorati) and the principal *enti* they control, either directly or
through nomination of representatives to their administrative councils.

Each component of the above list represents a center of autonomous political power, exercised in the pursuit of personal or factional
gain. The power of this vast bureaucratic apparatus and of the men
who direct it is immense. They control not only the hiring of personnel and the allocation of public funds in the form of contracts, concessions, subsidies, and credit, but also the many nonmonetary but
nonetheless critical functions of local government such as licensing,
zoning, tax assessment and collection, regulation of markets, and police vigilance over the enforcement of all of the above. Within local
government the elected assessors reap the direct political gains from
the manipulation of these multiple levers of power. The influence exerted by political appointees *inside* the bureaucracy, however, is of
equal importance, in spite of, or perhaps precisely because of, its relative obscurity. The key to the power of the bureaucrats is their control over the flow of *pratiche* – requests for building or commercial licenses, regional subsidies or credits, pension benefits, public
housing, and so on. What is in theory a purely bureaucratic function
becomes, in the southern Italian context, an act fraught with immense political implications. Here, where the Weberian conception
of an impartial bureaucracy has never penetrated, retarding or
speeding up a *pratica* – even one of minor economic import let alone

an application for a construction license or a bid on a public contract or concession where billions of lire may be at stake – is a clear-cut act of political favoritism, creating a corresponding political obligation that must sooner or later be repaid. The network of personal obligation built up by the individual bureaucrat can then, when elections approach, be used as a bargaining lever with political superiors in order to advance his own career. Top-level bureaucrats, especially at the regional level, also sit on a variety of external commissions and *consigli d'amministrazione* ("administrative councils") creating a network of interlocking and overlapping interests directly linking government functionaries (and through them their political protectors) to the administration of important centers of economic power like banks, public industries, hospitals, and *aziende municipalizzate*. In a resource-scarce economy, the DC has, as one observer has put it, created a new industry, the "industry of power."[10]

The politics of the *"raccomandazione"*

Chi mi dà il pane mi dà la vita.[11] [Sicilian proverb]

I receive an average of 1,000 *raccomandazioni* per year. The important thing, however, is not to place 1,000 persons per year – that is impossible and would be in any case counterproductive. You must place only 1 out of 20, 50 out of 1,000. In this way you keep in subjection the 950 from the preceding year together with the 1,000 new supplicants of the current year. [A DC deputy] [12]

One of the principal mechanisms of political support in postwar Palermo has been the manipulation of the public payroll by the DC and its allies. As more and more sectors of the urban economy have come under public or semipublic control, the *raccomandazione* ("political recommendation") has become a fundamental fact of life for every *palermitano*. The *raccomandazione* represents the purest expression of the DC strategy of individualistic consensus:

Where there is severe job shortage and an organized demand for jobs would provoke acute social conflicts, "individualistic incentivation" consists in presenting and distributing jobs as if it were a question of a concession to a privileged worker and not of the satisfaction of a collective need.[13]

The drama of job seeking and the *raccomandazione* reaches an extreme in an economic and political context like that of Palermo, where a substantial part of politics revolves around the *posto* ("job or position") and, as one highly placed political appointee put it, when all is said and done, "a job signifies a vote, and vice versa."[14] While this is undoubtedly an exaggeration, its common acceptance conveys the political climate of a city where politics is perceived as the only road to obtaining secure employment.

Elected officials and directors of important public agencies and

Table 4.5. *Organs of local government and their associated* ENTI

Commune	Province	Region
Assessorships	*Assessorships*	*Assessorships*
Urbanistica	Lavori Pubblici	Presidenza
Lavori Pubblici	Pubblica Istruzione	Enti Locali
Patrimonio	Igiene e Sanità	Bilancio
Pubblica Istruzione	Bilancio e Finanze	Finanze e Patrimonio
Servizi Tributari	Solidarietà Sociale	Lavori Pubblici
Finanze e Bilancio	Patrimonio	Agricoltura e Foreste
Aziende Municipalizzate	Personale	Industria e Commercio
Igiene e Sanità	Agricoltura	Pubblica Istruzione
Solidarietà Sociale	Lavoro, Contenzioso e	Sviluppo Economico
Annona	Espropriazione	Sanità
Traffico e Vigili Urbani	Turismo e Sport	Lavoro e Cooperazione
Polizia Urbana	Opere Delegate	Turismo
Lavoro e Sviluppo		
Economico	*Enti under partial or total*	*Principal regional enti (total*
Economato	*control of the municipal*	*of 86 in all of Sicily)*
Servizi Demografici	*and/or provincial govern-*	ESPI (Ente Siciliano per
Decentramento e Statistica	*ments*	la Promozione Indus-
Ville e Giardini	Ente Autonomo Porto di	triale)
Turismo, Spettacolo, Sport	Palermo	EMS (Ente Minerario
e Tempo Libero	Consorzio per lo Sviluppo	Siciliano)
	Industriale	ESA (Ente per lo Sviluppo
Aziende municipalizzate	Istituto Autonomo Case	Agricolo)
AMNU (garbage collec-	Popolari	AST (Azienda Siciliana
tion)	Croce Rossa (Red Cross)	Trasporti)
AMAT (public transpor-	Centro di Igiene Mentale	AZASI (Azienda Asfalti
tation)	Ente Provinciale del	Siciliani)
AMAP (water)	Turismo	Istituto Vite e Vino
Azienda del Gas	Azienda Turismo	
	Schools (buildings, sup-	
Commissions	plies, and all nonteach-	
Urbanistica	ing personnel): elemen-	
Edilizia	tary, intermediate, and	
3 commissions to super-	*liceo classico* by the	
vise the wholesale	Commune; *liceo scien-*	
markets for fruit and	*tifico*, technical and	
vegetables, fish and	professional high	
meat.	schools by the Province)	
	Variety of day-care insti-	
Banks and credit institutions	tutions, both municipal	
(Presidents and adminis-	and provincial	
trative councils nomi-	Istituto Assistenza	
nated by the regional	Infanzia	
government)	Teatro Massimo	
Banco di Sicilia	Orchestra Sinfonica	
Cassa di Risparmio		

Table 4.5. *(cont.)*

Commune	Province	Region
IRFIS (Istituto Regionale per il Finanziamento alle Industrie in Sicilia) CRIAS (Cassa per il credito agli artigiani)	Amici della Musica Museo Pitrè Palermo Calcio	
Hospitals (administrative councils nominated by the provincial and regional governments) Ospedale Civico (regional) Villa Sofia (regional) Ospedale Psichiatrico (controlled by the Prefect, but with financial contributions from the Province) Centro Tumori (provincial) Sanatorio Ingrassia (provincial) Ospedale dei Bambini (provincial) Ospedale "Cervello" (provincial) Ospizio Marino (provincial) Casa del Sole (provincial) Ospedale Ortopedico Traumatologico (provincial)		

publicly controlled firms are under intense and continuous pressure to satisfy the patronage demands of politicians, as well as of highly placed bureaucrats, bank directors, presidents of key *enti*, and so on, who hold the power to influence their careers. The sheer volume of the requests for jobs, no matter how weighty the recommendation, far surpasses the capacity for job creation of a chronically resource-scarce economy, despite the continual inflation of the public sector over the past three decades.[15] When asked by a local newspaper about the requests for jobs that they had received over the years, three influential local leaders during the 1950s and 1960s acknowledged an average of 25–30 *raccomandazioni* per day or a combined total of over 100,000 throughout their careers, of which they claimed to have satisfied only about 450. Asked how many of the people who approached him everyday asked for a job, one of these men, a regional assessor, replied, "In general I would say all of them. Everyone who approaches a regional assessor sooner or later asks for a job, either for himself or for someone else."[16]

While hope has clearly played a critical role in sustaining support for the machine even among those who have never directly experienced its benefits, a significant proportion of the middle classes in Palermo indeed owe their livelihood directly to the DC's transformation of the public bureaucracy into an immense reservoir of patronage. The most conspicuous founts of this public largesse have been the Region and the Commune, with the Province performing a more limited though no less virulent role. From the time of its establishment in 1947, the Sicilian regional government has, because of the concentration of its bureaucratic apparatus in Palermo, played a major role in local politics. Established in response to a powerful separatist movement and intended as an instrument of socioeconomic propulsion for a chronically depressed region, Sicilian autonomy evolved instead into a classic case of clientelism and corruption, squandering billions to further the political fortunes of regional presidents, assessors, and deputies and to maintain an elephantine bureaucracy, while Sicily fell ever further behind the rest of Italy in terms of economic development, and entire zones of the island's interior were relegated to abandonment and despair. With the setting up of an independent regional bureaucracy, a position, however lowly, in the regional administration became the ultimate aspiration of thousands of Sicilians in each successive generation – the dream, so fleeting in Sicily, of stable and dignified employment, of a regular salary and benefits, in sum, of security:

A position in the regional government is considered the fulfillment of all one's dreams and is the most efficacious instrument for placing friends, acquaintances, *galoppini* [ward-heelers] – in short for doing favors and forming a clientele. Every assessor, every deputy (apart from a few rare exceptions), almost without party distinction, has sought to create positions for his supporters.[17]

Thus, over the years, a massive influx of relatives, friends, political supporters, family, and friends of friends and of political supporters, without the least consideration of the applicant's qualifications for the job in question, other than family name or political loyalty, swelled the ranks of the regional administration to gargantuan proportions.

This uncontrolled expansion of the bureaucracy was made possible by the system of assuming personnel by *chiamata diretta* ("direct call"), which prevailed from the Region's inception in 1946 until 1962, when *concorsi* ("public competitions") for regional jobs became obligatory.[18] Under this system, each assessor had complete discretion, unlimited by any formal criteria of qualification, over hiring in his own department; in fact, it is widely held that the date of assumption of a regional employee can be determined by his accent, because every assessor and regional president, upon election to office, brings along with him a solid contingent of his local compatriots to staff his department. While the Sicilian Region has not yet produced a case so extreme as that of Caligula, who had his horse nominated to the Roman Senate, it has come a close second in the assessor of public instruction who created a special position in his department for his barber! Periodically, as total chaos threatened to overwhelm the regional bureaucracy, with burgeoning numbers of employees rapidly outnumbering tables and chairs, legislation would be passed to incorporate the new waves of appointees into the formal bureaucratic structure and to expand regional offices to accommodate them. The first such bill was passed in 1953, limiting the size of the bureaucracy to 1,474 employees and prohibiting, like all successive legislation, any subsequent hiring except by *concorso*. This was to no avail, however, since clientelistic hiring continued unabated; as a result, by 1958 a new law was required, expanding the bureaucracy to 3,567 positions. Only in 1962 were *concorsi* for the Region finally instituted, with 500–600 persons entering by this means between 1962 and 1971, after which a hiring freeze was passed in accordance with new legislation requiring a complete reorganization of the regional administration. Despite this hiring freeze, however, the effective strength of the regional bureaucracy at the end of 1976 was 6,149, an excess of 2,500 employees over the legal ceiling.

The example of the regional bureaucracy is emblematic of patterns of clientelistic hiring throughout the public sector. The techniques by which this tremendous swelling of public employment took place recur in substantially identical form regardless of the level of local government – region, province or city – or the type of *ente* – government offices, schools, hospitals, etc. – involved.[19] By the mid-1960s, the heyday of the *chiamata diretta* had passed, and the city's political leaders were obliged, in accordance with new legislation requiring *concorsi* in almost all sectors of the public administration, to devise more refined techniques of patronage hiring. The foremost instrument at their disposal has been that of *assunzioni fuori ruolo* – the hiring of persons on short-term contracts (usually six months) and outside regularly defined bureaucratic positions because their employment was allegedly temporary; in this way the *concorsi* required for all permanent administrative personnel could be circumvented. Once hired, however, the original contracts would be regularly renewed until, under the pressure of hundreds of "precarious" employees (the contingents mounting at the approach of every election), the unions would be compelled to demand their incorporation into the permanent bureaucratic structure. The following illustration of hiring by the Province describes a generalized practice among public offices in Palermo:

> In general employees have been hired on the basis of *raccomandazioni,* recommendations well calibrated . . . in terms of the balance of political forces and the interests of the various parties and of the factions within them . . . The candidate would have an interview (although this was often bypassed) and would then be hired as a temporary employee for a determined period of time. With the contract renewed regularly every six months, this precarious situation could drag on for years (the funds for the stipend, not always regularly paid, were often disguised under other categories of the budget, like "acquisition of paintings" or "paving of rural roads") until an assessor finally normalized their position with a special administrative act.[20]

From the viewpoint of the public-employee unions, anxious to justify their own presence and to recruit support in a traditionally hostile environment, support for such normalization, eminently fair insofar as the individual employee was concerned, was unavoidable. The overall effect of such actions, however, has often been to draw the unions as well as opposition parties into objective collusion with the very system of clientelistic power that ostensibly they were seeking to overthrow.

Another tactic by which the unions have been drawn into legitimation of clientelistic hiring is known in bureaucratic jargon as *svolgimento di mansioni superiori* ("performance of a job superior in rank to that for which one has been hired"). The key to the usefulness of this concept is the requirement of *concorsi* only for persons filling administrative positions, while for all other positions (clerks, typists, ushers,[21] doormen, janitors, gardeners, laborers, etc.), hiring can still take place on a direct personal basis. The weight of these subordinate positions within the bureaucratic structure is an indication of the enormous potential for patronage politics at this level; taking as an example the Comune di Palermo, out of a total of 3,056 positions (excluding *vigili urbani* or "city police") in 1976, 2,514 were of this type, as opposed to only 542 administrative positions requiring *concorsi.*[22] Hypothetically this supply of unskilled jobs in the public sector (supplemented by several thousand more in *aziende municipalizzate* like garbage collection and public transport) could serve, as it has to some extent, for drawing sectors of the urban working class and *sottoproletariato* into the DC machine. In reality, however, the vast majority of public-sector jobs in Palermo, even at these levels, have gone to members of the petty bourgeoisie or middle classes. The logic of such an apparent paradox lies in the concept of *mansioni superiori*. What this means is that, in order to circumvent the *concorso*, persons with high-school and even university degrees are hired as typists, ushers, or janitors. As such persons, however, could never be expected to perform menial tasks so far beneath their dignity and qualifications, they are rapidly assigned to appropriate administrative or technical functions, while continuing to be paid for the lower-ranking job. Eventually, as in the case of the *assunzioni fuori ruolo*, the unions are obliged to protest such exploitation, putting pressure on the administration to promote these persons to positions commensurate with the duties they are in fact performing. Because these persons are already *inside* the bureaucracy, however, this operation can take place either without a *concorso* or, in some cases, with a special *concorso* for insiders made to order for the particular individuals in question. As might be expected, the impact of such a system of hiring on the functioning of public offices is disastrous: despite continual hiring in these subordinate positions, many offices suffer such an acute shortage of clerical and maintenance personnel that they find it difficult to maintain a minimal level of services, both for their employees and for the public.

Another highly successful technique of job patronage has grown out of national legislation reserving 15% of all positions in the public administration for *invalidi* ("disabled"). As this legislation provides that a person certified as disabled can be hired without a *concorso*, the potential for political speculation, in a context like Palermo where anything is possible with the proper *raccomandazione*, is extremely high. At the approach of every election, large numbers of "disabled" persons are hired on short notice, providing hundreds and even thousands of dependable votes for certain well-placed candidates. The key to this operation is the medical commission of the city government's Office of Hygiene, which examines the applicants and provides the required certificate of disability. With the same party controlling both the certification of disability and subsequent hiring, the prospect of political gain from the hiring of the "disabled" can hardly help but prove tempting.

When all other avenues have been exhausted, the holders of power in Palermo must finally come to terms with the *concorso* itself. In most cases, fulfilling the letter of the law while totally negating its spirit has proved easier than might have been expected. In and of itself the *concorso* has failed abysmally in its purpose of providing a guarantee of impartiality in public hiring. Until the period of the "opening to the Communists" at the local level between January 1976 and June 1979, the commissions set up to judge *concorsi* were invariably dominated by representatives of the DC, to the complete exclusion, in flagrant violation of the law, of representatives of the opposition parties and of the public-employee unions associated with them. Under these circumstances, regardless of qualifications, the candidates with the proper *raccomandazioni* always seemed to finish first.

The real political value of the *concorso*, however, has been mainly in the breach. In 1976 the number of employees of the Commune of Palermo was 1,500 short of the official personnel requirements, the city administration having failed to complete any *concorsi* since 1968. Paradoxical as it may seem, for those who control the Commune *not hiring* may prove as politically expedient as hiring, particularly in periods when patronage resources are scarce and demand high. Just prior to the local elections of June 1975, for example, the city government announced a *concorso* for 1,000 positions – of the 35,000 persons who applied each was certain of his chances for success, secure in the *raccomandazioni* received from powerful local politicians in exchange for the preference votes of the applicants and their families. Like other "electoral" *concorsi* before it, this competition, as of mid-1977, still awaited completion, not a single position having been yet assigned; in the meantime it had sustained certain politicians through two elections. This example underlines the limitations of an analysis of the bases of machine power focusing primarily on the expenditure of public resources to create patronage jobs. In the last analysis, the system works less through the distribution of benefits to all-comers than through the astute management of *scarcity* and, above all, the critical element of hope. The key to the successful machine politician is not mass patronage but maintenance of the maximum clientele with the minimum payoff in terms of actual benefits.

With regard to those who actually do receive jobs in return for their votes, the ramifications of clientelistic hiring and the networks of political obligation created go far beyond the mere act of placing a person on the public payroll. Otherwise, it might be objected, how can the continuity of the patron–client bond be guaranteed once the original vote-for-job exchange is consummated, and the client is securely installed in a public-sector job from which he cannot, for all intents and purposes, ever be removed? The *raccomandazione* by which the public employee accedes to the object of his aspirations is only the first link in a chain of reciprocal obligation that will progressively bind him ever more irrevocably to his patron and protector. If he wishes not only to further his own career but also to provide the possibility of future employment for other family members, the public employee can ill afford to neglect his obligations to his patron once his own job is secure. Such insurance for the future requires sustained proof of loyalty, and such loyalty in Palermo is demonstrated above all in terms of preference votes.

As for career advancement, promotions and pay raises within the bureaucracy proceed almost exclusively on the basis of political favoritism. In theory, advancement for public servants in Italy proceeds according to seniority. In practice, what happens in an organizational structure like that of the Palermo city government, with 600 distinct *qualifiche* ("job classifications") and corresponding pay scales, is that the political game revolves around the attribution of the *punti di qualifica* ("points") that determine the rate of advancement, the more or less rapid passage from one *qualifica* to another making all the difference in the career of an individual bureaucrat. As the "commission of advancement," which controls all promotions, is composed of the mayor and the top bureaucrats in his administration, the overwhelming majority of whom are Christian Democrats (and often members of the dominant party faction as well), advancement in a bureaucratic career is decided in many cases on the basis of political rather than professional merit. In addition, the weight of one's *raccomandazione*, in a highly competitive situation where nearly everyone is "recommended" by one prominent politician or another, is directly proportional to the power of the patron, itself in most cases a direct function of the number of personal preference votes he has received in the preceding election. The employee's fate is thus directly linked to the continued electoral success of his protector, which in turn depends upon his own continued support.

Another manifestation of the impact of clientelism on the public administration is the phenomenon of *distaccati* and *imboscati*. *Distaccati* are persons on the public payroll who have been "detached" from their regular tasks and assigned instead to service on the personal staff of a prominent assessor or deputy or in the offices of one or another party faction – in short, they become electoral *galoppini* ("wardheelers") paid out of public funds. One step further along the *clientela* hierarchy is the *imboscato*. Unlike the *distaccato*, he is expected to perform no apparent service at all in return for the paycheck which he regularly receives at the end of each month. At least in the more notorious cases, the *imboscati* appear to be local politicians or family members of prominent political figures who remain on the public payroll while employed full time in totally different occupations. In 1976 the Communist Party prepared a preliminary list

of 600 *imboscati* in the regional administration, of which the following are among the more prominent cases:[23]

1. A high-level functionary of the Assessorato agli Enti Locali, who was also
   a Christian Democratic provincial councillor and delegate of the
   mayor to an outlying neighborhood of the city. Although he collected overtime in addition to his regular stipend, he did not even
   have an office in the Assessorato in question.
2. Another Christian Democratic provincial councillor, officially a member of
   the permanent staff of the Presidency of the Region, who had never
   once in the past 12 years been seen in those offices.
3. Another employee of the Presidency of the Region who was employed full
   time as President of the Center for Assistance to Migrants (another
   local center of clientelism) – coincidentally a relative of the former
   personal secretary of Restivo.

The impact of this mass of *distaccati* and *imboscati* (estimates of
their numbers in the city administration run as high as 30% of all
employees),[24] together with the other aspects of patronage politics
discussed earlier in this section, on the functioning of the public administration in Palermo has been disastrous. With *clientela* the pre-
eminent concern of those entrusted with the administration of local
government, chaos has increasingly come to reign in the myriad of
public offices and *enti* that dominate the life of the city. A superficial
indication of the prevailing anarchy is the fact that no organ of local
government possesses even a reliable and up-to-date census of its
own personnel; no one, not even the city government's Office of Personnel, can say with precision how many people are currently employed, how they are distributed among various departments, what
are their specific ranks and pay scales, and what is the actual percentage of *distaccati* and *imboscati*. Despite the massive patronage hiring
that has characterized Palermo politics over the past three decades,
offices are chronically understaffed, suffering particularly from shortages of employees with technical skills and the clerical and maintenance personnel essential to the day-to-day functioning of any administration: many offices in fact find themselves paralyzed by a lack
of secretaries to type and photocopy basic documents.

This situation is aggravated by the effect of such an atmosphere on
those employees who remain to staff public offices. Discipline and
punctuality are weak and lengthy coffee breaks and absences to run
personal errands often reduce effective working hours by up to one-
half (as it is, most public offices are only open from 8 A.M. until 2
P.M.). Shortly after the 1976 election of a new city administration
pledged to inaugurating a new style of government and to overturn-
ing the bureaucratic immobility of its predecessors, a disillusioned
neo-assessor complained bitterly of the stifling impact of such a *cli-*

entela-ridden bureaucracy on even the most ordinary administrative tasks, let alone on any serious initiative for change:

In order to obtain anything, one must request it as a personal favor . . . We survive on a day-to-day basis, and it is impossible to plan any-thing . . . There is no communication among the various city depart-ments, and therefore offices end up exchanging kilos of paper . . . without ever concluding anything.[25]

No wonder that performance of so many critical tasks of local govern-ment – garbage collection, construction of public housing and provi-sion of basic services to go along with it, utilization of the 65 billion lire (approx. US $108 million) allocated by the Cassa per il Mezzo-giorno and the Region for initiation of the long-overdue *risanamento* ("urban renewal") of the old city – grinds to a standstill, due in part to the paralyzing effects of political factionalism, but in equal mea-sure to sheer bureaucratic impotence.

The "salary jungle" and the spirit of corporatism

Central to an understanding of the bases of DC consensus among the white-collar middle classes is what has come to be called, after the widely debated book by Ermanno Gorrieri,[26] the *giungla re-tributiva* ("salary jungle"). Gorrieri's book demonstrates with a wealth of statistical data the privileged economic treatment both of public employees as a group and of particular sectors within the pub-lic sphere. In Italy, and in the South in particular, a public-sector job in and of itself conveys a sense of privilege insofar as it provides sta-bility of employment, a rare commodity in an economic context of extreme insecurity like that of southern Italy. In addition, at all but the highest levels, public employment offers a substantial salary ad-vantage with respect to an equivalent job in the private sector, with the disparity in compensation being most accentuated at the lowest skill levels (Table 4.6).

Not only are public employees privileged as a group with respect to workers in the private sector, there are substantial disparities in treatment among different sectors *within* the public sphere as well (Table 4.7). One of the outstanding characteristics of the Italian pub-lic administration, at all levels, is the lack of general norms regulating the organization of the bureaucracy in terms of job classifications and pay scales. In their absence, there has been an uncontrolled prolifera-tion of ranks and income levels, resulting in substantial salary varia-tions among people performing essentially the same functions. In Gorrieri's words,

Nothing is more fragmented and confused than the body of norms regulating the various categories and sub-categories of public employment. It is a "no

Table 4.6. Comparison of salaries in the private and public sectors (in thousands of lire per month)

Sectors	Unskilled workers	Skilled workers	Clerical personnel	Administrative personnel	Low-level management	Mid-level management
Private sector	121	145	182	271	354	682
Agriculture	98	124	185	256	—	—
Manufacturing	128	153	189	297	323	897
Construction	125	156	206	331	445	—
Commerce	134	150	149	200	296	468
Public sector	209	250	253	316	398	525
State offices	182	218	192	246	334	470
Autonomous state agencies (post office, railroads)	211	249	209	288	—	—
Parastato (local government, *aziende municipalizzate*, hospitals)	236	285	260	341	462	581
State telephone system	—	—	352	389	399	—
Banks	—	279	345	390	585	1271

Source: Gorrieri, *La giungla retributiva* (1972), p. 195.
Note: Dash signifies "not applicable."

Table 4.7. *Comparison of salaries across different sectors of public employment (in thousands of lire per month)*

Sector	Uscieri	Un-skilled workers	Skilled workers	Clerical personnel	Admin-istrative personnel
State offices	162	182	218	192	246
Autonomous state agencies	—	211	249	209	288
Parastato	228	236	285	260	341
Aziende municipalizzate	258	255	310	275	386
Hospitals	262	230	275	269	386
Local government	206	214	246	238	286
Social security offices	209	—	—	268	326
Chamber of Commerce	205	—	—	244	315

Source: Gorrieri (1972),p. 134.
Note: Dash signifies "not applicable."

man's land" which proliferates continually and which not even the experts understand in a complete and exhaustive fashion.[27]

In Sicily, because of the presence of the autonomous regional government, these inequalities are even more pronounced, with the employees of the special economic agencies of the Region (ESPI, ESA, EMS), of the Regional Assembly, and of the *aziende municipalizzate* far outdistancing civil servants in the regular administrative offices of local governments. Among them in turn, regional bureaucrats are in a privileged position relative to their colleagues in the offices of the city, the province, or the state (all of whom are covered by national contracts). These disparities in pay among different branches of the public administration are repeated within each branch, where the impenetrable maze of ranks and pay scales (600 *qualifiche* in the Commune alone) confounds any attempt to organize employees into more general functional categories. Despite its chaotic appearance, however, such a system of bureaucratic organization has played a critical role in the generation of individualistic consensus among the white-collar middle classes. A product of the clientelistic functioning of bureaucratic structures, the "salary jungle" at the same time reflects and reinforces the individualistic mentality pervading the ranks of public employees.

The case of the Sicilian Region provides a good illustration of the way such a system of individual incentives works.[28] The regular salary of regional employees (which already places them in a privileged position with respect not only to workers in the private sector but to the majority of public employees as well) represents only a proportion of their income, a proportion that grows progressively smaller as one rises through the ranks of the bureaucracy. To begin with, there is the question of overtime pay. According to regional regulations, overtime may be accrued from a maximum of 24 hours/month for the petty bureaucrat up to a maximum of 90 hours/month for top-level functionaries (the normal workday being only 6 hours, from 8 A.M. until 2 P.M.). The crucial fact about overtime is that its allocation to specific individuals proceeds, like everything else, on the basis of political favoritism, often having nothing to do with effective work loads or even with the actual presence of the employee in his office.

Unlike their counterparts in the private sector, all public employees receive an array of special indemnities over and above their formal salary; in the case of high-level functionaries these can have the effect, in the most extreme cases, of doubling or even quadrupling the official salary. The following examples attempt to give some idea of these highly lucrative income supplements, commonplace among the top bureaucrats of all branches of local administration:

> *Indennità di gabinetto* for those bureaucrats forming the personal staff of an assessor, the president of the Region or Province, or the mayor of the city.
>
> *Gettoni di presenza,* to the tune of 20,000–30,000 lire ($US 35–50) for every appearance of regional "experts" in the numerous external *consigli d'amministrazione,* commissions, etc., in which they participate. For example, those "experts" serving as judges in *concorsi* for hospitals or other local *enti* receive 100,000 lire ($US 165) for every *concorso* and may participate in 7–8 per year.
>
> *Indennità di collaudo,* a premium to the technical experts who are responsible for the inspection of public works projects, from a minimum of 3,000 lire ($US 5) per day for projects worth up to 50 million lire, up to 1% of the total cost of the project, or an average of 3 million lire ($US 5,000) for those valued over 50 million lire.
>
> A special indemnity of 3 million lire paid in every election year to selected employees of the Electoral Office of the Assessorato agli Enti Locali for the elaboration of the electoral results; this premium is paid as well to the director and *capo-gabinetto* of this office, who do not even participate in the task in question.

In addition to these already substantial benefits, top bureaucrats also receive severance bonuses and pensions, which at times reach truly astronomical sums. All this in addition to the special mortgage loans available to regional employees on extremely favorable terms (30 years with no interest), loans that were one of the determining factors in the construction boom that swept Palermo in the late 1950s and early 1960s.

At the upper levels of the administrative structure, patronage appointments and the privileges that go with them are not limited in their political payoff to the electoral support of the beneficiary and his family and friends. Much more importantly, they provide the patron with direct access to critical nodes of power within the bureaucracy and, thereby, with the means to extend even further his *clientela* network. The power of the bureaucrat, while obscure, is immense and can be a decisive factor in the outcome of cases ranging from a subsidy to a peasant to purchase a mule to the awarding of a public contract worth billions of lire. What has occurred in Palermo is an increasing politicization of the bureaucracy, not only because of the predominance of patronage appointments to public jobs but above all because of the progressive interpenetration of the local political class and the administrative organs of the city, province, and region. On the one hand, increasing proportions of the local leadership, not only of the DC but of all political parties (from section secretaries to members of the Provincial Committee to city councillors), are recruited from the ranks of public employees;[29] on the other, persons having made a career in politics are often nominated to head major public *enti* (banks, hospitals, etc.). The consequences of this interpenetration have been (1) the extension of direct political leverage throughout the bureaucracy; and (2) the establishment of a direct and privileged relationship both between the politician and a key constituency – public employees – and between the politician or section secretary *cum* bureaucrat and the individual citizen in his dealings with public offices or agencies.

The power of public employees, however, is not only that of the individual bureaucrat but of public employees in general as a political pressure group. Because of their numbers and their control over essential public services, public employees wield very real political clout with all parties, including the PCI. No party wants to risk incurring the wrath of such a concentrated and vocal sector of public opinion by defying public employees on issues deemed vital to their corporate interests. This fear helps explain the speed and unanimity with which provisions favoring public employees always seem to pass in local government assemblies, even in the face of severe budgetary constraints. As one observer explained:

Whenever there was a bill presented in favor of regional employees, the deputy who "took care of his sheep" (*"curava le sue anime"*) rushed to proclaim his support, to announce that the cause was sacrosanct; he would never have dared to risk an unpopular position. Only once was a proposal for economic benefits for regional employees rejected. As a result, the regional government was brought to the verge of a crisis. A few days later the same government presented the bill again and it was approved.[30]

A recent example at the city level further underlines the immense political leverage exerted by public employees. At the end of 1976, after vociferous condemnation of the clientelistic maneuvers of the DC, the opposition in the City Council voted in favor of a bill promoting all employees in the ranks of *ausiliari* ("janitors, ushers, etc.") who had, as of July 1970, performed *mansioni superiori* for at least one year. This Christmas bonus for hundreds of city workers was justified by the PCI as a demonstration of good will on the part of the City Council toward the public employees with whom, in the party's words, the PCI was seeking collaboration for a "new mode of governing."[31]

Discussion of the political weight of public employees leads to the issue of public-employee unions. In Italy, the nature and relative strength of these unions are a direct reflection of the structures of individual and group privilege that pervade the public sector. The predominance of personal ties in the internal functioning of the bureaucracy is a central factor in explaining the traditional weakness of public-employee unions in a city like Palermo. For example, prior to the 1975 local elections, city councillors of the DC and its coalition partners are reported to have organized electoral meetings among city employees at which they delivered the following message: "Have faith in us. We will take care of you, so forget about the unions. Vote for us and results will not be lacking."[32] The continued success of such a system of personalized political relationships in contrast to the strategy of collective bargaining represented by the unions is closely linked to the predominance among the middle classes of the ideology of individual advancement described by Pizzorno. For example, the national contract for municipal employees (signed nationally in 1973 but never applied until the end of 1976 in Palermo) provided for promotions only on the basis of internal *concorsi;* it was rejected in Palermo by the employees themselves, each of whom hoped to be able to profit more individually through the existing system than through collective guarantees.

As a result of such attitudes, the representation of the major national labor confederations (CGIL, CISL, and UIL) among public employees in Palermo has traditionally been quite low, in general ranging between 25% and 30% in the mid-1970s.[33] Among those public employees who are organized, the CISL, until recently considered a direct extension of the DC, predominates, followed by the CGIL which, starting from practically zero in the 1950s, made significant gains in the 1970s (Table 4.8). The most striking aspect of public-sector unionization in Palermo, however, is the presence of hundreds of "autonomous" unions. Taken one by one, these unions – at times limited to a single public sector, to a single local situation, or, at the extreme, even to a single *assessorato* or *ente* – may seem marginal, but

Table 4.8. *Union strength among public employees in Palermo*

	CISL	CGIL	UIL,[a] autonomous unions, or unorganized	Total employees
Region	561	400	5,539	6,500
Province	350	30	470	850
Commune	1,136	466	2,198	3,800
Hospitals[b]	2,456	898	3,646?	7,000?
AMNU (city garbage collection)	700	500	946	2,146
Total	5,203	2,294	12,799	20,296

[a] No exact membership figures are available for the UIL, but its strength among public employees is quite low. It is therefore included in the "catch-all" category of the "autonomous unions and the unorganized." The purpose of this category, in the absence of membership figures for the autonomous unions, is to give an idea of the tremendous scope for maneuver available to them.
[b] I was unable to procure exact figures on the number of hospital employees in Palermo. CGIL representatives give a minimum figure of 7,000.
Note: This table refers to membership figures as of the end of 1976 and includes the entire province; as the overwhelming majority of public employees and particularly those who are organized are concentrated in the city of Palermo, however, the figures are assumed to correspond fairly closely to actual levels of unionization in the city. Because of differences in the way the CISL and the CGIL organize different categories, this list does not include all public employees, but only those for which the two unions have equivalent categories.
Source: Data obtained from the provincial federations of the CISL and the CGIL.

in their entirety they represent a major political force, often outnumbering the national confederations on specific issues.[34]

Thus far, the evidence presented in this chapter has focused on the DC's strategy of "individualistic attraction" vis-à-vis public employees, that is, encouragement of purely individual channels of mobility, based on personal political ties. The other side of this strategy has been encouragement of a spirit of corporatism and group privilege. These two faces of the party's relationship with public-sector employees are not contradictory but complementary. The success of autonomous unions among public employees is a direct expression of the overlap between individual and corporate interests in this sector. The interests that autonomous unions champion are essentially individual interests – the defense and extension of existing situations of privilege within the category, not the "class" interests of public employees as a group – yet the articulation of these interests takes the form of collective organization among specific subgroups of public employees. In general, the strategy of the autonomous unions has been to exploit objective grievances to launch demands which, while extreme and demagogic, appeal to the immediate material interests of their constituency. Their goal is to mobilize the category along narrow corporative lines, undermining thereby the credibility of the national labor confederations, particularly the left-wing CGIL. Because of their affiliation with a nationwide labor movement (the CGIL, CISL and UIL having formed a unified labor federation in 1972) and with a national labor strategy aimed at affirming the unity and responsibility of the Italian working class, the local branches of the national unions have often found themselves the advocates of moderation and compromise in contrast to the intransigent local or sectoral demands of the autonomous unions. The latter then exploit this ostensible "sell-out" of their members' interests to discredit the national unions and to mobilize support for their own demands.

The success of these tactics derives from a combination of factors, organizational, structural and political: (1) the organizational chaos of the public sector, which permits the autonomous unions to manipulate the striking inequalities in treatment among different branches of the public administration; (2) the weakness of public authorities in the face of organized pressure from employees armed with the dual weapons of almost total job security and control over essential public services; (3) the frequent behind-the-scenes manipulation of the autonomous unions by competing factions in the internal power struggles of the DC. These factors, added to the corporatist mentality pervasive among public employees, have encouraged the autonomous unions in their most extreme and intransigent demands. In Gorrieri's words, "the corporatist spirit has led every category to make indiscriminate and unprincipled use of its bargaining capabilities and its contractual strength,"[35] generating an upward spiral of competitive demands that have repeatedly brought critical public services to a standstill and pushed local governments to the verge of bankruptcy.

The above discussion has attempted to bring out the complex interlocking of short-term material incentives with the broader sense of self-interest, both individual and corporative, which underlies DC support among public-sector employees. Support for the DC in this segment of the middle classes, more than in any other social group, is directly linked to the large-scale expenditure of public resources in the form of public-sector jobs, politically based promotions, and a system of compensation that creates entrenched positions of privilege, both for individuals and for the category of public employees as a whole. In the case of the white-collar middle class, however, support for the DC goes much deeper than just the buying of votes with patronage. There is also a deeper unity of perceived class interest, grounded in the ideology of individualism and of social privilege that pervades this social group. The bases of this ideology, both reinforcing and continually reinforced by the system of individual and corporative incentives constructed by the DC, are dual: (1) the conviction that one can get ahead only on an individual basis and through personal contacts, that *bisogna avere santi in paradiso* ("it is necessary to have saints in heaven"), and that one can rely only on an immediate and personalized relationship with an influential patron; and (2) the very real sense of privilege, in southern Italy, felt by the person who succeeds in securing a stable position. Only the unemployed or the "marginal" worker is considered "proletarian"; the janitor or garbage collector in the public sector, on the contrary, perceives himself not as a worker but as an employee, a "petty bourgeois." Once having attained this privileged position, his primary objective in life then becomes to protect it (against attack from the organized working class, for example), an objective that assumes particular intensity in situations of severe resource scarcity.

Politically, it could be argued that these two factors – the ideological and the material – produce support for the DC machine on the part of public employees at two different levels: on the one hand, the general party vote for the DC, which can properly be attributed as much to a perceived identity of class interest as to any specific clientelistic exchange; on the other, the preference vote for specific DC candidates, which is in most cases a direct expression of the individual patron – client bond. The utility of such a distinction can be demonstrated by comparing the ratio of party votes to preference votes in national and local elections, because the role of personalities tends to be greater in the latter case. Thus, in the 1975 administrative elections in Palermo, the ratio of DC party votes to the total of personal preference votes for each DC candidate was 1:2.9, while in the legislative elections of the following year, the ratio was only 1:1.5. Additional evidence emerges from comparison of the results of the administrative elections of 1975 and 1980. In 1980 the DC vote in Palermo reached unprecedented levels (167,620 votes or 46.7%, compared to 151,104 votes or 41.7% in 1975), yet the number of personal preference votes expressed fell sharply (from 442,182 in 1975 to 420,896 in 1980). Particularly striking was the collapse in the number of preference votes received by the DC mayoral candidate: from 20,111 in 1975 to only 12,026 in 1980.[36] One possible interpretation of this last set of figures is that, while the individual patron – client ties linking the voter to a specific DC candidate appear to be somewhat less compelling than in the past, the bond of perceived class interest between the DC and broad sectors of the middle classes has grown even stronger.

The current economic crisis, compounded in its effects by the as yet unresolved structural weaknesses of the Italian economy, could play a decisive role in determining the future of these support mechanisms, which have so far functioned so admirably. Increasing resource constraints have been accompanied by increasing corporative pressures, as each category seeks to maintain or improve its own position at the expense of the collectivity and of the overall reforms necessary to restructure the Italian economy. The paradox for the DC in all this is that, as resources become increasingly scarce, the dual ideology of individual advancement and corporative privilege that the party has so successfully disseminated over three decades of power could backfire. As public employees become increasingly well organized, those same corporative pressures encouraged by the governing parties as part of a strategy of "divide and conquer" vis-à-vis the national labor movement may, if the government proves unable to deliver, be turned instead against the DC and its allies. Despite their massive support for the governing parties, the politics of public employees, particularly in the South, consists less in loyalty to the DC as such than in the traditional southern *qualunquismo* (support for the most powerful contender.)[37] Given this type of "provisional" loyalty to the DC, as yet never seriously put to the test, the *impiegati pubblici* could potentially turn against the party if it proves unable to guarantee any longer the privileges it has led them to expect as their due. If this should happen, history indicates only too clearly in which direction the middle classes would be likely to turn; the worst fears of the Italian ruling class would be confirmed.

5

The local entrepreneurial class

Crucial to the political hold of the DC in Palermo are its linkages to the local entrepreneurial class. The relationship between political and economic elites is an issue that has stimulated significant interest and research activity, particularly among students of community power in the United States.[1] In contrast to American theories of a "power elite," which posit the domination of politics by business interests, what one finds in Palermo is the opposite extreme – the subordination of the entrepreneur to the politician and of economic rationality to the exigencies of party and factional struggle. The causes of this dependency relationship must be sought in three interrelated factors: (1) the nature of the southern bourgeoisie; (2) the model of postwar Italian economic development, which has perpetuated the subordination of the South to the needs of northern industry; (3) the expanding role of the state in the economy since 1945, particularly pronounced in the South because of the weakness of the private sector. As the latter two issues have been discussed at length in Chapter 2, this section will focus briefly on the problem of the southern bourgeoisie.

The new bourgeois class which came into existence in the South in the decades just before 1860 was in its outlook more closely wedded to the values of the landed aristocracy than to the independent initiative and propensity for risk characteristic of the entrepreneurial spirit, tendencies that have continued to mark the southern bourgeoisie until this day. Loath to invest without a maximum guarantee against potential losses, this class has preferred short-term speculative gain to long-term capital accumulation. In the words of Raimondo Catanzaro, the vocation of the southern bourgeoisie is essentially parasitic and the dominant orientation of the entrepreneurial class that of the *"entrepreneur comme rentier."*[2]

The unwillingness of the southern entrepreneur to undertake in-

111

vestment risks has meant that productive industrial investment in the South has been disproportionately the result of external, predominantly public, intervention. Even those firms that are formally part of the private sector are in most cases dependent for their survival upon some form of assistance from the state – be it special incentives or subsidies, privileged access to credit or public contracts, or discretionary use of licensing, zoning, and taxation powers. As a result, a truly private sector can be said to be practically nonexistent. Many firms exist for purely speculative purposes, being set up without any economic rationale, for the sole purpose of obtaining state or regional subsidies; once these funds are obtained, the firm goes bankrupt and is forced to close, while the subsidies find their way into foreign bank accounts (or, as happens frequently in Sicily, the firm is taken over by the Region in order to salvage the jobs of its employees).[3] In this way, the entrepreneur is assured a risk-free profit, his deficit being guaranteed by the state, while public resources are expended twice over with absolutely no return in terms of economic development. This emphasis on short-term, low-risk profit, combined with the paucity of externally induced industrial investment in the South, has meant that local entrepreneurial activity has been concentrated to a large extent in real-estate speculation and in the construction industry, which has come to symbolize "economic development" for much of the South.

The entrepreneurial class in Palermo consists primarily of the owners of small, relatively inefficient, and economically marginal firms, with rudimentary organizational structures and outlets limited almost entirely to local markets. To summarize briefly the argument of Berger and Pizzorno presented in Chapter 4: the key role attributed to these groups (together with the traditional commercial and artisanal middle classes) in the political strategy of the DC is a result less of their numerical strength in electoral terms than of the critical role of economic and political mediation they perform with regard to the marginal labor force. In the context of the southern Italian city, where the threat of mass unemployment is ever present, and public resources, despite mass patronage, fall far short of filling the gap, the independent middle classes play a central role in preserving the delicate economic balance upon which political and social stability depend. The fear of instability among the Italian ruling class has led the DC and its allies to protect these groups because of their special relationship with the marginal labor force, making both ultimately dependent primarily upon political solutions rather than market forces for their survival.

What, then, has been the nature of the linkage between the DC and local entrepreneurs? Lacking the resources for autonomous development, the southern economy has become increasingly dependent upon public intervention, in the form both of direct public investment and of various programs of incentives and subsidies for private investors. In each case, the intermediary role of the local political elite (at all governmental levels – municipal, regional, and national) has been a central factor. This does not necessarily imply the absence of entrepreneurship in the South, but rather an entrepreneurial class insufficiently autonomous to bargain on an equal basis with political elites. In the last analysis, the entrepreneurial function in the South has been assumed by the politician, who controls the access to all forms of public resources and who thereby holds the power to determine the success or failure of the individual economic actor.[4] As a result, a solid bond of reciprocal obligation is formed between the political intermediary and the entrepreneur, a confluence of interests having more to do with political power than with economic development. In the words of Alessandro Pizzorno, "The criterion of maximization is not the productive efficiency of the credit conceded, but rather the solidity of the bond of gratitude established and the type of service which will be made available in return . . . Economic credit, that is, generates a political debt."[5]

A study of another southern city, Salerno, in the early 1970s has produced extensive documentation on the nature and intensity of the contacts between the local political and entrepreneurial classes.[6] Through the use of survey data, this study demonstrates that political contacts are indeed more frequent and systematic for the marginal firm than for its modern, efficient counterpart. This does not necessarily mean that, in an economy as precarious as that of southern Italy, the majority of marginal firms are sustained by public intervention; in fact, in the Salerno study, 80% of the marginal firms surveyed reported only infrequent contacts with the local political class. On the other hand, if one looks only at those firms that do maintain political contacts, the greater intensity of these contacts in the case of the marginal firm is striking, with regard both to demands received from politicians and to demands transmitted to politicians. (Tables 5.1 and 5.2.) The most common type of request received by these firms is to provide jobs for individuals bearing political *raccomandazioni*. While it might seem paradoxical that it is the small marginal firm rather than the large modern enterprise that bears the brunt of political pressures for labor absorption, the explanation, according to the authors of the Salerno study, lies in the firm's very weakness. Unlike the modern industrial enterprise (often a subsidiary of a large northern company or publicly owned firm), which can resist local

Table 5.1. *Political demands according to type of firm and type of demand (percentages of firms in each category reporting a given type of demand)*

Type of demand	Marginal firms	Rational efficient firms
Individual *raccomandazioni*	62.5	50.6
General pressures for increased employment	42.0	30.6
Labor controversies	0.4	6.0

Source: S. Bonazzi et al., *Industria e potere in una provincia meridionale* (1972), p. 388.

Table 5.2. *Entrepreneurial demands according to type of firm and type of demand (percentages of firms in each category reporting a given type of demand)*

Type of demand	Marginal firms	Rational efficient firms
Intervention with suppliers	41.1	22.6
Financial and fiscal questions	53.9	37.9
Construction licenses	39.1	17.2
Public-works contracts	66.2	60.5

Source: S. Bonazzi et al. (1972), p. 389.

pressures because of its external market and its own political clout, the small firm has few arms with which to defend itself. As a result, it accedes to these pressures and, in so doing, reinforces its own inefficiency and marginality.

In return, the owners of these marginal firms transmit a variety of demands to local politicians: for special credit, for support in obtaining commercial credit, for public contracts, building licenses, tax reductions, and so on (Table 5.3). As a result of this exchange, the small firm with the requisite political contacts is protected and sustained, but at a substantial cost to the economy as a whole, because of the sacrifice of criteria of economic rationality in the distribution of these benefits. A recent study of entrepreneurial attitudes and behavior in the Province of Catania provides further evidence in support of the conclusions of the Salerno research.[7] Catanzaro and his *équipe* found the distribution of credit and other incentives and subsidies to be

Table 5.3. *Type of entrepreneurial demands reported by local politicians, distinguished by level of office held*

Level of office	Public contracts	Building licenses	Support for bank loans	Special credit	Tax reductions	Labor mediation
Local	7	17	10	9	13	10
Regional	2	4	4	7	3	2
National	8	5	8	11	3	2
Total	17	26	22	27	19	14

Source: S. Bonazzi et al. (1972), p. 417.

highly fragmented and to be directed predominantly at small and inefficient firms, for the most part in sectors related to construction, without prospects for further development but with an important role to play in limiting unemployment at the local level.[8] The only source of leverage of the individual firm is its control over the labor force, and the resulting threat (vis-à-vis the state) of an increase in unemployment if the firm is permitted to go under. This relationship of mutual dependence creates a situation where the element of risk inherent in entrepreneurial activity virtually disappears and, in Catanzaro's words, "assisted entrepreneurship becomes guaranteed entrepreneurship."[9]

In the end, where the goal of economic development has been subordinated to the interests of local power, political intervention, rather than breaking the vicious circle of underdevelopment, serves instead to reinforce it:

The goals of development end up by coinciding with the creation of an industrial apparatus capable of absorbing labor, but in no way efficient and rational with regard to production . . . In sum, the allocation of public funds serves latent functions of a welfare nature as well as sustaining local entrepreneurial groups for political ends, rather than promoting economic development.[10]

The result is a self-perpetuating process by which marginality, and with it the bases of clientelistic power, are continually re-created:

In a society in which the "hunger for work" is endemic, it is in the interest of local politicians to sustain firms which, because of their weakness, are unable to resist political pressures for increased jobs. On their part, these firms will request in exchange financial and fiscal incentives, building licenses and public works contracts. Thus a vicious circle is created, a process of non-de-

velopment which perpetuates one of the fundamental causes of marginality –
an excess labor supply – and with it the clientelistic bases of the party's
power.[11]

Public intervention in the southern economy has taken three general forms, which correspond to three distinct types of linkages between the DC and the local entrepreneurial class: (1) Direct public
spending by national, regional, and local governments. While this
form of patronage has been utilized by the DC above all to create a
huge politically dependent public bureaucracy in the South (see
Chapter 4), it has also been an important factor in allying certain sectors of the entrepreneurial class with the ruling parties. This public
spending has taken the form of incentives and subsidies as well as
special industrial salvage programs, on the one hand, and of favoritism and corruption in the awarding of the lucrative public-works
contracts of the Cassa per il Mezzogiorno and the Region, as well as
of the concessions let out by the city government for certain public
services (e.g., maintenance of streets and sewer lines), on the other;
(2) control of access to major channels of credit, both public and private; (3) discretionary implementation of the regulatory powers of
local government, particularly in the areas of urban planning, licensing, and taxation.

While alike in their generation of consensus on the basis of individualistic material benefits, these three instruments of patronage
politics imply very different relationships between the dominant political party and public resources. The first constitutes a direct and
substantial outlay of government funds, conforming to the traditional image of the machine as squandering public resources for political ends. The second, control of access to credit, while confirming
the critical intermediary role of the party, concerns resources that
emanate only in part from governmental sources. Finally, the third
category, discretionary use of the regulatory powers of local government, provides a striking example of the creation of a solid clientelistic bond without any drain at all on public treasuries. In contrast to
theories of clientelistic politics that point to high levels of resource-
flow over time as critical to the maintenance of the machine, the
above distinctions are essential for an understanding of the survival
of such a deeply rooted and enduring system of clientelistic power as
the DC machine in Palermo in an economic context characterized by
severe resource constraints. The remainder of this chapter and Chapter 6 examine in detail the functioning of each of these patronage
mechanisms as they relate to the local entrepreneurial class.

The uses of public funds

The most conspicuous example of large-scale dispersion of public funds to local entrepreneurs is the industrial development programs of the Sicilian regional government, the results of which unequivocally confirm the conclusions of the Salerno study regarding the impact of the clientelistic bond between the DC and the local entrepreneurial class on the general goal of economic development.

Over the past thirty years the Region has expended huge sums of money for industrial promotion, with few visible results either in terms of the island's productive capabilities or of increased industrial employment. The funds allocated over the years for industrial incentives or subsidies have been deployed in a chaotic, piecemeal fashion, without any attempt to fit them into a longer-term framework of development objectives, or even to conform to criteria of economic rationality in the choice of recipients. The allocation of funds has corresponded instead to the logic of political pressures from competing politicians and factions, each eager to consolidate or expand its own power base with the aid of the regional treasury. The end result, rather than the promotion of a network of self-sustaining small and medium enterprises capable of holding their own against outside competition, has been the creation and sustenance of firms operating completely outside the constraints of the market with regard to efficiency and competitiveness.

The instrument of the Region's industrial development program has been Ente Siciliano per la Promozione Industriale (ESPI), which has come to be regarded throughout Italy as a classic case study of the disastrous impact of clientelistic politics upon public programs for economic development.[12] Founded in 1967 upon the ruins of its bankrupt predecessor Società Finanziaria Siciliana (SoFiS) 1958–67, ESPI's purpose was to stimulate small- and medium-scale local industry by means of minority participation (up to 25%) by the regional government in the ownership of the firm. Shortly thereafter, the agency's statute was amended to permit, where deemed necessary, total public ownership in order to save a firm from bankruptcy, thereby signifying a shift in regional policy from industrial promotion to industrial salvage. Thus were born the *aziende* ESPI, a total of 45 small and medium industrial firms with approximately 7,000 employees throughout Sicily (concentrated primarily in Palermo and Catania) and a total deficit as of 1976 of 110 billion lire (approx. U.S. $180 million).

What ESPI has done is to take over and sustain failing firms by pumping in public funds to cover their deficits. The fatal flaw is that public ownership has not brought with it more efficient standards of management; on the contrary, the administration of the agency itself and that of the individual firms under its control have become prime pastures for clientelism, with criteria of sound management and economic rationality ignored in the rush for short-term political payoffs. Appointment to the administrative councils of these firms has been used as an important patronage prize by ruling parties, so that these positions have been awarded almost entirely on the basis of political merit rather than of technical or managerial competence. In 1973, between *consigli d'amministrazione* (responsible for the general management of the firm) and *collegi dei sindaci* (responsible for the overseeing of all financial procedures), the 45 ESPI enterprises boasted a total of 369 administrators, all but a handful political appointees. Precise data on the political affiliation of these appointees are available only for the 135 members of the *consigli d'amministrazione*, of whom 104 were nominated by ESPI and 31 by the minority private stockholders; with the exception of five technical experts, the 104 positions filled by ESPI were strictly apportioned among the parties making up the regional government majority, with 64 going to the DC, 24 to the PSI, 6 to the PRI, 4 to the PSDI, and 1 to the PLI.[13]

These positions have been widely used by political figures to engage in rampant patronage hiring as well as favoritism and corruption in buying and marketing practices. The result has been that, in addition to work forces swollen out of all proportion to their effective production needs, the *aziende* ESPI have been plagued by sheer managerial incompetence such that, rather than resolving the financial problems of the firms by public takeover, deficits have continued to mount at an even more alarming rate than before (one firm registering a deficit seven times greater than the total value of its production!). Under such conditions of gross mismanagement, corruption, and chronic bankruptcy, many of the firms in fact no longer produce. Regional funds continue to flow in just to maintain the salaries of the employees, while the productive function of the firm has been totally eclipsed.

The reasons for ESPI's failure to fulfill its primary objective – the creation of an autonomous entrepreneurial class in Sicily – as well as a complementary goal, the creation of a mature and responsible working class, are analyzed in the following passage, which underlines once again the considerations made at the outset of this chapter with regard to the nature of the southern bourgeoisie and the dominant role of the politician in the relationship between political and economic elites:

It is necessary that managers, at both intermediate and upper levels, comprehend that they must risk something of their own – their own careers, their own money if it has been invested – but above all they must know that only by hard work will they get ahead. If, instead, their activity is sheltered, because they are sure of the support of a patron-protector to whom in return they will provide a certain extra-industrial service – electoral and political – it is logical that they will never fully commit themselves, nor will they risk anything of their own, since whatever happens it will not be their responsibility. In this way, a true entrepreneurial class will never come into being.

Likewise, the worker who enters such a firm assumes the mentality of a pensioner. He never exerts himself on the job because his efforts have already been expended instead in making the rounds of all his "friends" to obtain the necessary recommendations.[14]

The *aziende* ESPI are an extreme but instructive example of the ways in which the demands of clientelistic politics can subvert the original purposes for which public programs of economic development are intended. Analyses of the ills of ESPI abound: the problem, still unresolved, is to find a politically viable solution. One of the most troubling lessons of the ESPI experience has been its demonstration of the self-perpetuating logic inherent in a strategy of development grounded in clientelistic premises. Despite the tremendous waste of public resources perpetrated by an agency like ESPI, a waste acknowledged by public figures of all political colors, such a program, once set in motion, inexorably gives rise to a wide range of entrenched institutional interests. These range from the bureaucrats and political appointees who run the agency and the individual firms to the trade unions who vigorously defend the workers' right to their jobs, placing almost insurmountable obstacles in the path of reform.

The other face of the use of public funds for patronage purposes – corruption in the awarding of public-works contracts and municipal concessions – is rampant throughout the South and has received extensive coverage in the Italian press. While this has been and remains an important link between the ruling parties and certain sectors of the entrepreneurial class (primarily, in this case, the larger, better-financed and equipped firms), the mechanisms involved should be sufficiently familiar from the American urban experience to require no further illustration. What *is* distinctive in the case of Sicily, and in recent years of Calabria as well, is the extent to which the public-works contracts of local and regional governments have been awarded to firms with only barely disguised mafia connections.[15] In many of these cases, public funds have indeed served to strengthen local entrepreneurial elites, but it is at least open to debate to what extent this kind of entrepreneurship will serve the interests of the South over the longer term. (For more detailed discussion of the entrepreneurial role of the mafia and its political ramifications, see Chapter 6.)

Control of access to credit

For the entrepreneurial class in general, not only in the South but throughout Italy, the primary link to public power in the postwar period has been that of credit. In Sicily, as in all of Italy, the most influential banks are publicly controlled and have constituted major centers of power for the Christian Democratic Party which, through its control of the state and of local administrations, has succeeded in appointing its representatives to the presidencies and administrative councils of the country's leading financial institutions.[16] This political domination of the banks, combined with extremely conservative standards of lending, has meant that the fastest and surest way to secure a loan has been to have an influential politician vouch personally for the client's reliability. The intermediary role of the DC between the entrepreneurial class and the commercial banking system remains an important element in the edifice of DC power, but it has, particularly in the South, been overshadowed by the establishment of even more direct instruments of economic and political power – the programs of *credito agevolato* ("special low-cost credit") set up by the national and regional governments for the purpose of benefiting small and medium firms unable to meet the stringent conditions and high interest rates (20%–25%) imposed by the commercial banks.[17] In both cases the concession of credit has been used to forge a solid bond of reciprocal obligation between the political intermediary and the entrepreneur.

However, while the overall importance of DC control over major channels of credit must not be underestimated, its significance for the local entrepreneurial class in Palermo and in Sicily more generally – an entrepreneurial class composed overwhelmingly of small marginal producers – is much less clear. Despite formal intentions to favor small and medium local enterprise, the lion's share of funds allocated for special credit in Sicily has in fact gone to large firms in the modern sector, as have the major public-works contracts of the Cassa and the regional government. While the Region does administer through the banks special programs of low-cost credit targeted to specific categories (small shopkeepers, artisans, and petty industrialists), the sums available have been so insignificant and the criteria so restrictive that the impact of these programs, in terms either of effective assistance to small firms or of political payoffs has been minimal. Instead, the keystone of special credit in Sicily has been Istituto

Regionale per il Finanziamento alle Industrie in Sicilia (IRFIS), established in 1954 as a joint venture of the Cassa, the regional government, and the major Sicilian banks for the purpose, as noted above, of providing low-cost credit to small and medium firms. Like the commercial banks, however, IRFIS has, despite its original goal of promoting small-scale firms, fallen victim to the triple forces of conservative criteria of financial management, bureaucratic red tape, and the strategy of favoring large, nonlocal industrial complexes (as expressed in the investment strategy of the Cassa) that have dominated economic development in Sicily since the late 1950s.[18] Not only has IRFIS repeated the stringent guarantees required by commercial banks (automatically excluding, for example, firms with under 100 million lire in fixed investments) but the agency's bureaucratic procedures are so lengthy and complex that the more efficient and profitable modern firm has a built-in advantage: even when a small firm succeeds in meeting the conditions for obtaining a loan (which, it should be added, are available only for fixed investments, not to cover operating costs, which constitute the most urgent need for many small firms), it may well succumb to bankruptcy before the funds arrive.

Perusal of the record of twenty years of IRFIS activity (1954–73) shows a total expenditure of almost 600 billion lire (U.S. $1 billion) for industrial credit, of which 59.0% has gone to the petroleum, petrochemical, and chemical industries (predominantly subsidiaries of national monopolies), a figure that rises to 83.4% if one looks at the year 1973 alone. As might be expected from such figures, 60% of all credit has been directed to the development poles of Catania-Siracusa and Messina, dominated by industrial giants with high capital intensity and minimal impact in terms either of employment or of "inducement effects" on the local economy.[19]

Given these figures on the distribution of publicly guaranteed low-cost credit, which, together with control of the commercial banking system, constitute the principal linkage between the DC and local enterprise, especially manufacturing firms, in most of the South, it is not surprising that many small businessmen in Palermo feel neglected and betrayed by politicians rather than protected and sustained. In both public and private statements small businessmen accuse the local political class, in Rome as well as in Palermo, of subordinating the interests of local enterprise to those of outside monopolies.[20] There is, however, an important exception to the general feeling of isolation and neglect among local entrepreneurs. This exception is the construction industry, which constitutes the real cornerstone of DC power among the entrepreneurial class in Palermo.

Because of the pivotal role of construction in the urban economy, it is above all to this sector that the dominant political elites have devoted their attention. Chapter 6 will demonstrate how, relying almost exclusively upon local levers of power – above all the licensing and zoning powers of local government, but also the concession of certain kinds of public contracts and the special relationship between the DC and local financial institutions[21] – the DC has created a solid partnership with the city's leading contractors, a partnership that in turn has formed the foundation of a far-reaching system of social alliances extending to almost every major segment of the urban population.

The powers of licensing and interdiction: the traditional middle classes

Before turning to the construction industry, however, it is necessary to consider another important facet of local governmental powers of licensing and interdiction in order to portray the full scope of the networks of power that can be built up through the exercise of such apparently bureaucratic functions. Not only building contractors but the traditional independent middle classes as well – small shopkeepers and artisans – have been solidly integrated into the dominant political regime by means of the distinctive regulatory powers entrusted to the city government, as well as through DC domination of the trade associations representing these categories.[22]

Before examining the specific patronage mechanisms at work in the case of the traditional middle classes, it is useful to reiterate the particular economic and social functions performed by these groups in the southern Italian city. In a situation of chronically scarce employment opportunities in other sectors of the economy, a situation aggravated in recent years by the onset of the economic crisis and the swelling tide of return migration it has provoked, petty commercial and artisanal activities have served and continue to serve to a significant degree as a "safety valve" against mass unemployment. As shown in Chapter 2, the distributive network in a city like Palermo is extremely pulverized, with at least 10,000 authorized retail outlets and 3,500–4,500 *abusivi* ("unlicensed sellers") in a city of about 800,000 inhabitants. The average shopkeeper leads a very precarious existence indeed, the mean life span of retail shops being only five years.[23] In recent years, because of the impact of the economic crisis on consumption levels, the prospects for successful commercial activity have become even dimmer, with bankruptcies increasing daily; yet, as of the end of 1976, 1,400 applications for new commercial licenses (predominantly for grocery and clothing stores, considered the sectors of easiest entry) awaited action by the city. Thus, despite the rapidly accelerating crisis of the sector and the excessive fragmentation of the existing retail network, pressures for entry continue to mount as more and more people turn to the mirage of their own shop as the only remaining alternative to outright unemployment.

In the light of the functions of economic and social stability attributed to the traditional middle classes, the policies of the dominant parties toward these groups can be seen as operating at two distinct levels: on the one hand, as outlined at the beginning of Chapter 4, a general political strategy aimed at maintaining a substantial role for these groups in contemporary Italian society; on the other hand, a more specifically clientelistic approach to these categories by the DC and its partners in local government. The former policy is exemplified by national legislation passed in 1971 to regulate the opening of new commercial outlets. This legislation was hailed as a major step toward rationalization of the excessively fragmented distributive system in Italy, because it requires cities and towns to elaborate detailed plans regulating the distribution of commercial outlets in their territory and makes the granting of a license requisite not only upon demonstration of professional capabilities but also upon the number of shops already in existence in any given neighborhood. In reality, however, this law, supported unanimously by all political parties in Parliament, actually represents a defense of the corporate interests of the existing commercial class; because of the obstacles it places in the way of granting new licenses, in particular for large supermarkets and department stores (the interests of small shopkeepers being strongly represented on the commissions that determine whether a license should be granted), the law has in fact obstructed rather than advanced the modernization of commerce in Italy.[24] The importance of the licensing power to both the bestower and the recipient of the license is captured in the following excerpt from an analysis of commercial policy in Bologna, where an alliance extending from the far Right to the far Left was mobilized to enact policies protecting small shopkeepers against competition from large retail outlets:

The commercial license represents the tutelage of a vassal; it is a feudalistic investiture of a few square meters of territory, by which to insure the shopkeeper "forever" from competition. It is the creation of a small monopoly . . . in sum, a reward to the good and faithful servant from the holders of local power.[25]

Within this context of general national policies to protect the traditional middle classes, local elites have utilized the regulatory powers of local government – specifically licensing and police powers – in such a way as to forge a direct bond of individual political obligation with the commercial and artisanal classes. In Palermo, until 1971, the granting of commercial licenses, as well as of special licenses for certain types of artisanal activities (e.g., barbers, hairdressers, bakeries) was entrusted entirely to the discretionary power of the municipal assessors of commerce and hygiene, positions upon which more than one political fortune has been built. In the absence of any clear-cut rules as to the number and type of retail outlets to be permitted in any section of the city or the specific requirements for obtaining a license (the only prerequisite being the absence of a criminal record), licenses were granted in a completely indiscriminate fashion calculated only to reinforce personal clienteles.

Six years after the passage of the 1971 law to regulate commerce, the city had yet even to begin elaboration of the required plan regulating the distribution of new commercial outlets. Under this law licenses are to be conceded only by authorization of apposite commissions set up by the Chamber of Commerce and the city government (including representatives of the trade associations) to examine applicants for their professional qualifications and to ascertain the need for additional shops in any given area. The pressure for new licenses is so intense, however, that, in the words of both the municipal assessor of commerce and the president of the major trade association, strict application of the law would be politically impossible; the existing structure of commerce is so irrational that application of the law would mean not only a ban on all new licenses but the exit from the sector of a significant proportion of those persons already exercising commercial activity.[26] The dilemma faced by these local administrators who now perceive the need for at least minimal rationalization of the distributional network underlines the kind of built-in pressures against reform that thirty years of clientelistic politics can generate.

Under this new system, if implemented, the manipulation of commercial licenses for clientelistic ends will become much more difficult. Another highly effective instrument, however, remains in the hands of local administrators – the surveillance and enforcement powers of the *vigili urbani* ("city police"). The potential political role of the *vigile* is underscored in the following statement by a member of the city police force: "A city administrator is always anxious to favor a *vigile* because each of us, underneath an anonymous uniform and helmet, can transform himself, if he wishes, into a *grande elettore*."[27] By what means, one might ask, can an ordinary city policeman exercise such political influence? On closer examination, it becomes clear that, in the course of his daily rounds, there are literally thousands of ways in which a vigilant police officer can either perform a favor or else make life miserable for a shopkeeper or street-vendor:

> If a cop wants to be fussy, he can ruin a shopkeeper. He can slap him with a fine of 30,000 or 40,000 lire if he lowers his grill five minutes later than the official closing time. He can levy another 50,000 lire fine if the price sign has fallen off the crate of oranges. And if the shopkeeper is very careful and commits neither of these infractions, the cop always has an ace up his sleeve. He need only express a doubt as to the sanitary conditions of the shop and its merchandise, and the merchant will never re-emerge from the troubles which beset him: controls, inspections, months of closing, endless expenses.[28]

Each of the above examples is, in and of itself, a relatively trivial matter – but one that can take on vital importance for the individual shopkeeper should the *vigile* decide to enforce the letter of the law. In practice the power of the *vigile* derives less from the controls he effects than from those he *omits* (failing to denounce, for example, an unauthorized shop or vendor), in return for either an immediate payoff or, more often, a debt of gratitude that will be repaid on a future, preferably electoral, occasion. One reason such a system of control over the individual shopkeeper or artisan has been so effective is that a large proportion of these people – especially at the level of small neighborhood grocery stores, owners of market stalls, and street-vendors – themselves come from the ranks of the *sottoproletariato*. Their ignorance of the law is compounded by an inbred fear of and deference toward the powerful, particularly if they wear a uniform. An able administrator can thus transform an automatic bureaucratic procedure (such as concession of a commercial license under the pre-1971 procedure or a permit for the occupation of public soil in the open markets) into a personal favor, just as the *vigile* can exploit the slightest infraction of the law, real or imagined, to create a network of personal obligation that he can then use as a bargaining arm with the holders of political power. For a policeman only the function of traffic control offers no potential for political exploitation – it is perhaps for this reason that a recent mayor assigned only 50 out of the 500 *vigili* at his disposal to direct the city's absolutely chaotic traffic.

Another instrument of power vis-à-vis the traditional middle classes has been DC domination of the trade associations representing merchants and artisans, as well as that of the small farmers (the *Coldiretti*); in nonurban areas of the South, the latter in particular has constituted one of the fundamental pillars of DC power throughout the postwar period. While competing trade associations have been created, particularly by the Left, thus far those controlled by the DC have succeeded, because of the party's identification with state and often local power, in retaining an overwhelming majority of the membership. An interesting example of this is the case of the Confcommercio (the DC-controlled association of merchants) in Palermo; occupying an entire floor of the building housing the local Chamber of Commerce (in Italy a direct emanation of the state), the Confcommercio has exploited this proximity to create the impression that it is *the* official representative of the category rather than only one among several competing organizations with diverse political leanings.

The formal power of these organizations is only a kind of trade-union representation of their members. Their real power stems instead from the intermediary function they perform between their membership and those public bodies that do in fact perform critical functions for the individual shopkeeper or artisan. The most important of these are the Casse Mutue, the special health and pension agencies representing the self-employed. Because the leadership of these bodies is decided through direct elections for which each of the trade associations presents a list of candidates, the predominance of the DC-controlled organizations has assured them the domination of the *mutue* as well. As in the case of the *vigili urbani*, the patronage potential of the *mutue* consists of petty favors – access to free hospital care, receipt of a pension or family allowance, acceptance into special job-training programs – but all favors that in the individual case create a lasting bond of gratitude.

The kind of power that can be exercised through such organizations, as well as the ways in which the DC has created a network of interlocking power throughout society, can be illustrated by the example of Giuseppe Guarino, president for over twenty years of the Associazione Artigiani (closely allied with the *fanfaniani*), which until 1968 monopolized representation of the artisans in Palermo. Although his high-handed manipulation of his position for political ends eventually gave rise to a revolt from within and the creation of competing organizations, Guarino still heads by far the largest of the artisanal associations. In addition to this position, he is president of the provincial and regional artisanal commissions, which supervise the registration and cancellation of artisans in the official professional lists kept by the Chamber of Commerce, registration in which is a prerequisite for assistance by the *mutua* (opponents estimate that about 40% of those so registered are false, presenting themselves as artisans only for purposes of assistance).[29] He is also president of the provincial and regional Casse Mutue for artisans as well as a member of the national council; president of the regional institute for professional training for artisans; member of the executive board of the Chamber of Commerce and of various commissions for the licensing of barbers, hairdressers, and the like; member of the municipal tax commission; and member of the local boards of the public-housing authority (IACP) and the state social-security agency (INPS). With such far-reaching influence, it is little wonder that he has maintained the kind of hold he has over the artisans of Palermo.

The evidence presented above as to the bases of DC support among the traditional middle classes reinforces the central theme of this chapter: the need to distinguish, in the analysis of clientelistic systems of politics, among types of patronage with very different resource bases. Apart from the regional industrial development programs discussed at the beginning of this chapter, the dominant factor in the other forms of linkage between the DC and the local entrepreneurial classes has not been the direct expenditure of public resources for political ends, but rather the critical intermediary role of the party as an obligatory middleman between the individual and a variety of benefits, only a portion of which imply an outlay of a monetary nature.

The case of the shopkeepers and artisans, like that of the building contractors discussed in Chapter 6, provides a prime example of the construction of a solid clientelistic bond that depends only in small part upon the expenditure of public funds and therefore constitutes only a very minimal drain on party or public treasuries. As these cases demonstrate, city governments possess a wide range of powers which, while conferring significant advantages or disadvantages of an economic nature, do not impose any *monetary* cost on the bestower.

This evidence shows how, through manipulation of the substantial regulatory powers of local government, a high level of clientelistically based consensus can be maintained over an extended period of time without necessarily provoking inflationary consequences. Naturally, contradictions will emerge over time in any such attempt to maintain political support predominantly through the use of short-term material incentives, as the weight of the chaotic nature of Palermo's urban expansion and of the city's distributive system on the rationalizing efforts of subsequent city administrators clearly demonstrates. It must be emphasized, however, that while these imply significant social costs, they are not constraints imposed by the exhaustion of available resources through patronage spending, nor do they necessarily imply the imminent collapse of the DC machine.

6

The mafia as entrepreneur: the politics of urban expansion and urban renewal

In Palermo, as in most other southern cities, development has been synonymous with the tremendous boom in construction activity that dominated the economic landscape of these cities during the latter half of the 1950s and the decade of the 1960s. The political, as well as the economic, weight of the construction industry in these cities cannot be underestimated. In contrast to other economic sectors, construction activity by its very nature has an exclusively local focus; correspondingly, the instruments of political power that can most decisively affect its success or failure – the issuing of construction licenses and the enforcement of building codes and zoning regulations – are the exclusive domain of local administrations. This local focus, both economic and political, has provided an excellent terrain for encounter between the economic interests of building contractors and the needs of a clientelistic system of local political power. This coincidence of interests is such that the ascent of the new generation of DC leadership in Palermo and throughout the South in the 1950s cannot be adequately understood without consideration of the critical role played by key real-estate and construction interests in the conquest and consolidation of its power.

The logic of speculative development

To understand the nature of this special relationship between the DC and the construction industry, it is necessary to reconstruct the history of the past thirty years of urban development in Palermo. At the end of the war, the dimensions of Palermo were still essentially those of the nineteenth-century city. At the core of the city lay the Quattro Mandamenti of the *centro storico*, where the urban *palazzi* of the Sicilian aristocracy sat side by side with the miserable one-room dwellings of the *sottoproletariato*, cut into four historic *quartieri* by the per-

128

pendicular axes of the city's two major commercial thoroughfares. To the north and west the *centro storico* was flanked by the fashionable bourgeois neighborhoods constructed in the last half of the nineteenth century, of which the central artery, the Via Libertà, with its masterpieces of Liberty architecture, was considered, along with the Champs Elysées, one of the most magnificent avenues of Victorian Europe. At the edge of these bourgeois neighborhoods, still within easy walking distance of the old center, the city gave way to the Conca d'Oro – the lush plain of citrus groves, already celebrated by the Arabs in the tenth century, separating the city on three sides from the surrounding mountains; scattered throughout the Conca d'Oro were dozens of small rural villages or *borgate*, made up predominantly of small peasant proprietors and agricultural day laborers. Palermo was the southern Italian city most severely damaged by the war, with 70,000 rooms destroyed in the bombing, and the one in which reconstruction proceeded at the slowest pace, with the ruins of the war still visible today in many areas of the old city. At the time of the first postwar census in 1951, Palermo had a population of about 500,000; of these, 127,000 were crowded into the decaying slums of the Quattro Mandamenti, while over 14,000 inhabited shantytowns and even caves, both on the periphery of the city and in bombed-zones in the center.[1]

This brief panorama of the city in 1951 sets the stage for the first act in a process of urban development that would, in the space of a decade, completely revolutionize the shape of the city and its politics. The end of the war and the establishment, in 1947, of the regional government with its capital in Palermo, provoked massive migration into the city from the provinces, in particular on the part of the provincial middle classes who arrived by the thousands to man the nascent regional bureaucracy; between 1951 and 1961 the population of the city increased by almost 100,000. Naturally, a population increase of this magnitude further aggravated the already severe housing shortage caused by the war. The aspirations for upward mobility of these new arrivals were condensed into one all-absorbing desire, *la casa* (symbolized by the modern high-rise apartment complex). This demand, sustained by the low-cost mortgages made available to all regional employees and reinforced by the wholesale flight of the remaining aristocracy and the traditional middle classes from the old city, laid the bases for an unprecedented boom of urban expansion.

The beginnings of this process go back to 1952, when the first DC municipal administration was elected after six years of rule by Monarchists and *qualunquisti*. At this time the DC in Palermo was still firmly in the hands of the traditional notables, landowners, and professionals: in the presidency of the Region Franco Restivo, in the city administration Francesco Scaduto and Pietro Virga (respectively mayor and assessor of public works), behind the scenes the immensely powerful Cardinal Ernesto Ruffini. These men and their followers constituted a small, tightly knit circle of power, composed primarily of members of the traditional elite they themselves directly represented. The beneficiaries of the initial speculative operations undertaken by the Scaduto administration were, on the one hand, prominent aristocratic families and, on the other, the Catholic Church (in the guise of the Società Generale Immobiliare, the huge real-estate trust controlled by the Vatican). The first and most notorious of these operations was that of Villa Sperlinga. In 1952 Villa Sperlinga was a large underdeveloped private park on the very edge of the city, zoned for public use by the Piano di Ricostruzione ("Reconstruction Plan") of 1947 in the absence of a general city plan. Scaduto, in the dual capacity of mayor and attorney, personally prepared an agreement between the city government and the representatives of the Immobiliare, the owners of the property, ceding 60,000 square meters for private development in return for a grant of the remaining 18,000 square meters to the city for a public park. Confronted with stubborn opposition in the City Council, which insisted on preservation of the entire area as a "breathing space" in what was already projected as a vast new zone of urban expansion, the mayor delivered a stunning *coup de grâce,* prophetic of the methods that would soon prevail in the competition for the enormous speculative gains to be realized from the tempestuous process of uncontrolled expansion about to sweep the city: "It is useless to continue the discussion," intoned Scaduto, "insofar as the park of Villa Sperlinga no longer exists. I must tell you some bad news: for some time, unknown vandals have been cutting down the trees."[2]

After Villa Sperlinga, which opened the door to the first wave of private speculation along the northwest axis of the city, the administration of the DC notables laid the groundwork for what would become one of the major instruments of public collusion in the speculative development of the city: the siting of public-housing projects. The scenario is the following: the city expropriates cheap agricultural land on the extreme periphery for the construction of public housing and proceeds to provide the major infrastructures (streets, water and sewage lines, electricity) necessary to link these areas with the city proper; overnight the intermediate areas, remaining under private ownership, increase as much as ten times in value, creating fortunes for certain well-placed proprietors. While the initial choice of areas for public housing may have been casual, dictated by the low cost of

Figure 6.1. Territory of the city of Palermo, indicating the *centro storico* (dark area), major public-housing projects (shaded areas), and rural *borgate* (designated by town names). The arrow indicates the primary direction of urban expansion in the 1950s and 1960s.

peripheral terrains, once it became clear that the construction industry would become the leading sector of the urban economy and provide the city's major source of wealth, the politics of public housing played a key role in promoting the speculative logic that would reign unchallenged over the process of urban expansion. The so-called satellite villages constructed by the IACP (the independent public-housing agency presided over for twenty-three years by Santi Cacopardo, a loyal supporter first of the DC notables and subsequently of Gioia), served as "'bridgeheads' established beyond the urban perim-

eter in order to subsequently exploit the increased value of the intermediate areas";[3] these bridgeheads traced a semicircle along the *circonvallazione* ("ring road") laid out in the early 1950s in the midst of
what was then open countryside (see Figure 6.1). The first of the
"satellite villages" was, appropriately enough, Villaggio Ruffini,
promoted and financed by the cardinal himself; situated in the countryside beyond the end of Via Libertà, it opened the way, along with
Villa Sperlinga, for the beginnings of the intense speculative development of what was to become the *Palermo nuova* – the "new Palermo" of block after block of luxury high-rise apartments, an entire
city springing up almost overnight, without parks, schools, community centers, or other basic social services, engulfing the Conca d'Oro
and the *borgate* in tons of cement.

It is not accidental that the great boom of urban expansion in Palermo, reaching its peak in the years 1957–63, moved in a single direction, along the northwest axis of the city in the area between the
circonvallazione and the prolongation of Via Libertà toward the fish-
ing village of Sferracavallo. From the first agreements of the city government with the Immobiliare and the two leading aristocratic families, the Terrasi and the Spatafora, in the early 1950s, to the *anni
ruggenti* ("boom years") of the early 1960s, certain clearly defined
property interests were at stake in the areas favored by the city administration for the public interventions that then paved the way for
massive private speculation (in contrast to the territory to the southeast of the city, dominated by small peasant proprietors). Fortunes
were amassed within a few years, with estimates of the gains to private speculators from the increase in land values alone in the range of
400 billion lire (approximately U.S. $660 million).[4] With such inter-
ests at stake, who gained or lost in the speculative game became
quite literally a matter of life and death.

Behind the seeming chaos and irrationality of Palermo's tempestuous process of urban expansion, a process that in a single decade
completely transformed the face of the city, a solid alliance was being
forged between the dominant faction of the DC and a new entrepreneurial class that seemed to appear almost overnight on the crest of
the building boom. To understand what happened in Palermo in the
critical years of the mid-1950s, it is necessary to go back to the takeover of the "young Turks" (Chapter 3). In the electoral campaign of
1956, focused on an appeal for renewal and moralization within local
government (an appeal directed particularly against the speculative
abuses of Scaduto), Gioia presented a program built around two fundamental elements – the *risanamento* ("urban renewal") of the old
city and the preparation of a general city plan – Piano Regolatore

Generale (PRG) – to regulate urban expansion. As the enactment of such a program would mean the expenditure of vast sums of money, both public and private, and the relaunching of the construction industry on a grand scale, it was clear that "the major source of urban income would soon be the construction industry, and therefore, that control of it would mean virtual control of the major financial levers of the city."[5] This meant that the key post in the new administration was assessor of public works (responsible at that time for the issuing of construction licenses and for all aspects of urban planning). In the period of intense urbanization that was about to commence, this office would become the focal point of local political life.

When, in 1956, Salvo Lima took over the Office of Public Works, he revolutionized the alliance system underpinning DC power. The doors of the *assessorato* were closed to the privileged clientele of the old DC notables, and all decisions passed directly through the assessor himself or his personal secretary, eliminating the petty trafficking by department functionaries which had been rampant under the old regime. What Lima did was to transform the essentially episodic operations of favoritism of the notables, undertaken without any broader strategic vision and limited to a restricted social elite, into a comprehensive strategy of urban expansion and of DC power, managed directly from key posts of power within the city administration. Within a few months of Lima's arrival, a whole new class of entrepreneurs had appeared on the scene, with names heretofore unkown in the ranks of the city's industrialists. A new era was about to begin in Palermo, an era of which the protagonists would be the duo Salvo Lima – Vito Ciancimino (the former assessor of public works until his election as mayor in July, 1958, the latter assessor of public works under Lima and his successor, DiLiberto, from July 1959 until July 1964).

Before 1960, no comprehensive city plan existed. Urban expansion proceeded under conditions of total chaos, with anyone capable of mustering minimal financial means fashioning himself a contractor and building apartments on the periphery of the city, with minimal interference on the part of the local administration apart from a "contribution" in order to obtain a speedy license. The events surrounding the elaboration, approval and implementation of the PRG in Palermo epitomize the evolving relationship between the DC and local entrepreneurs.[6] The critical years for such history are 1956–63, coinciding with the political domination of the city by Lima and Ciancimino. The years of the Lima – Ciancimino administration have been characterized as a period in which "the administration of the city of Palermo reached . . . unprecedented heights in the unrestrained disregard of the law, leaving behind irregularities of every kind."[7] Nowhere were these irregularities more pronounced than in the elaboration and implementation of the PRG and in the issuing of construction licenses. When Lima arrived at the Office of Public Works in 1956, one of his first acts was to set up a new planning office under his direct control and to completely revise the preliminary plan presented a few months earlier by the prefectoral "commissar" who had headed the city government for six months while the DC patched up its internal quarrels sufficiently to agree upon a new *giunta*. The new plan that was approved by the City Council in November 1959 was the end product of a no-holds-barred struggle for advantage in a sphere where everyone knew that immense fortunes were at stake. Under the incessant pressures of private interests, areas set aside for public use (parks, schools, community services, etc.) were bit by bit eliminated to make way for private development. A contemporary observer provides the following description of the maneuvering over the plan:

The battle rages. Prices have risen to the stars and the construction of a single school could mean a loss of millions. Thus, in a game of competing pressures and counterpressures, a school on the property of X is erased and relocated on the property of Y, who in turn rebels, seeks influential friendships and, if he is not clever, succumbs.[8]

The end result was a plan that not only failed abysmally in its purpose of superimposing the constraints of the public interest upon a hitherto chaotic process of expansion, but instead, in its final form, came itself to represent, in the words of its opponents, "one of the principal instruments of real-estate speculation."[9] Its effect was to legalize the private speculation that had hitherto taken place spontaneously (e.g., provision in zones of new expansion for building densities as high as 21 cubic meters/square meter, an average of 2,000 inhabitants/hectare, in contrast to a national norm of only 3.5 cubic meters/square meter in urban areas). The plan approved by the City Council incorporated about 600 "observations" or variations proposed by private citizens, all in the sense of removing restrictions for public use or increasing the building density permitted; a large percentage of these variations bore the names of prominent politicians and bureaucrats, of known DC supporters and mafia bosses, either directly or through family members.[10] When the plan was given final approval in July 1962 by the president of the Region, only about one-third of these variations were accepted as legitimate; in the intervening three years, however, the city government had continued to grant building permits on the basis of the 1959 plan, so that, by the time that plan took effect in its definitive form in 1962, its implementation was irrevocably compromised by the *fait accompli* of high-rise apartments in those zones set aside by the regional government for public use.

With the enactment of the PRG, then, speculation became legalized. Anything was still possible, but at the price of a definite *quid pro quo* with the holders of local power. Not only had the plan itself been radically reshaped to conform to private speculative interests but for those contractors with the proper connections, further violations of the plan were permitted. The most blatant example of the systematic "sacking" of the city in the interests of speculative gain is the case of Francesco Vassallo, who would come to symbolize the new entrepreneurial class that came to dominate Palermo in these years and its linkages to the new edifice of power being erected by the *fanfaniani*.[11]

Francesco Vassallo, who by 1969 would head the list of the most wealthy *palermitani*, began his career in the 1930s as a *carrettiere* (transporting sand and stone in a horse-drawn cart) in Tommaso Natale, a *borgata* of Palermo. After amassing an initial patrimony through black-market grain dealings during the war, Vassallo began his career as a contractor in 1952, when, with no prior experience, he won a city contract for the construction of the sewage line from Tommaso Natale to the neighboring *borgata* of Sferracavallo. The circumstances of the awarding of this contract which, together with the simultaneous opening of substantial credit by the Banco di Sicilia, sealed Vassallo's future in the construction industry, show the first evidence of the solid ties to various sectors of the public administration that would henceforth mark every phase of the ex-*carrettiere's* vertiginous career. Although not yet listed in the official city register of contractors, Vassallo was admitted to the bidding for the contract on the basis of a dubious declaration by the firms Saia-Bazan-Ferruzza (owners of the urban transport system before municipal takeover, boasting close ties to centers of both political and mafia power), attesting to the performance of construction work for their company; the son of Ferruzza would later become a partner in one of the speculative operations of Vassallo. The contract was awarded in private negotiations between Vassallo and the city government headed by Professor Gaspare Cusenza, after competitors suspiciously withdrew from the public bidding. With regard to this initial step in Vassallo's career, the parliamentary Antimafia Commission would later declare:

The entire procedure raises serious doubts . . . The suspicion of undue mafia pressures arises spontaneously . . . The beginnings of Vassallo's career are clouded by well-founded doubts as to the propriety of the actions of the administrative organs and the financial institutions with which he dealt.[12]

The second major boost for Vassallo, who by now had shifted his activities to the more lucrative sphere of private construction, came in 1958, when the Cassa di Risparmio (the second most prominent Sicilian bank), which until this time had been extremely cautious in dealings with Vassallo, performed a sudden about-face, granting credit of up to 700 million lire (approximately U.S. $1.2 million) without any of the normal guarantees required by the bank. This abrupt change in the bank's policy coincided with the nomination to the presidency of the Cassa of the same Gaspare Cusenza who had presided over the awarding of the original city contract to Vassallo, as well as being involved, both directly and through his four daughters (one of whom was the wife of Giovanni Gioia), in a series of profitable real-estate deals with the rising entrepreneur.

In the years that followed, thanks to the ever-increasing generosity of the banks, with which he had accumulated by 1963 debts of almost 2 billion lire (U.S. $3.3 million), and the acquiescence of the city administration in all manner of favoritism and outright illegality, Vassallo became master of half the city, building entire neighborhoods in the *Palermo nuova* and weaving ever closer ties with the representatives of local power. For Vassallo, both the restrictions of the PRG (limited though they were) and the guidelines of normal bureaucratic procedure were nonexistent. A 1964 investigation by the prefect of Palermo (known as the Rapporto Bevivino) cites case after case in which Vassallo obtained licenses for projects in violation of the PRG (building residential dwellings in areas destined for public use), altered projects after the initiation of construction (exceeding allowed volumes), and even went so far as to begin construction without a license – in every case with complete impunity, given the complicity of public officials, in particular the assessor of public works and the Provincial Control Commission, whose job it was to enforce observance of the plan. While other contractors waited months for approval of a project, on one memorable occasion Vassallo succeeded, on the very day on which he presented a project, in having it approved by the *commissione edilizia*, the official decision-making arm of the Office of Public Works, by the legal office of the Commune, and finally by the City Council – an amazing feat for a city in which the slowness of the bureaucracy is legendary![13]

By the late 1960s the market for private apartments was beginning to be saturated, so Vassallo turned to a more secure outlet for his *palazzi* – the public administration. A large proportion of his buildings were either bought or rented in advance by the Commune, Province, or Region to house public offices and schools, even though they had been built for private use and lacked the necessary infrastructures for public use; many of these contracts were stipulated from the day of the agreement rather than the day of consignment, which might be as much as a year later. In the year 1969 alone, Vassallo received rents of almost 190 million lire (U.S. $316,000) from the Commune and 210 million lire (U.S. $350,000) from the Province for fifteen sites to be used as schools.[14] Vassallo's new activity as a renter of locales for scholastic and other public uses was made possible by the acute shortage of schools in Palermo. The causes of this continuing shortage are dual: on the one hand, the distortions in the city plan discussed above, by which areas destined for schools and other social structures were sacrificed to private speculative interests; on the other, "the lack of any stimulus [on the part of the city administration] to undertake public works in the area of school construction, and a particular preference and solicitude instead for the solution of renting."[15] Thus, although both the Commune and the Province hold substantial sums allocated by the national and regional governments for school construction, these funds lie unused while the local administrations and the relevant control organs repeatedly approve vast expenditures for the rental of private edifices (particularly in those neighborhoods where speculative building has been most intense). With the complicity of the municipal and provincial administrations, Vassallo has thus been able to implement his own "personal city plan of school construction."[16] Not only did Vassallo realize immense gains both in the original speculative construction of his *palazzi* and in the excessively favorable contracts subsequently stipulated with various public bodies but he was actually praised as a benefactor by grateful administrators for having offered his *palazzi* to house the schools that the Commune and Province were unable to provide!

All these incidents point to a clearcut pattern of collusion between Vassallo and highly placed politicians within local government. In the mid-1960s, a newspaper published by a left-wing faction of the local DC went so far as to postulate the existence of a society called VALIGIO, of which the hypothetical partners were Vassallo, Lima, and Gioia:

This firm, whose owner passed with surprising rapidity from his initial status as a humble laborer to that of "boss" of Palermo industry, owes its lightning success to an acronym, VALIGIO . . . The abuses of the VALIGIO are common knowledge: it has built and continues to build where and as it pleases, without licenses, without finding any obstacles, and sells what it builds even before building it. Inevitably among its most conspicuous clients we find the Commune and the Italian Red Cross (headed by Gioia's brother). Let anyone who wants to make deductions do so.[17]

While the existence of such a society is mere invention, it expresses quite admirably the very real linkages between the entrepreneurial class symbolized by Francesco Vassallo and the new bosses of the DC.

The mafia and politics

Cu è surdu, orbu e taci, campa cent'anni 'mpaci. [Sicilian proverb][18]

To combat and destroy the kingdom of the mafia, it is necessary, it is indispensable, that the Italian government cease to be the *king of the mafia!* But the government has acquired too great a taste for the exercise of this dishonest and illicit authority; it is too practiced and hardened in its misdeeds. Have we come to a point where we can no longer hope for the cessation of the function without the destruction of the organ? [Napoleone Colajanni, 1900][19]

If it can be said that Vassallo symbolizes the new entrepreneurial class that emerged in Palermo concomitant with the takeover of local power by the *fanfaniani* of Gioia and Lima, it is not yet clear what made this rising entrepreneurial class so distinctive. The kind of collusion between public administrators and private speculative interests illustrated above is not peculiar to Palermo, because it marks the postwar politics of almost every large Italian city; what makes Palermo unique is rather the grafting of a certain segment of these speculative interests onto a preexisting criminal structure – the mafia – and the interpenetration between the mafia and key sectors of the public administration.

It is important to affirm at the outset that the use of the word "mafia" in this context does not refer to a hierarchically organized criminal society, but rather to the sum of the activities of individuals whose specific mode of behavior rather than their membership in a secret criminal organization is what defines them as *mafiosi*. The functions of the traditional mafioso originate in a set of subcultural norms that legitimize the use or threat of private violence to achieve certain ends in a context, like that of Sicily, characterized by the absence of effective state power. Although the defining characteristic of the mafia (distinguishing it, for example, from mere corruption) is this resort to private violence, the mafia boss is not considered a criminal but rather a "person of respect" within his own community, a prestigious figure to whom others turn both for protection of their persons and property and for mediation in a wide range of interpersonal transactions. The mafia boss himself is convinced of the necessity of the role he performs and sees himself as a "man of order" rather than a delinquent.[20] Apart from this subcultural legitimation, what distinguishes the mafioso most clearly from the ordinary criminal is the network of friendship and protection he has established with centers of formal institutional power, by means of which he further legitimizes his own position of private power. In all cases, however, the description of these activities in terms of a highly organized and hierarchically structured criminal society is an artificial construct imposed by outside observers upon a much more complex social reality, of which they had only a minimal understanding; the obvious parallels among the activities of various mafiosi reflect not the existence of a central mafia headquarters but rather the basic similarity in the social functions the mafia boss performed in each local setting.[21]

Until the end of World War II, the influence of the mafia was largely confined to the latifundial zones of the interior of western Sicily, where the typical mafioso served as an intermediary (*gabelloto*) between the absentee owners of the large estates and the peasant work force, as well as a guarantor of social peace in the countryside. This latter function assumed its most direct and brutal form in the immediate postwar period (1945–50) with a series of murders and intimidations of peasant activists and trade-union leaders involved in organization of the peasant land occupations that swept Sicily in those years.[22] With the enactment of agrarian reform in 1950, control of the land lost its critical economic and social function, and mafiosi turned their sights to new sources of gain, in particular the newly established programs of national and regional intervention, at that time oriented almost exclusively toward provision of rural infrastructures. Mafiosi rapidly came to dominate agricultural cooperatives, *consorzi di bonifica* ("land reclamation agencies"), and rural credit institutions, as well as controlling a disproportionate share of the public-works contracts of the Region and the Cassa per il Mezzogiorno. This rapid expansion of mafia influence within a far-reaching network of public and semipublic bodies (including bureaucratic positions within the regional government itself) was made possible, in the words of a contemporary journalistic inquiry by "the protection, collusion, and complicity of public offices, functionaries and government personalities, not only in Sicily but probably in Rome as well."[23]

By the mid-1950s, however, it had become clear to the rural elite, landowners and mafiosi alike, that the real potential for economic gain no longer lay in the countryside, already witnessing the beginnings of the mass exodus that would bleed it of its most vital forces during the next decade, but instead in the large coastal cities, whose tremendous population growth since the war had opened vast new possibilities for enrichment, particularly in the areas of real-estate speculation and the transport and marketing of agricultural produce:

The instrument by which the mafia passed from the countryside to the city was above all the monopolization of the harvest, sale and distribution of agricultural products. By this means and through its insertion into the speculative maneuvers associated with urban development, which concerned previously rural zones on the periphery of the large cities, the mafia, favored by the possibility of easy access to credit, established itself definitively in the city. In doing so, it joined and reinforced pre-existing nuclei of delinquency (especially in the *borgate*) and created the premises for new and even more profitable forms of gain.[24]

With its transfer to the city and its entry into new spheres of economic activity, the nature of the mafia's ties to political power underwent an important transformation as well:

In this period the mafia no longer represented, as it had before, the defense of certain class interests or positions; it sought, as always, stable and concrete ties with bureaucratic structures and political circles, but it sought them for the direct advantages which they could provide in the exercise of the mafia's own illicit activities . . . The personages compromised with the mafia found the counterpart to their support not only in the usual electoral and political advantages, but also in a concrete co-interest in certain business affairs and speculative deals. In certain cases, on the other hand, the new generation of mafiosi assumed positions directly in the administration of public affairs.[25]

By the late 1950s, the mafia's grasp extended into every sector of the economy of Palermo and its hinterland. While its strongholds remained the construction industry and the city's wholesale produce markets,[26] its dominion extended into such varied activities as cattle rustling and clandestine butchering, provision of water both for the city and for irrigation in the Conca d'Oro, control of the city's cemeteries from the sale of flowers to provision of caskets and tombstones, illegal commerce in contraband tobacco and drugs, municipal concessions for gasoline pumps, and intermediation in the provision of labor for the city's few large factories as well as in negotiations for land and water rights with firms located on the outskirts of the city.[27]

The nature of the linkages between the DC and this new urban mafia are manifested most clearly in the sector of real-estate speculation and construction, both because of the magnitude of the interests at stake and because of the direct responsibility of DC-dominated local administrations for regulation of these activities. Mafia penetration of this key sector of the urban economy took place at several levels: (1) preferential access to credit, both from commercial banks and regional credit institutions like IRFIS; (2) the winning of lucrative public contracts, from the public-works projects of the Region to the services contracted out by the city to private firms; (3) the complicity of the municipal administration, as shown above, in repeated abuses with regard to the elaboration and implementation of the city plan, the awarding of building permits, and surveillance over the conformity of construction activity to existing regulations; (4) a tight system of control over construction sites themselves, by which the mafia serves as an obligatory intermediary in the provision of building supplies and manpower, as well as imposing its own "protection system" (known as *guardiania*) on all firms, with the price of refusal at best an exemplary theft and at worst a charge of dynamite.

Investigations promoted by both the regional and national governments during the 1960s demonstrated beyond a doubt that the new class of entrepreneurs who came to dominate the process of urban expansion in Palermo in the mid- to late 1950s were a very particular group of people indeed. The investigation carried out in 1964 by the Prefect of Palermo (the Rapporto Bevivino) shows, for example, that out of 4,025 construction licenses approved by the assessor of public works between 1957 and 1963, 80% had been issued to only five persons, the two most prominent of whom (1,653 and 703 licenses respectively) were revealed upon further investigation to be a bricklayer and an ex-vendor of general merchandise and coal, clearly registered as contractors under false pretenses.[28] Upon interrogation by the Antimafia Commission of the Italian Parliament, the former, who would become doorman in one of the edifices for which he had signed the license, made the following statement:

I signed the documents to favor "friends." They are good people and help me out: what do you want, I do my best to get along [*mi industrio*].[29]

The conclusion of the Rapporto Bevivino in the face of such evidence was unequivocal:

In the presence of such a monumental quantity of work, . . . one cannot help but wonder with what unlimited financial capacities and imposing technical facilities the firms of the ex-vendor of general goods and coal and the bricklayer were endowed. The Commission found itself before an obvious case of "fronts." In effect, the activity of these "fronts" was limited to the signing of the project proposal or, more frequently, the countersigning of the license.[30]

Both the falsification of building permits to conceal the true interests lying behind them and the identities of the beneficiaries of the over 600 variations to the PRG approved by the City Council in 1959 (as well as of the perpetrators of subsequent violations of the plan) point to the immense leverage of known mafia elements within local government, as well as to the direct involvement of prominent personalities within the DC in the lucrative speculative dealings of the period. The background to the incredible acts of favoritism and corruption that characterized the regulatory activities of local government was the explosion, in the late 1950s, of a full-blown war between rival *cosche* ("mafia gangs") for control of the increasingly profitable economic opportunities brought about by rapid urban growth – in particular, land speculation and construction, wholesale markets, and the growing drug traffic. The prospect of the enormous gains to be reaped from these activities undermined the boundaries of the traditional zones of influence of the various mafia *cosche* (based primarily in the rural *borgate* where the persistence of a predominantly agricultural economy had preserved the figure of the traditional mafia boss), as well as the traditional relationships of respect and deference among mafiosi, leading to the emergence in the mid-1950s of a new generation of mafiosi, avid and unscrupulous in their drive for personal enrichment:

> The young and more enterprising mafiosi competed ruthlessly over building areas, and eventually even the old bosses of the *borgate* were obliged to join the fray. Their traditional prestige was no longer an automatic guarantee of control over everything that happened; the immense amounts of money at stake shattered the old organizational structures of the agrarian mafia. The processes of succession became ever more rapid and ever more bloody.[31]

The outcome of this breakdown of the established order was a bloody struggle for supremacy, of which the protagonists were the two rival clans, the Grecos and the La Barberas.[32] The Grecos, with their base in the *borgata* of Ciaculli, represented the traditional agrarian mafia, "camouflaged with respectability";[33] beginning as *gabelloti*, they had risen to become prominent landowners and dealers in citrus fruits, enjoying high social prestige within the *borgata* and a network of friendship and protection in influential commercial, banking, and political circles. The La Barbera brothers and their followers, on the other hand, were the prototype of the "new mafia." More openly criminal and interested only in rapid enrichment, they had abandoned the traditional model of the mafia boss as a "person of respect" (*uomo di rispetto*) for what can be best described as gangsterism, along the lines of American organized crime. In their rivalry with the Grecos, they introduced levels and methods of violence heretofore unknown among the mafia *palermitana*, which had always preferred compromise to outright violence and, if violence became necessary, the traditional *lupara*[34] to the machine guns and dynamite charges of the new generation. Beginning as common criminals, the

La Barberas in the early 1950s went into the business of transporting building supplies, and within a few years accumulated sufficient wealth to set up their own construction firm and to lead a life of conspicuous luxury; this meteoric success was based largely on extortion and violence (e.g., obliging contractors to pay for each load of sand four or five times over), coupled with instrumental friendships in high places. After several years of skirmishes, in 1962–3 the rivalry between the Grecos and the La Barberas erupted into open warfare for control of the city. The ferocity of the struggle was unprecedented, reaping over 100 victims in less than two years[35] and culminating in the "massacre of Ciaculli" on June 30, 1963, when an automobile loaded with high explosives, left outside the home of one of the Grecos, exploded and killed seven police officers sent to defuse it.

The tremendous public reaction to this event was a determining factor in provoking the immediate convocation, only six days later, of the special parliamentary commission to investigate the causes of the reemergence of mafia violence in Sicily (the Antimafia Commission), which had been established six months earlier but never convened because of conflicting political pressures. In its attempt to uncover the causes of this ferocious rekindling of mafia violence, the Antimafia Commission, itself subject to intense political pressures, sought to avoid attribution of political responsibility for the countless irregularities and illegalities encountered in its investigations of local government in Palermo and for the outbreak of mafia violence that accompanied them. The Commission provided copious documentation of mafia infiltration into key sectors of the urban economy and into the administrative bodies responsible for their regulation and surveillance, yet forever fell short of drawing the logical implications with regard to the responsibility of the political figures most directly involved. The tone of the conclusions of the Antimafia Commission, accusatory but at the same time evasive, is clear from the following excerpts from the sections of the two successive reports of the Commission (1971 and 1976) regarding the city of Palermo:

The inquiry conducted by the Commission has ascertained that: (1) in particular, construction activity and the acquisition of building areas have constituted, with the determining contribution of the administrative irregularities uncovered in the areas of urban planning and the concession of construction licenses, a most propitious terrain for the prospering of illicit activities and of an extra-legal power exercised by private interests in the form of parasitic intermediation and of a policy of favoritism encountered with striking clarity and frequency;
(2) in a brief span of years, persons of obscure origins emerged in the area of construction activities, becoming wealthy so rapidly as to induce suspicion;

(3) a substantial proportion of the irregularities, in particular in the area of building licenses, benefited persons indicated as mafiosi by police reports or by subsequent criminal or judicial events;

(4) some of the protagonists of the most notorious criminal episodes in the Palermo area have participated in the buying and selling of building areas and are indicated, in some reports, as persons capable of exerting a notable influence on the administrative organs of the city.[36]

In the face of such facts, one cannot help but think of the mafia, a mafia that had taken possession of the sector of real-estate speculation and was unwilling to retreat from the positions it had conquered, even at the cost of the most ruthless violence. The administrative irregularities discussed above offered a propitious terrain for the success of the mafia and for the power it exercised, through organized pressure groups, to obtain every form of favoritism and to profit from the parasitic intermediation connected with construction activity and with the acquisition of building areas. In addition, although the particular intensity in those years of criminal activity in the city of Palermo was certainly an effect of the struggles which broke out among the various *cosche* for domination of the various zones of the city, one cannot ignore in this regard the objective parallels between the sequence of criminal events and the recurrent anomalies and omissions in the administration of the Commune of Palermo.[37]

One prominent DC politician in Palermo, however, did achieve national notoriety as a result of the revelations of the Antimafia Commission. This was Vito Ciancimino, assessor of public works from 1959 until 1964, considered by many the principal architect of the unrestrained speculative boom that swept the city in those years. While his more influential protectors within the DC managed to escape any direct implication in the seemingly endless procession of scandals uncovered by the Antimafia Commission, Ciancimino – only the most glaring example of a phenomenon with much deeper roots in the entire system of alliances sustaining the DC in Palermo during those years – was made to serve as a scapegoat in order to deflect further and potentially much more dangerous probing by the parliamentary commission. The case of Ciancimino is, however, emblematic of the forces shaping the DC as a whole in the critical period from the mid-1950s until the late 1960s; above all, his career epitomizes in its most unambiguous form the intimate interrelationship between public administrators and private economic interests to the point where, in the conduct of local government, public and private interests became virtually indistinguishable.[38]

Born in Corleone (an agricultural town in the interior of the province of Palermo) in 1924 to a family of modest economic conditions, Vito Ciancimino began his professional life in 1950 with the establishment of a small business for the transport of railway cars. Thanks to the personal intervention of a prominent DC notable, Bernardo Mattarella, then undersecretary of transportation in Rome, in 1951 Ciancimino was granted the concession for the transport of railway cars within the city of Palermo. The terms of the contract, awarded by the Ministry, were fixed in private negotiations with Ciancimino after three competing forms were excluded from the bidding because of "insufficient guarantees"; this contract was regularly renewed, each time without competitive bidding, until June 1971. Contrary to the assurances as to the technical and financial superiority of his firm that won Ciancimino the contract, at the outset he was obliged to rent equipment from the railway system itself in order to carry out the service. Within a few short years, however, Ciancimino's economic situation would improve so dramatically that his firm would boast a stock of vehicles worth hundreds of millions of lire.

Ciancimino's professional takeoff preceded by only a few years his rise to prominence within the local DC. In 1953, after Gioia defeated the notables to become provincial secretary, Ciancimino, together with his protector Mattarella, became a *fanfaniano*. In 1954, Ciancimino was nominated "commissar" of the DC's municipal committee, giving him absolute power over all party sections in the city until a new committee could be regularly elected. In fact, a regular municipal committee was never elected, and Ciancimino retained this "interim" position until 1970, thus concentrating in his hands a critical lever of power that would prove immensely important both in internal party struggles and in electoral campaigns. In 1956 Ciancimino was elected to the City Council with 6,874 preference votes (6th place in the DC list), without ever having made a single public appearance. He was elected leader of the DC group in the City Council, a position he continued to hold until 1975, as well as assessor responsible for the *borgate* and the *aziende municipalizzate* (serving from June 1956 until July 1959). In 1959 Ciancimino took over the key post of Assessor of Public Works in the Lima administration (rumor has it that this post was Ciancimino's price for reconciliation with Gioia after a brief rift in early 1959).

Thus, beginning in 1959, Ciancimino became one of the primary shapers of the process of urban expansion in Palermo, a process in which the speculative fever would reach unprecedented intensity precisely in the years in which Ciancimino presided over the Department of Public Works. First-hand witnesses have described the frenetic climate that prevailed in this key department of city government during Ciancimino's "reign": "His office was always crowded and full of confusion, making it almost impossible to speak to him. A mob of contractors, *capi-elettori* and *galoppini* always awaited his arrival . . . The password in the Office of Public Works was the following: 'For the needy sections of the DC.' "[39] One of the most sensational cases to occur under Ciancimino's administration was that of the construction firm Aversa, which denounced the assessor for having illegally denied the firm a building permit in order to favor a competing firm, the Sicilcasa; the six owners of the Sicilcasa were intimate friends of Ciancimino, and the firm was widely regarded as a front for the assessor's own personal business interests. In the midst of the legal proceedings against Ciancimino, the representative of the Aversa unexpectedly withdrew all charges, having suddenly decided (or been convinced) that the copious evidence he had presented against Ciancimino was all false. A similar fortuitous coincidence saved Ciancimino from another potentially embarrassing investigation – shortly after the regional government had ordered a special inquiry into the conduct of the Department of Public Works, unknown thieves mysteriously broke into the department's offices, removing critical documents concerning the elaboration of the PRG.

By 1964, however, the investigations of the Antimafia Commission had rendered the post of assessor of public works so uncomfortable and had so tarnished Ciancimino's public image that he opted to resign temporarily from public life (although remaining DC leader in the City Council) in order to devote himself more fully to party affairs. Throughout it all, his personal electoral success continued unabated – he was regularly reelected to the City Council, with 11,038 preference votes in 1960, 9,266 in 1964, and 11,182 in 1970; following the break with Lima in 1968, Ciancimino served as Gioia's surrogate to insure control of local government by the *fanfaniani*.

Building on two critical pillars of power – his control over local party sections[40] and the special relationship with the representatives of real-estate and construction interests cemented during the years at the Department of Public Works – Ciancimino had over the years, however, consolidated a position of independent personal force within the DC. He had constructed a broad-based clientele (including virtually all the key bureaucrats in the division of urban planning and suspicious concentrations of "friends" in the rural *borgate*) loyal to him personally rather than to any of the formal faction chiefs and thus an essential force to be dealt with in intraparty struggles. The importance of this independent power base of Ciancimino has emerged most dramatically in recent years. In October 1970, public opinion in Palermo and in the nation as a whole was stunned by the announcement of the election of Vito Ciancimino, then under three

Figure 6.2. Vito Ciancimino, on the occasion of his election as mayor of Palermo in 1970. *Source:* Nicola Scafidi (Palermo).

separate indictments for his previous activities as a public administrator, as mayor of Palermo (see Figure 6.2). The Antimafia Commission, which had compiled copious dossiers on the ex-assessor of public works, defined his election as "a provocation and a challenge, both to the city of Palermo and to the Commission itself."[41] Ciancimino had been elected by only one vote, with numerous defectors in the ranks of his own party, but, backed by Gioia, he refused to give way even before the raging debate that threatened to tear the party apart (the mayoralty, as rumor has it, having been the condition for

Ciancimino's continued support of Gioia in his bitter struggle with Lima). Thus, Ciancimino became a national *cause célèbre*, an object of bitter controversy among opposing parties and factions in Rome as well as in Palermo; the case even brought down the regional government, which resigned rather than be obliged to pronounce judgment on Ciancimino. Finally, after two months of acrimonious political debate, Ciancimino stepped down, but the divisions created by the scandal ran so deep that it proved impossible to form a new administration to replace him until April 1971.

With the approach of the local elections of June 1975 – regarded both in Italy and abroad as a key test for the upcoming national elections of 1976 – Ciancimino's political demise seemed to be assured. In an attempt to counter left-wing propaganda based on appeals for "good, honest government," the DC national leadership decided to refurbish the party's public image by excluding from the electoral lists a few of the party's most compromised personalities; in Palermo, the axe fell on Ciancimino. Despite his own exclusion, however, Ciancimino's personal power at the base of the party has remained intact; in both 1975 and 1980, he succeeded in electing seven of his own men to the City Council, giving him representation equal to that of Gioia and Lima and thereby guaranteeing him an influential voice within the city government. In retaliation for his exclusion from the party's list, Ciancimino broke with Gioia, thereby consigning the *fanfaniani* to the minority in the Provincial Committee and opening the way for the formation of a "new majority" (based on an alliance between Lima and the "left" faction of Forze Nuove), which proceeded in January 1976 to elect, for the first time in twenty years, a municipal administration not dominated by the *fanfaniani*. Seeing the prospect of the critical levers of local power passing definitively out of their hands, however, Gioia and Ciancimino soon recomposed their differences; with their combined force they succeeded once again in reducing both the city and provincial administrations to immobility.

By late 1976, however, the balance of power within the local DC was shifting inexorably toward Lima, the proponent of a new policy of "opening to the PCI" in local government in contrast to the intransigent anti-Communism of the *fanfaniani*. Ciancimino was not slow to perceive the direction the winds were blowing; in a dramatic move, he broke once more with Gioia and carried his key votes to the new majority, sealing the defeat of the *fanfaniani* and demonstrating once again his continuing pivotal function within the local DC, undiminished either by the Antimafia Commission or by the official censure of the national party leadership.[42] Thus, only a year after he was considered definitively banished from political life, Ciancimino re-emerged as a key figure in DC politics; his reserve of personal influence has proven so critical to the delicate balance of power within the DC that even the Communists, who once denounced him in the most unequivocal terms, were forced to come to terms with him in order to advance their own strategy of an "historical compromise" with the DC. That "Don Vito" remains a formidable force in local DC politics was demonstrated most recently by the results of the administrative elections of June 1980, in which Ciancimino reelected a solid core of supporters to the City Council, showing once again that the votes controlled by him constitute the critical balance for the formation of both party and local government majorities.

Ciancimino has come to symbolize one essential aspect of DC power in Palermo – the intricate network of interlocking interests through which the party, in the 1950s and 1960s, succeeded in cementing a solid alliance with key sectors of the local entrepreneurial class and thereby insured its own control over critical sources of income and employment.[43] While it would be inexact to define the activities of Ciancimino and others like him as themselves "mafioso," these individuals and the party that continues to protect and reward them are unquestionably responsible for a profound penetration of the public administration not only by illegitimate private interests but by unmistakable criminal elements, creating the premises for the bloody gang wars which have terrorized the city. The last word on Ciancimino and the system of power he represents I leave to the judge who acquitted a local journalist before him on charges of slander:

One could conclude that, while the rival mafia *cosche* were preparing for war, Assessor Ciancimino predisposed, to the advantage of one side or the other but always in total disregard of the public interest, variations to the city plan or unauthorized construction licenses. The Court certainly does not sustain that Ciancimino bears sole responsibility for the chaotic expansion of Palermo, from which the mafia was able to draw substantial profit; it does retain, however, that the defendant, not by stupidity but by deliberate intention, was one of the major architects of this chaos, which derived from illegitimate acts, tainted by favoritism and benefiting the power of the mafia . . . The case of Ciancimino is symbolic of a much vaster phenomenon which, during the 1960s, contaminated the political and administrative life of Sicily. This contamination was due to the self-interested confluence of the mafia into public life and to the attempts by politicians, both for electoral ends and for internal party struggles, to recuperate the support of the traditional forces of the agrarian bloc and of political figures compromised by familiarity with the mafia.[44]

In the glare of publicity that accompanied the Antimafia Commission's initial investigations, with the threat of criminal indictments hanging over mafiosi and their political protectors alike, the incidence of visible mafia activity subsided significantly, to the point where a witness testifying before the Commission in the mid-1960s could dismiss the problem as a relic of the past. But the interests at stake in the struggle for dominion over the "new Palermo" were not defunct, only temporarily submerged. In 1969 the still unresolved rivalry between the Grecos and La Barberas reexploded with increased intensity, this time in the "massacre of Via Lazio," when four followers of La Barbera were gunned down in the office of a prominent Palermo contractor.

The reemergence of Vito Ciancimino into public life with his sensational election as mayor of Palermo in 1970 thus coincided with a renewed outburst of mafia violence. A reign of terror gripped Palermo, transforming the city into a replica of gangland Chicago in the 1930s. Via Lazio, one of the major arteries of the "new Palermo," would gain national fame as the symbol of the seemingly endless chain of violent clashes that shook the city's new *quartieri;* the once flourishing citrus groves of the Conca d'Oro were rapidly being destroyed by ever-advancing blocks of cement, and each new high-rise tower paid its price in blood. Palermo's notoriety was further enhanced by the disappearance of the prominent local journalist Mauro De Mauro, in September 1970, and the assassination of Pietro Scaglione, Procuratore della Repubblica (the highest-ranking magistrate in Palermo), in broad daylight in May 1971. Never before had the mafia struck so high. With the murder of Scaglione, the burning issue of the relationship between the mafia and the state could no longer be covered up. While the whole truth will probably never be known, Scaglione had clearly been deeply involved, during his thirty-year career as the island's chief magistrate, in the cases of several prominent mafia bosses and in the network of political complicity that had protected them from conviction and imprisonment; it may be because he knew too much about potentially explosive issues that Scaglione had to be eliminated.

With the death of Scaglione, the reign of terror that had haunted the city for over a decade reached its final paroxysm. The reasons for the subsidence of mafia violence were dual: (1) the success of the Grecos in virtually eliminating their major competitors; and (2) the end of the construction boom that had fueled the speculative frenzy of the previous fifteen years. The respite was brief, however. In the late 1970s, a new wave of mafia violence exploded in Palermo, reaping fifty-eight victims in the first ten months of 1979 alone. This time the focus of the struggle had shifted from real-estate speculation and the private construction industry to the drug traffic and the public-works contracts of local government. By 1979, it became clear that there was a new pattern in the victims of mafia violence as well. Whereas previously violence had been directed primarily at rival mafia gangs, during 1979 and 1980 a succession of public figures – a local journalist conducting an investigation of the "new mafia," a left-wing magistrate and ex-PCI deputy of national renown, two high-ranking police officials, the provincial secretary of the DC, and, finally, the Christian Democratic president of the Sicilian Region[45] – were gunned down by mafia killers. In virtually all these cases the victims, unlike Scaglione, had been responsible for police, judicial, or political operations that threatened to strike at the heart of mafia interests. What appears to be happening, for the first time on such a scale, is a concentrated mafia attack on the representatives of the state and of the party which for so long guaranteed them political protection. The message is clear: if the mafia can no longer rely on the unquestioned complicity of public officials, it is prepared to engage in an all-out struggle to reestablish its privileged relationship with public power.

The reconstruction of the old city

Continued access to centers of local power is especially important to the mafia because of the prospect of billions of dollars in public contracts associated with a massive commitment of national and regional funds for reconstruction of the *centro storico* of Palermo. By the beginning of the 1970s, the extensive urban development of the past decade, dominated by the logic of private speculation, had reached its peak. Not only was further expansion blocked by natural obstacles but the market for private luxury apartments that had sustained the speculative boom was nearly saturated. In the 1970s the housing market in Palermo was marked by a fundamental contradiction: the coexistence of an excess supply of high-cost private apartments with an immense unsatisfied demand for low-income housing (17,000 applications for public housing in 1976, while in the *Palermo nuova* 8,000 new luxury apartments lay empty).[46] The construction industry in Palermo (overwhelmingly dependent on the private market) entered a period of severe crisis, the extent of which can be measured by the drastic contraction in the ranks of construction workers: from a peak of 40,000–50,000 in the boom years of the 1960s, they had been slashed by the mid-1970s to a mere 15,000–18,000 (of whom only about one-third was employed).[47]

With construction activity – the motor of the local economy – almost at a standstill, and public pressures for low-income housing mounting steadily, local politicians turned their attention to a perennial unresolved issue of Palermo politics – the *risanamento* ("urban renewal") of the *centro storico*. Already severely damaged by the war and the effects of decades of neglect, the *centro storico* (by now inhabited almost solely by the poor) was dealt a final devastating blow by the earthquake that ravaged western Sicily in January 1968. Within a year, thousands had fled the crumbling alleys and courtyards of the old city in a mass movement of spontaneous occupations of recently completed, but as yet unoccupied, public-housing projects on the periphery of the city (see Chapter 8). As a result, the population of the *centro storico* was drastically reduced (from a high of about 200,000 at the end of the war to only about 50,000 by 1974), but, given the extensive damage inflicted by the quake, conditions of hygiene and overcrowding actually worsened, not to mention the ever-present danger of *crolli* ("cave-ins") in those dwellings (the vast majority) suffering lesions from the quake. Whole sections of the old city have come to resemble ghost towns; entire blocks have been abandoned and walled up, while in others, hundreds of families continue to live in the shadow of buildings where the only protection against collapse is constituted by long wooden beams braced against the opposite *palazzo*. In the long years of public indifference since 1968, the list of *crolli* and resulting deaths and injuries (in particular of children with nowhere else to play but in the ruins of crumbling buildings) has inexorably mounted. The center of the city has thus been reduced to a zone of the most abject urban degradation, economic as well as physical (see Figure 6.3). All but the most marginal of the artisans and shopkeepers who once formed the backbone of the traditional economy of these neighborhoods have fled, leaving behind only the most wretched of the city's poor.

In the face of the ever-mounting degradation of the *centro storico*, what has been the response of the city administration? In practical terms, as yet nothing. Over a decade has passed since 1968, a decade in which the old city has continued to crumble inexorably away. The most important effect of the earthquake was to rekindle, after decades of empty electoral rhetoric, the old debate over *risanamento*.[48] In 1970, Parliament passed a comprehensive package of earthquake relief for western Sicily, one provision of which was to delegate implementation of the *risanamento* of Palermo to the Cassa per il Mezzogiorno, which was to carry out the project through a concession to a company owned by public capital. Under the terms of the agreement (*convenzione*) stipulated between the Cassa and Italstat (a member of the IRI group) in 1971, and approved by the municipal *giunta* in July,

Figure 6.3. The legacy of neglect in the *centro storico* of Palermo.

Table 6.1. *Summary of major provisions regarding* risanamento *of* centro storico

1. *1959*: Approval by City Council of general city plan (PRG) including indications for *risanamento* of *centro storico*.
2. *1962*: Parliament passes laws no. 18 and no. 28, defining the *risanamento* of Palermo a "project of supreme national interest" and providing financing of up to 10 billion lire (approx. U.S. $16.6 million) for public housing and associated public works.
3. *1970*: Parliament passes law no. 21 delegating implementation of the *risanamento* to the Cassa per il Mezzogiorno, by means of a concession to a company controlled by public capital.
4. *July 1973*: Final approval of the *convenzione* among the Commune, the Cassa, and Italstat (IRI), creating the concessionary Risanamento Edilizio Palermo (REP) and specifying the terms under which the *risanamento* would proceed. Realization of the project is to be governed by the criterion of *economicità di gestione*.
5. *November 1973*: City Council approves a series of amendments to the *convenzione*, with the purpose of asserting the priority of the criterion of the general public interest over that of *economicità* as the guiding principle of the *risanamento*.
6. *May 1976*: The national and regional governments allocate a total of 65 billion lire (approx. U.S. $108 million) to Palermo for the concrete initiation of the public works associated with the *risanamento* of the *centro storico*.
7. *February 1977*: The municipal administration of Palermo denounces the REP as *inadempiente* ("in default") and decides to assume directly the responsibility for the initiation of the *risanamento*, utilizing the 65 billion lire allocated by the national and regional governments in May 1976.

1973, the concessionary – *Risanamento Edilizio Palermo* (REP) – would assume responsibility for the preliminary works of expropriation, demolition, and provision of necessary infrastructures, for which it would subsequently recuperate its costs by auctioning the areas thereby rehabilitated to private buyers. (See Table 6.1 for a summary of recent legislation regarding *risanamento*.)

The criterion that was to guide the entire operation was *economicità di gestione* ("economic management"), in other words, profit maximization; in short, the agreement conformed to the same logic of private speculation that had guided the urban development of the 1960s. In operational terms, this would mean the wholesale razing of the old city, the expulsion of its residents to the peripheral ghettos of public housing, and their replacement by luxury apartments and offices. The speculative intent of the *convenzione* was made manifest by the two initial "experimental" projects elaborated by the REP, for the purpose of testing the profitability of limited interventions in the *centro storico* before making a commitment to *risanamento* on a grand scale. The first of these, involving the utilization of public funds targeted for *risanamento* in a zone not even within the boundaries of the *centro storico*, was the covering-over of the river Oreto (essentially an open sewer), in order to open to speculative development the agricultural land lying beyond the river (areas in which, not coincidentally, members of the Gioia "clan" hold important interests). This focus on the areas beyond the Oreto as a zone for new expansion was reinforced by the revision of the Piano Territoriale di Coordinamento (PTC) – a kind of metropolitan development plan – to provide for the construction of major highway linkages connecting this area directly with the peripheral transportation arteries of the city.

The condition imposed by the REP for undertaking the Oreto project and the second "experimental" intervention in the *quartiere* San Pietro (a bombed-out zone near the port) was the elimination in both areas of existing land-use restrictions for public housing; the acceptance of this condition reduced the already minimal provisions for low-income housing within the *centro storico* to a derisory level (only 6 hectares out of a total area of about 240 hectares, with a population capacity of only 900). The plan presented by the REP for the San Pietro project envisaged the construction of 500 new dwellings, of which not a single one was to be destined for the present low-income residents of the neighborhood. Such a beginning pointed to the wholesale transformation of the socioeconomic character of the *centro storico* if the strategy of the REP and its political supporters (specifically, the *fanfaniani* and their ally, the PRI) were to be implemented.

In November 1973, after a series of public debates on the *convenzione*, the City Council approved an amendment to the agreement providing that "the criterion of *economicità* must be limited by the prevailing public interest, and to such an end the City Council, at the time of elaboration of detailed plans, reserves the right to request variations whose approval need not depend upon conformity with this norm."[49] The amendment called in particular for the safeguarding of the historical-artistic patrimony of the *centro storico* and for the preservation of its existing socioeconomic fabric through provision of public housing to maintain at least 20,000 of the present residents within the *centro storico* and the setting up of special zones to be reserved for petty artisans and shopkeepers. This attempt, however limited, to undermine the profit basis of the *risanamento*, combined with the political uncertainty deriving from the intensification of internal contrasts within the DC, led to another three years of complete immobility.

Because of the failure of the REP to undertake any concrete initiatives to fulfill its obligations, the new city administration elected in January 1976 (excluding the *fanfaniani* for the first time) denounced the *convenzione* with the REP in early 1977 and moved toward implementation of *risanamento* directly by the Commune and the IACP. This effort found financial support in the allocation in May 1976 of 65 billion lire (approximately U.S. $108 million) in national and regional funds for the immediate realization of the public works associated with *risanamento;* these funds could be employed directly by the city government for provision of basic infrastructures, restoration of publicly owned buildings, and construction of low-income housing within the *centro storico.* These funds have since been supplemented by over 300 billion lire (U.S. $500 million) from the Cassa per il Mezzogiorno for the Progetto Speciale ("Special Project") for the metropolitan area of Palermo, as well as by national funding for public-housing construction. Incredibly, with such extensive financial resources available to the city government for projects related to the *risanamento,* at the beginning of 1981 not a single project had yet been initiated.[50]

How can one explain such total inertia when the potential patronage gains from the spending of such vast resources are so great? Part of the answer is the technical incapacity of the city government to deal with a project of this type. With the technical offices of the Commune suffering from a drastic shortage of qualified personnel, largely as a result of years of unrestrained patronage hiring, the planning capability necessary to carry out a project like the *risanamento* of the old city is simply nonexistent. More importantly, the city government has been paralyzed since 1976 both by conflict among the coalition partners and by the internal power struggles within the DC. The interests at stake in the *risanamento* of Palermo are enormous – estimates of the total cost of the *risanamento* and the Progetto Speciale run as high as 1,700 billion lire (almost U.S. $28 billion) over a 10–15 year period.[51] In an economic situation like that of Palermo, where chronic depression has been further aggravated by the disastrous effects of the current economic crisis, such a massive injection of resources into the key sector of construction could well determine the relaunching of the entire urban economy. With such a prize at stake, the clash of political and economic interests over the critical questions of who will get the contracts and what social groups will benefit from the reconstruction will not be resolved easily.

With the accession to power of the *fanfaniani,* speculation, previously a matter of individual instances of favoritism or corruption, was transformed into a general strategy for mobilizing mass support around the DC. In one way or another, almost every social or economic group in the city found it had something to gain from the tumultuous, unregulated expansion that completely transformed the face of Palermo in the space of a decade. The *blocco di potere* ("power bloc") consolidated by the DC in these years represented a broad cross-section of the major social and economic forces of the city:

1. The great speculative interests – landowners, real-estate brokers, building contractors
2. The myriad of artisans and small manufacturing firms supporting the construction industry – especially producers and transporters of building supplies
3. Firms dealing in the production and commerce of all types of home furnishings (e.g., fortunes were amassed through the importation and sale of modern kitchen and bathroom components, previously virtually unknown in Sicily)
4. The working class proper and the thousands of *sottoproletari* who found employment in construction in the years of the boom, as well as the building-trades unions, whose self-interest clearly coincided with that of the industry in stimulating maximum construction activity
5. An important sector of the professional and technical middle classes – engineers, architects, surveyors, draftsmen, and so on
6. The white-collar middle classes, especially public employees, for whom the great speculative boom provided the means for the realization of their aspirations for social prestige, expressed above all in the desire for a modern apartment
7. The masses of low-income inhabitants of the *quartieri popolari* of the old city and the *borgate*, who saw in the endless promises of public housing the answer to their desperate need for decent, sanitary living conditions

In general, these same groups, with the exception of that part of the middle classes whose demand for housing has already been satisfied, today constitute a constituency for the *risanamento* of the *centro storico* and the Progetto Speciale. In recent years, they have been reinforced by two other significant groups: the growing ranks of unemployed youth, for whom *risanamento* represents the only real hope for jobs, and the large number of peasant proprietors (as well as large landowners) in the area beyond the Oreto, where declining agricultural incomes have made the sale of land to speculators increasingly attractive.

This broad-based mass support for the DC's urban development policy has been a fundamental factor in sustaining the party's power in Palermo over the past twenty years. The process of rapacious speculative development promoted and sustained by the new generation of DC leaders who took control of the party in the mid-1950s was totally destructive of the "public interest," in the sense either of providing decent low-cost housing and eliminating the appalling slums of the old city or of the quality of urban life more generally (in terms of population densities, social services, open spaces, etc.). Yet, despite the total devastation of the city in human terms, the DC proved amazingly successful in mobilizing the short-term material interests of a substantial portion of the city's population behind such a policy. The extent of this support was such that the opposition (for the most part by the Communists and Socialists) to the speculative outrages and illegalities perpetrated by the DC and its allies was vocal but ineffectual. Not only were protests brutally overruled by the sheer force of numbers in local elective bodies and by the complicity of the control organs responsible for supervising the legitimacy of local government actions, but would-be opponents found their opposition undermined by the recalcitrance of important sectors of their own organizational and electoral bases, above all the construction workers and their unions, the largest in the city and among the principal sources of left-wing organizational strength.

The construction industry is emblematic of the ways in which the Christian Democratic Party throughout the South, by means of its control of local government, has used the bureaucratic powers of licensing and interdiction to weave a network of clientelistic bonds linking the party solidly to the leading sector of the local economy and through it to a broad cross-section of the urban population. In Chapter 7, which analyzes the relationship between the machine and the urban poor, the intermediary role of the party is once again of primary importance. In this case, however, political mediation has less to do with the regulatory powers of local government, although these do retain a certain importance, than with direct personal intervention to break through the impenetrability and inertia of the bureaucracy to resolve the day-to-day problems of the city's low-income population.

7

The urban poor: poverty and political control

In Palermo, which of all European cities reflects most faithfully the economic and class structure of the preindustrial metropolis, the urban *sottoproletariato* forms the most distinctive of the city's social groups, yet, because of the myriad and continually shifting nature of its economic pursuits, the least susceptible to precise definition. Although the *sottoproletariato* of Palermo continues to be concentrated in the slums of the old city, the urban poor inhabit as well the lurid shantytowns along the banks of the Oreto, the peripheral public-housing projects whose population was swelled by refugees from the crumbling *centro storico* in the wave of illegal occupations that followed the 1968 earthquake and, to a somewhat lesser degree, the rural *borgate* ("traditional peasant communities"), now increasingly engulfed by urban expansion. This chapter lays out the basic parameters – economic, social, and political – of life among the urban poor in Palermo. This initial descriptive overview will be followed in Chapter 8 by a more detailed examination of the particular configuration – in terms of both socioeconomic context and patterns of political participation – of the three distinct types of *quartieri popolari* ("low-income neighborhoods") to be found in Palermo: the center-city slum, the peripheral public-housing project, and the rural *borgata*.

The socioeconomic context

The word the poor in Palermo use to describe their condition is *la miseria* – not just poverty, but the seemingly unbreakable vicious circle of precarious employment, inadequate housing and sanitary facilities, malnutrition, disease, and illiteracy that relegates them to a permanent position of marginality and subordination with respect to the rest of society and inexorably shapes the passivity and fatalism, broken only rarely by spontaneous but short-lived rebellions, which characterize their outlook on life and politics. The descriptive material that follows is drawn for the most part from data on the slums of the old city and the zones of *baracche* ("shantytowns"); with the exception of housing, however, these descriptions are valid for the majority of the public-housing projects and the *borgate* as well (where relevant, the specific differences will be brought out in the discussion of the individual neighborhoods).

Lack of stable employment

Economic uncertainty is the critical structural variable shaping the attitudes and behavior of the urban poor. In a 1975 survey of residents of four *quartieri popolari* (Table 7.1), stable employment among adult males (ages 15–55) ranged from a low of 24.0% to a high of only 57.5% (the latter in a public-housing project with a relatively high proportion of lower-middle-class residents). The predominant occupations in these neighborhoods are manual labor in construction, street-vending, and the myriad of precarious day-to-day trades described by Rochefort (see Chapter 2, "The Urban Sottoproletariato"), and, last but not least, theft and contraband – all activities that provide not only low but, above all, highly irregular sources of income.

Housing

Official estimates placed the number of *palermitani* living in substandard housing at about 100,000 in 1976.[1] The housing situation among the urban poor in the center-city slums remains essentially that described by Danilo Dolci in the mid-1950s:

The living conditions in the *quartieri* of the old city are those of the *catoi* or the *bassi* of Naples: one or two rooms at the most, deprived of the most elementary sanitary facilities – without a bathroom, a proper kitchen, running water, and sometimes even electricity. These rooms are cold and humid, without sunlight or fresh air, filled with dust from the streets and courtyards, and permeated by the stench which rises from the open drains below. Such conditions, together with the appalling overcrowding and consequent promiscuity, have produced a state of physical and moral degradation which can, without fear of exaggeration, be described as horrifying.[2]

These conditions have been exacerbated by the severe damages inflicted upon the already decaying dwellings of the *centro storico* by the 1968 earthquake. Hundreds of families continue to live in buildings declared "unhabitable due to imminent danger of collapse" by the city authorities, who lack the means, however, to provide alternative shelter. Conditions in the *baracche* are even worse: here dwellings consist of a one-room shack of cardboard, reinforced with

Table 7.1. *Employment status of residents between ages 15 and 55 in four* quartieri popolari, *1975 (in percentages)*

| Type of activity | Sex | Neighborhoods[a] | | | |
		Oreto	Guadagna	Capo	Villa Tasca
Stable employment	M	46.7	24.0	28.7	57.5
	F	10.0	2.2	5.9	11.8
Precarious employment	M	29.0	40.0	43.8	9.1
	F	1.6	2.2	4.4	4.0
Unemployed	M	19.3	26.0	19.4	15.1
	F	86.6	88.6	85.4	71.8
Retired	M	4.8	8.0	5.4	—
	F	1.6	2.2	1.4	1.9
Students	M	—	0.5	2.7	18.3
	F	—	—	2.9	10.5

[a] Oreto is a zone composed primarily of *baracche*, Guadagna an ex-*borgata* now completely swallowed up by the city, Capo a center-city slum, and Villa Tasca a public-housing project with a relatively high proportion of lower-middle-class residents, many of whom are public employees.
Note: Dash signifies insufficient data.
Source: Survey conducted by students of the Faculty of Medicine of the University of Palermo, 1975–6.

pieces of laminated aluminum or scrap metal, and completely deprived of even the most basic services. In contrast to a city-wide average of 1.3 inhabitants per room, indices of population density in the *centro storico* and the shantytowns reach a mean of 2.5–3.5 inhabitants per room, with numerous reported cases of 10–15 persons crowded into a one-room dwelling.[3]

Sanitary conditions

In contrast to the Palermo of Dolci's study, where the overwhelming majority of the city's low-income inhabitants still used chamber pots, which were emptied daily into open drains, and had access to water only from the neighborhood fountain, today most dwellings in the city proper are hooked up to the municipal water and sewer lines (even if, as is often the case, sanitary facilities consist only of a toilet squeezed into a corner of the kitchen). In the shantytowns, however, residents are still completely without running water and indoor plumbing; wastes are emptied directly into the adjacent river which, because of the city's total lack of sewage treatment facilities, has been reduced to a vast open sewer carrying a large pro-

portion of the city's wastes out to sea. As a result of the peculiar politics of public housing in Palermo (see Chapter 8), many of the new
housing projects have been left for years without linkages to the city
sewer lines, so that here, too, the wastes of hundreds of families
empty into open canals or even, in one case, directly into tanks in the
basements of the apartment buildings. In many neighborhoods running water arrives for only 2–3 hours per day, and it is not at all rare
in the summer for water to arrive for only a few hours every 2–3 days.
These conditions are aggravated by the extreme inadequacy of garbage collection throughout the city, a problem that is particularly accentuated in the low-income neighborhoods, where mountains of
refuse accumulate for weeks or even months at a time, providing an
excellent breeding ground for rats and insects as well as a playground
for the children, who have no other place to go.

Malnutrition and disease

Given the appalling conditions of sanitation and hygiene in
the *quartieri popolari*, it is not surprising that the threat of epidemic
haunts the city every year as summer approaches. Digestive disor-
ders from inadequate diet, infectious diseases like typhus and hepa-
titis caused by contamination from sewage and garbage, and respira-
tory ailments produced by the extreme humidity of the fall and
winter months in dank dwellings without sunlight, heat, or fresh air
are all endemic among Palermo's poor. Another index of the degradation of living conditions in these neighborhoods are levels of infant mortality, which in certain zones approximate those of Third
World countries (Table 7.2).

Illiteracy

Illiteracy among adults in the *quartieri popolari* ranges as high
as 50% and, despite laws making education obligatory through
grade 8, levels of scholastic evasion among children of school age remain appallingly high, both because parents send their children out
to work and because families may be unable to afford the shoes and
clothing necessary to send the children to school (for data on child
labor and scholastic evasion, see Chapter 2). Among those children
who do attend school, levels of grade repetition are far above the city
average; in one neighborhood of the *centro storico*, 70% of the children repeat the first grade at least once.[4]

The outstanding characteristic of all the *quartieri popolari* of Palermo – with the partial exception of the *borgate*, where the traditional structures of peasant society have to some extent persisted – is
their extreme social and economic fragmentation and the absence of

Table 7.2. *Disease and infant mortality among residents of four* quartieri popolari, *1975 (percentages of those surveyed reporting a given disease within the past year)*

| Medical condition | Neighborhoods[a] | | | | |
	Oreto	Guadagna	Capo	Villa Tasca	City average[b]
Chronic bronchitis					
in all age groups	20.1	14.3	13.2	4.3	n.a.
among children aged 0–12 years	20.8	19.0	18.5	13.6	n.a.
Recurrent tonsillitis	8.3	11.9	4.5	6.0	n.a.
Bronchial pneumonia	1.3	3.3	4.2	0.2	n.a.
Tuberculosis	0.3	0.4	0.3	0.0	0.01
Arthritic disorders	20.5	20.5	13.0	14.6	n.a.
Typhoid and typhus	0.7	0.0	2.1	1.0	0.01
Viral hepatitis	1.1	2.3	1.2	2.3	0.07
Gastroenteritis	4.9	9.0	9.3	8.0	0.00
Infant mortality (deaths/1,000 live births)					
in the first 15 days	67	37.6	34	46	21.2
in the first year[c]	134	65.8	69	85	31.8

[a] For a description of the neighborhoods, see Table 7.1.
[b] The city-wide figures refer to the year 1974.
[c] The national average was 22.9/1,000 in 1974.
Sources: The neighborhood figures are from a survey conducted by students of the Faculty of Medicine of the University of Palermo in the fall of 1975. The city-wide figures are from *Panormus 1974*, while the national figure for infant mortality is from ISTAT, *Annuario di Statistica 1975*.

any associative structures that could serve as poles of aggregation for the population. This fragmentation stems above all from the lack of stable employment among the *sottoproletariato*. The traditional economic structure of the old city was based primarily on the artisanal guilds or confraternities, which not only served as instruments of economic solidarity but performed an important function of social and cultural cohesion as well; as the street names of the old city still testify, each trade was concentrated in a specific neighborhood, clustered around the church of its particular patron saint, which in turn served as the focal point for the social and cultural life of the *quartiere*. With the disintegration of the traditional economy, the social and cultural fabric associated with it largely disappeared as well, leaving behind entire zones of the *centro storico* cut off from the mainstream of the city's economic life and relegated to abandonment and decay, both physical and moral. Those economic activities that remain are dispersed in thousands of individual expedients for day-to-day survival. The absence of centers of employment within the *quartiere* or of any form of occupational aggregation outside it (e.g., stable factory employment) deprives the residents not only of any sense of collective economic interests but also of one of the primary aggregative structures through which political and other organizations can gain access to a mass base.

Patterns of political participation and political control

The absence of aggregative occupational structures (once again, with the partial exception of the *borgate*) is reflected in the almost total lack of organized social, political, or recreational activity in these neighborhoods. There are no social or community centers, neighborhood clinics, or recreational clubs; only the local *bettole* ("taverns") provide a place where people can get together, and this only for men, of course. Except in the new public-housing projects, party organizational structures are virtually nonexistent, and in general those that do exist open their doors only on the occasion of electoral campaigns.

On the part of the DC, this is a reflection of a general disregard for the role of the party section as a center of political discussion and popular participation, resulting from the party's almost exclusive reliance on the levers of local governmental power to maintain support; in general the sections serve only to legitimate the false membership figures that play such a critical role in local and national factional struggles. Even during electoral campaigns, the section often takes a back seat to the "electoral committees" of the individual candidates which, in the *quartieri popolari* at least, are the real centers of electoral activity.

As for the Left, traditionally it has been weak, both organizationally and electorally, among the *sottoproletariato*, whose votes have gone primarily to the DC and its minor coalition partners. This weakness, in part an expression of the absence of points of access within the *quartieri* for organization on a collective as opposed to an individual basis, reflects as well the more general neglect and mistrust of the *sottoproletariato* that permeates Marxist theory and practice. The attitudes toward the "lumpenproletariat" expressed in the following citations from Marx and Engels tended, until very recently, to characterize the perceptions and strategy of the Italian Left toward the urban *sottoproletariato*:

The lumpenproletariat . . . in all large towns forms a mass sharply differentiated from the industrial proletariat, a recruiting ground for thieves and criminals living on the refuse of society, people without a definite trade, vagabonds, . . . varying according to the degree of civilization of the nation to which they belong, but never renouncing their *lazzaroni* [dregs] character.[5]

The lumpenproletariat, this scum of depraved elements from all classes, with its headquarters in all the big cities, is the worst of all possible allies. This rabble is absolutely venal and absolutely brazen.[6]

The "dangerous class," the social scum, that passively rotting mass thrown off by the lowest layers of the old society, may, here and there, be swept into the movement by a proletarian revolution; its conditions of life, however, prepare it far more for the part of a bribed tool of reactionary intrigue.[7]

At least partially as a result of such preconceptions, the Communists have had difficulty in elaborating a strategic approach to the problems of the urban poor in cities like Palermo, concentrating their efforts on the organized working class which, limited though it may be, is accessible through the factories and the unions. In those neighborhoods where the PCI does maintain a functioning section, it is the only party to sustain a continuous presence. In general, however, because of the party's lack of any organic linkages to the life of the *quartiere*, this organizational presence is often provided by students or in any case persons external to the neighborhood, thereby exacerbating the already substantial structural difficulties in reaching the residents and involving them in the political initiatives of the party.

The difficulty of party organizations in establishing stable linkages to the *quartieri popolari* is also due in part to the extreme mistrust among the urban poor of the state in general and of political parties and politicians in particular. Throughout Sicilian history the state has been an alien entity, the expression of foreign domination, whose presence was felt only in the oppressive acts of tax collection and military conscription. In the view of many Sicilians, Italian unification was simply the substitution of the Bourbons by another foreign power. The subsequent experiences of the majority of the urban poor with the representatives of national or local government have given them little reason to alter this historical perception of the state as an alien and unresponsive presence. In general the parties, regardless of their ideology, fare no better among the residents of the *quartieri popolari*. The most common judgment heard in these neighborhoods is one of exasperated disillusionment and mistrust: "The parties are all the same: the politicians come before election day and make all kinds of promises to get your vote, and then are never seen again for another five years."

In this bleak landscape of economic and social disintegration, only the Church continues to provide a center of social life, however minimal, for the *quartiere*. As a result, the parish priest remains a key figure in many low-income neighborhoods, in many cases the only institutional link between the *quartiere* and outside centers of power, as well as the source, through the charitable societies linked to the Church, of much of the charity that sustains many families in the absence of a public welfare system. The only real social events in these neighborhoods are the annual festivals for the local patron saints; these festivals are still organized by the traditional religious confraternities, the last surviving vestiges of the old artisanal society and the only remaining source of anything that could be described as neighborhood pride or solidarity. Apart from the annual religious festivals, however, the Church can no longer wield the kind of influence it once did among the urban poor. The social fabric of the *quartieri popolari*, especially in the old city and the new housing projects, has been irrevocably eroded; in the absence of more organic social bonds, even the Church has come to play an increasingly marginal role in the life of the *quartiere*. This obviously varies to some extent from *quartiere* to *quartiere*, but in those cases where the Church continues to play an important social role, it is due much more to the personal involvement of individual priests than to the centrality of the Church as an institution to the lives of the inhabitants.

The changing role of the Church can be seen as well in its relationship to the DC. Until the mid-1960s the Church in Palermo, under the leadership of Cardinal Ruffini, was a direct and highly efficacious arm of DC power, especially in the *quartieri popolari*. In the past decade, however, this relationship has become increasingly ambiguous, partly because of the reluctance of the Church to identify itself with the venality and corruption of DC power in Palermo, partly because of the increasing openness of individual priests, particularly in low-income neighborhoods, to common social and political action with the Left to resolve the dramatic problems of their *quartieri*. As a result, the direct electoral role of the Church in support of the DC, while not to be ignored, has greatly diminished in recent years.[8]

In the absence of alternative structures to aggregate and mobilize collective interests, every individual seeks to resolve his problems on his own, through whatever personal channels are open to him. People are convinced, on the basis less of cultural conditioning than of direct experience, that nothing can be obtained from the existing power structure without direct personal intervention by an influential "patron." As there are few structures for collective organization, there is little sense of collective efficacy. Even in those collective organizations that do exist, for example unions, the cohesion of the membership in many cases is due less to support for the ideology or programmatic goals of the organization than to a series of parallel individual ties to the leader, who carries this personal following with him even if he changes party or union organization. Success in obtaining one's goals depends on individual clientelistic linkages, linkages, however, in which the personal bond created may ultimately transcend the specific act of exchange. Such long-term personal relationships are seen as the essence of the *clientela* bond in the following statement by a local PLI deputy:

> The term "clientele" must include the totality of the friendship relationships which one establishes in life, human relationships which are transferred into the field of politics as well. In this sense even I have a personal clientele. Its defining characteristic is stability, the personal bond which is independent even of the party and which is expressed in a vote of trust.[9]

Pizzorno has argued that the critical element for understanding clientelism is not the concrete exchange relationship but rather this more general personal bond that underlies it. In his view, this personal link – often institutionalized in the form of *comparaggio* ("ritual kinship") – is independent of any specific act of material exchange which, while serving to reinforce it, is not necessary to the survival of the relationship. It is in this ability to endure over time without continual reinforcement by concrete acts of exchange that Pizzorno sees the essence of the clientelistic relationship; it is less the specific immediate benefit received that maintains the relationship than the constant anticipation of possible future favors as a result of the personal tie. Such an analysis underlines the importance of the element of hope in sustaining a clientelistic system of power in a context of limited resource availability. Instead of shifting their votes to another party in accordance with the model of the "rational voter," people continue to vote for a politician even in the absence of immediate material benefits, because of their recognition of the potential future utility of the personal bond to an individual in a position of power. Thus, they are not necessarily voting in exchange for or anticipation of any specific benefit but rather to confirm the possibility of future access to favors, should they become necessary.[10]

Because of the social disaggregation of the *quartieri popolari* and the general exclusion of the poor from the occupational centers of *clientela* power (like the shopkeepers', artisans' and small farmers' associations), the relationship between the DC and the *sottoproletariato* tends, at least superficially, to be more sporadic and more exclusively electorally oriented than that with the public employees, the local entrepreneurial class, and the traditional middle classes. This distinction emerges clearly from the very different ways in which electoral campaigns are managed with regard to the various social groups. Before entering into these distinctions, however, it should be emphasized at the outset that the electoral campaigns of the DC in Palermo are very different from those of other political parties. Public appearances, rallies, speeches, or debates by party leaders are extremely rare, in general occurring only on the occasion of a campaign stop by a national political figure like Fanfani or Moro. Apart from the distribution of the campaign materials sent from Rome, there is no real electoral campaign of the Christian Democratic *party* in Palermo; rather there are dozens of campaigns organized by competing factions and individual candidates, each involved in a desperate struggle to maximize the number of personal preference votes obtained.

Although they never make a public appearance or engage in a political debate, the electoral activity of local party leaders like Gioia and Lima is frenetic, but it all takes place behind closed doors – in private meetings in party sections, parish halls, and special electoral "buffets" where the candidate makes a brief appearance to reaffirm his ties with the local activists and *capi-elettori*. The following description of the activities of Gioia in the campaign for the municipal elections of June 1975 is characteristic of the electoral role of the local faction chief:

> Gioia covered the entire city, zone by zone, party section by party section, one *capo-elettore* after the other. He asked each one how it was going, listened to their response, gave neither advice nor directives. What mattered was the fact of his presence, the limousine which pulled up, his personal entourage, the *capi-elettori* who line up to see him, the handshakes. Few words were necessary.[11]

The efficacy of such a strategy is demonstrated by the example of Ciancimino who, after having been excluded from the party's list for the 1975 elections, succeeded in electing every one of his own men to the City Council, in the place of the "good government" candidates supported by the official party apparatus.

The role of the *capo-elettore* is critical to an understanding of the functioning of the DC electoral machine. The *capi-elettori* are individuals bound to a given candidate, in general because of favors either received or expected, who put their services at the disposition of the "patron" during the electoral campaign. The *capi-elettori* are in most cases the critical link between the candidate and the individual voter. One explanation of the efficacy of the DC machine is the capillarity of its networks of *capi-elettori* – there are an estimated 1,000–1,500 *capi-elettori*, each of whom controls 300–500 votes, votes he has every interest in producing, because his own access to future benefits will depend on the outcome.

The way in which this system of *capi-elettori* works can be illustrated by examining the functioning of the municipal garbage collection agency (AMNU), one of the few public agencies in Palermo to recruit a significant number of workers from the *quartieri popolari*. For organizational purposes, AMNU has divided the city into eight zones, each of which is headed by a *capo-zona*, a sort of foreman who oversees the work of all the garbage collectors and street sweepers assigned to that zone. The powers of the *capo-zona* over the individual worker are immense:

A *capo-zona* of AMNU is more than a boss. Every morning he marks the presence of the men who work under him, he distributes the work to be done, decides who will work overtime or night shift, assigns days off and holidays, and at the end of the month hands out the pay in cash with his own hands.[12]

With such powers at his disposal, the *capo-zona*, often a "person of respect" in his own right, constitutes a pivotal link in the *clientela* networks of the faction or politician which controls AMNU: with 200–250 workers under his control each *capo-zona*, by marking an absent worker present or by assigning a street sweeper 500 meters as opposed to 3 kilometers of street to be cleaned, can control blocks of hundreds of votes, taking into account the family and friends who will be influenced by each *netturbino* ("garbageman" or "street sweeper"). Because of the inflated size of the agency (about 2,500 employees, the same number as in Milan, where about three times as many people are served) and its linkages to the *quartieri popolari*, control of AMNU has always been a key bone of contention among competing DC factions. As a result, the agency has played a pivotal role both in internal party struggles and in the individual electoral success of those candidates linked to it.

Having clarified the role of the *capi-elettori*, we can now examine the very different ways in which this highly articulated electoral machine functions with respect to different social groups. In middle-class neighborhoods electoral activity is virtually nonexistent. The control of the middle class, predominantly public employees, passes almost exclusively through the *clientela* networks within each public office, with electoral hiring and promotion the order of the day, as well as the reaffirmation of all existing bonds of gratitude or of hope (see Chapter 4). The basis of these exchanges is explained in the following dialogue between a journalist and a DC organizer:

Organizer: Electoral control is exercised through the public offices . . .
Journalist: But aren't you ashamed to beg for votes?
Organizer: We don't understand each other. Who begs for votes? They hold in their hands the fate of entire families, not only in terms of jobs but for a hundred other equally important things. They don't ask for votes; they say, "Help me and I'll help you in return." It's very simple: in the last analysis, it's a form of solidarity.[13]

By contrast, electoral activity at a ward or neighborhood level is concentrated almost entirely in the *quartieri popolari* of the city, the votes of which are hotly contested by competing candidates.

The techniques of electoral competition that prevail in the *quartieri popolari* take the most varied forms, but all share one common element: the exploitation of the powerlessness, ignorance, and need of the city's poor for personal political ends. The most conspicuous of these techniques is that of petty electoral corruption of the most squalid kind – a cynical buying and selling of votes in return for a kilo of pasta, bills of 5,000 or 10,000 lire (1,000 lire = U.S. $1.00-U.S. $1.50), or coupons for gasoline, for the cinema and, in one classic case, even for prostitutes. The distribution of pasta is a time-honored electoral technique in the slums of Palermo, and one whose popularity, regardless of its actual efficacy, seems not to have declined at all with the passage of time. In every *quartiere* the arrival of the truck of pasta, accompanied by thousands of ballot facsimiles with the candidate's name and number, is still the high point of every electoral campaign. The usual practice is that, at the outset of a campaign, a candidate will be approached by enterprising individuals from a given neighborhood who offer, in return for a certain sum of money, to set up an electoral committee in the candidate's name and distribute pasta. This process, common to all the low-income neighborhoods of the city, is described in detail in the following first-hand accounts:

The dozens of electoral committees which spring up like mushrooms at the moment of the elections are the products of individual initiative. Two or three desperate individuals get together, for a month and a half leave their regular jobs as street-vendors, and rent a locale, a table and some chairs. They procure – it's not difficult – the electoral lists for a group of precincts, including the name, address, and the polling place in which each elector will vote; then, with this in hand, once having selected the candidate, the bargaining begins. They came to me with 1,300 voters from the Capo. Their demands: 4 trucks of pasta, a truck of canned tomatoes and oil,. . . plus the costs for rent, electricity, and pay for the "lads" – this besides the facsimiles and some extra money for "needy cases." For them it's a good deal, and in general it is for the candidate as well; they really work hard, even if it's not by such means that a candidate is assured of election. [A DC candidate][14]

It's like a seasonal job: they leave their usual trade and put themselves at the service of the highest bidder. In the Albergheria [a zone of the old city] a rascal now in prison "worked" for three different candidates – one Monarchist, one Christian Democrat, and one Republican. In the same way others worked simultaneously for Liberals or Christian Democrats who promised jobs as garbage collectors or doormen . . . By these means in the *quartieri popolari* a candidate can obtain from 30%–50% of his votes.[15]

The "old man" [the local *capo-mafia*] in one of the center-city neighborhoods makes a deal with the candidate for two million lire with the proviso that he supply the "lads"; in addition, the candidate must provide him with two tons of pasta and sometimes find a job for one of the "lads" as well. At the beginning we "lads" receive 10,000 lire apiece to make our services available; then after two weeks another 5,000 or 10,000 lire. When the campaign is over, everyone hopes for a job, but hardly anyone ever gets one. Each of us in the last election procured 50 to 200 votes in this way, and in our *quartiere* alone we were 10 "lads" working.[16]

Despite the unabated recourse to such methods of electoral persuasion in the *quartieri popolari* of the city, it is generally accepted that their efficacy is no longer what it once was. Increasingly people accept the pasta or other electoral bribes and proceed to vote as they please:

In the Albergheria they were passing out movie tickets and 5,000 lire bills, and people were running in every direction as if there were a raid. Where were they all running? The Communists to the local party section, the others to the parish priest, all asking if they could accept the money. The reply was: "Accept the money, deny the vote."[17]

Given the amount of money that politicians continue to spend for such purposes, it would be rash to conclude that they no longer produce results. A more accurate appraisal would rather be that these kinds of electoral bribes are intended above all to shift a certain fringe of marginal votes rather than to assure election in and of themselves. The reason such tactics can continue to produce results, even in the absence of any dependable means for controlling whether an individual does in fact vote as he has promised, is that many among the urban poor remain so totally alienated from the political system that they see no particular reason to prefer one party or candidate over another. Given such an outlook, a kilo of pasta or 5,000 lire is as good a basis as any other for deciding how to vote.

Underlying the well-established ritual of the dispersal of tons of pasta in the slums of Palermo, however, there are other more serious and more reliable mechanisms linking the urban poor to the holders of local power. Here again, consensus is maintained primarily through the manipulation for electoral ends of the DC monopoly over virtually all centers of local power. This monopoly has provided the DC, and in particular certain factions, with a permanent and highly efficacious electoral machine. As an election approaches, the personnel of many public offices are mobilized on a grand scale to assist in the campaign of one or another candidate (depending on which faction controls that particular office); regular business grinds to a halt as employees devote themselves full time to filling and addressing envelopes or distributing electoral propaganda. At the same time, the normally sluggish procedures of local government bureaucracies experience an abrupt surge of energy. Hundreds of openings for public jobs are announced and, although the numbers of *sottoproletari* who ever receive such jobs are extremely limited, promises abound. Requests for assistance that have lain buried for months in various public offices are suddenly processed by the hundreds. Each response is accompanied by a letter, of which the following is a typical example, communicating the positive outcome of the request and containing facsimiles bearing the number of the assessor, who just happens to be a candidate in the upcoming election: "I am pleased to inform you that – as a result of my personal interest in your problem – you will receive a subsidy of 5,000 lire. Vote DC."[18]

The most strategic center of power for the purposes of "electoral beneficence" is the regional Assessorato agli Enti Locali. In addition to the oversight of local government, the functions of this department include jurisdiction over all charitable institutions in Sicily, a total of 19,000 (over double the national average), which provide assistance to minors, the elderly, and the handicapped. These institutions are in their entirety religiously affiliated, providing important links between the holder of this key office and the local parishes, through which the funds are channeled. The regional budget allocates about 5 billion lire (app. U.S. $8.3 million) annually for this purpose, the distribution of which depends entirely upon the discretion of the assessor. Given such power, it is hardly accidental that the men who have filled this position have consistently reaped the highest number of personal preference votes among DC candidates in the subsequent regional election.[19] At the level of individual benefits, the most important arm of the Assessorato agli Enti Locali is Ente Comunale di Assistenza (ECA), which provides the only semblance of public welfare in Italy – cash benefits of 5,000–10,000 lire per month and a limited program of meals and dormitory facilities, primarily for the indigent elderly. The funds, however minimal, that ECA has to distribute are also under the total discretionary control of a "commissar" appointed by the prefect (because the City Council has never succeeded in nominating the administrative council required by law).

Another important source of electoral support, particularly among the residents of the decaying slums of the old city, has been the local public-housing authority (IACP). Given the desperate shortage of public housing in Palermo, what exists has always been a primary instrument of electoral speculation, with completed apartments being held empty for months or even years in order to assign them just prior to an election. Electoral promises of public housing rival those of jobs in the *quartieri popolari* and are just as rarely maintained: "Public housing? They ask for our vote and make us believe that any day we will be assigned an apartment. Then they never come back."[20]

The inventiveness that the pursuit of electoral success can instill in the holders of public power is illustrated by the following exploit of a municipal assessor of taxes. During the campaign for the 1971 regional election, for which the assessor was a candidate, thousands of citizens, in particular residents of the *quartieri popolari*, received exceptionally high tax assessments. Upon presenting appeals, these citizens were notified that they should come directly to the office of the assessor to resolve the problem. Upon their arrival, the assessor proceeded to annul the "mistaken" assessment, requesting in return that the individual vote for the DC and presenting him with his personal facsimiles.[21]

A final illustration of the uses of public offices for electoral ends goes back to the regulatory powers of local government discussed in Chapter 5. Because of the importance of the neighborhood markets to the economy of the *quartieri popolari*, the mechanisms linking shopkeepers, street-vendors, and artisans to the DC are an important part of the networks of political obligation within these neighborhoods. In addition to those aspects of local regulatory powers that affect these groups, there are other functions performed by the policeman that touch more directly the immediate needs of the urban poor. The most effective of these in terms of political payoff is that performed by the *vigile* assigned to the sector of "social solidarity." His task is to ascertain, through direct visits to the home, the authenticity of the need attested to by those requesting a subsidy from ECA, recovery in a hospital at the expense of the city, or the placing of a child in a public institution or summer camp. At this point the outcome of the request depends entirely upon the decision of the *vigile*. As in the case of the shopkeepers, the *vigile* can in this way create a solid network of friendships, friendships he reaffirms when he returns house by house to distribute electoral certificates (legal documents certifying the individual's eligibility to vote, necessary for access to the polling booth) and, very often, to hand out facsimiles for a particular candidate at the same time.[22]

The above examples are just a few of the ways in which a municipal or regional assessor, through his control of channels of public spending, however trivial in the individual case, or of certain of the regulatory powers of local government, can create a solid personal clientele through the distribution of a wide range of petty favors. Be-

174 The social bases of the machine

cause of the importance of such favors, every public official, from the national deputy to the municipal assessor, maintains copious and detailed files recording every favor ever performed. These files, which can run into the tens of thousands of cases for prominent politicians with long public careers, are then activated during every electoral campaign, with letters sent out to every beneficiary reminding him of the past services of the candidate and soliciting his vote in the current election. The critical importance of these files is illustrated by the case of a prominent politician whose files were stolen by his own personal secretary, with the ultimatum that they would not be returned unless the secretary were placed in the party's list for the upcoming municipal elections. Not surprisingly, the secretary not only became a candidate but was elected with almost 9,000 preference votes.[23]

Probably the most important linkage between the DC and the urban poor, however, is that of bureaucratic intermediation. To some extent this is an extension of the preceding discussion of the utilization of public offices for the purpose of petty clientelism. The difference is that here we are dealing not with the discretionary distribution of public funds or the selective implementation of certain regulatory codes, but rather with intervention in the processes of ordinary administration. This is by its very nature a much more continuous relationship than that produced by the dispensation of benefits just prior to elections. The possibility of such intervention in bureaucratic procedures for political ends can be explained in part by the nature of the southern Italian bureaucracy. In contrast to Weber's model of rational, impartial bureaucratic conduct, all relationships are highly personalized and politicized, even those regarding the most trivial administrative procedures. As a result, the citizen's legal right is transformed into a personal favor and used as an instrument of pressure to obtain votes:

The "intermediary" attempts to convince his client that he is on friendly terms with the functionary (even when this is not really the case), presenting this friendship as the determining motive for the positive outcome of the request. And likewise the functionary, wherever possible, presents an act due the client by law as a "favor," conceded by his good will alone.[24]

One reason this system functions so well is that the bureaucracy in Italy, and especially in the South, is such an inefficient, slow-moving apparatus, bogged down in endless red tape, that it is indeed only by the personal intervention of an influential intermediary that one can obtain any immediate result. In this way what might strike the outside observer as a pathological dysfunction of the bureaucracy serves in reality as a highly efficacious instrument for generating and maintaining political support. For practically every necessity of life – the innumerable documents required for even the most trivial public act in Italy; eligibility for a welfare benefit, pension, or family allowance; admission of a family member to a day-care center, hospital or other public institution; application for public housing or a public-sector job – the individual citizen finds himself confronted by an impersonal and unresponsive bureaucracy. In such a situation ordinary citizens, and the poor in particular, disadvantaged by their illiteracy and lack of experience in dealing with bureaucratic institutions, are constrained to seek assistance from a higher-status patron who can intervene directly on their behalf. In a system where the functioning of the public bureaucracy has been so entirely subordinated to the logic of personal political gain, the individual simply has no alternative but to seek a personal solution to his problem. Thus, once again, consensus is rooted in the critical intermediary role of the party or the individual politician in the relationship between the citizen and the state.

The above patronage mechanisms may seem familiar to anyone acquainted with the history of the big-city political machines in the United States. What distinguishes the machine in the low-income neighborhoods of Palermo, apart from the broader political context, is a final type of linkage between the party and its electorate, one that depends upon a series of intermediary networks within each neighborhood, which function independently of any direct personal relationship between the candidate and the individual voter. The superficial version of such linkage mechanisms takes the form of the petty electoral corruption described above, where votes are essentially sold to the highest bidder, without the slightest regard for the individual candidate, his party, or the political positions, if any, he represents; because of the system of preference voting, many people in fact vote only for a number, with no idea of the candidate to whom it corresponds.

The real networks of electoral influence within these *quartieri*, however, are of a quite different nature; they are based on the ties linking a person of influence within a given neighborhood – the local *capo-mafia*, the parish priest, a doctor, or prominent merchant – to a particular party or candidate. The nature of this link – friendship, *clientela*, or an outright exchange of cash – varies according to the case. What is important is that the *grande elettore* is capable of mobilizing blocks of votes through his personal influence alone, an influence that may be based equally on respect or fear, without any exchange of benefits between the candidate and the individual voter. These votes, which depend entirely on the prestige of the local influence broker, are thus, in their pure form at least, independent not only of the individual candidate and the political party but also, and most importantly, of all the traditional patronage levers of local power. The nature of these interpersonal ties and their political consequences are admirably expressed in the following statement by Genco Russo, the *capo-mafia* of an agricultural town in the interior of Sicily and reputed to be one of the island's most powerful mafia bosses until his recent death. Although the context is that of a peasant village rather than an urban slum, the relationships in question are virtually identical in the two settings:

People ask me how to vote because they feel an obligation to ask advice in order to demonstrate a sense of gratitude. They feel themselves to be ignorant of the candidates and parties, and want to conform to the views of the persons who have done them a good turn.[25]

A concrete illustration of the role of such a neighborhood "boss" when he decides to put his personal influence to political ends is that of "Don" Alberto Aliotta, secretary of the PCI section in the Capo and city councillor since 1970. After Aliotta's "conversion" to the PCI in 1968, the party's votes in the neighborhood increased from 900 to 2,500 in 1975. The example of Aliotta demonstrates not only the universality of certain patterns of political behavior in Palermo, regardless of party allegiance, but also the overlapping of the various types of support mechanisms that have been differentiated here for analytical purposes. The case of Aliotta is an example of the confluence in the same person of the two roles of neighborhood boss and political intermediary, which in general remain quite distinct. While in this regard this is a somewhat exceptional case, it is worth recounting because it provides a vivid first-person account of political relationships in a typical *quartiere popolare*:

Before being elected to the City Council, I was esteemed, I was loved, I was respected by virtually the entire *quartiere*, because I was born in this *quartiere*, I am sixty years old, and I still live where I was born – thus everyone knows me well. Since I have been city councillor, I have recruited many new members to the Communist Party, many of whom had never before been members of the party . . . In the City Council I was elected to the Commission on Commerce and the City Police. As a result, people from the *quartiere* came to find me, and I obtained for them licenses or permits to occupy public soil in the markets. I succeeded quite justly in annulling many fines because the poor cannot pay these fines, just because they were selling illegally a basket of fruit or fish, and some *vigile* came along who wanted to levy a fine in order to enrich the Commune. The people of the *quartiere* have always turned to me to be helped, and I have always done the best I could . . . Many people have sought me out even in my place of work, a shoe factory, saying that the *vigili* had given them a fine of 10,000 or 15,000 lire, and that they couldn't pay it. These are poor people, people who are desperately trying to earn those extra 100 or 1,000 lire in a trade for which they are not authorized just in order to provide a plate of pasta for their hungry children . . . Many people had been my friends and many more drew close to me when I was elected city councillor . . . They understood that my being elected to the City Council from this *quartiere* was an historic event. I am the first city councillor ever to be elected from this *quartiere*. I have become an historic personage: when I walk by, the people say: "We have the mayor of Palermo in our *quartiere*, our friend Alberto Aliotta."[26]

Having completed this overview of the principal mechanisms of political support among the urban poor, we can now turn to a more detailed analysis of political participation in three typical low-income neighborhoods. What is most fascinating about the *quartieri popolari* of Palermo is the ways in which, within the general framework of *clientela* relationships presented in the preceding pages, the different types of low-income neighborhoods have developed distinctive patterns of political behavior, in terms of both voting patterns and the outcomes of attempts at alternative models of political mobilization. Chapter 8 will describe and attempt to explain these differences.

8

The urban poor: three neighborhood studies

Low-income neighborhoods in Palermo fall into three distinct categories: the center-city slum, the new public-housing projects on the urban periphery, and the rural *borgate* of the Conca d'Oro, which as a result of the tempestuous urban expansion of the past two decades are being progressively engulfed by the city proper. While they share many of the general characteristics outlined in the previous chapter, each of these neighborhoods presents distinctive patterns of social interaction and political participation, linked to its peculiar structural setting. In all three types of neighborhoods there have been in recent years attempts to mobilize the inhabitants against the machine. This chapter analyzes the different political outcomes of these neighborhoods in the light of the more general question of the prospects for change in clientelistic regimes.[1]

The Capo: a center-city slum

The Capo is one of the four historic *mandamenti* of the *centro storico* of Palermo, lying just behind the cathedral in the angle formed by the intersection of the city's two main thoroughfares. Reflecting the progressive decay of the old city, the population of the Capo has declined from over 30,000 at the end of the war to only a little over 10,000 in 1976, an exodus that has been most dramatic in the years since the 1968 earthquake. Despite its central location, the Capo is one of the most disaggregated and emarginated of the *quartieri popolari*. Practically everyone who has succeeded in securing a stable income has fled the *quartiere*, including the majority of the merchants and vendors in the local market, who, while continuing to work in the Capo, now reside elsewhere. The market, lining several of the major arteries of the *quartiere*, constitutes the only viable economic activity remaining in the Capo. The Capo once constituted an important artisanal center, particularly in the shoe and furniture trades, but these activities have largely disappeared, crushed by outside competition; the few artisans who remain are engaged in a desperate struggle for survival against overwhelming odds. A large proportion of the men of the Capo are either unemployed or engaged in petty theft and contraband; many families are sustained primarily by the women, who work in large numbers as domestic servants or prostitutes, or by the children, who probably make up the bulk of the neighborhood's active labor force.

Each of the four *quartieri* of the old city constitutes in many ways a closed social system, with many residents, particularly women, passing their entire lives within the narrow boundaries of the neighborhood or even of a single street with little or no contact with the rest of the city. This isolation – and the corresponding neglect by the rest of the city and its administrators – have given rise to a strong sense of diffidence toward outsiders and at times even toward persons coming from a different section of the same *quartiere*, together with an intense mistrust of public authority in all its forms. In contrast to the overall social disaggregation of the *quartiere*, however, there exists a strong sense of neighborhood solidarity centered around the individual *vicolo* ("narrow street or alley"). Each *vicolo* has created its own system of collective survival, a kind of mutual aid society among relatives and neighbors that carries each family through those periods when it has no source of income, as well as supplying on a reciprocal basis many of the basic social services the city has failed to provide:

If, for example, you have no money and you go into the street in the old *quartiere*, you have the possibility of getting a loan of 1,000 lire from an acquaintance, a cup of coffee in a bar from a friend, words of comfort from another. In case of a sudden illness, there is someone there to help; the neighbors keep an eye on your children. In short, there is a kind of solidarity.[2]

The politics of the Capo, like that of the other neighborhoods of the *centro storico*, has traditionally constituted a kind of ideal type of the mechanisms of bureaucratic intermediation backed up by petty electoral corruption described in the preceding pages. It is here that the "electoral committees" spring up most densely and the appearance of the pasta trucks becomes a regular ritual in the weeks preceding every election. In terms of votes, this kind of politics has benefited not only the DC, because of its domination of the levers of local power, but also its minor coalition partners like the Republicans and the Social Democrats, who, on the strength of candidates who hold important municipal assessorships or simply are willing to engage in

large-scale electoral corruption, tend in these neighborhoods to receive levels of votes significantly above their city-wide average.

In contrast to cities like Catania and Reggio Calabria, where the
urban *sottoproletariato* has constituted a substantial reservoir of votes
for extreme right-wing parties like the MSI, in Palermo support for
the neo-Fascists comes primarily from the bourgeois neighborhoods
of the new city. The residents of the *centro storico*, on the contrary,
have, since the collapse of the strong right-wing movements of the
immediate postwar period, provided consistent majorities for the
parties of the ruling coalition. Because, however, of the contingent
nature of the linkages between the DC and large numbers of the
urban poor (in contrast to the more stable relationship between the
party and the middle classes), the political behavior of the *sottoproletariato* is potentially highly volatile. Thus far, however, this instability has been manifested primarily in shifts of votes among different
parties and candidates within the majority coalition rather than in
support for "antisystem" parties of either the Left or the Right (for an
analysis of electoral results by type of neighborhood, see Table A.3).

This successful combination of political passivity and clientelistic
intermediation was unexpectedly disrupted in the wake of the local
elections of June 1975, in which the local Christian Democrats, in
contrast to the advance of the Left in every other major Italian city,
actually increased their seats on the City Council. The stimulus behind this disruption was the issue of housing, which, apart from the
constant struggle for economic survival, constitutes the most deeply
felt problem among the residents of the Capo, as of all the neighborhoods of the old city. The majority of the inhabitants live in over-
crowded, unsanitary conditions in decrepit dwellings, many of
which are officially condemned and in constant danger of collapse
due to the combined effects of decades of neglect and the damages
inflicted by the 1968 earthquake. The deterioration of housing conditions since 1968 has been so severe that the need for decent housing,
felt with particular intensity by the women, has generated an unprecedented degree of popular anger and mobilization for direct political action among the ordinarily passive and diffident residents of
the old city. The political movement that resulted will be discussed
in detail in the following section.

The *movimento per la casa*

In the fall of 1975, an extraordinary political movement shook
the tranquillity of political life in Palermo. It was called the *movimento
per la casa* ("the housing movement")[3] and consisted of several hundred families, predominantly from the *centro storico* but including

Figure 8.1. The *movimento per la casa*: a mass demonstration along the main street of Palermo. *Source: L'Ora.*

some residents of the peripheral shantytowns as well (see Figure 8.1). These families had been organized by a loose coalition of student groups to the left of the PCI (the so-called extraparliamentary Left) to demand decent housing for all families living in conditions of physical peril, overcrowding, or inadequate sanitary facilities. The housing situation in Palermo is so critical that these groups, proposing immediate occupations of both empty units of *case popolari* ("public housing") and unrented private apartments, found a fertile terrain for organization among the residents of the city's slums, people exasperated by years of unfulfilled electoral promises and by the mounting numbers of partial cave-ins or outright collapses in the dwellings of the old city. Not only did the movement achieve striking success in mobilizing the presumed "unorganizable" urban *sottoproletariato* but, even more importantly, it was the women of the *quartieri popolari* who made up the real backbone of the movement, demonstrating a degree of aggressiveness and combativity that shocked party leaders and city administrators accustomed to a much more passive and submissive female constituency.

At the outset, the tactics of the movement were two-pronged: on the one hand, a series of illegal occupations both of private apartments and of *case popolari* in a recently completed project where it was suspected that the apartments were being held back for later "electoral" distribution; on the other, a mounting campaign of mass demonstrations along the major thoroughfares of the city and in front of key public offices (in particular, the City Hall and the IACP). The momentum of this popular mobilization was such that the movement soon succeeded in involving the left-wing parties, the labor unions, and students in a broad political coalition around the issues of unemployment and the *risanamento* of the old city, culminating in a general strike and massive public demonstration on November 10, 1975. Although initially taken by surprise, the PCI had moved quickly to insert itself into the growing movement, utilizing it as an instrument of pressure in its own strategy to bring down the municipal *giunta* dominated by the *fanfaniani* and to initiate a new "opening to the Communists" in the city government similar to the programmatic accord reached at the regional level a few months before.

The initial response of the city administration to this unprecedented wave of popular protest was to nominate a special commission, composed of representatives of all the political parties present in the City Council, of the three labor confederations, and of the two national tenants' unions (one of which, the SUNIA, is essentially an organizational arm of the PCI), to visit the *quartieri popolari* and prepare a list of the most urgent cases (giving priority to those dwellings in most imminent danger of collapse). To provide for these families the prefect had requisitioned the 328 *case popolari* currently available plus a block of 35 private apartments (in both cases, those that had been previously occupied by the protesters, who had been forcibly dislodged by the police). The nomination of the commission, criticized by the *extraparlamentari* as a tactic for pacifying the masses and dividing the movement, and the requisition of the apartments for immediate distribution, marked the end of the first phase of the *movimento per la casa,* which culminated in a major political victory for the movement – the formation in January 1976 of a new Center-Left city government supported by the Communists. Popular support for continued struggle then fell off as the focus of the problem shifted from mass mobilization to the bureaucratic procedures associated with the commission's visits to the various *quartieri* and the selection of the families to receive the requisitioned apartments. Thus, having obtained this initial institutional response through mass protest, people once again lapsed into passivity, awaiting resolution of the problem from above. The formation of the commission served to reaffirm a perception of the issue as an individual rather than a collective problem; with thousands of families in desperate need of housing and only 363 apartments available, the poor were pitted one against the other in often bitter competition to gain the favor of the commission, which took on an almost godlike quality among the residents of the old city.

In the meantime, the *extraparlamentari,* who had been denied representation on the commission, criticized its functioning in the following terms: first, that it considered only cases where dwellings had actually collapsed or were in imminent danger thereof and not those of severe overcrowding or lack of sanitary facilities; second, that the methods of the commission had degenerated into the usual clientelistic maneuvers, with the available apartments being divided up for distribution among the various parties present in the commission. In support of the latter contention, they pointed to the random and unannounced nature of the commission's visits to the various *quartieri,* citing cases where entire streets had been bypassed or where, in a condemned building inhabited by several families, some would be placed on the list and others (often supporters of the leftist groups) arbitrarily excluded. As the only political party to have an organizational presence in these neighborhoods (the success of the *extraparlamentari* having stimulated a sudden revitalization of the heretofore largely dormant PCI sections in the *centro storico*), the PCI bore the brunt of these criticisms. In one neighborhood in particular the leader of the PCI section built up a substantial personal following of her own, the residents being convinced that if they followed the PCI, she would personally procure them an apartment. Feeling the party's credibility severely threatened by the success of the *extraparlamentari* in mobilizing a mass base, certain PCI leaders had clearly encouraged such misperceptions in their zeal to lure away the followers of the leftist groups; they would subsequently pay the price for this zeal in the backlash against the party in certain zones where people felt they had been tricked into supporting the party, once the initial allotment of apartments had been completed, by unfounded promises of nonexistent *case popolari* still to be assigned. In order to forestall such clientelistic maneuvers, the *extraparlamentari* demanded systematic house-by-house coverage of each neighborhood and a public calendar of the commission's visits, in order to permit supervision of their activity by representatives of the groups and by citizens' committees from each *quartiere*.

Such demands came to naught, however, as already by March 1976 the activities of the commission had ground to a standstill. After a first round of visits, which had produced an initial list of 252 families, the commission found, as it prepared to undertake a second round, that it was confronted with over 3,000 requests for visits and only 107 remaining apartments to be distributed. Faced with the impossible task of choosing the most deserving among all these families and thereby setting off a "war among the poor," the commission refused to proceed any further until a decision could be reached on the requisition of private apartments to fill the gap, utilizing the 1,400 million lire (approximately U.S. $2.3 million) that had been allocated to the city for that purpose by the regional government. With the commission out of the picture, the remaining apartments were assigned by the Prefect, on the basis of police reports of evictions from buildings that had already suffered collapses, a procedure that gave rise to a second chorus of protests over alleged cases of fraud and discrimination (e.g., persons who had allegedly obtained a *casa popolare*, then sold or sublet it, moving back into a crumbling tenement in order to procure a second one).

At this point the mass movement, which had lapsed for two to three months while the commission was completing its work, was revived, but with a quite different character. The PCI, having succeeded in its previous strategy of imposing a new municipal *giunta* that it supported, had every interest in keeping the movement within established institutional bounds, and clearly regarded the renewal of activity by the *extraparlamentari* as a potential threat. Thus, in contrast to its earlier collaboration, this time the PCI did everything in its power to isolate the movement and to prevent the formation of a unified popular front like that of the previous fall. Tensions between the party and the leftist groups rapidly intensified, with the PCI publicly accusing the *extraparlamentari* of demagogic extremism in their slogan of *"la casa per tutti"* ("a house for everyone") which, they said, deliberately misled the masses, ignoring the fact that there was simply no more public housing available and that the only real solution to the problem was a long-term one, the *risanamento* of the old city. The party even more vehemently condemned the groups for their continued advocacy of illegal occupations which, in the words of a party spokesman, constituted "adventurist" tactics, "carrying with them the risk of grave divisions within the popular movement, offering a fertile terrain for provocations of every sort and, above all, failing to guarantee any criterion of justice for all citizens aspiring to a decent home."[4]

The dangers to which this statement refers are above all those of conflict between the legitimate assignees and the illegal occupants of public housing, a constant preoccupation of the PCI since the massive wave of occupations following the 1968 earthquake. There is a strongly rooted tradition in Palermo that those who occupy *case popolari* have a good chance of remaining; thus, once an apartment has been assigned, the legal assignees often mount a 24-hour guard against intruders until they themselves can move in. When illegal occupants have succeeded in gaining access to apartments, however, the Communists have found themselves in a very uncomfortable position, caught between two competing groups of "proletarians" with equally legitimate demands. Given this tradition of housing occupations and the urgency of the individual need for decent housing, tensions emerged within the ranks of the *extraparlamentari* as well with regard to the form that occupations should take. The question at issue was whether occupations should be undertaken primarily as symbolic gestures, that is, as tactical maneuvers to gain public attention and exert pressure on other parties and on the city administration, or whether they should be seen instead as potentially permanent solutions for the families concerned. Although the latter interpretation had clearly been the stimulus behind the previous waves of housing occupations in Palermo, the *extraparlamentari* attempted to refute such an individualistic posing of the issue and to present the occupations as simply a tactical weapon in a broader political struggle.

The grass-roots reaction to such an approach was one of incomprehension and uncertainty. In one neighborhood meeting, for example, the question was raised as to the purpose of occupying apartments if the occupants would only be promptly thrown out by the police; in reply, the representative of the groups explained that the occupations had a political value regardless of the outcome and that, if the police intervened, it was useless to resist because they disposed of overwhelming physical force. After the meeting the organizer was severely reproached by one of the neighborhood activists in the following terms: "If you don't give people the hope of being able to remain in the apartment they occupy, no one will participate; no one wants to struggle and then see the benefits go to someone else." These tensions broke into the open in the spring of 1976, when, as the movement became increasingly isolated and fragmented, increasing numbers of spontaneous occupations and roadblocks took place, completely outside the control of either the established parties or the leftist groups.

As it became clear that the available stock of *case popolari* had been exhausted (with a waiting list of 17,000 applicants and only 3,000 additional units of public housing projected for the foreseeable future), the protest movement focused increasingly on the issue of the requisition of private apartments. It is a tribute to the political force wielded by the movement that such a question – heretofore taboo in Palermo where the forces of private speculation have dominated urban development – was ever even raised to the status of a political issue. The reaction of property owners and building contractors was predictable: they denounced requisition as a threat to the sanctity of private property, affirmed that in any case there were no apartments available (contrary to statistics showing 8,000 luxury apartments unoccupied), and made barely veiled threats to close down construction sites if requisition were authorized, attempting thereby, as they had done so often in the past, to mobilize the construction workers' fear of unemployment in order to promote speculative interests. The conflict was exacerbated by the insistence of the *extraparlamentari* on requisition at political prices rather than at market value, so as to be able to rent more apartments with the available funds and to avoid rewarding speculators who held empty apartments in order to keep prices high.

While the debate over requisition of private apartments went on (a debate, not surprisingly, never resolved), the desperation of those condemned to wait in crumbling tenements or primitive shacks increased; expectations had been aroused and people wanted results. While the PCI (through SUNIA) and the *extraparlamentari* continued to mobilize their followers in competing demonstrations on the steps of City Hall, scattered groups of *sottoproletari*, exasperated by the months of ineffectual bargaining among the parties, took affairs into their own hands, setting up roadblocks across key intersections and carrying out spontaneous occupations of empty apartments, from which they were promptly dislodged by the police, although not without resistance. In two of the most dramatic cases, twenty-seven families occupied an unused municipal day-care center for over six months, without water, electricity, or sanitary facilities, while at the same time another five families, evicted by force from their condemned homes and having nowhere else to go, set up makeshift tents in the square outside the City Hall, where they remained for four months until they were relocated by the city to a decrepit building in almost as dilapidated condition as the hovels they had left.

At this point the movement, already badly fragmented, ran up against an even more formidable obstacle – the approach of the June 1976 elections for Parliament and the Regional Assembly. The force of the movement was inexorably siphoned off into electoral channels, as the perennial tactic of promises and *raccomandazioni* to obtain a *casa popolare* entered into high gear. Recourse to such methods was possible because of the failure of the IACP to maintain its commitment – extracted through intense movement pressure – to publish before the end of May a permanent list of the 17,000 families awaiting public housing ranked in order of priority (according to a point system based on the condition of the current dwelling, the size of the family, employment status, etc.). The publication of such a list, heretofore nonexistent in Palermo, had throughout the months of struggle been one of the foremost demands of both the leftist groups and the SUNIA, who saw it as an indispensable weapon which, by informing people exactly where they stood with regard to public housing, could prevent precisely the kind of electoral manipulation of the tremendous housing need that in fact ensued.

Although in the end it was preempted by the usual electoral maneuvers, the *movimento per la casa* did constitute a new political phenomenon in Palermo. The *extraparlamentari* claimed that the movement demonstrated the creation of a new political consciousness among the urban poor:

For the first time the struggle for housing in Palermo has resisted a rapid degeneration into a war among the poor, into becoming not a moment of unification but of further disaggregation . . . The action of the extra-parliamentary groups demonstrates that the presence of an avantgarde with real roots among the popular masses can succeed, despite lags and uncertainties, in overcoming the individualistic and corporative limits of previous struggles . . . The combativity of the protesting masses and the political dimension which the struggle rapidly acquired are indications that there is taking place . . . in the consciousness of the masses a change of great importance – a break with clientelism, with resignation, with a spontaneous "rebellionism" full of anger but easily turned back into passivity and inertia.[5]

Although, in the light of later developments, such an appraisal appears overly optimistic, it cannot be denied that, in its initial phase at least, the *movimento per la casa* did constitute a clear step beyond the spontaneous revolts of the past. Why, it may be asked, was the movement able to assume the force it did at this particular moment? While the housing conditions of the majority of the residents of the *centro storico* were and remain desperate, these conditions have been at a critical level since at least 1968. After the initial wave of mass occupations following the earthquake, however, the tide seemed to have subsided and the old passivity and dependence on individual solutions to have reasserted themselves. What was it, then, that overcame the traditional diffidence of the *sottoproletariato* and made the latent despair and frustration of the poor explode into collective action?

Any attempt to answer this question must take as its point of departure the prior absence of any organized political force in the *quartieri* with an interest in mobilizing popular anger for direct political action. Apart from the PCI, the presence of the other political parties was limited strictly to electoral campaigns. As for the Communists, not only was the party traditionally weak in the neighborhoods of the old city but its general strategic line – encouragement of popular protest only insofar as it could be channeled by the party into support for its own role as privileged mediator between the masses and official institutions – made it very difficult for the PCI to muster mass support in the *quartieri popolari,* where the people had long since lost faith in the value of such mediation. Because of the importance attributed by the party at this time to eventual compromise with the DC, PCI support for any radical initiatives was limited by the political context, both national and local. At a moment when all the party's efforts were geared toward realization of an "historic compromise" with the DC, the PCI focused its activity primarily on its own insertion into existing institutions and viewed with suspicion any popular initiative likely to have a negative effect on such an eventuality. Free from any such preoccupations and anxious to build up a mass base of their own, the *extraparlamentari* were thus the only political group to have any real interest in organizing the residents of the *centro storico* and the *baracche.* That they were so successful can be attributed to the strategy of direct action they proposed, in contrast both to the perennial electoral promises of the DC and to the appeals of the left-wing parties to rely on action within formal institutional channels, procedures that, as the poor knew only too well, had thus far failed to produce any concrete results.

The fundamental issues raised by the *movimento per la casa* in Palermo are those of the relationship between relatively powerless groups and the organized political system: (1) How can spontaneous popular protest be channeled into an effective and continuous political organization? (2) How can the momentum of a movement organized around demands for immediate material benefits be maintained? The nature of the objectives posed by the movement clearly constituted a source of strength in the short term – most people participated not because of ideology or a broader political vision, but because they were presented with a definite goal, corresponding to their own most immediate needs, and with a strategy of direct action to obtain it, in contrast to the usual political practice of endless meetings and discussions at the expense of action. While both the PCI and the leftist groups debated at length how to broaden the objectives of the movement into a more general political strategy for launching a new model of urban development, their mass base understood little of such debates – they knew only that they desperately needed decent housing. The outlook of the majority of the residents of these neighborhoods is described in the following observation of a long-term neighborhood militant:

The people I know in the neighborhood in general want a job and decent housing – there isn't anyone who discusses the prospects for or the shape of a new society . . . They aspire to a better life but never pose the question of the shape either of the groups, of the city, of the state, or of anything.[6]

In the wake of the movement's first victory – the nomination of the commission to prepare the list of families to receive the first lot of *case popolari* – the ambiguities in mass perceptions that had been obscured in the first wave of popular enthusiasm began to emerge. In the absence of broader political goals to hold the movement together, the formation of the commission was sufficient to demobilize the movement's base, as people once again put their faith in an individualistic solution. Despite its initial impetus, the cement holding the movement together turned out to have been less political consciousness than desperate need. In many cases, participation did not imply a clear political choice, but rather the willingness to follow anyone who seemed to hold out the promise of concrete results, as illustrated by the not infrequent cases of women who divided their efforts between the PCI and the *extraparlamentari*, carefully hedging their bets so as to maximize their chances of success from one side or the other.

The real weakness of both the PCI and the *extraparlamentari*, and the ultimate cause of the movement's demise, was their inability to harness the pent-up frustration and anger expressed in the protest movement to a longer-term political strategy centered around the general issue of the *risanamento* of the old city. Outside the context of a commitment to a radically different concept of *risanamento* than the one that had thus far prevailed – that is, a *risanamento* that would preserve the "popular" character of the *centro storico*, revitalizing the traditional commercial and artisanal economy and maintaining a large proportion of the existing low-income residents within the center-city – the question of housing in and of itself was susceptible to resolution through conventional welfare channels. If not confronted in conjunction with the general problems of *risanamento* and the revival of the urban economy, demands for public housing risked promoting the very speculative designs the movement was attempting to defeat: isolation of the poor in proletarian ghettos on the extreme periphery of the city, far from even those minimal sources of economic sustenance by which they now managed to survive, and liberation of the center of the city for a new wave of speculative development. A comprehensive strategy for urban renewal in the old city was critical for another reason as well – the existence of a thriving market in condemned dwellings. Unless, upon the transfer of a family to a *casa popolare*, their previous residence were to be immediately demolished, the chances are that it would forthwith be reinhabited by another equally desperate family, thus perpetuating the problem the assignment of *case popolari* was meant to eliminate. Limited to the immediate objective of housing, the initial radical thrust of the movement was diverted relatively quickly into traditional clientelistic channels, with the following consequences: (1) with only a limited number of apartments to be distributed, the degeneration of popular unity into individual competition for material benefits and resulting animosity between those who received an apartment and those who did not; (2) the "buying off" of individual participants who, once they had obtained an apartment, no longer saw any reason to participate in the movement; (3) fragmentation of the movement and loss of political direction when, after the first lot of apartments had been assigned, the prospects for further immediate results dimmed.

A final limit of the movement is inherent in the very nature of the "extraparliamentary" groups that organized it. The initial victories of the movement were due to its capacity to draw in other political and union forces with direct access to and leverage in centers of institutional power, centers of power from which the *extraparlamentari* were excluded. Because of this dependence on the support of outside forces in order to gain access to the policy-making process, the movement was left, when these forces abandoned it, with no other political resource but disruption. Without a broader political front behind it, such disruptive activities could with relative impunity be either repressed or ignored.

What general conclusions can be drawn from the case of the *movimento per la casa* with regard to the efficacy of protest as a political resource for the urban poor? In his study of the rent strike movement in New York in the 1960s, Lipsky concludes that protest movements are inherently unstable because of four competing demands on their leadership: organizational maintenance, maximization of public exposure, gaining the support of influential third parties, and obtaining concrete results from target groups.[7] This analytical framework provides useful insight into both the successes and the failures of the *movimento per la casa* in Palermo. The problem of organizational maintenance was a critical one: the scarcity of organizational resources, both human and material, the dependence on the voluntary services of outside sympathizers, in this case the students of the extraparliamentary groups, and the crucial importance of being able to point to immediate tangible results in order to sustain participation, made creation of a stable, cohesive, political organization extremely difficult.

The second two factors, maximization of public exposure and third-party support, are highly interdependent in the Palermo case. The extent and nature of media exposure varied directly with the involvement of outside forces, the left-wing parties and the unions, in the struggle, because this involvement gave the demands of the movement a legitimacy they would not otherwise have had. The support of these third parties was essential to the success of the movement because of their access to the policy-making process, from which the representatives of the movement were excluded. This creates a dilemma for such a movement, however, since the broader its goals, the greater the possibility of attracting such crucial third-party support but, by the same token, the greater the difficulty in maintaining one's own organizational base, which is attracted precisely because of the concreteness and immediacy of the movement's goals. As the availability of third-party support is often linked to factors outside the movement's control, the success of a protest movement over time depends on its ability to develop stable and independent political resources so that it does not need to depend on such outside support in order to gain access to institutional channels. The problem is that these are precisely the kinds of resources that are most difficult for a movement based on the poor and powerless to generate.

This brings us to the final issue: the response of target groups. In the case of Palermo, as for Italian protest movements more generally, the targets of protest at the local level tend to be, because of the centralization of decision making, the official representatives of local government, that is, the mayor and the *giunta*. The official response to the *movimento per la casa* strongly reinforces Lipsky's observations about the possibility of responding to protest in such a way as to blunt the cutting edge of the movement without, however, making a commitment to the large-scale resource expenditure that would be necessary to resolve the general problem at the root of the protest. The response of the city administration to the protest movement in Palermo took two forms: symbolic responses and token satisfactions. On the one hand, public expressions of concern, the nomination of the commission, and a series of encounters with movement representatives served as symbolic reassurances to placate popular anger while concrete initiatives to resolve the problem were continually postponed to an indefinite future; with any luck, given the instability of protest movements, there was a good chance that popular pressure would have subsided before the administrators would be compelled to undertake any substantial policy revisions. On the other hand, token satisfactions – responding on an individual basis to "crisis" cases while leaving general conditions unchanged (the distribution of the first lot of 363 apartments) – were used with equal effectiveness to defuse mass discontent into individual channels.

This capacity of the city administration to absorb a potentially threatening protest movement into conventional institutional channels points to the limited ability of excluded groups to exert political influence through protest. Protest by the poor may raise important issues, but, because they lack the resources to enter the bargaining arena directly, they are forced to rely for a solution upon the intervention of third parties; as a result, they have very little impact on the way in which the problem is ultimately resolved. Consequently, such movements, although producing results in individual cases, generally fail to alter the prevailing balance of power or distribution of resources in any meaningful way. In fact, their propensity to produce only symbolic or token solutions without any perceptible change in underlying conditions may in the end so disillusion the movement's supporters that their original apathy and political passivity, and with it their powerlessness, may actually be reinforced.

That this has been at least partially the case is suggested by the results of the June 1976 elections in the low-income neighborhoods of the *centro storico*. Although the Left made marginal gains, the capacity of the DC to recuperate the clientelistic votes of the past after months of a virulent protest movement directed explicitly against the party and its conduct of local government was impressive. Despite its unquestioned political impact in the short run, the *movimento per la casa*, once it subsided, seems to have left barely a trace in terms of more enduring patterns of political behavior. In the new *quartieri* of public housing, on the contrary, similar popular struggles have produced quite different political results. The following section will attempt to explain why.

Borgo Nuovo, CEP, and ZEN: the new ghettos

The setting:

> Borgo Nuovo: Constructed 1956–66, approximately 25,000 inhabitants, of which only about 10% *abusivi* ("illegal occupants"). Social composition: about equally divided between workers, primarily from the Cantiere Navale, and public employees.
>
> CEP (Centro di Edilizia Programmata): Completed 1967, approximately 12,000 inhabitants, of whom about two-thirds are *abusivi*. Social composition: a handful of public employees (many of whom garbage collectors) and factory workers, about 25% construction workers, mostly unskilled, and the remainder *sottoproletariato*.
>
> ZEN (Zona Espansione Nord): Completed 1968–71, approximately 13,000 inhabitants, of whom 90% *abusivi*. Social composition: 10% petty employees, 10% factory workers, remainder unskilled construction workers and *sottoproletariato*.

As shown in Chapter 6, the politics of public housing pursued in Palermo since the mid-1950s has favored the construction of huge projects (ranging from 10,000 to 25,000 inhabitants) on the extreme periphery of the city while relegating the *centro storico* to progressive abandonment and decay. The choice of such a strategy, as opposed to the *risanamento* of the old city, has been largely dictated by the interests of private speculation. Such interests have been promoted, on the one hand, by the siting of public housing in such a way as to increase the value of the intermediate terrains through the provision of the basic infrastructures (streets, water, and electric lines) by the city, whereas ordinarily the provision of such services would have to be paid by the private developer; and, on the other, by the long-term goal behind such a policy – the removal of the poor from the center-city, thereby liberating the *centro storico* for private speculative development (in contrast to left-wing demands for substantial public housing within the *centro storico* as an integral part of the projected *risanamento*).

In Italy the responsibility for the construction of public-housing projects is divided among different levels of government: while the buildings themselves are in general financed by state or regional funds, the procurement of the land and the provision of infrastructures, both primary and secondary, are delegated to local administrations. The prevalence of speculative interests in the determination of public-housing policy in Palermo has meant that once the houses were completed and the minimal infrastructures (streets, water, and electric lines) required to satisfy speculative needs provided, the projects were completely abandoned by the city administration and the IACP (the local public housing authority). As a result, entire blocks of apartments might be held empty for months or even years awaiting action by the city to provide the necessary services to render them inhabitable. Thus, while on paper these projects were model *quartieri*, complete with all the social structures of a self-contained modern city, in reality they were barren cement deserts, completely isolated from the rest of the city and devoid of even the most elementary infrastructures for civilized existence.

Given the severe housing shortage in Palermo, public housing has since the mid-1950s played an important role in the clientelistic politics of the city, both for the DC and the PSI, which has held the presidency of the IACP since 1968. Not only have promises of *case popolari* abounded in the city's slums at the approach of every election, but an apartment in public housing has traditionally been one of the most common rewards for the services of *capi-elettori* and *galoppini*. This use of public housing as a patronage reward explains why so many of the low-income residents of the city remain without decent housing while a significant proportion of the inhabitants of public housing are low-level public employees.

Such electoral manipulation of public housing came to an abrupt halt in January 1968. In the wake of the earthquake, as the entire old city threatened to collapse upon them, thousands of families, evicted from their homes by order of the prefect and offered no other shelter but makeshift tents in the municipal stadium, assaulted by force unoccupied blocks of public housing (see Figure 8.2), many of which had lain empty for months, not only because of the lack of the necessary infrastructures but because they were being reserved for distribution during the campaign for the upcoming parliamentary elections. After an initial attempt to remove the occupants by force had met with fierce resistance, the city administration, under the pressure of continued demonstrations by the earthquake victims (organized by the PCI), gave in; the over 3,000 apartments that had been illegally occupied were requisitioned by the prefect and assigned on a provisional basis to the *abusivi*. Similar waves of illegal occupations continued at regular intervals through 1973, every time a new block of public housing neared completion; in some cases, even unfinished apartments, without plastering, windows, or doors, were occupied as well, so desperate was the need to secure a solid roof for one's family. Despite the city's concession before the *fait accompli* of thousands of illegal occupations, the stipulation of regular contracts

Figure 8.2. A group of families from the *centro storico* "invades" an unfinished public-housing project. *Source: L'Ora.*

was perennially postponed so that the occupants remained for years under the constant threat of possible eviction, a situation that was exploited in turn for electoral advantage. Regularization of the status of the *abusivi* was finally achieved only after several years of continual mobilization and protest (in 1973 in the ZEN, while in the CEP the problem still remained unresolved at the end of 1976).

After this desperate struggle to secure a *casa popolare*, the first reaction of the residents of these new *quartieri* was one of relief and joy at finally having, after years of existence in a crumbling tenement or a makeshift shack, a real roof over their heads and a clean modern apartment worthy of a civilized existence. This joy soon turned to bitter disillusionment and anger, however, when the residents realized that, apart from the new modern facade of the apartments, they had been transferred to a new ghetto, if anything, even worse than the one they had fought so hard to leave. The physical distance between the public-housing projects and the rest of the city, with the nearest bus line at a distance of several kilometers, made getting to one's job, buying food, or getting the children to school a daily ordeal. Because of the total isolation of the *quartieri* from sources of employment, especially for the *sottoproletari*, whose means of subsistence, however meager, were closely tied to the economy of the old city, some residents were actually constrained to give up the apartment so dearly won and move back to the old slum in order to make a living. Because the projects had been occupied illegally and the occupants therefore had no formal legal status, they were denied at the outset even the most elementary necessities of existence – running water and electricity; because of the speculative design discussed above, the water and electric lines were indeed in place, but could not be hooked up until the residents' status had been formalized (in the interim, water was provided in small amounts by trucks from the city and electric lines were tapped illegally until an agreement was reached between the IACP and the responsible city agencies to provide regular service). Sewer lines were nonexistent, so that sewage either ran off in open canals or, as in the case of the ZEN, was collected in inadequate tanks which regularly overflowed into the basements of the apartment buildings, often filling up to ground level and producing an incredible stench and constant fear of epidemics; in addition, the projects had neither paved streets, outdoor lighting, nor regular garbage collection. The residents thus found themselves cut off from the rest of the city, without running water and electricity, submerged in mud, sewage, and garbage, beset by rats and insects, and afraid to venture forth in the total darkness that enveloped the *quartiere* as soon as the sun set (see Figure 8.3). The following comments by residents of the CEP are typical of the reaction to the conditions in which the new *quartieri* had been abandoned:

The ghettos have been transferred here with the same ills as before and even worse . . . We carried our poverty along with us to the CEP, but once here we found, even worse, the possibility of drowning in mud and refuse, of dying of typhus.[8]

They have sent us here to die . . . We have been abandoned in a desert, deported to an island, like in the Stone Age, worse than in a cemetery.[9]

Secondary social services – schools, shops, public offices, first-aid

Figure 8.3. The new ghettos: "model" public-housing projects where the areas designated for social services have become garbage dumps instead.

stations or clinics, recreational facilities – were equally nonexistent. Apart from the shops, the absence of which was quickly compensated for by the setting up of makeshift shacks (unauthorized, of course) to sell basic foodstuffs, the most acutely felt lack was that of schools. Because of the distance separating the projects from the nearest schools and the absence of public transportation, children in a *quartiere* like CEP missed up to two years of school before facilities, still far from adequate for the number of children present, were finally built in the *quartiere*. A survey conducted in the CEP in 1969 not only showed appalling levels of scholastic evasion and illiteracy but demonstrated that the situation had actually worsened since the transfer of the residents from the old city where, despite equal pressures for sending a child out to work, there was at least always a school nearby.[10] The medical situation was equally disastrous – without a pharmacy, first-aid station or clinic in the *quartiere*, there was a very real risk of dying in an emergency before help could be obtained.

Cut off from the city and deprived of all the necessities of civilized life, the sense of isolation and emargination was even more intense than that experienced in the slums of the old city. The solidarity of the *vicolo*, which had played such an important role in mitigating the material deprivation of life in the old neighborhoods, was here nonexistent. The dominant social characteristic of the projects was instead a pervasive sense of atomization and uprootedness, a dissolution of all social bonds and a return to an almost Hobbesian state. Nostalgia for the old *quartiere*, which many returned to visit on a regular basis, remained strong. Whereas in the old neighborhood people lived their lives in constant interaction with their neighbors, in the new *quartieri* they were isolated in individual apartments in impersonal high-rise buildings, from which they departed in the morning and returned only at night. As far as social life was concerned, the projects offered nothing but other identical high-rise structures – no markets, cafes, or even taverns where people could meet to talk, relax, or just pass the time of day.

The social isolation created by the physical structure of the projects and the absence of any aggregative centers was aggravated by the confluence of persons coming from every section of the old city, bringing with them their own distinct customs and traditions and their instinctive diffidence toward the residents of other neighborhoods. The "promiscuity" of the *vicolo* was replaced by the model of the bourgeois family, cloistered in its own private affairs in a social context of anonymity and mutual distrust:

In the new *quartiere* there is a kind of *embourgeoisement* of the poor; they have become atomized, each one on his own. It may seem as if all the families in a single large building live together, but in fact each one is isolated, and all together they are like prisoners at the margins of the city, having lost even their old communal life.[11]

Before, the food shop was right next-door and everyone knew everyone else. Here people don't even speak when they pass on the landing.[12]

These comments are reinforced by data from the CEP survey showing 74% of those interviewed to have no social relationships within
the *quartiere,* while 72% judged their neighbors to be persons with
whom they would not associate.[13] This lack of social solidarity within
the *quartiere* was reflected as well in the external relationships of the
residents, particularly with regard to the inhabitants of the nearby
borgate; mostly small peasant proprietors, the latter treated the new-
comers with intense suspicion and dislike, regarding them as "lumpenproletariat" in the precise Marxist connotation of the term.

What distinguishes the public-housing projects most sharply from
the other *quartieri popolari* of Palermo has been their unusually high
level of electoral support for the PCI, ranging from 30% to 40% of the
vote, in contrast to a city-wide average of only about 17% before
1976, when the PCI vote in Palermo rose to about 24% (see Table
A.3). Particularly striking is the contrast with the slums of the *centro
storico* – the place of origin of the overwhelming majority of the residents of *quartieri* like CEP and ZEN – where with an almost identical
socio-occupational structure, patterns of voting and political participation are radically different.

What factors account for these differences? At the outset it is important to distinguish between two types of public-housing project:
on the one hand, projects where the majority of the apartments were
regularly assigned, like Borgo Nuovo, and where the inhabitants are
for the most part skilled workers or low-level public employees (this
because certain categories of workers pay contributions to a public-
housing fund and therefore have first priority in the distribution of
apartments); on the other hand, *quartieri* like CEP or ZEN, which
from the outset were inhabited almost entirely by illegal occupants
from the *centro storico.* The first case is relatively easy to explain. The
workers from the Cantiere Navale, who represent the majority of
non–white-collar assignees in projects like Borgo Nuovo or Borgo
Ulivia, represent the labor aristocracy in Palermo and are a traditional stronghold of both union and PCI strength. Thus, upon transfer to the new *quartieri,* they not only retained their traditional political loyalties but drew upon their experience of union organization
in the work place to constitute strong and active Comitati di Quartiere ("neighborhood committees") both to mobilize the *quartiere* to
exert pressure on the city government to obtain essential services
and to undertake self-improvement projects within the *quartiere*
(e.g., in Borgo Ulivia the residents have transformed the bare courtyards between the buildings into miniature formal gardens, complete
with statuary, benches, and makeshift lighting).

Projects like these, however, constitute the exception rather than the rule. The situation in projects like CEP and ZEN is very different. These are populated primarily by the classic *sottoproletariato* of the center-city slums, with its deeply rooted mistrust of political parties and collective action and its traditional vulnerability to the petty clientelism of the DC and its coalition partners. How, then, can one explain the remarkable shift in political orientation that accompanied the transfer of these families from the slums of the old city to the new public-housing projects on its extreme periphery? The first factor to consider is the way these people got into the projects. Although they began as a spontaneous movement born of mass desperation in the wake of the earthquake, the illegal occupations were quickly organized and, even more importantly, defended by the PCI, even at the price of battles with the police, in clear contrast to the party's later position with regard to the *movimento per la casa* in 1975–6. The question may then be raised as to whether the high levels of PCI electoral support that ensued should be attributed to a genuine process of politicization resulting from the experience of the occupations, or whether what happened was instead a process of self-selection among potential occupants, such that those persons who in fact participated in the illegal occupations came disproportionately from the minority in the old neighborhoods who were already politically conscious or indeed outright Communist supporters. The answer to this question probably lies somewhere between these two alternatives, as will become clearer from the following discussion.

All available evidence suggests that the unusual electoral strength of the Communists in the public-housing projects is above all a result of the intense struggles that were necessary, first simply to remain in the occupied apartments, and subsequently to obtain even the most elementary infrastructures and social services. When these families arrived in the new *quartieri*, not only did they have to engage in bitter struggles with the police to defend their right to remain, but they found themselves in a virtual desert, with modern apartments to be sure, but nothing else. At this point the urgency of immediate need overcame the legacy of passivity and diffidence, and spontaneous committees (which would later come to be dominated by the Communists) were formed to defend the occupations and mobilize the residents in successive waves of protest to secure the necessities of everyday life – attachment of the water and electric lines, the paving of streets and installation of outdoor lighting, then garbage collection, public transportation, schools, and other services. Each of these essential services was extracted from a recalcitrant city administration only after bitter and prolonged protest, with certain critical problems, like that of the sewer system in the ZEN, still the object of a bureaucratic stalemate almost ten years later.

Although born of exasperation, these struggles, which often saw the women and children in the front line, performed a critical function of political socialization. Even more so than the occupations themselves, which in the last analysis constituted less a mass movement than the sum of thousands of individual solutions, the years of struggle to obtain the basic necessities of everyday life not only impressed upon people the total indifference of the DC-dominated administration, apart from rare electoral appeals, to their most urgent needs (needs which, unlike that of housing, could not be met in an individualistic manner), but demonstrated for the first time the efficacy of collective action to obtain results. As in the case of the *movimento per la casa*, the political mobilization of the residents of the new *quartieri*, while initiated by the *extraparlamentari*, was by 1970–1 dominated for the most part by the PCI. It is important to note, however, that in all of the housing projects protest activities have been conducted not in the name of individual political parties, but rather in that of the Comitato di Quartiere, which includes all sympathetic political and social forces (in most cases the PCI, PSI, the local priest, neighborhood social workers, representatives of the schools – only in rare cases, however, is the DC present in a formal way).

It may well be that the very isolation and atomization of life in the new projects, and the lack even of those basic services the center-city slum had offered, stimulated a recognition of collective interest born of shared adversity, expressing itself in the formation of the first spontaneous committees to organize the struggles for water and electricity. Unlike the apartments themselves, the essential services for which struggles were conducted in the ensuing months were *collective* goods, which could not be obtained through traditional patron – client channels; the urgency of the common need thus broke down traditional diffidences and hostilities within the *quartiere* and brought the residents together in a united and combative front. That the PCI has been the beneficiary of these struggles is less a question of ideology than of the party's superior organizational skills and its capacity to exert leverage within institutional channels for the resolution of certain kinds of problems. The high level of electoral support for the PCI in these *quartieri* is thus in part recognition of the leading organizational role of the party in the successful struggles of the past, and in part probably a generic vote of protest against the neglect of the *quartiere* by city administrations dominated by the DC.

Although the years of struggle have left a clear political mark in the sustained electoral dominance of the PCI, which in many of the projects remains the only political party to maintain a permanent organizational presence, the problems of creating a long-term political movement on the basis of episodic protest have been the same here

as in the case of the *movimento per la casa*. With the resolution of the
most pressing problems, popular response to political initiatives has
fallen off as people once again give priority to their personal pursuits. Beneath the surface, the temper of a *quartiere* like the ZEN remains potentially explosive; with regard to recurrent and directly felt
problems like water shortages and the nonfunctioning of the neighborhood elementary school, for example, the *quartiere* will mobilize
on an immediate and spontaneous basis. In these cases, the problem
confronting the left-wing parties and groups is not how to stimulate
popular protest but rather how to channel and control it. In general,
however, a certain semblance of normality has been achieved in
these *quartieri* and, while electoral support for the Left has as yet not
been affected, both the PCI and the *extraparlamentari* complain of increasing difficulty in mobilizing popular support for political initiatives not directly linked to the immediate needs of the *quartiere*.

Apart from the inherent difficulties of constructing a broader political movement on the basis of immediate material demands, part of
the explanation for the limited scope of the protest movements in
these *quartieri* must be sought in the global political strategy of the
PCI, which has been the principal political force behind these activities. Because of its growing ties to the existing institutional framework, the PCI, while eager to mobilize popular pressures to enhance
its own leverage in local decision making, has consistently sought to
limit such mobilization to immediate concrete demands that can be
dealt with through institutional channels, rather than organizing a
more general attack on global problems whose resolution would require more far-reaching political changes. As with the *movimento per
la casa*, such a strategy in effect passes the initiative to the city administration, which specializes in defusing protest either through
symbolic reassurances or by means of stop-gap emergency measures
that permit it to postpone more serious action until the next crisis
breaks out. As a result, despite increasingly vocal protests over the
past few years, the fundamental structural problems underlying the
city's dismal record of service delivery seem never to be confronted.
Thus, while the emphasis on very concrete, particularized demands
may facilitate mobilization and in the short run increase the perceived efficacy of protest, it leaves both the balance of political power
and the general condition of public services for the poor, not to mention critical underlying problems like unemployment, essentially untouched. In the public-housing projects the poor have learned to organize effectively to exert pressure for the bureaucratic resolution of
specific problems, but they remain excluded from the determination
of the broader policies which in a much more profound way shape
their lives.

The rural *borgate*

The third and final type of *quartiere popolare*, the rural *borgata*, which has retained to a large degree the characteristics of traditional peasant society, constitutes a kind of foil against which to project the social and political reality of the inner-city slums and the new *quartieri* of public housing. Roccella, Brancaccio, and Ciaculli-Croce Verde are three neighboring *borgate* lying along the south-southwestern perimeter of the city in the heart of the Conca d'Oro. Despite increasing encroachment by urban expansion, the primary pursuit of the population, totaling about 30,000 among the three *borgate*, remains agriculture – truck farming for urban markets along the coast and cultivation of citrus groves, primarily tangerines, in the interior areas. The physical structure of the *borgata* is quite distinct from that of the rest of the city. It consists of two single rows of typical two-story peasant dwellings stretched for a distance of 2-3 kilometers along either side of the major arteries connecting Palermo to the adjoining communities; this linear structure is intended to detract as little land as possible from productive uses and to facilitate communications among residents of the *borgata*. There are dozens of such *borgate* scattered throughout the Conca d'Oro surrounding Palermo, each a self-contained and relatively self-sufficient community, quite separate from the rest of the city, at least until the boom of urban expansion beginning in the 1960s, which has increasingly engulfed many of the *borgate*, (see Figure 8.4).

The socioeconomic structure of the *borgata* is essentially that of the traditional peasant village in miniature – a few large landowners, a handful of white-collar employees and professionals, with the overwhelming majority of the population made up of small peasant proprietors and *braccianti* ("agricultural day laborers"). In contrast to the impoverished agriculture of the interior, these are very fertile areas producing high-income crops; as a result, even the small peasant proprietor has traditionally been relatively well off, while the *braccianti*, many of whom own a small plot on the side, are employed year-round and earn quite good wages. Because of the advance of the city into the surrounding countryside and the reluctance of young people to work the land, this traditional socioeconomic structure has been subject to progressive disintegration over the past decade. Of the three *borgate* considered here, Ciaculli-Croce Verde, the most isolated, is the only one to have preserved essentially in its pure form the traditional structure of the *borgata*. Roccella and Brancaccio, because of their greater proximity to the city, have undergone more far-reaching transformations; while the majority of the population is still engaged in agriculture, a rapidly growing minority is made up of

Figure 8.4. The traditional peasant dwellings of the *borgata*, progressively engulfed by speculative development.

white-collar employees or workers in public jobs like the *aziende municipalizzate* (e.g., garbagemen and bus drivers) and the railroads, which have a large locomotive depot in Brancaccio. The breakdown of the self-contained rural community has been further accelerated in the case of Roccella by the construction, beginning in the mid-1970s, of two huge public-housing projects, for which the farmlands of many of the residents of the *borgata* were expropriated. As a result, not only was a large part of the traditional economy of the zone destroyed but thousands of families from the *centro storico*, with an entirely different cultural background and occupational status, were abruptly brought into the *borgata*, causing profound dislocations and hostility on both sides (for discussion of the political repercussions, see later in this section).

Despite the increasing disintegration of the economic unity of the *borgate*, thus far the traditional structures of influence have remained largely intact. The social and political life of the *borgata* still revolves around two central institutions – the Church and the mafia. Like the other *quartieri popolari* we have examined, the *borgate* lack a developed network of associational structures and social services; in their absence, the Church constitutes the only aggregative structure in the community, the center of all social and recreational activity. In the *borgata* the Church retains a much greater social and political role than in the other *quartieri popolari*, because of the closely knit character of the community and the strength of traditional religious sentiment among the predominantly peasant population; in this regard the *borgata* resembles more closely the peasant villages of the interior than the typical urban *quartiere popolare*. As a result, the Church continues to perform a key political function on behalf of the DC, a role that has greatly diminished over the past decade in other parts of the city.

Rivaling the social and political importance of the Church is that of the mafia. The influence structure of the *borgata* remains rooted in traditional patron–client relationships, based on the independent economic power and personal prestige of the notable, who in this case is represented by the *capo-mafia* of the *borgata*. In the *borgate*, the model of the classic agrarian mafia, of the "person of respect" to whom everyone in the community turns for assistance and advice, remains intact. Despite socioeconomic changes, the majority of the inhabitants of the *borgate* still depend for their very existence on the local mafia boss who controls land, employment, credit, the marketing of produce and, most important of all for the small peasant proprietor, access to water for irrigation. All the water resources of the Conca d'Oro are in the hands of the mafia, constituting a constant instrument of blackmail against the small farmer, whose economic survival depends upon having the right amounts of water at the right times.

Apart from these traditional levers of control over the local economy, the *capi-mafia* of the *borgate* have succeeded in penetrating virtually all the public agencies concerned with local agricultural affairs. A classic example, dating from early 1960s, is that of the massive campaign mounted by the regional government against the Argentine ant, a deadly citrus fruit parasite. The regional assessor of agriculture established a special consortium made up of committees from each commune of the coastal plain and each zone of *borgate* to organize the campaign. This consortium, with 120 million lire (U.S. $200,000) at its disposal, provided each committee with a stock of the insecticide and the necessary equipment for its application, as well as delegating to it the task of hiring and paying the required workers. Each committee was headed by the "most representative" personalities from the zone – in each case, the local mafia bosses together with representatives of the DC and the Coltivatori Diretti. The *capi-mafia* thus became comanagers of an important public program with vast economic consequences for the individual cultivator. The substantial public resources that had been allocated for the program never reached the bulk of the small growers; instead they were concentrated in the hands of a small elite of political and mafia bosses who used them to favor a restricted circle of "friends" as well as selling large amounts of the insecticide at a profit on the private market.[14]

As illustrated in Chapter 6, in the course of the 1960s there occurred a tight interpenetration between the mafia and certain sectors of the DC. Nowhere was this penetration more complete than in the *borgate*. Originally linked to the Monarchists in the immediate postwar period, the *capi-mafia* of the *borgate* soon sensed the direction in which the wind was blowing and either directly shifted their allegiance to the DC or else supported those Monarchist bosses who had themselves joined forces with the DC. Because of the function of the local *capi-mafia* as *grandi elettori*, the electoral predominance of the DC in the *borgate* has, since the mid-1950s, been overwhelming, with the other parties reduced to little more than a token presence (see Table A.3 for electoral results).

The immense economic leverage of the mafia over the individual peasant or *bracciante* is reinforced by three direct institutional supports for the DC, which form a kind of interlocking system of power together with the Church and the mafia. The first and most powerful of these is the Coltivatori Diretti, the DC-controlled organization of small peasant proprietors, analogous to the associations of shopkeepers and artisans discussed in Chapter 5. The Coldiretti performs a central intermediary role between the peasant and the state in matters of pensions, credit, etc., as well as controlling the all-important Cassa Mutua, the official organ of health insurance and medical assistance for the peasantry. Throughout the South, the Coldiretti has constituted the key electoral arm of the DC in the countryside, a stronghold for the party's most conservative factions as well as a personal fiefdom for certain powerful politicians. In the South, the Coldiretti holds a virtual monopoly over the organization of the peasants; in the province of Palermo, for example, it controlled 97.3% of the votes for the administrative board of the Cassa Mutua in 1976, the remainder of the votes being divided among the two competing associations on the Left.[15]

An analogous role to that of the Coldiretti has been played by the FISBA (the agricultural laborers' union of the CISL) among the *braccianti*. In the *borgate* the FISBA is a mass organization, recruiting not only *braccianti* but many small proprietors as well, who are falsely registered as *braccianti* in order to obtain family allowances and unemployment benefits, from which the union leader receives a substantial cut in return for his complicity. Like the Coldiretti, the FISBA has served as a direct patronage extension of the DC, in collusion with rather than in opposition to the local mafia bosses. Rather than organizing union struggles on behalf of its members, the FISBA, like its counterpart in the CGIL, limits its activities in the *borgate* to assistance. With regard to more serious matters, a tacit agreement has been reached between the unions and the mafia, such that the *braccianti* receive higher than contractual wages in return for a guarantee of noninterference on the part of the unions.[16]

The final center of DC influence in the *borgate* is the *delegazione communale*, a kind of little City Hall with the power to issue a range of personal documents and to perform certain routine bureaucratic procedures. While these powers are formally quite limited, they constitute, together with the symbolic function of the *delegato* ("the mayor's representative"), a direct link between the populace and the mayor, a significant reserve of petty favors that can be used with great effect to build up a personal clientele for the *delegato*, who is appointed directly by the mayor. The following remarks by an employee in one of these *delegazioni* are indicative of the potential scope of such influence:

Since Bronte [the *delegato*] is a good fellow and wants to help people out, he makes us do things that we aren't supposed to do (e.g., issuing a document without the required investigation as to the validity of the information provided, or accepting the signature of a relative for an individual who is aged or ill, since the *delegato* knows the individual personally). What can we do, *signorina*, these are poor people who need our help. [To which remark a fellow employee added, with obvious pride, "These things don't happen in other places!"][17]

With these discretionary powers, however trivial they may seem, the *delegato* in a very real sense takes on the prestige of the mayor in the eyes of the residents of the *borgata*; he is the personification of the power and authority of the city administration. Each of the levers of power discussed in the preceding paragraphs reinforces the others; their combined effect, together with the network of lifelong personal relationships binding their representatives to the rest of the population, has been to create a virtually unchallengeable DC monopoly stretching across the *borgate* of Palermo.

Into this world of peasant self-sufficiency and mafia *prepotenza*, marked by extreme diffidence toward outsiders and the traditional *omertà* of the Sicilian countryside, politics, apart from the ritual of voting on election day, rarely enters. Both the land occupations of the immediate postwar period and the great union struggles of the *braccianti* in the 1960s – the two high points of left-wing mobilization in postwar Sicily – left the *borgate* virtually untouched. Here there is no tradition of struggle, the organizations of the peasants and the *braccianti* existing only for corporative and welfare ends. Yet, beginning in the summer of 1975, and continuing through 1976, the *borgata* of Roccella was gripped by an intense political controversy, one which brought into question the very bases of the city's policies for public housing and urban expansion.

The roots of the controversy go back to the early 1960s and the approval of the PRG, which designated, on the southern flank of the city, the areas on the seaward side of the *circonvallazione* for large installations of public housing, and those between the *circonvallazione* and the mountains for private development; this dividing line corresponded to a predominance of small peasant proprietors in the former area, and large estates – one of which linked to the family of none other than Gioia himself – in the latter. At the time the plan was formulated, there was little protest, because everyone hoped to be among those who would profit by the increase in land values resulting from the construction of the *case popolari*. When, in mid-1975, however, the moment of truth arrived and hundreds of small farmers were notified that their lands, among the most fertile in the entire Conca d'Oro, were to be expropriated, the *borgata* rose up in a state verging on open warfare with the city authorities. Apart from bitterness at the loss of their lands, which at this point was irreversible, the real focus of the protest was the question of compensation: in contrast to the going speculative rate of 20,000–30,000 lire/sq. meter, the rate for public expropriation of agricultural land was only about 1,000 lire/sq. meter.

Underlying the protest was the conviction of political favoritism in the selection of the areas to be expropriated, with the small peasant proprietors accusing the administration of having drawn up the plans in such a way as to expropriate the mass of smallholders while excluding neighboring terrains belonging to large landowners with political connections, lands that would thereby be opened to lucrative speculative development. The PCI, which might have been expected to exploit such an opportunity to make things difficult for the *fanfaniani*, who at this time still controlled the city administration, made only a token effort to defend the peasants, both because this was a zone in which they felt that they stood to gain very little politically and because they were under pressure from the construction workers' union and the growing protest movement of residents of the *centro storico* to support the immediate realization of the proposed public housing. Thus, "betrayed" by their own party and finding nowhere else to turn for support, the protesters finally accepted a compromise solution of 2,500 lire/sq. meter, a price still below even the agricultural value of the land, and even so, months passed before many of them were in fact compensated.

The construction of the *case popolari* in this area, following, as in the past, the logic of private speculative interests, demonstrated, by its destruction of one of the few remaining viable sectors of the local economy and by the hostility it provoked among a traditional DC electorate, the potential contradictions in the system of social alliances built up so effectively by the DC over the previous twenty years. The bitterness produced by this episode runs very deep, especially as many of those who were expropriated had been faithful clients of the DC and even, in some cases, *capi-elettori* and *galoppini*. During the campaign for the 1976 elections, the traditional DC candidates in the zone were greeted by angry protesters. When the electoral results came in, they showed a strong backlash against the former "protectors" of the *borgata;* because of the unwillingness of the PCI to enter the struggle on behalf of the peasants, however, this backlash resulted less in a large-scale loss of votes for the DC as such than in a massive shift of preference votes away from the traditional DC "patrons." While this time, due to the absence of effective alternatives, the DC suffered only minor losses, the danger signs were clear – a first ominous crack had appeared in the heretofore monolithic structure of DC control in the *borgate*.

The three neighborhood studies presented above demonstrate the potential for strains within the DC system of consensus – on the one hand because of the inability of the local administration to provide adequate public services, on the other because of the emergence of conflicts among different sectors of the DC's social base (e.g., the interests of private speculation vs. demands for the *risanamento* of the *centro storico* and preservation of the agricultural economy of the *borgate,* or the contrasts between the residents of the *borgate* and the new public-housing tenants). They demonstrate as well, however,

the resilience of the machine and the extreme difficulty facing the opposition in attempting to go beyond episodic protest to create a
broader political alternative. Given the social disaggregation of the
quartieri popolari, which thus far have been the focus of protest
movements against the local administration, success in organizing
people for other than immediate material demands – demands that
thus far have been absorbed with relative ease by the existing clientelistic regime – has been very limited. The problem, it would seem,
is one of perceived alternatives. With key resources concentrated in
the hands of the DC and its allies, the Left has little to offer but a
generic vote of protest or a long-term prospect of social and political
change. It is not that most of the poor do not understand the largely
one-sided nature of their relationship with the DC, rather that they
see no better alternative. In a situation of severe resource constraints
like that of Palermo, the choice between ideology and the possibility
of immediate concrete benefits, however limited, through personal
ties is only too clear. In the words of a Sicilian proverb, "Megghiu 'u
tintu canusciutu ca 'u nuovu a canusciri" ("Better a known evil than
an unknown good").

9
Why does clientelism survive?

The image that emerges from the preceding chapters is one of a stagnant, immobile political system, in which political control is so complete as to make change from within almost impossible. Such a conclusion, pessimistic though it may be, is, I believe, the only one possible on the basis of the evidence presented here and any reasonable projections as to developments in national politics in the foreseeable future. The justification for such a conclusion is to be found in the particular strengths of clientelism as an instrument of political mobilization and in its relationship to fundamental economic and social structural variables.

The strength of the machine as an organizer of consensus lies above all in its incentive structure which, because of the direct particularistic bond linking the machine to its electorate, maximizes the incentive to individual participation. Mancur Olson's *The Logic of Collective Action* (1968) provides an excellent theoretical basis for understanding the strength of the patron – client bond as an instrument of political support. Taking as a point of departure the premise of the rational and self-interested behavior of individuals, Olson points to a fundamental obstacle to group formation: while the members of a group may have a common interest in the potential gains from group activity, there is no incentive for any individual member to assume the costs of participation necessary to achieve the goals of the group, because he will in any case participate in any collective benefits attained. Olson argues that, in order to function, voluntary organizations must offer their members "some separate incentive, distinct from the achievement of the common or group interest," an incentive that "operates not indiscriminately, like the collective good, upon the group as a whole, but rather selectively toward the individuals in the group,"[1] so that those who do not contribute to the organization can be excluded from this incentive. According to Olson's analysis, the smaller the group, the greater the incentive to individual participation, because the relationship between the input of the individual member and the benefits he receives is clearer, and the greater the possibility of control over the contribution of each member.

It follows that, from this perspective, the patron–client relationship, based on a direct exchange of favors between two actors, is the optimal social group, because the incentive to individual participation is maximized. The strength of the machine as an instrument for mobilizing political support is identical to that of the simple patron – client relationship. As it is based on the direct exchange of short-term material benefits, "striv[ing] mainly for benefits that accrue to particular individuals, rather than for the common interests of any large group,"[2] the machine represents, in Olson's terms, the only type of political organization to which it makes sense for a "rational" individual to adhere.

Essential to discussion of the incentive structure of the machine is the question of the resource base required to support a clientelistic system of political power. As indicated in the Introduction, many studies have argued that, because mass support is based on the distribution of short-term material benefits, such political systems require access to an expanding resource base in order to sustain power over time. These inevitable inflationary tendencies are seen as posing an inherent limit to the scope and duration of systems of political support based on clientelistic incentives, a limit to be found either in the restricted resource base of the economy (the case in most developing countries) or in the impact of economic crisis. With regard to the specific case of southern Italy, proponents of this argument sustain that, while until the present a flow of resources from the state (in the form of local government spending, transfer payments, and development funds from the Cassa per il Mezzogiorno) has compensated for the severe resource constraints of the southern economy, the current economic crisis, by shrinking the resource base available for patronage politics, will progressively undermine the local political machines that dominate much of the South.[3]

The evidence presented in the preceding chapters on the bases of support for the Christian Democratic Party in Palermo demonstrates the limits of such an analysis. Because of the severe resource constraints under which local government operates and the broad base of consensus generated by the DC, Palermo can be viewed as a kind of test case for a theory of clientelism that links sustained support to an expanding resource base. That there has been a tremendous expenditure of public resources for patronage purposes in Palermo cannot be denied. In fact, it could be argued that, although state spending has been quite limited in Sicily, it has been compensated for by a sustained flow of resources from the regional government which, because of the special status granted to Sicily in 1946, has a degree of both political and financial autonomy unparalleled in any of the regular regional governments (instituted only in 1970). Such an argument is supported by data on the size and compensation of the regional bureaucracy as well as by the scope of regional expenditures for public works, low-cost credit, and industrial salvage programs like ESPI. The beneficiaries of this patronage spending by the Region, which has drained resources that might otherwise have been invested in public services or economic development projects, have been above all public employees and certain sectors of the entrepreneurial class. On the other hand, the limitations of the resource argument become manifest when one considers the cases of the building contractors, the traditional middle classes, and the urban poor. Each of these groups has constituted an important pillar of DC power in Palermo and yet, in terms of direct patronage spending, has received practically nothing. In addition, far from incurring ever-larger expenditures in its quest for clientelistic consensus, the Sicilian Region has in fact been plagued since its inception with massive *residui passivi* ("funds allocated but never spent"), totaling 1,369,636,000,000 lire (over U.S. $2.2 billion) in 1978.[4]

The key to the strength and durability of the DC machine in Palermo, I would maintain, lies in the nature of the linkages between the DC and groups like the building contractors, the traditional middle classes, and the urban poor. Here, as in the case of public employees, the relationship is based on a direct exchange of short-term particularistic benefits, but in this case the benefits, although implying significant economic advantages or disadvantages for the individual recipient, are not necessarily *monetary*, and therefore do not require any expenditure of public resources. Patronage mechanisms like the issuing of construction and commercial licenses, variations to the city plan, the wide range of police powers of local government, and bureaucratic intervention on behalf of the urban poor are central to the maintenance of DC power, but, in terms of direct public spending, cost nothing. (This is not to say, of course, that they may not imply a high social cost in the long run, because of the favoring of individual benefits at the expense of broader social policy and of private at the expense of collective interests, but this is another issue.)

Looked at from this perspective, it is clear that the essence of DC power lies not in the quantity of resources the party is able to distribute, but rather in its monopoly hold on all resources, whatever their level, and in its control over all the critical interstices of society – political, economic, and social – so that the party becomes an obligatory intermediary in all transactions between the individual and public power. With regard to the nature of patronage resources, it is important to reaffirm as well the personal bond underlying the clientelistic relationship. In many cases, once created, this personal bond can endure over relatively long periods of time without continual reinforcement by subsequent acts of exchange. It is not that the nature of the relationship has been transformed from an instrumental one into one based purely on affective ties, but rather that the affective element sustains the bond in expectation of future benefits, even if immediate rewards are not forthcoming.

Given, then, such a monopoly of resources in the hands of the dominant party, combined with important nonmonetary sources of clientelistic support – the regulatory powers of local government, the function of bureaucratic intermediation, and the enduring nature of the patron–client bond – not only is an expanding resource base not essential to the survival of the machine but economic crisis alone is not a sufficient condition for the disintegration of a system of political support based on clientelistic bonds. This is not to say that the machine may not, and often does, have inflationary consequences, but rather to argue that such consequences are not a *necessary* component of the machine as a model for the mobilization of political consent. The critical case for understanding the nature of the machine must be sought not in a situation of relative abundance, when the machine may well produce high levels of resource expenditure, but rather in a situation of economic crisis, when that resource base is drastically reduced. It is under such circumstances (epitomized by southern Italy since 1973–4) that, I would argue, the essence of the machine emerges most clearly. Far from destroying the bases of support for the machine, the impact of economic crisis may be just the opposite. As the already restricted resource base of the society shrinks even further, the role of the dominant party as the privileged channel of access to the few remaining resources may actually be enhanced.[5]

A second crucial element explaining the strength of clientelism in Palermo and throughout much of the South is the relationship between local and national power. The first consideration in this regard must be that of the progressive expansion of state intervention in the postwar period, which has permitted the party holding governmental power to extend its control into a wide range of social and economic activities that elsewhere are confined to the private sphere. The second important consideration is the centralization of the Italian state and the uninterrupted control of the national government by the same party that dominates local politics in most of the South, thereby providing privileged access to the resources of the state by the holders of local power. In this context it is necessary to distinguish between domination by the DC as a party and domination by one faction within that party. The most important factor for understanding the monopoly power of the *fanfaniani* in Palermo between 1956 and 1976 is the structure of power within the DC. While the sources of electoral support for the machine in Palermo are clearly local, the total domination of the party by a single faction and the methods by which opposition has been stifled within both the party and the local government arena would not be possible without the protection of the local DC bosses by the national party leadership. This protection continues, despite national scandals involving personalities like Gioia, Lima, and Ciancimino, because of the logic of factional struggle within the DC. So long as the votes that leaders like Gioia and Lima can carry to the national party congress are essential to the success of their respective "patrons," meaningful change from within the DC at the local level is highly unlikely.

In the final analysis, however, the perpetuation of clientelism in southern Italy is dependent upon national power and policy in an even more fundamental way. A key variable underlying DC power in Palermo is the economic structure of the city and the social fragmentation associated with it, which impede the aggregation of political demand and the organization of collective interests necessary for the emergence of an alternative model of political behavior. The monopolization of economic resources in the hands of the DC is possible because of the absence of an autonomous resource base at the local level and the consequent dependence of the local economy on the resources of the state. Once all centers of both local and extralocal power are centralized in the hands of one party, an expanding stock of resources is no longer necessary; indeed, the power of the party rests rather on the manipulation of *scarcity*, on maintaining large numbers of people in competition for scarce resources, all of which are channeled through the party. In such a situation, there is little incentive for the party to stimulate productive investment. It is in fact economic development rather than economic crisis that presents the greater threat to a clientelistic regime, because it offers the possibility of creating alternative sources of economic goods that might eventually elude strict political control, as well as an industrial working class which, even if subject to clientelistic control in the short run, provides a potential focus for alternative models of political aggregation and mobilization.

While the possibility for a clientelistic model of politics to take root in the South at the end of World War II was clearly related to a preexisting state of economic underdevelopment, the situation since then can be described as one of a mutually reinforcing bond between the structure of political power and the socioeconomic base upon which it rests. Through its political control the DC has sought to perpetuate the very conditions of resource shortage and social fragmentation upon which the survival of the system of power it has created depends. The types of investment policies that have been implemented in the South support such an hypothesis. While there has been substantial industrial investment in the South over the past twenty-five years, it has been limited for the most part to investments with only a minimal impact on the local economic and political context, so as not to undermine the bases of local clientelistic control. Similar conclusions can be drawn from the studies of the relationship between politicians and entrepreneurs in Salerno and Catania cited in Chapter 5 or the case of regional industrial development programs in Sicily: public funds intended to promote economic development have been employed instead in such a manner as to reinforce the conditions of economic marginality and dependence they were supposed to overcome. Thus, while described by many scholars as a transitional form of political organization, this evidence demonstrates that a mass-based clientelistic party, having once established control over key resources, can block precisely that process of autonomous economic development which is seen as bringing about its eventual demise, thereby perpetuating the structural bases of its own power.

This analysis suggests that social and economic change sufficient to break through the vicious circle of marginality and dependency in which the South is caught cannot come about without a prior transformation in the structure of political power. The evidence presented in the preceding chapters minimizes the probability of political change from within the DC, at either the local or the national level. If that is the case, the only alternative to the machine in southern Italy would seem to be the Left (this means, in the Italian context, primarily the Communist Party). Although the Left has proved impotent in Palermo and other major Sicilian cities like Catania and Messina, the largest southern city, Naples, provides a concrete example of the defeat of the machine by a left-wing coalition led by the Communist Party. Part III will first explore the causes of that defeat and then assess the successes and failures of left-wing rule in Naples in the period 1975–80, in an attempt to bring the experience of Naples to bear on the more general issue of the strengths and weaknesses of clientelism both as an instrument of mobilizing mass political support and as a system of urban government.

Part III

The prospects and the limits of change

10

Naples under the Left

The picture just painted of a deeply rooted clientelistic regime in Palermo and the pessimistic conclusions as to the possibility of political change at the local level could have been written equally well with reference to Neapolitan politics in the early 1970s. And yet, in 1975 the Christian Democratic machine in Naples suffered a stunning electoral defeat, being replaced as the city's leading party by the Communists. This chapter will seek to explain why, in contrast to the conclusions of Part II on the strengths of clientelism in a socioeconomic context like that of southern Italy, the machine lost its mass base in Naples. It will then assess what the first five years of left-wing rule have meant for Naples, as well as raising, on the basis of this experience, the question of the degree to which the change in administration has succeeded in transforming the fundamental contours of political life in the South.

The reign of the machine

To understand Naples under the Left, it is necessary first to look briefly at Neapolitan politics before 1975. Throughout the postwar period Naples constituted a major stronghold of right-wing strength in Italy. In the institutional referendum of 1946, almost 80% of Neapolitans voted for the monarchy (in contrast to a national figure of only 46%), and from 1952 until 1958 the city gave overwhelming support to the Monarchist administrations of the shipping magnate Achille Lauro, whose appeal was based on a combination of populist antistatism and petty clientelism. Only in 1958, when Lauro's administration was dissolved by prefectural decree after a long history of scandals and corruption, were the Monarchists displaced as the city's leading party by the Christian Democrats.[1] From the early 1960s until 1975 both the local DC organization and the municipal and provincial administrations were dominated by a powerful machine in the hands of the Gava family, local representatives of the *doroteo* faction of the DC.[2] At its peak the Gava machine seemed omnipotent, extending its control into every aspect of social, economic, and political life and monopolizing the levers of political and economic power in the city. Like the DC machine in Palermo, the Gavas consolidated their power through manipulation of the resources of local government and control over the local labor market, creating a far-reaching network of patronage linking virtually every social group in the city (with the partial exclusion of the industrial working class) to the party.

At the height of its power, in the early 1970s, the Gava machine seemed even more powerful than its counterpart in Palermo, because of the close ties to national power of the Gava family. Silvio Gava, the "patriarch," one of the founders of the DC in 1943, has been a member of the party's national executive council since 1944, a senator since 1948, and a high-ranking member of almost every government from 1949 until 1973 (he served in the key position of minister of industry from 1970 to 1972); his son, Antonio, who runs the family's affairs at the local level, was named in 1975 to head the DC's national office for local government affairs and then, in 1980, himself became a minister in the first Forlani government.[3] This direct access to centers of national power and thereby to channels of state spending gave the Gavas control over critical sectors of the Neapolitan economy, in particular banking and credit, public works, and the state-controlled firms that account for 70% of Neapolitan industry. Given the weight of the public sector in the Neapolitan economy, the Gavas' political empire seemed virtually unassailable.

And yet, in June 1975 the Gava machine suffered a stunning defeat, losing control of one of the principal pillars of its power, the municipal and provincial administrations. The Communist Party became the city's first party, winning almost 33% of the vote and, after three months of bitter and inconclusive negotiations with the DC and its former coalition partners, formed a minority administration with the Socialist Party (PSI), later joined by the Republicans (PRI) and Social Democrats (PSDI), in order to save the city from total administrative paralysis. In the parliamentary elections of June 1976, after less than a year in office, the Communists went on to reap an astonishing 41% of the vote in Naples, a figure heretofore reserved for traditional Communist strongholds like Bologna and, to many observers, inconceivable in this city notorious for its steadfast support first of Monarchist and then of Christian Democratic bosses. (See Table A.4 for electoral results.)

How can such a rapid and radical shift in the political orientation of a city like Naples be explained? At the most obvious level, one could point to the scandals and misgovernment of the previous DC administrations, to the crisis of local finance in Italy, which, combined with the more general economic crisis, has narrowed the margins for the politics of mass patronage upon which the city's rulers had relied for the past thirty years, and to the growing discontent provoked by the impact of the worsening economic crisis on the already fragile economic structure of the city. None of these factors can be entirely disregarded, but their explanatory value is undermined by the example of Palermo, where each of these factors weighs at least as heavily, if not more so, than in Naples, and where the local DC machine actually strengthened its position in the administrative elections of 1975 and 1980. Why, then, did such an unexpected political upheaval occur in Naples? Why in Naples, in contrast to Palermo, was the DC monopoly over key centers of political and economic power no longer sufficient to guarantee electoral success? What can the defeat of the Gava machine and the subsequent experience of Communist-led administrations in Naples tell us both about the strengths and weaknesses of clientelism as an instrument for mobilizing mass political support and about the potential and limitations of left-wing rule as an alternative model of local government?

The turn to the Left

Despite the overall weakness of the industrial sector in the Neapolitan economy (see Chapter 2), Naples has, because of the presence of large publicly sustained firms like the Italsider steelworks and, more recently, the Alfa Sud automobile factory, traditionally had a small, but compact and combative, working-class nucleus, a focal point for trade-union and left-wing political organization that has been much weaker in a more purely tertiary city like Palermo. As a result, the PCI has throughout the postwar period maintained a much stronger grass-roots presence in Naples than in Palermo. Although, before 1975, the DC and the Right dominated all local administrations, the PCI vote had since 1960 approximated the national average (23%-28%);[4] in addition, because of the unusual strength of the neo-Fascist Right (MSI) in Naples, the gap between the PCI and the DC has consistently been narrower than in other southern cities.

Even given this preexisting organizational and electoral base, however, the PCI gains of 1975 and 1976 were extraordinary (a gain of 13 percentage points between 1972 and 1976). To a certain extent, it can be argued that the 1975 and 1976 votes in Naples were the

product of the broader swing to the Left that swept Italy in 1975, itself the result of two converging factors: (1) a shift to the left of a significant segment of the Italian bourgeoisie (in particular professionals and intellectuals); and (2) an increasing bipolarization of
Italian politics, as a large proportion of the vote previously going to
the minor parties of the Right and Left was absorbed into the two
major mass parties.[5] This latter trend was particularly noticeable
with regard to the Left in Naples, where the Socialists, reduced to
less than 5% of the vote in 1976, have been completely eclipsed by
the Communists. The conformity of the Neapolitan vote in 1975 and
1976 to the general outlines of the national results was welcomed by
many observers as evidence that, 100 years after Italian unification,
the political unity of North and South had finally been achieved.

However, while transformations in the social and political climate
at the national level clearly played a part in the Neapolitan vote, a full
understanding of the causes of the PCI victory requires a closer analysis of the local situation after 1970. Although, already by 1970, there
were growing signs of division and discontent within the local
Christian Democratic organization, there was little reason to believe
that the DC (with 34% of the vote in the 1970 administrative elections) would not easily retain the relative majority in 1975. Observers
on both sides of the political fence agree that the "moment of truth"
arrived in August-September 1973, when Naples was struck by a
sudden outbreak of cholera and, for a few agonizing weeks, the
threat of a major epidemic loomed over the city. The crisis situation
created by the cholera outbreak, in its exposure of the shocking degradation of the city's sanitary structures (for example, Naples' sewer
system is still that of 1888, even though the city's inhabited area has
doubled just since World War II), laid brutally bare the consequences
of twenty years of clientelistic power. As in Palermo, between the
1950s and the beginning of the 1970s the already precarious sanitary
situation of the city was further exacerbated by wave after wave of
uncontrolled speculation, with entire neighborhoods the size of
small cities springing up on the periphery without the most basic
urban infrastructures. At the same time the slums of the *centro
storico*, already infamous 100 years ago for their crumbling housing,
extreme overcrowding, and appalling conditions of health and hygiene, were abandoned to ever more rapid decay. Even before the
cholera outbreak, the levels of infant mortality and infectious diseases in Naples were the highest in Italy and rivaled those of Third
World cities.[6] From this perspective, what was surprising about the
cholera outbreak was not its occurrence, but rather its failure to develop into a full-blown epidemic.

Above all, the crisis exposed the total incapacity of the incumbent DC administration. In the face of an emergency situation, the "establishment" was paralyzed. Into the void stepped the PCI, rising to the occasion with an impressive demonstration of organizational capacity and administrative efficiency. As the total disorganization of the authorities became evident, the party mobilized both the Provincial Federation and the neighborhood sections to maintain calm among a panicked population, set up inoculation centers, and organized special precautionary hygienic measures. Throughout the cholera crisis the PCI projected the image of a "party of government," a party capable of honest and efficient administration in contrast to the incompetence and immobility of the DC and the established power structure. As the secretary of the PCI Federation at that time put it, "In those critical days we *were* the government of the city. Even the Prefect was calling the Federation to ask what to do."[7]

In terms of the local situation 1973 was clearly a turning point, even if the magnitude of the changes in public opinion that had occurred was not revealed until June 1975. The key social groups behind the electoral shift of 1975 in Naples were, on the one hand, the white-collar and professional middle classes and, on the other, the *sottoproletariato*. While the PCI advanced substantially in all neighborhoods of the city, surpassing 60% of the vote in some working-class neighborhoods, a breakdown by neighborhood shows the most substantial increases in 1975 and 1976 in middle-class neighborhoods and in the slums of the old city (see Table A.5). A warning of the changing attitudes of the middle class, heretofore a moderate and highly traditional force in Italian politics, especially in the South, came in the 1974 referendum on divorce. For the DC, which had campaigned vigorously for repeal of the existing divorce legislation, the outcome was a major shock; 59% of Italians voted in favor of divorce and over 60% of Neapolitans who, because of the city's reputation as a stronghold of the Right, had been expected to provide especially strong support for the antidivorce forces.

These results demonstrated the increasing autonomy of the traditional Catholic electorate, which had heretofore constituted one of the principal pillars of DC power. Among a significant segment of the Italian middle class, this new-found autonomy related not only to issues of individual conscience, like divorce or abortion, but had a more general political component as well; fed by a growing disgust with DC corruption and inefficiency, it reflected an increasing openness to the possibility of Communist participation in government. Although in general this trend was less evident in the South than in the North, in Naples it was reinforced by the vivid experience of the cholera crisis, in terms both of the demonstrated incapacity of the DC administration to protect the middle class from the threat of epidemic and of the contrasting display of organization and efficiency on the part of the PCI. So long as the degradation of the urban fabric had been perceived as primarily a matter of the low-income neighborhoods of the old city or the urban periphery, the political outlook of the middle class had been little affected by scandals over real-estate speculation, substandard housing, and inadequate water and sewage facilities. When such conditions threatened to set off a city-wide epidemic, however, the fruits of misgovernment became much more immediate and the prospect of an alternative more attractive.

The case of the urban poor, the second major pillar of the PCI victories of 1975 and 1976, provides a fascinating example of the potential for crisis within a deeply rooted system of clientelistic power. A critical factor for the understanding of Neapolitan politics after 1970 is the changing relationship between the working class and the *sottoproletariato*. Traditionally, Naples' vast "marginal" labor force had constituted a reservoir of votes for demagogic right-wing movements and unscrupulous machine bosses. However, in the wake of the intense workers' struggles of Italy's "Hot Autumn" of 1969 (struggles bitterly fought by Naples' working-class nucleus as well), a part of the *sottoproletariato* began to become politicized. An explanation for such politicization must be sought in the neighborhood structure of the city. Within the low-income neighborhoods of Naples, whether the slums of the old city or the new public-housing projects of the periphery, it is often difficult to make a clear distinction between the stable industrial working class and the "marginal" labor force; within the same neighborhood and often within the same family, one finds the steel or automobile worker side by side with the street-vendor, junk collector, or unemployed day laborer. After 1969 the effect of contagion, which had traditionally been one of hegemony of the attitudes of the *sottoproletariato* upon the working class, began to work in the opposite direction; the lesson of organization learned from the successful workers' struggles began to make inroads upon the traditional cynicism and individualism of the Neapolitan slum. These changes were hastened by the fact that, with the onset of the economic crisis, increasing numbers of the unemployed were no longer the traditional *mille mestieri*, but rather ex-factory workers or youth with high-school or even college diplomas, who brought with them a very different attitude toward, and experience of, collective action.

Here, too, the real turning point came in 1973 in the wake of the cholera outbreak. The economic damage inflicted by the crisis was immense and struck directly at the heart of the city's "marginal" economy. As, according to official reports, the virus had been brought into the city by contaminated shellfish, one of the few initiatives taken by the authorities was a series of dramatic police actions against the fishermen and the hundreds of street-vendors and owners of small bars and restaurants who could not demonstrate compliance with official standards of hygiene. The effect was to reduce drastically the margins of subsistence for thousands of Neapolitan poor. The immediate reaction was desperate, but doomed, mass resistance to the police actions. Subsequently, however, the unemployed and the underemployed, under the leadership of student groups of the "extraparliamentary Left," began to organize a new movement, the *disoccupati organizzati* ("the organized unemployed"), which within a few years would revolutionize the face of Neapolitan politics.[8]

Heretofore the very heart of politics in Naples had been the ability of the dominant party to exert an almost iron-clad control over the local labor market. In a situation of mass unemployment, the need for a political patron in order to obtain a job had provided a large and reliable mass base for the DC and its centrist allies (in southern Italy the small lay parties – PSDI, PRI, PLI – are generally deeply involved in clientelistic politics at the local level). The creation of an organized movement of the unemployed challenged the very foundations of clientelistic power in Naples. Boasting 10,000–15,000 active members at its peak (1975–6), the movement was based upon a radically different conception of the *posto di lavoro* ("job or position"), no longer regarded as an individual favor to be conceded by the powerful but rather as a fundamental right to be conquered through collective struggle. The unemployed imposed their own "lists of struggle" upon the state employment office, insisting that those who actively participated in the protest demonstrations, which soon became a daily and increasingly violent fact of life in Naples, should have first priority when jobs became available. This entrance of collective organization into a sector of society previously characterized above all by its lack of any poles of social or political aggregation marked a first critical breach in the old structure of power.

The Left in power, 1975–9

Thus, on the crest of two very different but converging movements, the shift to the left of important sectors of the middle class and the birth of new forms of mass struggle among the urban poor, two key pillars of DC power in Naples were seriously weakened, and the PCI became the city's first party, forming a minority administration with the Socialists. The record of left-wing power in Naples is a very mixed one. Naples is a city with problems of phenomenal proportions. Apart from its chronic economic problems, the city boasts the highest population and traffic density, the largest number of rats, the highest concentration of substandard dwellings, and the highest levels of atmospheric and noise pollution, infant mortality, and infectious diseases of all Italian cities.[9] In addition, the new administration inherited the fruits of thirty years of misgovernment and corruption, exemplified by the ravages of unrestrained speculation and the decay of the old city.

The catastrophic problems facing the city when the Left took power were compounded by yet another catastrophe – the state of local finances. The clientelistic politics of the "old regime," together with the inability of local governments in Italy to levy their own taxes, had brought the city to the verge of bankruptcy. The first year of the new administration, until passage of national legislation to reform local finances, was marked by continual confrontation with the state simply to obtain sufficient funds to meet monthly payrolls. As a result, one of the first priorities of the new administration was to put local finances in order. Although this necessarily meant extreme austerity during the first few years, this goal has been achieved. From a situation of total financial chaos, with Naples the most indebted city in Italy, unable to pay either its creditors or its employees, not only was the 1980 budget balanced but it provided for 12% of expenditure in the form of new capital investment as opposed to only 1% under the previous administration.[10]

Upon moving into the city offices, the would-be reformers found a bureaucratic machine swelled by successive waves of patronage hiring (over 34,000 employees), a bureaucracy built up over a period of thirty years not for the purposes of honest and efficient administration, but rather as an electoral machine for party bosses, first Monarchist and then DC. A large percentage of the city employees were not only unqualified for the task of administering the city, but strongly organized as well in defense of corporatist privilege (in addition to the three national labor confederations, eight distinct "autonomous" unions are present among city employees, each dedicated to preserving and extending the privileges of its narrow constituency).

Faced with such a situation, the first task of the PCI and its allies was an attempt to put some order into the administrative chaos around them, to inaugurate a new style of rigor and morality in the public sphere. Among the first initiatives were a clampdown on all nonessential costs (e.g., the widespread private use of city cars and telephones), distribution of former patronage plums like commercial and construction licenses with strict impartiality, and, of particular symbolic value after twenty years of public collusion with private speculation, the demolition of several buildings erected in violation of the city plan. An attempt to enforce new standards of work upon the city's civil servants, however, illustrates the difficulties against which the initial moralizing and rationalizing impulse of the new administration all too frequently ran aground. Contrary to the practice of previous administrations, which had looked the other way not only at employee lateness but at widespread absenteeism as well, the new junta immediately announced a crackdown on lateness and began deducting a half-hour's pay from the check of every late employee. The guilty employees, rather than accept the payroll deduction, retaliated by taking the *entire* day off as sick leave, for which they received full pay. The attempt to enforce punctuality soon provoked absentee rates of up to 35%, and the junta was forced to back down. Although seemingly trivial, this case symbolizes the difficulty even of insuring more rational and efficient administration with a bureaucratic structure built on patronage and privilege, let alone attempting to inaugurate any more radical policy changes.

In terms of substantive policy issues, unemployment has clearly been the most critical problem facing the administration, even though in a highly centralized political system like that of Italy the formal powers of local government in this sphere are quite limited. In a situation like that of Naples, this problem lies at the very center of political attention and mobilization, as well as providing an accurate mirror of the changing relationship between the PCI and mass protest movements like the "organized unemployed" as the party moved from a role of opposition to a role of government. Although the PCI itself never directly organized the unemployed, the movement (like the housing struggles of the early 1970s), breaking as it did the traditional bond between the DC/Right and the urban poor, clearly played a fundamental role in the Communist advances of 1975 and 1976. Among the unemployed the formation of the left-wing administration was greeted with intense joy and expectation, reflected in the oft-repeated slogan of those first enthusiastic days, "Finally we will go to work."

Once the new administration took office, however, the relationship between the party and the unemployed became strained rather quickly. This was because, in the absence of any concrete prospects for the creation of new industrial jobs, the "organized unemployed" set as their immediate goal a position, however humble, in the public administration. Given the weakness of the private sector in the

South, economic demands are focused directly on the organs of the state, symbolized at the local level by the City Hall. Thus, from leadership of the struggles of the unemployed when in the opposition, the PCI, as the dominant force in the new administration, suddenly found itself manning the other side of the barricades.

In this city where the promise of a patronage job in the public sector has been at the center of politics for decades, PCI leaders emphasize with pride that they have eliminated hiring by political recommendation. Although to a certain extent this is true, the reality of the situation is more complex. With local finance in a shambles and the bureaucracy already overinflated, the number of jobs the new city government could provide was derisory in relation to the magnitude of the unemployment problem. As a result, the desperation of the unemployed, having nowhere else to turn, expressed itself in increasingly vocal and at times violent demonstrations against the administration and the PCI.[11] With regard to those jobs that *are* available, the PCI and the unemployed have clashed over the criteria by which they should be assigned. While the "organized unemployed" insist that jobs be assigned on the basis of their own "lists of struggle," the PCI and the unions counter that hiring must take place strictly in accordance with the lists of the state employment office, based on the length of time the applicant has been unemployed. Our struggle, insist the Communists, must not be, as in the past, to procure a position for the individual, but rather to promote new investment so as to create jobs for all the unemployed. Thus, the PCI has denounced the position of the "organized unemployed" as narrowly corporatist, as acceptance of a "welfare logic" in contrast to a broader strategy of struggle to expand the productive base of the local economy. While such a position clearly has its merits, it does little to resolve the immediate problem of those who are unemployed *today*. As a result, representatives of the DC as well as of the neo-Fascist Right have stepped into the widening gap between the PCI and the "organized unemployed," organizing competing lists of the unemployed (a kind of mass clientelism as opposed to the individual clientelism of the past), which they have used to maintain social tensions at a fever pitch and to channel the discontent of the unemployed against the left-wing administration.

In the face of this situation, and in the absence of any serious initiative on the part of the regional and national governments with regard to the employment problem,[12] the local administration has increasingly come to terms with the necessity, in the short term at least, of using the city government as an instrument of "assistance" to absorb unemployment. Thus, in 1979–80 over 6,000 young people were hired by the city government (under the aegis of national legislation for youth employment)[13] for such tasks as garbage collection, park maintenance, restoration of monuments, and various programs of assistance for children and the elderly, or else admitted into "courses of professional formation" whose purpose, in the absence of eventual occupational outlets, has more to do with welfare than with job training. This example illustrates the extent to which, in a context like that of Naples, the Left has found itself constrained, in order to maintain consensus, to use local government institutions for what its opponents have not hesitated to define as clientelistic ends.

The constraints on initiatives for reform posed by the structural weaknesses of the Neapolitan economy are evident in other policy areas as well. The dilemmas confronting the PCI are underlined by the following episode. The sanitary conditions of the city having remained unaltered since 1973, Naples faced the threat of a second cholera outbreak in the summer of 1977. In order to forestall such a possibility, it was agreed that strict controls over the cultivation and sale of shellfish and rigorous enforcement of hygiene in the city's open markets would be necessary, measures that would have put approximately 30,000 persons out of work. In the absence of any alternative prospect of economic development to reabsorb the persons thereby displaced, the administration felt that implementation of such measures would create dangerous social and political tensions and risk bequeathing a mass base of maneuver to the neo-Fascists. Faced with such a prospect, the administration chose what it perceived as the lesser of the evils – to take a chance and do nothing. A similar case is that of the estimated 50,000 Neapolitans who make a living from contraband, with their boats docked along the waterfront in full view of the customs police. The authorities watch and do nothing, not because they condone contraband, but because they know only too well that any attempt to move against it would deprive tens of thousands of families of their only means of subsistence.

Under such circumstances, how can the "new way of governing" promised by the Communists take concrete form? At what point can one break into the vicious circle of underdevelopment to transform a city like Naples? Given the overwhelming problems facing the city and the limited power and resources available to local government to deal with them, together with the inexperience of most of the new administrators, the left-wing administration found itself increasingly accused of immobilism. Despite the generally unquestioned honesty and dedication of the Communist administrators, the PCI's attempt to inaugurate a "new way of governing" in Naples had by 1978–9 produced few concrete results.

The tide turns back

In the slums of the old city and the squalid housing projects of the urban periphery as well as among the "progressive" sectors of the Neapolitan middle class, the victory of the Left in 1975 was greeted with intense enthusiasm and almost utopian expectations. By 1978, however, there were serious indications that the political climate of the city was changing once again. In May 1977 and again in May 1978 partial administrative elections concentrated disproportionately in the South resulted in serious setbacks for the Communists and substantial gains for the DC.[14] The erosion of the PCI's electoral base in the South suggested by these results was dramatically confirmed, both in general and with regard to the specific case of Naples, by the outcome of the June 1978 national referendum for the repeal of two laws – one providing public financing for political parties and the other the *Legge Reale*, a strong law-and-order bill originally pushed through by the DC but later, in the wake of Italy's rising terrorist wave, supported by the Communists and Socialists as well. Repeal of the two laws was opposed by all the major parties (including the PCI, which supported the national government majority from 1976 to 1979); only the neo-Fascist MSI, the tiny Radical Party (which had initiated the referendum), and the groups of the extraparliamentary Left were in favor of repeal. The parties opposing repeal thus represented over 90% of the Italian electorate (on the basis of parliamentary seats), as well as all the power and prestige of the Italian political establishment.

Yet, despite a heavy-handed campaign dominated by the PCI, which accused opponents of the laws of favoring terrorism on the one hand and attempting to undermine Italian democracy on the other, the outcome was the following:

	Public financing	*Legge Reale*
Against repeal	56.3%	76.7%
In favor of repeal	43.7%	23.3%

Although neither of the laws was repealed, turnout was very low by Italian standards (81.4%), and the final result, even on the *Legge*

Table 10.1. *Results of the June 1978 referendum (in percentages)*

	Public financing		Legge Reale		
	In favor of repeal	Against repeal	In favor of repeal	Against repeal	Turnout
Italy	43.7	56.3	23.3	76.7	81.4
North	39.9	60.1	20.2	79.8	87.3
Center	41.0	59.0	20.9	79.1	85.9
South	52.7	47.3	30.7	69.3	70.2
Palermo	64.0	36.0	36.0	64.0	67.8 (Sicily)
Naples	59.7	40.3	30.1	69.9	69.8 (Campania)
Rome	54.9	45.1	26.9	73.1	83.3 (Lazio)
Turin	51.2	48.8	26.5	73.5	84.3 (Piedmont)

Source: Corriere della Sera (June 13, 14, 1978).

Reale, was closer than anyone, including the sponsors of the referendum, had expected. In Naples, where the PCI alone had won 40.8% of the vote in 1976, throughout the South, and in major northern cities like Rome, Milan, and Turin, a majority actually voted to repeal the law on public financing of the parties; the gravity of these results is reinforced by the figures on turnout, which fall sharply as one moves from north to south (see Table 10.1). The outcome of the referendum was unmistakably a slap in the face for Italy's major parties, above all the PCI, which had borne the brunt of the electoral campaign.[15] The outcome on the law for party financing was particularly alarming, both because of its symbolic value as an indicator of public attitudes toward the parties and because of the magnitude of the gap it revealed between the leaders of Italy's major parties and their mass base, a gap that had become a veritable chasm in the South.

The danger signals for the PCI implicit in the 1977–8 results were amply confirmed a year later in the parliamentary elections of June 1979. These elections, held two years in advance of the normal date, were precipitated by Communist withdrawal of support for the Andreotti government in January 1979. When all attempts to resolve the ensuing governmental crisis failed, early elections were called to break the impasse. The PCI hoped through these elections to reinforce its claim to full governmental participation, while the DC appealed to the electorate to return a clear centrist majority, eliminating the need to deal with the Communists by returning them to a role of permanent opposition. The results of the elections fulfilled neither of these hopes, but rather reconfirmed the political stalemate that has paralyzed successive Italian governments since the early 1970s. At the national level the relative strength of the Left and the Center-Right blocs remained virtually unaltered. Contrary to most predictions, the DC failed to increase its share of the vote beyond the 38% reached in 1972 and 1976. While the small Center parties (PSDI and PLI) did make gains (reversing the trend toward bipolarization of the electorate that had characterized the 1976 elections), these were insufficient to provide a clear centrist majority. Substantial voting shifts took place instead within the Left, with the loss by the PCI of about 4% of its 1976 vote, the meteoric rise of the Radical Party, and lesser gains by the Socialists and the New Left. A final important feature of the 1979 elections was the abstention rate of over 10%, a heretofore unheard-of figure in a country where voting has always been considered almost obligatory. This figure underlined the pervasive climate of apathy and disillusionment present among many Italian voters, reconfirming the earlier signals of discontent expressed in the referendum of June 1978. (See Table A.1 for the national results.)

Perhaps the most striking aspect of these elections, however, was the disintegration of the political unity of North and South that had been hailed as one of the most important outcomes of the 1976 elections. In 1979 what one saw instead were two very different political processes taking place in the North and in the South. In the North both the PCI and the DC suffered substantial losses, particularly in large cities, with the PCI losing young voters and many workers either to the Radicals or through abstention, while the DC lost a significant portion of its middle-class electorate to the small lay parties of the Center. In the South the image that emerges from the electoral data is quite a different one. Abstention rates rise dramatically as one moves from north to south, PCI losses are substantially higher than in the North, and the DC increases its share of the vote almost everywhere.[16] Communist losses in the South are not fully compensated for by the gains of other leftist parties; unlike the North, there is evidence of a direct transfer of votes from the PCI to the DC and the small lay parties.

In Naples the collapse of the PCI between 1976 and 1979 is extraordinary (10 percentage points), the largest loss for the party in any major Italian city, even though the Communists remain, by a hair, the city's leading party (see Table A.4). Although, as elsewhere, the PCI lost substantially both to other left-wing parties and through abstention, there remains a significant percentage of the Communist losses that can be accounted for only by a shift of left-wing votes to the DC, the small lay parties, and the MSI. Analyses of the Neapolitan vote by the party's own spokesmen emphasize the widespread disillusionment with the left-wing administration, above all among youth and the urban poor, both pillars of the Communists' 1975 and 1976 victories.[17] It is interesting to note that in Naples, like many northern cities, PCI losses were heavier in the slums of the old city and in the low-income neighborhoods of the periphery than among middle-class voters won over to the party in 1975 and 1976, with some of the most serious losses coming precisely in the PCI's traditional strongholds, like certain public-housing projects where the party had long reaped over 40% of the vote (see Table A.5).[18] Although these results are for national parliamentary elections, they clearly reflected the prevailing mood of Neapolitan politics as well as the national political situation. Consequently, they were interpreted by both the PCI and its adversaries as sounding a clear and present danger for the future of left-wing rule in Naples, to be decided in administrative elections in June 1980.

What went wrong? The limits of left-wing rule in Naples

How can the collapse of the PCI vote in Naples in 1979 be explained? What had happened since 1975–6 when over 40% of the Neapolitan electorate had placed its hopes for change in the Communist Party? The electoral results of 1978–9, combined with a renewed flare-up of social tensions in Naples, revealed a growing disillusionment with the PCI not only among those social groups – like the *sottoproletariato* and, to a lesser extent, the middle class – whose support had been pivotal for the party's earlier victories, but among growing sectors of its traditional electorate as well. In many cases the support for the Communists in 1975–6 from groups outside the party's traditional working-class base had been more a vote of protest against the "old regime" than an expression of a stable alliance with the PCI. Particularly in the case of the "organized unemployed," the PCI had supported the movement for electoral purposes, but without fully integrating these new voters into the party's organizational structure. It could also plausibly be argued that many new PCI voters, especially among the urban poor (and probably including some grass-roots party activists as well), saw a vote for the Communists in terms less of a coherent program of social change than of a new clientelism of the Left, changing the beneficiaries but not the basic style of local government. Less ideological and less organizationally molded, the allegiance of these new Communist voters among the middle classes as well as the urban poor was more contingent on concrete results than was that of long-time party militants and, as a result, potentially more subject to fluctuation. The Communist electoral successes in 1975 and 1976 provoked a tremendous wave of popular enthusiasm in Naples. Four years later it was not the desire for change that had faded, but rather its credibility.

Why was the PCI unable to deliver on the promises of change that had brought it within the "area of power" at both the local and national levels? To understand the situation in which the PCI found itself from 1976 on, we must first examine the national political context. From 1973 to 1980 the PCI's national strategy was based on the formula of the "historic compromise"– collaboration among the country's three mass parties, the Communists, the Socialists, and the Christian Democrats.[19] In line with this strategy the PCI consistently rejected the idea of a left-wing alternative, insisting instead on a government of national unity including all the major political forces. From the summer of 1976 until January 1979 the PCI participated in the government majority (first through abstention and then through direct support), but without sharing executive responsibility. The Communists were thus caught in the dilemma of responsibility without control – while participating publicly in the formation of government policies, the PCI, excluded from ministerial responsibility, had no power over their implementation. In the eyes of the masses the Communist Party had become a full participant in government, yet many, including a growing number of long-time party militants, increasingly came to feel that nothing had changed but the political formulas.

In Naples as in Rome, Communist strategy was determined until the beginning of 1979 by the goal of the "historic compromise." Although the Communists agreed to form a minority left-wing administration after the failure of months of fruitless negotiations with the DC, their goal remained that of an eventual reentry of the DC into the majority. (An agreement to this end was finally reached in June 1978, whereby the DC would support the majority but without participation in the junta, essentially the reverse of the national situation.) The justification for such a policy, at both the local and national levels, was (1) that the problems facing the city (or the country) are so critical that they can be resolved only through a unified effort of all the major political forces; and (2) that to exclude the DC would allow it to avoid its responsibility for the current state of affairs and to engage in demagogical opposition. In both cases this strategy meant endless negotiations and extreme caution on the part of the PCI to prevent any actions that might threaten the goal of collaboration. Collaboration with the DC became the Communists' top priority, to which the demands for change coming from below were subordinated; as a result, party activity became increasingly dominated by top-level interparty negotiations. This policy provoked growing friction between the PCI leadership and the party's mass base, many of whom felt that their vote for the Communists in 1975–6 had been a call for a political alternative, not for compromise with the old ruling parties.

The DC in Naples took advantage of this situation to play the game on both sides. While proclaiming its availability for a "programmatic accord" with the PCI, the DC engaged the Communists in lengthy and exasperating negotiations, at the same time conducting an obstructionist policy with regard to the concrete activities of the left-wing administration. Having, from the unaccustomed perspective of opposition, "rediscovered its ties with the masses," the DC (or, more accurately, its conservative wing, the Gavas) organized groups of the unemployed to protest against the administration's failure to provide jobs, supported corporatist unions in extravagant demands on the already bankrupt city treasury, and promoted strikes by essential city services in an attempt to discredit the administration.[20] The PCI thus found itself caught between the increasing mobilization of social tensions and corporatist pressures by its opponents. As a result, the Communists found it increasingly difficult even to insure the functioning of normal administrative activities, while initiatives for change were to a large extent blocked by the search for compromise with the DC. Once again, one of the consequences was a widening gap between the PCI and those sectors of the population that had brought it to power.

The relationship between the party apparatus and its mass base is a critical issue for a party like the PCI when – with its history, organizational structure, and raison d'être, as it were, all those of an "anti-system" opposition party – it suddenly finds itself called upon to assume governmental responsibility within a capitalist state. During this period the PCI defined itself as a "party of government and of struggle," but the two roles were not easy to reconcile, either in the party's activities or in the minds of its supporters and activists. A serious problem where, as in Naples, the PCI directly participates in power, has been the identification of the party with the institutions it administers, greatly limiting its capacity to mobilize the masses against these institutions and transforming the role of the party apparatus into a passive support structure, organizing grass-roots consensus for the left-wing administration. This situation was aggravated in those cases, like Naples, where the party's sudden electoral success was out of proportion to its organizational strength. On the one hand, this meant that the party faced a serious shortage of qualified and experienced personnel to fill the top positions in local government; on the other hand, as a result, the best cadres were funneled into the administration, leaving little time, energy, or talent to attend to purely party concerns. In a sense, the party was absorbed into the administration.

As might have been expected, the "party of struggle" became increasingly difficult to realize when it became a question of organizing protest against the PCI-dominated administration. Motivated by fear of creating additional troubles for the administration in a difficult moment or of placing obstacles in the path of compromise with the DC, PCI organizers in many cases either abandoned mobilization of the masses altogether or, at the very least, attempted to contain protest within limits not threatening to the city's delicate political equilibrium. The party's caution in this sphere provoked growing frustration among grass-roots activists, as well as a move by other political forces to fill the void left by the PCI's organizational absence. This trend was most obvious in the case of the "organized unemployed," who, as we have seen, constituted a major source of support for the new administration in its early days. Since early 1977, however, the movement has become increasingly fragmented and anti-Communist, as the weakening of the PCI's organizational hegemony has opened the door to an escalation of protest against City Hall by competing groups of the unemployed under the leadership not only of groups to the left of the PCI but of neo-Fascists and displaced DC notables as well.

A related but distinct problem is the issue of grass-roots participation in local government. The PCI's promise of a "new way of governing" included not only a commitment to honest and efficient administration but also the inauguration of a new relationship between governmental institutions and their constituents, one based on direct citizen involvement in decision making. Translated into a far-reaching program of decentralization of the functions of city government to neighborhood councils, this idea was first introduced by Communist administrators in Bologna and translated into national legislation in 1976. Such a "democratization" of local government was seen as especially important for the South, where the state has long been perceived by the populace as an alien entity, foreign to its needs and aspirations. The PCI saw its participation in power as a break in this tradition – the beginning of a new kind of organization of the endemic protest of the southern masses, no longer to be directed *against* the state as such, but aimed instead at a *transformation* of the state. Attempts at implementing decentralization, however, ran up against serious political resistance, with direct election of neighborhood councils, passage from consultative to deliberative powers, and effective decentralization of municipal services scheduled to take place only in 1980. Consequently, the left-wing administration found itself caught in the traditional pattern: delegation of responsibility by the citizenry to the PCI and the junta and continued perception of City Hall not as an instrument of the people's will, open to the participation of all, but rather as the seat of *power*, where one goes only to petition or to protest. A leading PCI spokesman and administrator depicted the party's dilemma in the following terms:

At the institutional level we have overemphasized the element of "good government" and "clean hands," of efficiency based on the rigor and spirit of sacrifice of our administrators . . . , without giving top priority to the question of participation and popular control . . . This has generated a new form of delegation of responsibility and passive expectation on the part of the citizenry vis-à-vis those local institutions where our presence is determining . . .[21] The city government is a sort of island under siege, at the center of all the social and economic tensions of the city, but without the capacity to give the responses which the people expect. In this way are created attitudes of extreme trust, which are then followed by extreme disillusionment.[22]

If the PCI does not succeed in building a new kind of relationship between the masses and the state, he goes on, "the traditional rebelliousness of the South may re-emerge, but this time directed against the Left."[23]

A return to clientelism?

Juxtaposed against the mounting difficulties of the PCI in Naples was a resurgence of clientelistic appeals on the part of the Christian Democrats and the Right, the success of which was reflected in the electoral gains of the DC throughout the South in the period 1977–9. This turn of a significant segment of the electorate back to clientelistic parties reinforces the arguments presented in Part II with regard to the strengths of clientelism in a socioeconomic context like that of the South. The reasons for this resurgence of clientelism must be sought in the structural constraints posed by the nature of the southern economy, in the linkages between political and economic power in Italy, and in the impact of the economic crisis.

Underlying all the myriad and pressing demands bombarding Naples' left-wing administrators is one fundamental and overriding problem: the weakness of the urban economy, plagued by chronic unemployment (an official figure of 126,000 at the end of 1980) and surviving to a large extent on *lavoro nero* ("black" or clandestine labor), which, prior to the earthquake of November 1980, provided work for at least 60,000 people.[24] The preeminence of the employment issue as a focal point for mass mobilization in Naples emerges clearly from the preceding pages. This, however, is a basic structural problem, which political power at the local level, regardless of the party which controls it, is not in a position to resolve by other than clientelistic means. This is due in part to the highly centralized administrative structure of the Italian state, which delegates neither substantive powers nor resources to local government in the area of economic policy. Even more important, however, is the interpenetration of political and economic power in Italy over the past thirty years and the success of the Christian Democratic Party in monopolizing key sectors of the economy and shaping them into solid pillars of its own hegemony. This aspect of DC power has been – and remains – of central importance in the South, where the economy depends overwhelmingly on the public sector. What this means for the Left is spelled out in the following statement by Maurizio Valenzi, the Communist mayor of Naples:

> It must be made clear that, just because the Left controls local government, this does not mean that it "holds power" in Naples. The left-wing parties participate in the city and provincial administrations, it is true, but the decisive aspect of power – i.e., the levers of economic power, still remain in the hands of the DC.[25]

Thus, despite the political victory of the Left, all major centers of economic power in Naples – the Ministry of State-Controlled Industry (which controls about 70% of Neapolitan industry), the Bank of Naples and other major credit institutions, ISVEIMER (the regional agency for publicly subsidized credit), the Port Authority, the Consortium for Industrial Development, the Chamber of Commerce, and the Union of Industrialists – as well as the regional government of Campania, continue to be controlled by the DC.[26] The combination of continued DC domination of the national government and the DC monopoly over the major levers of economic power has made it virtually impossible for the Communists to transform the basic structural constraints of the Neapolitan situation. Without a serious national commitment to economic development in the South, a commitment that PCI participation in the national government from 1976 until 1979 proved incapable of producing, left-wing control of local government in Naples has as yet been able to do little to affect the most critical problems facing the city (employment and housing); the most it has been able to do in these areas is to use local institutions as levers of pressure to extract resources from the national and regional governments. Under these circumstances, the left-wing administration found its activity increasingly limited to normal administration – undoubtedly more honest and somewhat more efficient than that of its predecessors, but normal administration nonetheless.

Even that was rendered precarious at times by the enormity of the problems facing the city, the inexperience of the Communist administrators, the obstructionism of certain sectors of the DC and the Right and, most recently, the disastrous consequences of the earthquake of November 1980, which devastated the slums of the old city and added close to 100,000 homeless to the city's already colossal problems. Under these conditions, and with important levers of power still in the hands of the old machine bosses, the continuing strength of clientelistic appeals is not surprising.

In contrast to those theories that have seen economic crisis as a major factor in the collapse of clientelistic regimes, the resurgence of clientelism in Naples and in the South more generally since 1977–8 appears to be directly correlated with the dramatic worsening of the southern economy as a result of the economic crisis.[27] The southern vote for the PCI in 1975–6 was in large part a vote for change, a protest against decades of neglect by the national government and a demand for new priorities and policies to transform the South from an eternally assisted area into a productive component of the national economy. Instead, the southern economy deteriorated still further after 1975, and national politics and policies seemed little affected by the presence of the Communists in the "governmental area." As a result, confidence in the changes promised by the PCI had turned by 1979 to frustration and despair. Not only the inability of the Communists to provide solutions for the dramatic problems of Naples and the South but their unwillingness, in the absence of broad social and economic change, to hold out even the prospect of an individual solution, left the door open to a return of the forces of the "old regime," more than willing to exploit the resulting disillusionment.

The key to the enduring strength of clientelism in an area like southern Italy, in the absence of the prospect of broader social change, has been the element of hope, and it is precisely on this terrain that the Communists found themselves at a disadvantage vis-à-vis their opponents. Mayor Valenzi recounts the following episode as a symbol of the dilemma of the PCI in Naples. He was approached by a middle-aged woman who explained that she had shifted her vote from the DC to the Communists because, after years of electoral promises by the DC, her son was still unemployed. "You Communists are good people," she said, "and I know that you can find my son a job." The mayor patiently explained that he personally could do nothing, that her son would have to go to the state employment office and there go through regular channels. The woman turned away in anger and dismay: "But then you want to take even *hope* away from us!" The tragedy for the PCI, Valenzi notes bitterly, is that

240   *The prospects and the limits of change*

"if you deny them hope, the old patron is right there ready to extend it, because *his* game revolves around hope."²⁸ If the PCI proves unable to fulfill the expectations which it has created, another Communist leader explained, southerners may turn back to the "traditional image of the city government as a 'mediator' of assistance and favors between a South in need of everything and a distant and hostile state." If that happens, he concludes, "who better than a certain sector of the Christian Democratic Party, with the formidable apparatus of party and state behind it, can perform such a function?"²⁹

Thus, as the economic crisis reduces available resources, privileged access to remaining resources – concentrated in the hands of the DC and its allies – becomes more important than ever. More concretely, when the prospect of work for all begins to fade, many turn back to the desperate search for a patron, in order to insure at least an *individual* solution. People begin to look with nostalgia to the "good old days" when, with the proper connections, one could at least obtain *something*. As one observer put it, "Better a clientelistic system than no system at all."³⁰

1980–Whither Naples?

On the eve of the June 1980 administrative elections, the mood of the Neapolitan Communists was somber, and the thesis of a "return to clientelism" was of foremost concern for both the PCI and the DC. During the campaign, national attention was centered on Naples as a symbol of the counteroffensive mounted by the DC and the Right against left-wing rule in Italy's major cities. Not only did the DC focus its hopes for victory on Naples (in 1979 only 1,000 votes had separated the DC from the PCI, as opposed to 80,000 three years earlier) but the neo-Fascist MSI as well – counting on a broad-based wave of protest against the left-wing administration – mounted a massive campaign to make its national secretary, Giorgio Almirante, the next mayor of Naples. The results confirmed neither the optimistic hopes of the DC and the Right nor the worst fears of the Communists. The PCI managed to hold its own with regard to the local and regional elections of 1975 and to reverse slightly the disastrous losses of 1979, but fell one seat short of obtaining an absolute majority for the left-wing coalition that had governed the city since 1975. On the other hand, the Neapolitan DC suffered one of the worst losses in the entire country (−5.3% with respect to 1979), while the MSI, although failing in its promise to make Almirante mayor of Naples, increased its vote from 18.7% in 1975 to 22.3% in 1980. (See Table A.1 for the national results and Table A.4 for the local results.) After an initial period of consultation among the parties, the leftist administration (PCI, PSI, PSDI, PRI) was reconfirmed; because, as in the period 1975–80, the coalition does not have an absolute majority, the vote of the DC remains essential for critical issues like the passage of the budget.

Given the preceding analysis of the dilemma confronting the PCI in local government and the evidence supporting the thesis of a return to clientelism, how can these results be explained? How, given the PCI's disastrous losses in 1979, which reflected not only disillusionment with the party's national strategy but profound discontent with the record of the left-wing local administration as well, did the party succeed in recuperating sufficient support to maintain its hold on local government and forestall the predicted victory of the DC and the Right? As we have seen, from 1976 until 1979 the Left in Naples found itself progressively cut off from its mass base and engaged in little more than guaranteeing normal administration, while garbage mounted in the streets, traffic became more chaotic than ever, and the ranks of the unemployed continued to swell. In the wake of the 1979 electoral losses, the PCI, at both the national and the local levels, underwent a profound process of self-criticism, with respect not only to its strategy vis-à-vis the DC but to the broader question of the relationship among institutions, party organizations, and mass base as well. Having resumed a role of opposition at the national level and concomitantly abandoned its fixation on agreement with the DC at the local level, the PCI in Naples proved able to revitalize the energies of its grass-roots activists, to begin to restore its ties with local struggles (particularly in the fields of housing and youth unemployment), and to promote a series of new initiatives on the part of the city government during the last half of 1979 and the first half of 1980. These included a program of free cultural events in the summer of 1979, new programs of assistance for the elderly, approval of a far-reaching plan for the redevelopment of the urban periphery and, most importantly, reconsideration of the major dilemma facing the party – how to deal with unemployment.

Like the party in the rest of the South, the PCI in Naples, together with the unions, had consistently rejected the provision of public-sector jobs for the unemployed as "assistance," insisting instead on a broad-based struggle for new productive investment. After the 1979 elections, however, the Neapolitan Communists came to terms with the necessity, in the short run at least, of using the city government as an instrument of assistance to absorb unemployment. Thus, as discussed earlier in this chapter, between June 1979 and June 1980 over 6,000 young people were hired by the city for a variety of public-service jobs or else admitted into publicly financed job-training programs. Given the magnitude of the problems facing Naples, even these initiatives were primarily symbolic, with the Communists themselves admitting that the first five years of left-wing rule should be seen more as an indication of direction than as a record of concrete accomplishments.[31] However, on the basis of the new wave of dynamism evident in the year preceding the June 1980 elections, the Communists seem to have succeeded in reconvincing Neapolitans that a "new way of governing" may indeed be possible. In the words of Antonio Bassolino, the PCI regional secretary, "the left-wing administration has not done everything, but it has at least restored hope,"[32] a hope that a year earlier had seemed irrevocably lost.

With regard to the DC and the Right, the analysis is more complicated. The electoral results of 1980 indicate a clearcut distinction between Naples and the rest of the South. On the one hand, the PCI vote in Naples is in sharp contrast to the substantial losses suffered by the party in the rest of the South; on the other, the DC, which loses badly to the neo-Fascist Right in Naples, advances significantly elsewhere in the South, as well as in the region of Campania outside the Province of Naples. The divergence in political outcome between Naples and the rest of the South can be traced to two factors. First, although from the opposite perspective, the Naples results seem to confirm the thesis of the Palermo research that control of the institutions of local government is the keystone of clientelistic power in southern Italy. Despite the continuing control of the Gavas over major levers of economic power in Naples and the strengthening of their ties to national power since 1975, the loss by the DC of a key center of patronage like the city government seriously undermined its capacity to mobilize grass-roots support, even in the presence of widespread disillusionment with the left-wing administration.

A second and related peculiarity of the Neapolitan situation is the capacity of the MSI, rather than the DC, to attract those sectors of the population dissatisfied with the Left. The 1980 total of 22.3% for the MSI in Naples contrasts sharply with a figure of only 8.5% in Palermo, the latter more representative of neo-Fascist support in southern Italy as a whole. The most vigorous electoral campaign in Naples in 1980 was in fact that of the MSI, which mounted an impressive door-to-door operation of petty clientelism in the slums of the old city, mobilized protest demonstrations of homeless families against City Hall, organized numerous meetings with specific occupational categories from doctors and lawyers to shopkeepers and cab drivers, as well as capitalizing upon the charismatic personal appeal of its national leader, Almirante, who won more personal preference votes than the incumbent Communist mayor.[33] Traditionally the South has oscillated between two distinct models of political behavior: on the one hand, the search for individual solutions through clientelistic channels, and on the other, the spontaneous explosion of protest against a state perceived as alien and exploitative. Although there are elements of clientelism present in the neo-Fascist as well as the Christian Democratic vote, in general the Neapolitan vote of 1980 (combined with an abstention rate of 15%) seems to indicate a resurgence less of clientelism than of the right-wing populist antistatism deeply rooted in certain sectors of the middle class and the urban *sottoproletariato*. If this analysis is correct, what the Neapolitan vote signals is a widening gap between the citizen and the state, a growing sense of frustration and alienation from democratic institutions even more alarming in its implications than a revival of the machine politics of the Gavas.

Thus, whereas for the South as a whole the thesis of a return to clientelism is amply confirmed by the 1980 elections, in Naples the Gavas seem to have lost their hold on the city, which more than ever is polarized between Left and Right. With regard to the prospects for the Left until the next elections (1985), the renewed dynamism of the administration after mid-1979 momentarily stemmed the wave of skepticism and frustration that seemed about to engulf it. The precariousness of the Neapolitan situation was dramatically exposed, however, by the earthquake that devastated southern Italy in November 1980. The quake, like the cholera outbreak of 1973, laid bare the shortcomings of successive local governments, above all the tendency, of the Left as of preceding administrations, to deal with problems on an ad hoc, day-to-day basis rather than seeking broader long-term solutions. With the low-income neighborhoods of the old city in ruins, close to 100,000 homeless living in containers along the waterfront or in 177 occupied schools, and the traditional *economia del vicolo* ("slum economy") that provided the margin of subsistence for the poor almost totally destroyed, Naples in the first half of 1981 was a city daily on the brink of anarchy. Demonstrations by the homeless and the unemployed mounted continually in size and violence as popular anger and desperation exploded against the city's administrators. The billions to be spent for relief and reconstruction have offered a propitious terrain for the flourishing of both traditional clienteles and the *camorra*, the Neapolitan equivalent of the mafia, while the demands of the homeless have provided the wedge by which terrorist groups have made their entrance onto the Neapolitan scene.[34] Under these conditions, the left-wing administration once again has its back against the wall, and the space for maneuver by extremist groups of both the Right and the Left grows daily. For Naples, as for the rest of the South, the prospects for the next five to ten years depend above all on policy decisions at the national level. The combination of economic crisis and chronic political immobilism in Rome offers little ground for optimism. Given the continued absence at the national level of either the political will or the necessary resources to confront the ever more drastic problems of the South, there is little reason to expect that the social and political tensions of the last several years will be alleviated in the foreseeable future. As a result, the political gap between North and South may well continue to widen, with incalculable consequences for Italian democracy.

11

Conclusion

Over the past three decades southern Italy has presented the observer with a variety of often contradictory images. Islands of development and backwaters of feudalism, models of mass consumption alongside the age-old traditions of peasant society, cities where modern thoroughfares lined with office buildings and luxury shops open onto teeming slums where the conditions of life bear more resemblance to the Third World than to the rest of Europe. These contradictions are reflected in political behavior as well. On the one hand the traditional South, stronghold of the Monarchy and then of powerful and unscrupulous machine bosses, its history punctuated with spontaneous, but short-lived, revolts against the state; on the other the South of the peasant land occupations of the immediate postwar period and, over two decades later, of left-wing electoral victories in cities like Naples and Taranto.

How can these juxtaposed processes of continuity and change be explained? What conclusions can be drawn from the concrete experiences of the two "capitals" of the Mezzogiorno, Palermo and Naples, with regard to southern Italy more generally as well as to the larger question of the role of clientelism in developing nations? As a point of departure, it is necessary to recall the regional differences in political behavior in Italy since 1975. At the national level, the Christian Democratic Party, which has governed the country uninterruptedly throughout the postwar period, has in recent years been subject to increasing strains, ranging from major defeats on issues like divorce and abortion to recent scandals like the appalling inadequacy of earthquake aid in the South or the revelations of the secret activities of the P2 Masonic lodge, and culminating in June 1981 in the nomination for the first time in the history of the Republic of a non-DC prime minister. These strains have been reflected in substantial electoral losses for the DC in the northern and central regions of the

245

country since 1975, losses that have been especially accentuated in major urban centers, in most of which the Communists have become the leading party. In the South, however, the processes of electoral change have been reversed. After significant gains by the Communists in 1975–6 (gains that led to premature predictions of the political unification of the country), the PCI has suffered drastic losses throughout the South (with the exception of cities like Naples and Taranto), while the DC vote, already above the national average, has increased still further in many areas.

The differences in political behavior in the North and the South reflect the growing gap in the socioeconomic bases and prospects of the two regions. As discussed in Chapter 2, it is a mistake to view the South of the 1980s as a stagnant, backward, agricultural society. Over the past two decades southern society has undergone tremendous processes of change and modernization, the most important of which has been rapid urbanization, transforming the South by the 1970s into a predominantly urban society. The fundamental problem is that this has been for the most part a process of modernization without development – creating a modern society in terms of models of consumption and, most importantly, of expectations, but without providing the productive base to sustain those levels of consumption.[1] As a result, large areas of the South have been relegated to the status of an *area assistita*, dependent for survival on various forms of assistance from the state.[2] Under the impact of the economic crisis, the character of the South as an *area assistita* has been still further accentuated, leading many southern leaders to fear that, if concrete action to promote productive investment is not taken soon, much of the South may be destined to remain forever at the margins of national life.

This model of an "assisted society," dependent for survival upon its links to political power, is a product of DC power and in turn reinforces it, at both the local and national levels. In the first place, as argued in Chapter 9, clientelistic power thrives in a context of economic scarcity and social fragmentation. In lieu of economic development, there has been instead a proliferation of welfare measures, sustaining levels of consumption for the products of northern industry, but at the same time maintaining much of the South in a position of economic and political dependency. At the same time, mass clientelism has promoted the fragmentation of society into a multitude of competing individual and corporative interests, impeding the formation of stable class alignments. In such a society the one stable point of reference is the party that holds power and thereby controls the distribution of the pensions, subsidies, and the like, which have provided the margins of subsistence for much of the southern population. Thus, for many, in the absence of any realistic prospect of development, a vote for the DC is a vote for the continuation of the flow of welfare benefits that has sustained levels of consumption far in excess of the region's contribution to national income.[3]

Beyond the creation of a miniature welfare state, in which virtually every family receives some form of pension, there is another critical component of the kind of society that has taken shape in the South over the past thirty years. When the DC campaigns in the South as the "party of liberty," this slogan has implications going beyond the usual anti-Communist rhetoric. While the type of development that has taken place in much of the South (characterized, for example, by the "cathedrals in the desert" and the uncontrolled speculation that has ravaged cities like Palermo and Naples) has produced tremendous distortions and inequities, it has also created a society in which, because of the absence of clearly defined social roles and of corresponding rights and obligations, certain margins of freedom, of maneuver, and of privilege have been guaranteed to key social groups – a society in which anything is possible with the proper connections. This applies not only to obvious cases like public employees and certain sectors of the entrepreneurial class (culminating in the impotence of the state against manifestations of organized violence like the mafia and the *camorra*) but even to not insignificant segments of the urban poor, whose means of earning a living seldom show excessive concern for the fine line between legality and illegality. The chaos of the existing system, however appalling its overall effects on the quality of urban life, holds out the possibility of individual gain to all those who can succeed in forging a personal tie, however tenuous, to the holders of power. Although the nature and scope of the benefits in question vary greatly, this is a system that cuts across class barriers, creating a base of support for the ruling party that represents a true cross-section of society.

The continued and even reinforced support for the DC in the South in the face of a devastating economic crisis, which has shrunk the resource base for mass patronage on a grand scale, requires a reconsideration of conventional theories of the nature of clientelistic power. While the exchange of the vote for concrete short-term benefits (or at least the promise thereof) remains an essential factor for explaining DC success in southern Italy, support for the machine is not directly correlated to resource expenditure. Part of the answer lies in the argument made in Chapter 9 about the availability of nonmonetary forms of patronage and the importance of control of *access* to resources as opposed to the quantity of resources distributed. Thus, in a situation of scarcity, and one in which the margins of survival, already minimal, have been further reduced by the economic crisis, the vote for the DC is a vote for a concrete connection to the powerful and the possibility of access to the resources that connection represents, even in the absence of an immediate personal payoff. The critical factor is not the actual payoff but rather the widespread perception of the need for a personal link to those in positions of power, even in the face of incontrovertible evidence demonstrating that only a few actually benefit from such a relationship.[4]

The DC vote in the South, however, is not just a vote for the individual patron who promises concrete favors, whatever their nature. It is also a vote for the party whose continued dominance at both the local and the national level guarantees the perpetuation of a society in which the margins of personal maneuver and privilege discussed above will continue to exist. Evidence in support of this argument is provided by comparison of the results of the 1975 and 1980 administrative elections in Palermo (local elections in the South traditionally constituting the prime terrain for the expression of the individual patron – client tie through the personal preference vote).[5] In 1980 the DC vote in Palermo reached the highest level of the postwar period (46.7% or 167,620 votes, compared to 41.7% or 151,104 votes in 1975). At the same time, the total number of personal preference votes for DC candidates was considerably lower than in 1975 (442,182 or a ratio of 2.9 preference votes for every party vote in 1975, as opposed to 420,896 or a ratio of only 2.1:1 in 1980). This evidence suggests that, in Palermo at least, the traditional individual patron – client bond may have weakened (perhaps in part because of the uncertainty produced by continuing factional struggle within the local DC), but people continue to vote for the DC as guarantor of a society that remains fundamentally clientelistic in its conception of the relationship between the citizen and the state.

The other side of the coin is the credibility of the alternative offered by the opposition in the South. Forces for change do exist in southern Italy, as the examples of the *movimento per la casa* and the *disoccupati organizzati*, as well as the left-wing victories in Naples in 1975 and 1980, clearly demonstrate. At the same time as the economic crisis, by lowering expectations and by reinforcing the intermediary role of the dominant party, has strengthened the machine, it has also given rise to a desire to transcend the constraints of the existing situation. The prospect of a renewed commitment to productive investment in the South, backed up by pressures for increasing Communist leverage at the national level, gained the PCI unprecedented electoral support in the South in 1975–6. But, while this desire for change may be present among certain sectors of the southern population, there is, in addition to the difficulties of organization inherent in a situation of extreme social and economic disaggregation, a low threshold of risk built into southern society. People may desire change, but they want that change to be assured and credible. It is above all on these two criteria that the Communists, the only viable opposition force, have failed in their attempt to mobilize a mass base for a political and socioeconomic alternative in the South. PCI opposition in the South has focused almost exclusively on the long-term prospect of massive industrial investment to transform the structural bases of DC power. As the likelihood of such a transformation receded ever further into unreality under the impact of the economic crisis, and Communist participation in government at the national level produced few concrete results for the South, the PCI alternative, increasingly abstract and rhetorical, suffered a progressive loss of credibility. Dismissing tertiary activities as unproductive, if not parasitic, and equating assistance with clientelism, the PCI has been unable to offer any immediate and concrete alternative to the existing society, in which for the foreseeable future most people will continue to depend for a living precisely on the tertiary sector or on assistance, nor can it replace the short-term benefits, however limited, that the DC can provide. Thus, as the credibility of the alternative the PCI represented in 1975–6 has faded, people have sought above all stability and security, a terrain on which the natural advantage lies with the ruling party. This underlying search for stability and security emerges quite clearly from the following analyses of the 1980 vote in Palermo, even though they come from opposite ends of the political spectrum:

In a country which lives on very little, the DC represents certainty, even if minimal. [DC mayoral candidate][6]

Once the thrust for change has waned, the decisive factor becomes who governs, who engages in political mediation. It is these levers which are held by the DC, which therefore extends and reinforces its power. [Secretary of the Provincial Federation of the PCI][7]

On the other hand, as demonstrated by the case of Naples, clientelism in southern Italy is not eternal or immutable. The potential for change does exist, even though for the present the forces of continuity have proven remarkably resilient. The Neapolitan experience seems to suggest that, given the obstacles to change discussed above, a catastrophe like the cholera outbreak of 1973 may in many cases provide an essential stimulus to change. Despite corruption and inefficiency, in the absence of a crisis the forces of stability and conti-

nuity seem to maintain the upper hand. An emergency situation performs a kind of catalytic function: on the one hand laying bare the
immediate human consequences of misgovernment, and on the
other, as in Naples, providing the opposition with an opportunity to
demonstrate in an immediate and concrete way its ability to offer a
more honest, efficient, and hopefully more human, form of government. Thus, one could argue that in Naples what ultimately made the
left-wing victory of 1975 possible was the opportunity provided the
Communists by the cholera crisis to demonstrate a concrete capacity
to govern and to offer a viable and nonthreatening alternative to the
machine – precisely those qualities whose absence has condemned
the PCI in most of the rest of the South to sterile and increasingly
isolated opposition. Similarly, in the year preceding the 1980 elections, it was the display of activism with regard to concrete policy
issues, in contrast to the immobilism of the previous three years, that
saved the left-wing administration from what otherwise would have
been almost certain defeat. On the other hand, as the aftermath of the
tragic earthquake of 1980 demonstrates, the forces of progress are not
necessarily the beneficiaries of catastrophe. The chaos, anger, and
frustration resulting from the earthquake provide ample scope not
only for a revival of traditional *clientela* networks but also for even
less desirable forces of the extreme Right and the extreme Left.

Thus, although the symbolic value of left-wing rule in Naples
should not be underestimated, the experience of the city from 1975 to
1980 underlines the fragility of change in a structural context like that
of southern Italy. Even in those cases where political change has
taken place, the socioeconomic structure of the South exerts a continual blackmail over attempts to use political power at the local level to
initiate broader processes of social change. It is not inconceivable
that, in a situation of widespread frustration and deepening despair,
the Left could succeed in winning other positions of local power in
the South. The more important question is what the consequences of
such a change in political alignment would be. It is at this point that
the linkages between local and national power assume a determining
role. Just as, under normal circumstances, the interlocking of local
and national power has given DC machines in the South remarkable
resiliency, so these linkages make the margins for change at the local
level very narrow. Even if the machine is defeated at the periphery,
clientelistic power on a much larger scale (exemplified by the logic of
sottogoverno that permeates the Italian political system) remains intact at the center. Thus, basic change in the structural constraints that
now shape politics in the South depends above all on a fundamental
shift in power and policy at the national level.

The critical issue here is the relationship between clientelistic power and socioeconomic structure. Thriving upon poverty and social fragmentation, the machine, through its ties to national power, can perpetuate the conditions of dependency and underdevelopment in which it is rooted and which impede the mobilization of mass support along alternative lines. The hold of clientelism on southern Italy can be broken only by the presence in Rome of a governing coalition with the political will and the necessary resources to launch a process of autonomous development in the South, creating centers of economic power no longer dependent upon links to political power for their survival. Given the peculiarities of the Italian political system, what would be needed would be a Socialist government in order to create a dynamic capitalism in the South.

Italy is a classic case of economic and political dualism, an unparalleled example of internal dependency in which modernity and backwardness are inextricably intertwined. As such, the Italian case is of major importance for development theory, because it represents the paradigm toward which much of the Third World is presently moving – a model of development in which, within a single country, a "center" of advanced capitalism linked to world markets coexists with and thrives upon a backward "periphery" doomed to exploitation and emargination. In such a context of both external and internal dependency, the role of clientelism in development is an issue of fundamental importance. Some students of clientelism have argued that, especially in the early stages of modernization, the machine makes a positive contribution to both economic and political development, by circumventing obstacles to entrepreneurship, by integrating populations with no prior experience of political participation, and by defusing potential class, racial, or ethnic conflicts.[8] The case of southern Italy demonstrates both the virtues and the limits of such an analysis. With regard to economic development, thirty years of DC rule have indeed produced undeniable processes of development in the South. However, because DC power in the South is based primarily on clientelistic exchange, which in turn is rooted in dependency and the manipulation of scarcity, it is unlikely that governments controlled by the DC will ever promote autonomous processes of development that could eventually undermine the structural bases of the party's power. As for political integration and social stability, the DC machine in southern Italy, like New York's Tammany Hall, has performed an important function of political socialization for poor, uneducated, often recently urbanized populations. In fact, in the Italian case, the success of clientelism in integrating low-income groups into the existing system and in guaranteeing social and political stability in a potentially explosive socioeconomic context has been considered by one analyst as "the major political achievement of the DC."[9] At the same time this process has integrated these groups into the existing system on terms of subordination and manipulation, exploiting their immediate individual needs so as to impede their mobilization on a collective basis in pursuit of more radical social, economic, and political goals.

The machine is thus above all an instrument for the preservation of the political and socioeconomic status quo. It will limit socioeconomic change within boundaries that do not threaten political control over essential resources, as well as perpetuating a society constructed on the exacerbation of individual privilege on the one hand and on mass deprivation and collective squalor on the other. The consequences of such a system of political support can be clearly seen in the degradation of the conditions of urban existence in cities like Palermo and Naples, in the total neglect of collective needs in the frenzied pursuit of individual gain. This growing gap between individual benefits and social costs is the major internal contradiction of the system of power constructed by the DC in the South. By the 1970s these social costs (unemployment, the shortage of low-income housing, inadequate public services) had begun to give rise to outbursts of popular anger (especially among the poor) which, although periodically assuaged by short-term clientelistic rewards, carry within themselves the potential for change. It is just such popular anger that brought the Left to power in Naples, and will judge it equally harshly if it fails to deliver on its promises.

Whether the political contours of the South a decade hence will resemble more closely those of Palermo or of Naples depends above all, as discussed earlier in this Conclusion, on the configuration of national politics. It is nonetheless true, however, that the performance of the Left in Naples will have reverberations throughout the rest of the South. Notwithstanding the constraints of economic structure and national power, two critical goals confront the Left in Naples: (1) to begin to redress the neglect of collective goods and services which has devastated southern cities; and (2) to lay the bases for a radical transformation in the relationship between the citizen and the state, overcoming the age-old alienation of the South with new forms of popular participation at the grass roots. Should the Left fail to achieve even these limited goals, the political future of the South provides little cause for optimism. On the one hand, the forces of clientelism could find a ready point of reentry; on the other, a crisis of the DC combined with the failure of the Left could offer a propitious terrain for either the demagogic appeals of the neo-Fascist

Right or the nihilism of the terrorist Left. The latter possibility is given some credibility by the phenomenon of steadily rising abstention rates in the South since 1976, which points to a growing gap between the population and existing political institutions. While in the short run abstention could reinforce the electoral hold of the machine, in the longer term it signals a break in the integrating and stabilizing functions performed thus far by clientelism. If neither the DC nor the Left succeeds in restoring the credibility of democratic institutions, the South may well prove to be the Achilles heel of Italian democracy.

Statistical appendix

A methodological note

This book is based on thirteen months (January 1976–February 1977) of intensive fieldwork in Palermo and on subsequent research visits to Palermo and to Naples in the summers of 1978 and 1980. Because of the nature of the research and the absence, in the case of Palermo, of any published works on local politics apart from the abundant but, with a few exceptions, not very useful literature on the mafia, the research methodology leaned heavily on a combination of personal interviews and participant observation, supplemented by material from the local press. Because of the lack of secondary sources, the local press was particularly important in Palermo for reconstructing local political life from the late 1940s to the mid-1970s. There are two daily newspapers in Palermo – the *Giornale di Sicilia*, of a Center to Center-Right tendency, and *L'Ora*, associated with the Left. The latter, taking into due account the possibility of political bias, was especially useful for information on the functioning of and the internal power struggles within the local DC, and for in-depth investigative reporting on the events surrounding the elaboration of the city plan and the subsequent speculative development of the city in the mid-1960s. In Naples such extensive reliance on the local press to reconstruct local history was unnecessary because of the existence of a number of well-documented studies of Neapolitan politics before 1975, as well as first-hand accounts by leading participants of the political life of the city in the early years of the left-wing administration (1975–7). Given this more solid point of departure for the Naples research, the press served primarily as a means to keep abreast of current events during the period of 1978–80.

Official sources of data on both cities included the Censuses of the Population and of Industry and Commerce, electoral results at both the city and the neighborhood level, and various documents of the city government. In Palermo, apart from census data (the inadequacies of which are discussed in Chapter 2), other official sources of information proved extraordinarily hard to come by. I would argue that this is a direct by-product of the clientelistic organization of local government. Because of clientelistic hiring, the city bureaucracy is characterized by such a degree of organizational chaos that it is equipped neither to collect data in any systematic way nor to make whatever data may exist available to the public. Basic information, like the exact number of city employees and their distribution among departments, was a mystery even to the head of the Personnel Office of the Commune, to whom I arrived armed with the requisite "recommendations." This brings me to the second critical aspect of clientelism as it affects the conduct of research in a city like Palermo. To extract even the most trivial piece of information from a public office requires an affidavit of political trustworthiness from someone in a position of responsibility, a process that is often both frustrating and time-consuming. Thus, for example, when I arrived on my own at the Electoral Office of the Commune to collect electoral results at the neighborhood level, it required a lengthy effort of persuasion with the department head in order to convince him that I was not a spy for a political party and therefore could be trusted with access to what are by law "public" documents. In Naples, on the other hand, the city government was much more efficient in this regard, publishing a wide variety of statistical information at both the city and the neighborhood level in an annual yearbook. Whether this achievement is to be attributed to the left-wing administration, I cannot say, but the contrast with the difficulties encountered in Palermo was striking.

In both cities, however, what published works or statistical data were available served primarily as background material. The principal concerns of the research – in Palermo the nature of the linkages between the DC and various social groups and in Naples the causes of the Communist victory and of the party's subsequent difficulties – were, as indicated above, of such a nature as to require a methodology relying heavily on personal interviews and, with regard to the chapter on the politics of the urban poor, on participant observation. In Palermo local journalists proved to be an invaluable source of information on the political life of the city, both past and present. More formal interviews were conducted with members of the provincial leadership of the major political parties and labor unions, with city councillors and assessors, and with representatives of the local associations of shopkeepers, artisans, and small farmers. At the neighborhood level, informal conversations were held with activists of both the DC and the PCI, with representatives of the *comitati di quartiere*, and with people like priests and social workers, who had both a detailed knowledge of the neighborhood and a certain position of influence therein. These sources were supplemented by participant observation at meetings of the *comitati di quartiere* and of Communist Party sections in several low-income neighborhoods, by first-hand involvement in the *movimento per la casa* and the electoral campaign of 1976, and by direct personal experience of the conditions of life in the slums of the old city. In Naples, because of greater time constraints, the field research was based primarily on interviews with local party elites (both DC and PCI) and with neighborhood activists of the PCI and the extraparliamentary Left, as well as with students and scholars at the University of Naples who were themselves involved in sociological, political, or economic research at the local level. Participant observation, which played a major role in the Palermo research, was limited in Naples to coverage of the 1980 elections.

Table A.1. *National Electoral Results (Camera dei Deputati), 1948–80 (percentages of vote)*

	1948	1953	1958	1963	1968	1972	1976	1979	1980 (regional elections)
DC	48.5	40.1	42.3	38.3	39.1	38.8	38.8	38.3	36.8
MSI/Mon-archists	4.8	12.8	9.7	6.8	5.8	8.7	6.1	5.3	5.9
PLI	3.8	3.0	3.5	7.0	5.8	3.9	1.3	1.9	2.7
PRI	2.5	1.6	1.4	1.4	2.0	2.9	3.1	3.0	3.0
PSDI	7.1	4.5	4.6	6.1	14.5[b]	5.2	3.4	3.8	5.0
PSI	31.0[a]	12.7	14.3	13.9		9.6	9.7	9.8	12.7
PCI		22.6	22.7	25.3	27.0	27.2	34.4	30.4	31.5
Radicals	—	—	—	—	—	—	1.1	3.4	—
New Left	—	—	—	—	4.5	2.9	1.5	2.2	2.1
Turnout	—	—	—	—	—	93.2	93.4	89.9	87.7

[a] The PCI and the PSI presented a joint list in elections from 1947 until 1952.
[b] In the 1968 election the PSI and the PSDI were unified under the name Partito Socialista Unificato (PSU).
Note: Dash signifies no list presented. For turnout, dash signifies no figures available.
Source: Ministry of the Interior.

Table A.2. *Electoral results for the city of Palermo, 1946–80 (percentages of vote)*

	DC	MSI/Monarchists	PLI	PRI	PSDI	PSI	PCI	Radicals and New Left	Other
1946 (Constituent Assembly)	25.3	39.1[a]	16.9	3.1	—	4.4	2.6	—	8.6
1946 (municipal)	14.5	44.3[b]	11.5	—	—	9.8	12.1	—	7.8
1948 (national)	45.9	23.2	7.1	2.4	4.0	12.5[e]		—	5.0
1952 (municipal)	25.0	41.1	3.9	1.3	4.5	22.5		—	1.7
1953 (national)	33.1	35.6	3.7	0.8	2.4	4.9	17.2	—	2.3
1956 (municipal)	35.8	28.8	3.9	0.4	5.4	8.6	16.2	—	0.9
1958 (national)	42.3	20.7	3.4	0.9	4.4	9.9	18.1	—	0.3
1960 (municipal)	37.9	17.7	4.1	(See PSI)	4.4	7.1[c]	13.8	—	14.9[f]
1963 (national)	36.0	15.2	11.0	2.2	5.0	10.0	17.4		3.2
1964 (municipal)	44.4	10.1	9.8	4.7	6.2	6.0	13.0	2.3	3.5
1968 (national)	41.7	12.1	7.1	5.3	10.4[d]		17.3	4.8	1.4
1970 (municipal)	40.7	9.5	6.0	8.6	6.4	9.7	13.5	3.3	2.2
1972 (national)	40.3	19.1	4.5	3.6	4.4	7.4	17.2	1.7	1.7
1975 (municipal)	41.7	10.4	3.9	7.0	4.8	9.4	18.4	1.4	3.1
1976 (national)	43.8	12.2	1.8	3.8	3.5	6.7	24.4	3.4	0.0
1979 (national)	44.8	11.0	2.5	4.5	4.7	6.9	16.5	7.8	1.3
1980 (municipal)	46.7	8.5	4.2	6.8	6.1	11.6	15.4	—	0.7

ᵃ Monarchists, Uomo Qualunque, and Separatist movement.

ᵇ Monarchists and Uomo Qualunque.

ᶜ Joint list of PSI, PRI, and Radicals.

ᵈ In the 1968 election the PSI and the PSDI were unified under the name Partito Socialista Unificato (PSU).

ᵉ The PCI and the PSI presented a joint list in elections from 1947 until 1952.

ᶠ The entire other vote is represented by Unione Siciliana Cristiano Sociale (USCS), a DC splinter group.

Note: Dash signifies zero.

Sources: 1946–72, official data from the Ministry of the Interior; 1975–80, L'Ora (June 17, 1975; June 22, 1976; June 5, 1979; June 11, 1980).

Table A.3. Palermo, electoral results by type of neighborhood, 1970–6 (in percentages)

	DC	Right	PLI, PRI, PSDI	PSI	PCI	Radicals/ New Left
Middle-class neighborhood (Sciuti)						
1970	38.4	12.8	27.1	8.6	7.1	2.7
1972	36.2	26.1	18.5	6.5	9.3	1.3
1975	39.9	15.2	17.1	9.3	13.3	1.9
1976	45.6	16.3	11.2	6.5	15.0	5.1
Old city/Sottoproletariato						
Kalsa						
1970	39.5	10.7	18.9	9.6	14.5	2.4
1972	42.4	19.8	9.9	7.2	17.7	2.1
1975	44.6	10.2	15.6	7.6	17.8	—
1976	47.6	11.4	9.0	5.6	24.4	3.0
Capo						
1970	37.4	12.6	22.5	8.5	13.1	3.5
1972	37.7	22.6	12.7	5.9	17.6	2.6
1975	39.8	13.8	16.9	7.2	18.5	1.3
1976	39.2	13.4	8.3	4.6	31.9	2.6
Borgate						
Villagrazia						
1970	59.5	5.7	18.6	4.5	7.3	1.8
1972	57.8	9.7	15.3	3.6	11.4	1.6
1975	60.3	3.5	16.9	5.9	11.1	0.6
1976	67.5	6.1	5.2	3.0	13.6	2.4
Roccella						
1970	45.9	5.3	19.7	8.3	16.4	3.3
1972	48.7	12.5	8.3	6.1	20.2	2.9
1975	48.3	6.0	13.1	7.4	21.3	1.1
1976	51.9	7.1	6.6	4.8	26.6	2.5
Public-housing projects						
Borgo Nuovo						
1970	30.5	6.6	15.6	14.7	25.1	—
1972	30.6	13.5	8.8	12.6	30.6	2.6
1975	33.4	6.6	14.1	13.4	28.4	1.2
1976	32.1	8.0	7.8	9.8	39.2	2.5
CEP						
1970	24.5	5.4	17.6	23.3	25.0	2.8
1972	26.6	11.5	9.4	14.2	34.0	3.0
1975	29.5	4.9	17.3	13.4	28.9	2.6
1976	30.7	6.8	9.2	11.5	39.1	2.5
ZEN						
1970[a]						
1972	32.9	11.1	9.2	10.0	29.4	5.5
1975	36.3	4.6	12.7	10.0	29.8	3.0
1976	34.6	5.1	8.4	7.5	41.4	2.6

[a] ZEN did not exist as a distinct electoral section in 1970.
Note: Dash signifies zero. Results broken down by neighborhood are not available for the 1979 and 1980 elections.
Source: Compiled from data from the Electoral Office of the Commune of Palermo.

Table A.4. *Electoral results for the city of Naples, 1952-80 (percentages of vote)*[a]

	DC	MSI/Mon-archists	PLI	PRI	PSDI	PSI	PCI	Radicals and New Left	Other
1952 (municipal)	23.9	42.9	4.1	0.4	1.5	3.0	21.5	—	2.6
1953 (national)	30.3	36.5	2.7	0.4	1.5	5.2	21.3	—	2.2
1956 (municipal)	16.4	56.9	1.7	—	0.8	4.5	19.2	—	0.6
1958 (national)	32.0	31.2	2.0	0.5	1.4	6.9	25.0	—	1.1
1960 (municipal)	26.2	39.2	2.1	—	2.0	6.0	23.4	—	1.6
1962 (municipal)	27.8	36.5	2.7	—	3.2	8.4	20.9	—	0.5
1963 (national)	30.2	19.4	8.5	0.7	4.0	11.5	25.0	—	0.8
1964 (municipal)	34.7	18.6	8.0	—	5.7	6.6	24.6	1.7	0.2
1968 (national)	29.2	19.5	6.3	2.0	10.1[b]		28.1	3.0	1.9
1970 (municipal)	34.0	15.8	4.6	2.6	7.1	7.4	26.0	1.8	0.8
1972 (national)	28.4	26.3	3.2	2.3	3.7	5.6	27.8	1.2	0.5
1975 (municipal)	28.4	18.5	2.0	3.1	6.9	6.9	32.3	1.5	0.4
1976 (national)	29.9	15.5	1.0	2.6	2.1	4.8	40.8	3.1	0.2
1979 (national)	30.5	16.4	1.4	2.8	4.0	5.9	30.7	8.1	0.2
1980 (municipal)	25.3	22.3	1.8	3.0	6.5	7.7	31.7	1.6[c]	0.1

[a] Results for the Constituent Assembly in 1946, the municipal elections of 1946, and the parliamentary elections of 1948 were not available.

[b] In 1968 the PSI and the PSDI were unified under the name Partito Socialista Unificato (PSU).

[c] The Radical Party, which accounted for the bulk of the "Radical and New Left" vote in 1979, did not present a list for the 1980 local elections.

Note: Dash signifies zero.

Sources: 1952-68, *Bollettino di statistica* (Naples, 1978); 1970-76, Ministero dell'Interno; 1979-80, *Corriere della Sera* (June 5, 1979, and June 11, 1980).

Table A.5. *Naples, electoral results by type of neighborhood, 1972–80 (in percentages)*

	PCI	DC	Right	Radicals
Middle-class neighborhood (Vomero)				
1972	14.2	29.7	31.8	—
1975	21.4 (+7.2)	30.0 (+0.3)	23.0 (−8.8)	—
1976	25.3 (+3.9)	34.9 (+4.9)	19.5 (−3.5)	2.4
1978	"Yes" on repeal of public financing, 65.3			
1979	18.4 (−6.9)	33.5 (−1.4)	15.6 (−4.0)	9.8 (+7.4)
1980	23.7 (+5.3)	24.6 (−8.9)	28.2 (+12.6)	—
Old city/sottoproletariato (Montecalvario)				
1972	26.8	26.2	32.0	—
1975	29.3 (+2.5)	28.4 (+2.2)	23.7 (−8.3)	—
1976	39.5 (+10.2)	28.9 (+0.5)	19.4 (−4.3)	1.2
1978	"Yes" on repeal of public financing, 62.4			
1979	28.7 (−10.8)	30.6 (+1.7)	18.8 (−0.6)	5.2 (+4.0)
1980	29.2 (+0.5)	25.0 (−5.6)	27.4 (+8.6)	—
Industrial zone/working class (S. Giovanni)				
1972	48.8	22.3	16.3	—
1975	52.4 (+3.6)	21.6 (−0.7)	10.7 (−5.6)	—
1976	63.4 (+11.0)	19.0 (−2.6)	8.9 (−1.8)	0.5
1978	"Yes" on repeal of public financing, 43.4			
1979	55.8 (−7.6)	19.6 (+0.6)	8.8 (−0.7)	2.9 (+2.4)
1980	56.0 (+0.2)	16.6 (−3.0)	12.2 (+4.0)	—
Urban periphery/public housing (Secondigliano)				
1972	36.3	23.8	21.8	—
1975	36.4 (+0.1)	24.4 (+0.6)	14.5 (−7.8)	—
1976	49.5 (+13.1)	25.0 (+0.6)	12.5 (−2.0)	0.7
1978	"Yes" on repeal of public financing, 62.1			
1979	35.5 (−14.0)	27.0 (+2.0)	12.6 (+0.1)	3.7 (+3.0)
1980	33.8 (−1.7)	23.9 (−3.1)	18.2 (+5.6)	—

Note: Dash signifies zero.
Sources: 1972–6, *Bollettino di Statistica* (Naples, 1977); 1978–80, data from Neapolitan Federation of PCI.

Notes

Introduction

1 An excellent anthology, including both the anthropological and the political science literature on clientelism, is Steffen W. Schmidt et al., eds., *Friends, Followers and Factions: A Reader in Political Clientelism* (Berkeley: University of California Press, 1977). See also the anthology edited by S. N. Eisenstadt and R. Lemarchand, *Political Clientelism, Patronage and Development* (Beverly Hills: Sage, 1981).

2 James C. Scott, "Patron–Client Politics and Political Change in Southeast Asia," *American Political Science Review*, 66 (March 1972): 92.

3 For a detailed theoretical analysis of the nature of clientelism, see Luigi Graziano, "A Conceptual Framework for the Study of Clientelism," *European Journal of Political Research*, Vol. 4, no. 2 (June 1976): 149–74. Graziano in turn relies to a large extent on Peter Blau, *Exchange and Power in Social Life* (New York: Wiley, 1964) in elaborating his model of clientelistic exchange.

4 On the American experience, see Edward C. Banfield and James Q. Wilson, *City Politics* (New York: Random House, Vintage Books, 1963); Ira Katznelson, *Black Men, White Cities* (London: Oxford University Press, 1973); Robert K. Merton, *Social Theory and Social Structure* (New York: Free Press, 1957), pp. 70–82; Martin Shefter, "The Emergence of the Political Machine: An Alternative View," in Willis D. Hawley et al., *Theoretical Perspectives on Urban Politics* (Englewood Cliffs, N.J.: Prentice-Hall, 1976), pp. 14–44; and Raymond E. Wolfinger, "Why Political Machines Have Not Faded Away and Other Revisionist Thoughts," *Journal of Politics*, 34 (May 1972): 365–98. On machine politics in developing nations, see, in addition to the Scott article cited above, Wayne A. Cornelius, *Politics and the Migrant Poor in Mexico City* (Stanford University Press, 1975); Elizabeth Leeds, "Forms of 'Squatment' Political Organization: The Politics of Control in Brazil" (M.A. Thesis, University of Texas, 1972), Chapter 2, "Games Favelas Play"; Joan M. Nelson, *Access to Power: Politics and the Urban Poor in Developing Nations* (Princeton University Press, 1979), Chapter 5, "Traditional Leaders, Patrons, and Urban Political Machines"; James C. Scott, "Corruption, Machine Politics and Political Change," *American Political Science Review*, 63 (December 1969): 1142–58.

5 See, for example, Scott, "Corruption" (1969); Francine R. Frankel, "Democracy and Political Development: Perspectives from India," *World Politics*, Vol. 21, no. 3 (April 1966): 448–68; and Myron Weiner, *Party-Building in a New Nation: The Indian National Congress* (University of Chicago Press, 1967), pp. 368–370. This argument is made with regard to the specific case of southern Italy in Mario Caciagli et al., *Democrazia Cristiana e potere nel Mezzogiorno* (Florence: Guaraldi, 1977).

6 In addition to Caciagli et al. (1977), see Percy Allum, *Politics and Society in Post-War Naples* (Cambridge University Press, 1973), and Sidney Tarrow, *Peasant Communism in Southern Italy* (New Haven, Conn.: Yale University Press, 1967).

7 Important exceptions are Wolfinger (1972) and Allan Rosenbaum, "Machine Politics, Class Interest and the Urban Poor" (unpublished paper delivered at the 1973 annual meeting of the American Political Science Association, New Orleans, September 4–8, 1973), with regard to the American case. Although most of the Latin American literature has focused on the machine as it relates to the urban poor, one exception is the Mexican case, where the entire political system has been likened to a political machine. See John F. H. Purcell and Susan Kaufman Purcell, "Machine Politics and Socio-Economic Change in Mexico," in James W. Wilkie et al., eds., *Contemporary Mexico* (Berkeley: University of California Press, 1976), pp. 348–66.

8 Good examples of this approach are Banfield and Wilson (1963); Michael Bamberger, "A Problem of Political Integration in Latin America: The Barrios of Venezuela," *International Affairs* (London), Vol. 44, no. 4 (October 1968), pp. 709–19; and Oscar Lewis, *The Children of Sanchez* (New York: Random House, 1961) and *La Vida* (New York: Random House, 1965).

9 Banfield and Wilson (1963), p. 123.

10 See especially Cornelius (1975); Anthony and Elizabeth Leeds, "Accounting for Behavioral Differences: Three Political Systems and the Responses of Squatters in Brazil, Peru, and Chile," in John Walton and Louis H. Masotti, eds., *The City in Comparative Perspective* (Beverly Hills: Sage, 1976), pp. 193–247; Janice E. Perlman, *The Myth of Marginality: Urban Poverty and Politics in Rio de Janeiro* (Berkeley: University of California Press, 1976).

11 Martin Shefter, "The Electoral Foundations of the Political Machine" (unpublished paper, Cornell University, October 1972), pp. 53–4.

12 Such a model is explicit in Allum (1973), and in Luigi Graziano, "Patron–Client Relationships in Southern Italy," *European Journal of Political Research*, Vol. 1, no. 1 (April 1973), pp. 3–34, and implicit, it would seem to me, in Tarrow, *Peasant Communism* (1967).

13 For exploration of this issue from a cross-national perspective, see Eisenstadt and Lemarchand (1981).

14 For an excellent discussion of the nature of the Italian state, see Giuseppe Di Palma, "The Available State: Problems of Reform," in Peter Lange and Sidney Tarrow, eds., *Italy in Transition: Conflict and Consensus* (London: Frank Cass, 1980), pp. 149–65.

Chapter 1. Politics in the South, 1860–1943

1 The major contributions to the discussion of the *"questione meridionale,"* from the nineteenth century to the present, are included in the excellent anthology compiled by Bruno Caizzi, ed., *Nuova antologia della questione meridionale* (Milan: Edizioni di Comunità, 1975), which provides ample references to the original works. For a deeper understanding of southern Italian and, in particular, Sicilian history, see Rosario Villari, ed., *Il Sud nella storia d'Italia*, 2 vols. (Bari: Laterza, 1972); Leopoldo Franchetti and Sidney Sonnino, *Inchiesta in Sicilia*, 2 vols. (Florence: Vallecchi, 1974); and Dennis Mack Smith, *A History of Sicily*, 2 vols. (London: Chatto and Windus, 1968).

2 In their book *Contro la questione meridionale* (Rome: Samonà e Savelli, 1972), E. Capecelatro and A. Carlo argue that in 1860 the North and the South were at very similar levels of economic development and that the *"questione meridionale"* is therefore a result purely of postunification economic policies. While the evidence they present as to the industrial development of cities like Naples and Palermo prior to 1860 is an important corrective to the prevailing conception of a totally backward South, the South in general in 1860 was still overwhelmingly characterized by a feudalistic agrarian economy. I agree with their argument about the impact of postunification policies, but see them as aggravating an existing disparity rather than creating one where none existed.

3 Giuseppe Tomasi di Lampedusa, *The Leopard* (New York: Pantheon, 1960), p. 40.

4 Tarrow, *Peasant Communism* (1967), pp. 13–14.

5 Antonio Gramsci, "Alcuni temi della quistione meridionale," in *La questione meridionale* (Rome: Editori Riuniti, 1966), p. 149.

6 Feudalism was legally abolished in the continental Mezzogiorno in 1806, during the French occupation, and in Sicily in 1812, under pressure from the British government. In both cases the socioeconomic reality of feudalism was much more difficult to eradicate, persisting in many parts of the countryside until 1945.

7 An excellent literary prototype of this rising bourgeois landowning class is the figure of Calogero Sedara in Lampedusa's novel *The Leopard*.

8 The term "agro-town" refers to the settlement pattern of densely populated rural agglomerations prevalent in southern Italy, in contrast to a pattern of scattered settlements with peasant families living directly upon the land. For a discussion of the origins of the agro-town, see Anton Blok, "South Italian Agro-Towns," *Comparative Studies in Society and History*, 11 (1969): 121–35.

9 Sidney Sonnino, "Condizioni generali dei contadini in Sicilia," in Caizzi (1975), pp. 217–21.

10 For a more detailed discussion of the fragmentation of the peasantry, see Manlio Rossi-Doria, *Riforma agraria e azione meridionalistica* (Bologna: Edizioni Agricole, 1948).

11 For a good overview of the literature on clientelism, see the anthology edited by Schmidt et al., *Friends, Followers, and Factions* (1977).

12 For contemporary descriptions of *trasformismo*, see Pasquale Turiello, "La vita politica nel Mezzogiorno," and Gaetano Salvemini, "Lo Stato italiano e la vita politica meridionale," in Caizzi (1975), pp. 349–66; and Leopoldo Franchetti, "Il governo e le influenze locali in Sicilia," in Villari (1972), pp. 118–27.

13 W. A. Salomone, *L'età giolittiana* (Turin: De Silva, 1949), p. 14.

14 Gaetano Salvemini, *Scritti sulla questione meridionale* (Turin: Einaudi, 1955), p. 48.

15 Giampiero Carocci, *Giolitti e l'età giolittiana* (Turin: Einaudi, 1971), p. 22.

16 Francesco Crispi, *Scritti e discorsi politici* (Rome, 1890), p. 575 (cited in Allum [1973], p. 69).

17 It is important to note that the feudal system disintegrated much more quickly in the continental Mezzogiorno than in Sicily. As a result, the rise of a new class of wealthy bourgeois landowners was more marked on the mainland, while in large parts of Sicily feudal patterns of social stratification continued to prevail.

18 Franchetti and Sonnino (1974), Vol. 1, p. 210.

19 Ibid., p. 194.

20 Peasant rebellions were endemic in southern Italy both before and after unification. Short-lived but violent, they left a permanent mark on southern society in the form of widespread brigandage and a deeply rooted sense of alienation from the state. For further discussion, see Dennis Mack Smith, *Italy: A Modern History* (Ann Arbor: University of Michigan Press, 1959), and Franco Molfese, *Storia del brigantaggio dopo l'unità* (Milan: Feltrinelli, 1964).

21 On the role of the Prefect, see Gaetano Salvemini, "La piccola borghesia intellettuale nel Mezzogiorno d'Italia," in Caizzi (1975), especially pp. 387–9.

22 Guido Dorso, *La rivoluzione meridionale* (Turin: Mondadori, 1969), pp. 153–4.

23 Recounted by Rocco Zerbi, a Neapolitan journalist, to Giustino Fortunato (cited in Allum [1973], pp. 67–8).

24 Allum (1973), p. 70.

25 For a general overview of the Fascist period, including its impact on the South, two excellent works are Adrian Lyttelton, *The Seizure of Power: Fascism in Italy, 1919–1929* (London: Weidenfeld and Nicolson, 1973), and Edward R. Tannenbaum, *The Fascist Experience: Italian Society and Culture, 1922–1945* (New York: Basic Books, 1972).

26 Michele Pantaleone, *The Mafia and Politics* (London: Chatto and Windus, 1966), p. 43.

27 Ibid., p. 35.

28 Anton Blok, *The Mafia of a Sicilian Village, 1860–1960* (New York: Harper and Row, 1975), p. 182.

29 The term *mandante* refers to a person who pays another to commit a crime for him.

Chapter 2. The southern economy

1 The legislative mandate of the Cassa per il Mezzogiorno, which was due to expire in 1976, was renewed for another four years thanks to an agreement between the Christian Democrats and the Communists, as a result of which Communist representatives for the first time received seats on the Cassa's administrative council. At the end of 1980, as this new mandate ran out, a heated debate over the Cassa's future (Should the Cassa continue to exist at all? Should its functions be primarily technical rather than financial? What should its relationship with the new regional governments be?) raged among Italy's political parties. For an excellent overview of the institutional structure of the Cassa, its legislative mandate, the details of its industrial incentive policies, and an analysis of Cassa investments from 1950 to 1975, see Gisele Podbielski, *Twenty-Five Years of Special Action for the Development of Southern Italy* (Milan: Giuffrè Editore, 1978).

2 Total Cassa expenditure between 1951 and 1975 (at constant 1975 prices) was 17,685,400,000 lire (approximately U.S. $29.5 million, taking 600 lire to the dollar); during this period Cassa expenditure fluctuated between 0.6% and 1.5% of GNP (Podbielski [1978], pp. 74, 76).

3 In 1951 the rate of labor force participation was 41.1% in the South and 48.9% in the Center-North; in 1975 the figures were 32.5% for the South and 38.7% for the Center-North (Podbielski [1978], p. 112).

4 Net emigration from the South was 1,755,000 between 1952 and 1961, and 2,665,000 between 1962 and 1975 (Podbielski [1978], p. 113).

5 Data on investment from Claudio Grosso, "Per una storia della Cassa per il Mezzogiorno," *Quaderni Siciliani* (October 1973): 63.

6 For a detailed examination of the changing industrial incentive policies of the Cassa, see Podbielski (1978), pp. 60–72.

7 For an excellent analysis of one such project, see E. Hytten and M. Marchioni, *L'Industrializzazione senza sviluppo: Gela, una storia meridionale* (Milan: Franco Angeli, 1970). See also Jane Hilowitz, *Economic Development and Social Change in Sicily* (Cambridge, Mass.: Schenkman Publishing Co., 1976).

8 Podbielski (1978), pp. 171–3.

9 Alberto Statera, "Chi semina miliardi raccoglie onorevoli," *L'Espresso* (June 23,

1974), pp. 116–17. See also the discussion of the Cassa in Tarrow, *Peasant Communism* (1967), pp. 300–42.

10 Ada Collidà, "Aspetti clientelari dell'intervento straordinario nel Mezzogiorno," in Luigi Morelli, ed., *Sviluppo e sottosviluppo nel Mezzogiorno d'Italia dal 1945 agli anni '70* (Naples: Morano Editore, 1972), pp. 182–7.

11 Ibid., p. 186.

12 Data on the impact of the economic crisis from *Rapporto sul Mezzogiorno, 1977*, prepared by SVIMEZ (Associazione per lo sviluppo dell'industria nel Mezzogiorno) and presented in Naples on June 25, 1978.

13 Salvatore Cafiero, *Sviluppo industriale e questione urbana nel Mezzogiorno* (Milan: Giuffrè Editore, 1976), pp. 25–6.

14 Eric Hobsbawm, *Primitive Rebels* (New York: Norton, 1959), p. 114.

15 Fernand Braudel, *The Mediterranean and the Mediterranean World in the Age of Philip II*, 2 vols. (New York: Harper and Row, 1972), Vol. 1, p. 347.

16 For an excellent analysis of the role of the "city mob" in European history, see Hobsbawm (1959), Chapter 7, "The City Mob."

17 Ibid., pp. 115–16.

18 Ibid., p. 124.

19 Detailed figures on population movements for all southern Italian cities during the periods 1951–61 and 1961–71 can be found in Cafiero (1976), p. 64.

20 The Italian census defines "active population" in the following way: the total of the employed, the unemployed due to loss of a prior job, and young people seeking their first job. The figures presented in the text refer to the active population *"in condizione professionale,"* i.e., excluding those in search of first employment. This is consistent with the way the term is used in most Italian analyses and is necessary in order to calculate the sectoral distribution of the labor force, as those in search of a first job cannot be categorized. The census figures for the active population cannot, however, be considered an accurate indicator of the true dimensions of the labor force, because they exclude both "hidden employment" (those workers in various forms of precarious employment that elude census documentation) and "hidden unemployment" (those who would be willing to work if opportunities were available, but who have withdrawn in discouragement from the official labor market and are therefore classified by the census as "inactive"). In the absence of more accurate data, the census figures are still useful as an indication of the diversity of economic structure in various parts of the country, a contrast that emerges quite clearly even with very inadequate data.

21 See the articles by Giuseppe De Meo, Luca Meldolesi, Marcello De Cecco, Massimo Paci, and Luigi Frey in Salvatore Vinci, ed., *Il mercato del lavoro in Italia* (Milan: Franco Angeli, 1974); Giorgio La Malfa and Salvatore Vinci, "Disoccupazione palese e disoccupazione nascosta," in A. Graziani, ed., *L'economia italiana, 1945–1970* (Bologna: Il Mulino, 1972), pp. 331–6; and Massimo Paci, *Mercato del lavoro e classi sociali in Italia* (Bologna: Il Mulino, 1973).

22 Theoretical discussion of the functions of productive decentralization for Italian capitalism can be found in Suzanne Berger and Michael Piore, *Dualism and Discontinuity in Industrial Societies* (New York: Cambridge University Press, 1980), especially Chapter 4. For a review of the Italian research on this question, see Judith Chubb, "The Functions of Economic Marginality: The Case of Italian Industry" (unpublished paper delivered at M.I.T., September 1975).

23 With regard to the limitations of Italian data on employment, see note 20. Indicative of the difficulties facing the researcher in pursuit of more reliable figures on unemployment is the following comment by a functionary of the Department of Labor

(Assessorato al Lavoro) of the Sicilian Regional Government: "Figures on unemployment? Believe me, this is a tragedy. We ourselves don't have any, nor have we succeeded in procuring any." (*L'Ora*, December 9, 1976).

24 The official figures for Palermo are from the Ufficio Provinciale del Lavoro, while those for Naples were cited in "Vedi Napoli che muore," *Panorama* (February 9, 1981), p. 49. The unofficial estimates are from interviews with trade-union leaders.

25 The state of economic statistics at the communal level is near disastrous. The only official sources are the Census of the Population, which breaks down the labor force into broad economic categories (agriculture; extractive industries; manufacturing; construction; electricity, gas and water; commerce; transportation and communications; services; and public administration) and the Census of Industry and Commerce, which reports the number of firms and employees for each of the above categories and their subcategories. The Census of Industry and Commerce also gives figures on the distribution of firms by size (i.e., number of employees), but at the city level this data is reported only for the general categories of "industry," "commerce," and "other." The categories employed by both censuses are so general as to be of little assistance to one who seeks a detailed understanding of the occupational structure of the city.

A search for alternative sources of economic data – from the municipal and regional governments, from the Chamber of Commerce, and from the university – proved to no avail. The only interesting and useful source uncovered was a 1974 publication by INPS (the state social security system) in Palermo, which outlined the economic situation of the city and the province using data compiled on the basis of social security contributions. Unfortunately, neither this nor the census, because of their built-in biases toward registration of the regularly employed, has any reliable information regarding the substantial portion of the population employed in the "marginal" labor market. Finally, the statistical data presented by these various sources is grossly inconsistent, not only among the three, but at times even within any one of them. Such confusion is maddening and advises against undue reliance on the exactitude of any of the data to be presented.

26 Cafiero (1976), p. 31. For tables providing comparable figures for all southern and northern cities, see ibid., pp. 74–5.

27 An estimate of "marginal" employment can be obtained by comparing the results of the Census of the Population and the Census of Industry and Commerce. While the former is carried out door-to-door, asking the occupation of every member of the family, the latter collects its data from the individual firm. The former thus has the possibility of registering certain forms of "marginal" labor, while the latter reports only those workers with a minimally stable position. Comparison of the two can thus give a rough approximation of the size of the "marginal" work force and its distribution by economic sector. Where the results of the industrial census are in excess of those of the population census, this is an indication of pendolarity – i.e., workers who are employed in the city while residing elsewhere.

28 The following data are not meant to be exhaustive, but merely to give an indication of the impact of the economic crisis in the South. In Palermo, of a sample of 104 food-processing plants present in 1971, only 58 were still in operation at the end of 1976 (*L'Ora*, September 20, 1976); within the same period the shoe industry, once an important source of exports, had almost totally collapsed (interview with a trade-union leader, December 7, 1976). In Naples over 8,000 workers in small and medium-sized firms were laid off between June 1977 and June 1978 alone. Statistical data regarding the impact of the crisis on the southern economy can be found in SVIMEZ, *Rapporto sul Mezzogiorno, 1977*.

29 The Cassa Integrazione is a mechanism by which the state maintains the wages of workers temporarily laid off in times of economic crisis, thereby avoiding outright firing of the workers and consequent increases in unemployment.

30 Interview with a trade-union leader (November 2, 1976).

31 Ibid.

32 Ibid.

33 Comitato Provinciale INPS Palermo, *Annotazioni sulla situazione socio-economica della Provincia di Palermo* (Palermo: Author, 1974), p. 174.

34 Comune di Palermo, *Panormus 1974* (Palermo: Author, 1976), p. 18; Comune di Napoli, *Bollettino di Statistica 1977* (Naples: Author, 1978), pp. 560–2.

35 The estimate of the number of *abusivi* ("unlicensed vendors") in Palermo is from an interview with the director of the Federazione Provinciale dei Commercianti (Confcommercio) on December 17, 1976. For Naples, I assumed approximately the same percentage of *abusivi* as in Palermo, calculated against the figures for total commercial licenses provided by the city government.

36 *L'Ora* (November 20, 1973).

37 See especially Lisa Peattie, "Tertiarization and Urban Poverty in Latin America," in W. A. Cornelius and F. M. Trueblood, eds., *Urbanization and Inequality: The Political Economy of Urban and Rural Development in Latin America* (Beverly Hills: Sage, 1975), pp. 109–24. For further discussion of the "marginal" labor force in Third World cities, see David G. Epstein, *Brasilia: Plan and Reality* (Berkeley: University of California Press, 1973), and T. G. McGee, "The Persistence of the Proto-Proletariat" (Comparative Urbanization Studies, University of California at Los Angeles, 1974).

38 Hobsbawm (1959), pp. 113–14.

39 For Palermo I am using as a point of departure the study by Renée Rochefort, *Le travail en Sicile* (Paris: Presses Universitaires de France, 1961). Although her estimate refers to the late 1950s, there is no evidence to suggest that the ranks of the urban poor have significantly diminished since then. As for Naples, a 1975 report by members of the left-wing factions of the local DC to the party's provincial secretary claims that at least half of the urban labor force is either unemployed or underemployed, thus for the most part falling into the general category of *sottoproletariato* ("La necessità di un impegno politico e sociale a Napoli" [mimeograph, 1975]).

40 Rochefort, *Le travail en Sicile* (1961), and Danilo Dolci, *Report from Palermo* (New York: Viking Press, 1970). Even though both studies are dated, the overall picture they paint of the mechanisms of survival among the urban poor is as relevant today as it was when the research was carried out in the 1950s.

41 Lello Mazzacane, ed., *I "bassi" a Napoli* (Naples: Guida Editori, 1978), reports the results of a study of seven slum neighborhoods in Naples carried out by a team of sociology students from the University of Naples. Thomas Belmonte, *The Broken Fountain* (New York: Columbia University Press, 1980), is a first-hand account of life in the Neapolitan slums during Belmonte's one year of field research.

42 *L'Espresso* (May 3, 1959), cited in Allum (1973), pp. 47–8.

43 Rochefort, *Le travail en Sicile* (1961), p. 312.

44 A 1975 survey performed by students of the Faculty of Medicine of the University of Palermo in one typical slum neighborhood revealed that only 28.7% of adult males had stable employment. A similar study in Naples (Mazzacane, 1978) produced a figure of only 18.2%.

45 Renée Rochefort, "Les bas-fonds de Palermo," *Annales, Economies, Sociétés, Civilisations* (April–June 1958): 352.

46 Dolci, *Report from Palermo* (1970), pp. 24–5, 74–5.

47 Mazzacane (1978), p. 28.

48 The overall figure for scholastic evasion in the city of Palermo is about 8% (this includes children up to the 8th grade, which is the limit of compulsory education in Italy). Reports by social workers in slum neighborhoods, however, show percentages of working children in the elementary classes as high as 50%–80% (*L'Ora*, May 23, 1969).

49 *L'Ora* (May 6, 1969).

50 With regard to child labor in Palermo, see a six-part inquiry in *L'Ora* (May 6–23, 1969). For Naples see, in addition to Mazzacane (1978), the article by Camilla Cederna, "Spettabile ditta Scugnizzi & C.," *L'Espresso* (December 2, 1979).

Chapter 3. Christian Democracy in the postwar South

1 The following works give a good overview of the evolution and role of the DC at the national level: Lidia Menapace, *La Democrazia Cristiana: Natura, struttura e organizzazione* (Milan: Gabriele Mazzotta Editore, 1975); Ruggero Orfei, *L'occupazione del potere: I democristiani '45/'75* (Milan: Longanesi, 1976); Arturo Parisi, *I democristiani* (Bologna: Il Mulino, 1979); Alan S. Zuckerman, *The Politics of Faction: Christian Democratic Rule in Italy* (New Haven: Yale University Press, 1979).

2 This situation was not unique to the DC; in many local situations even the parties of the Left found themselves obliged to depend on local notables to lead party sections. As a result, party struggles often had little to do with ideology, reflecting instead the traditional factional divisions of the town.

3 For a detailed account of the absorption of the local mafia bosses into the DC, see Pantaleone (1966), pp. 195–225.

4 For a detailed account of local government in Naples under the Monarchist administrations of Achille Lauro, see Allum (1973), pp. 274–89, 307–15.

5 Cited in Tarrow, *Peasant Communism* (1967), p. 306.

6 As president of the Sicilian Region, Franco Restivo headed a series of Center-Right governments between 1949 and 1955.

7 The following paragraphs on Fanfani's reforms in the South draw heavily on Tarrow, *Peasant Communism* (1967), pp. 300–42.

8 Cited in ibid., p. 308.

9 Ibid., p. 309.

10 Ibid., p. 308.

11 The takeover of power by Gioia in Palermo was paralleled by a similar ascent of the "young Turks" throughout the South. Documentation of this process in two other major southern cities can be found in Allum (1973) and in the in-depth study of the DC in Catania by Mario Caciagli et al., *Democrazia Cristiana e potere nel Mezzogiorno* (1977).

12 *L'Ora* (February 12, 1959).

13 Literally, the term *"ascaro"* comes from the word used by the British in East Africa for tribal chiefs who fought in the colonial armies. In the Italian context, it is used as a derogatory term to describe a local politician who is considered to have "sold out" the interests of his region in return for access to national power.

14 *Corriere della Sera* (November 7, 1973).

15 For a detailed denunciation of the means utilized by the *fanfaniani* to secure and maintain power, see the document prepared by the left-wing factions of the DC in Palermo and sent to the national party leadership, "Libro bianco della DC, "*L'Ora* (December 11, 1970).

16 The membership figures for the DC in Palermo were obtained from the National Organizational Office of the DC in Rome. Only membership data for the current year is kept at the party's provincial headquarters in Palermo.

17 *Corriere della Sera* (November 7, 1973).

18 "Libro bianco della DC," *L'Ora* (December 11, 1970).

19 From an article by Lino Jannuzzi in *L'Espresso* (cited by Giuliana Saladino in *De Mauro: Una cronaca palermitana* [Milan: Feltrinelli, 1972], p. 96).

20 See note 11.

21 The numerous *enti* operating under the tutelage of the various levels of government in Italy are referred to in Italian as *sottogoverno*. The presidencies and administrative councils of these bodies are strictly divided up among the parties making up the governing coalition at the city, provincial, regional, or national level. Control of these *enti* is so important for patronage purposes that government crises are often protracted for weeks or even months before the parties can agree on the division of these critical levers of power.

22 The political career of Salvo Lima is described in detail in a three-part series of articles in *L'Ora*, "Il sindaco degli anni violenti" (January 24, 25, and 28, 1963).

23 The electoral network of a DC candidate can be divided into three levels: the *grandi elettori*, the *capi-elettori*, and the *galoppini*. The position of the *grande elettore* is analogous to that of the traditional notable, e.g., the deputy, the mayor, the local mafia boss, the parish priest, who is in a position to exert widespread influence among a variety of social groups. Beneath him in the hierarchy is the *capo-elettore*, who is usually the leader of a single group network, e.g., a neighborhood "boss" or a leader of a single union like construction workers or city employees. Finally we come to the *galoppino*, who is paid either in cash or patronage to perform petty electoral services like the distribution of pasta or facsimiles for the candidate. The operation of these networks is described in detail in Allum (1973), pp. 170–7.

24 The City Council became in effect an appendage of the DC. It was convened in accordance not with administrative regulations, but rather with the logic of the internal factional struggles of the DC. When disaccord reigned within the Provincial Committee of the DC, months would pass without a meeting of the City Council; the entire administrative life of the city would be paralyzed until the competing cliques within the party could recompose their differences. When the City Council was convened, the arrogance of the DC was such that hundreds of items would be approved on a voice vote without giving the opposition recognition to make an objection; on one occasion 2,700 items were passed within a period of 20 minutes. Domination of the Provincial Control Commission by the DC guaranteed that any challenges to such procedures would go unheeded.

25 Since 1952 the Palermo city government has been controlled continuously by the DC, either in shifting coalitions with centrist and right-wing parties (PSDI, PRI, PLI, PNM) or occasionally (April 1971–January 1972, December 1977–November 1978) through minority DC administrations. The only breaks in this pattern have been three periods of Center-Left rule with the participation of the PSI (January 1965-December 1966, January 1976–December 1977, November 1978–July 1980). In none of these periods was either the substance or the style of local government significantly altered by the sharing of power with the Socialist Party.

26 *Testo integrale della relazione della commissione parlamentare d'inchiesta sul fenomeno della mafia*, Vol. 1 (Rome: Cooperativa Scrittori, 1973), p. 43.

27 *L'Ora* (February 13, 1959).

28 Cited in Tarrow, *Peasant Communism* (1967), p. 311.

29 Ibid., pp. 325–6.

30 See Franco Cassano, *Il teorema democristiano* (Bari: De Donato, 1979) for an anlysis of the role of the DC in postwar Italy in terms of the contradiction between the demands of capital accumulation and the demands of legitimation (popular consensus). Cassano argues that, after the failure of the attempt to introduce a majoritarian electoral system in 1953, the DC turned to a strategy of mass clientelism in order to reconcile the conflicting interests of its electoral base (composed of both the most modern and the most backward sectors of the Italian bourgeoisie, as well as important strata of the white-collar middle classes, workers, and peasants). In the absence of a coherent ideology, the DC promoted the fragmentation of Italian society into a multitude of corporative interests, all considered equally legitimate and all competing for a share of the resources of the state. Eventually the acceleration of public expenditure that this strategy entailed diverted resources from productive investment and produced even larger budget deficits, thereby undermining the accumulation process and creating a specifically Italian variant of the "fiscal crisis of the state."

31 Tarrow, *Peasant Communism* (1967), p. 332.

32 CISL (Confederazione Italiana dei Sindacati Lavoratori) is the Catholic laborunion federation; ACLI (Associazione Cristiana dei Lavoratori Italiani) is a cultural-recreational association for workers associated with the left-wing factions of the DC; the Coltivatori Diretti is the association of small peasant proprietors.

33 For extensive discussion of this issue, see Joseph La Palombara, *Interest Groups in Italian Politics* (Princeton University Press, 1964), and Giuseppe Di Palma, "The Available State: Problems of Reform," in Lange and Tarrow, eds., *Italy in Transition: Conflict and Consensus* (1980), pp. 149–65.

34 Luigi Graziano, *Clientelismo e sistema politico: Il caso dell'Italia* (Milan: Franco Angeli, 1980), p. 69.

35 Tarrow, *Peasant Communism* (1967), p. 327.

36 Cited in ibid.

37 This model is explicit in Allum (1973), and in Luigi Graziano, "Patron–Client Relationships in Southern Italy" (1973). It is also implicit, it would seem to me, in Tarrow, *Peasant Communism* (1967).

38 Tarrow, *Peasant Communism* (1967) and Allum (1973).

39 The men who succeeded Lima as mayor of Palermo between July 1966 and January 1976 were without exception colorless second-rank politicians who served as fronts for the personal power of Gioia.

40 Despite the fact that Lima's new majority coalition included the "left-wing" factions of Forze Nuove and the *morotei* and supported a more open policy toward the Communists at the local level, the management of power within the party continued to be based on the techniques perfected by the "right-wing" *fanfaniani*.

41 Giovanni Gioia has been a member of the Consiglio Nazionale of the DC since 1956 and of the party's Direzione Centrale since 1964; from January to October 1969 he served as national vice-secretary of the DC. Gioia also served as undersecretary of finance from February 1966 to December 1968, as minister of the postal system from June 1972 to July 1973, as minister for relations between the government and parliament from July 1973 to November 1974, and as minister of the merchant marine from November 1974 to July 1976. Salvo Lima was undersecretary of finance from June 1972 to November 1974 and undersecretary of the budget from November 1974 to July 1976; he has been a member of the Direzione Centrale of the DC since 1976.

It would be misleading, however, to ignore Lima's own links to national power in explaining his ultimate ascendancy over Gioia. After his split with Gioia, Lima aligned himself with the Andreotti faction at the national level. It is hardly coincidental that Gioia's exclusion from ministerial rank and Lima's own accession to the national leadership organs of the DC coincided with the inauguration of the Andreotti government in July 1976. Both Gioia's fall from grace and Lima's ties with the new prime minister clearly played a part in the factional realignment at the local level which, like its counterpart at the national level, was played out around the issue of Communist participation in the government.

Chapter 4. The white-collar middle class

1 See Scott (1969); Frankel (1969); and Weiner (1967), pp. 368–70. This argument is made with regard to southern Italy in Caciagli et al. (1977).

2 In addition to Caciagli et al. (1977), see Tarrow, *Peasant Communism* (1967) and Allum (1973).

3 The Uomo Qualunque was a short-lived right-wing political movement that flourished, especially in the large southern cities, in the immediate postwar period, appealing primarily to the lower-middle class and the urban poor.

4 For a more detailed discussion of the relationship between the traditional middle classes and the marginal labor force, see Alessandro Pizzorno, "I ceti medi nei meccanismi del consenso," in Fabio Luca Cavazza and Stephen Graubard, eds., *Il caso italiano* (Milan: Garzanti, 1974), pp. 327–8.

5 See Pizzorno (1974); Berger and Piore (1980), Chapter 4; Ermanno Gorrieri, *La giungla retributiva* (Bologna: Il Mulino, 1972); Paolo Sylos-Labini, *Saggio sulle classi sociali* (Bari: Laterza, 1975).

6 Pizzorno (1974), p. 322.

7 Ibid.

8 Ibid., pp. 330–1.

9 Comitato Provinciale INPS Palermo (1974), p. 174.

10 *L'Ora* (September 28, 1967).

11 "He who gives me bread gives me life."

12 *L'Ora* (September 30, 1967).

13 Luigi Graziano, "Partito di regime e clientelismo di massa," *Rinascita* (August 8, 1975): 14.

14 *L'Ora* (September 28, 1967).

15 It is unfortunately impossible to document the increase in the size of the city and provincial bureaucracies, for both of which it proved impossible to obtain reliable data on employment prior to 1976. At the end of 1976, municipal employees (including the *aziende municipalizzate*) numbered about 9,500, while the number of provincial employees was about 850. At the end of 1980, after a five-year period in which hiring had virtually ground to a halt, the city administration revealed a plan to hire 10,000 new employees. This would bring the total number of employees of the Comune di Palermo (excluding the *aziende municipalizzate*) to 12,226, making it the largest "industry" in Sicily (*Corriere della Sera*, October 6, 1980). For figures on the expansion of the regional bureaucracy, see p. 95.

16 *L'Ora* (September 28, 1967).

17 Danilo Dolci, *Chi gioca solo* (Turin: Einaudi, 1967), p. 188.

18 The following paragraph is based primarily on information obtained in an interview with the provincial secretary of the union of regional employees of the CGIL (October 27, 1976). With regard to the extent of patronage hiring in the regional bureaucracy, the 1976 report of the Antimafia Commission revealed that, from 1946 to 1963, 8,236 out of a total of 8,887 (92.7%) regional employees entered on the basis of personal recommendations; of these 73.2% came from the "mafia" provinces of western Sicily, which account for only about half of the island's population. Senato della Repubblica, *Commissione parlamentare d'inchiesta sul fenomeno della mafia in Sicilia, Relazione conclusiva* (February 4, 1976), pp. 205–6.

19 The discussion of techniques of patronage hiring that follows is based on information from the following sources: interview with the provincial secretary of the regional employees' union of the CGIL (October 27, 1976); interview with the provincial secretary of the municipal employees' union of the CGIL (October 23, 1976); Dolci, *Chi gioca solo* (1967); and local press accounts.

20 Dolci, *Chi gioca solo* (1967), pp. 192–3.

21 The figure of the *usciere* ("usher") is fundamental to an understanding of the functioning of public bureaucracies in Italy and, in particular, of a clientelistic system of power like that of Palermo. The *usciere* is a ubiquitous figure in every office (there are 82 in the offices of the city government alone), but his precise functions are difficult to discern. First and foremost, the position of *usciere* represents the epitome of job patronage, requiring no other quality but physical presence. The *usciere* does, however, perform an important – and to the public often exasperating – function, that of controlling access to public offices and in particular to persons in high positions. This role of "guardian of the sanctuary" has symbolic as well as functional aspects: the *usciere* personifies the social and political gap between the official and the individual citizen, who is instilled with appropriate awe as he is shuttled from one *usciere* to another before finally gaining access to the "inner chamber." Finally, the *usciere* serves an important communications function, carrying messages and documents from one office to another in a bureaucracy with no institutional links between different departments.

22 Data from the Office of Personnel of the Comune di Palermo.

23 These examples were cited in an interview with the provincial secretary of the regional employees' union of the CGIL (October 27, 1976).

24 *L'Ora* (November 10, 1976).

25 *Giornale di Sicilia* (March 12, 1976).

26 Gorrieri (1972).

27 Ibid., p. 131.

28 The following paragraph is based on information from an interview with the provincial secretary of the regional employees' union of the CGIL (October 27, 1976) and from a special inquiry of *L'Ora* on the top-level bureaucrats of the regional government (October 11, 13, 16, 18, 20, 23, 25, 27, and 31, 1972).

29 At the end of 1976, 16 out of 35 DC city councillors and 40 out of 59 DC section secretaries in the city of Palermo were public employees.

30 Dolci, *Chi gioca solo* (1967), p. 188.

31 *L'Ora* (December 13, 1976).

32 *L'Ora* (May 9, 1975).

33 Interviews with the provincial secretaries of the municipal and regional employees' unions of the CGIL (October 23 and October 27, 1976).

34 For a more detailed discussion of public-sector unions in Italy, see Gorrieri (1972), pp. 132–3, 238–41.

35 Ibid., p. 133.

36 Sources for the electoral data on Palermo are *L'Ora* (June 17, 1975; June 22, 1976; June 10, 1980). For a detailed analysis of the role of the preference vote in Italian politics, see Alvaro Ancisi, *La cattura del voto: Sociologia del voto di preferenza* (Milan: Franco Angeli, 1976).

37 This tendency has been demonstrated by the periodic large-scale transfers of allegiance by public employees, especially high-level bureaucrats, in the ongoing struggle for power between Gioia and Lima in Palermo. As belonging to the right faction is critical to the success of a bureaucratic career, bureaucrats have been quick to follow every shift in the balance of power between the two. Most recently, as the victory of Lima in the upcoming Provincial Congress of May 1977 became increasingly probable, scores of top bureaucrats changed from *fanfaniani* to *limiani* overnight.

Chapter 5. The local entrepreneurial class

1 For a pluralist perspective, see Robert Dahl, *Who Governs?* (New Haven: Yale University Press, 1961), and Edward C. Banfield, *Political Influence* (New York: Free Press of Glencoe, 1961). For an approach based on the concept of elite dominance, see Floyd Hunter, *Community Power Structure* (Chapel Hill: University of North Carolina Press, 1953), C. Wright Mills, *The Power Elite* (New York: Oxford University Press, 1956), and Peter Bachrach and Morton Baratz, *Power and Poverty: Theory and Practice* (New York: Oxford University Press, 1970).

2 For analysis of the *"entrepreneur comme rentier,"* see Raimondo Catanzaro et al., *L'Imprenditore assistito* (Bologna: Il Mulino, 1979), pp. 281–90. This study also provides survey data documenting the attitudes of local entrepreneurs toward various forms of investment, pp. 266–71.

3 Personal conversations with Franco Vaccina, Professor of Social Statistics at the University of Palermo, and Alberto Spreafico, Professor of Political Science at the University of Catania. For further discussion of the industrial salvage programs of the Sicilian Region, see "The use of public funds."

4 For discussion of the relationship between the politician and the entrepreneur, see Carlo Donolo, "Sviluppo ineguale a disgregazione sociale: Note per l'analisi delle classi nel meridione," *Quaderni Piacentini*, no. 47 (July 1972): 122–3; S. Bonazzi, A. Bagnasco, and S. Casillo, *Industria e potere in una provincia meridionale* (Turin: L'Impresa Edizioni, 1972), Chapter 13; and Catanzaro et al., *L'Imprenditore assistito* (1979), especially Chapters 5 and 9.

5 Pizzorno (1974), p. 330.

6 Bonazzi, Bagnasco, and Casillo (1972).

7 Catanzaro et al., *L'Imprenditore assistito* (1979).

8 Ibid., Chapter 5, "Intervento pubblico e riproduzione della marginalità," pp. 183–212.

9 Ibid., p. 298.

10 Raimondo Catanzaro, "Potere e politica locale in Italia," *Quaderni di Sociologia*, Vol. 24, no. 4 (October–December (1975): 291–2.

11 Graziano, "Partito di regime e clientelismo di massa" (1975), p. 14.

12 More detailed information on SOFIS and ESPI can be found in P. Pumilia and M. Buscemi, *Il volto di una classe dirigente: Uomini e responsabilità nella realtà ESPI* (Palermo: Centro Regionale Studi CISL, 1971); Dino Grammatico, *Processo alla Regione Siciliana* (Milan: Edizioni del Borghese, 1974), pp. 24–42; and the "Rapporto Rodinò" (a report by the special commissar of ESPI to the president of the Region), published by *L'Ora* (September 17, 1969).

13 *L'Ora* (April 12, 1973).

14 Cited in Pumilia and Buscemi (1971), p. 31.

15 Extensive documentation of the corruption in the awarding of the public-works contracts of the City of Palermo can be found in *Mafia e potere politico: Relazione di minoranza e proposte unitarie della commissione parlamentare d'inchiesta sulla mafia* (Rome: Editori Riuniti, 1976), pp. 74–91, 243–7. With regard to the entrepreneurial activities of the Calabrian mafia, see Pino Arlacchi, "Mafia e tipi di società," *Rassegna Italiana di Sociologia* (January–March 1980): especially 32–48.

16 The presidency of a major bank is such an important political prize that it is bitterly contested among competing factions within the DC. In some cases, like that of the Banco di Sicilia, the factional struggle is so intense that years may pass before the party succeeds in agreeing upon a candidate. After the expiration of the term of the bank's last president in 1968, over a decade of bitter intraparty struggle ensued before a successor could be agreed upon.

17 For a detailed analysis of the distribution of publicly guaranteed credit in the Province of Catania, see Catanzaro et al., *L'imprenditore assistito* (1979), pp. 183–212.

18 The last attempt to affirm an investment strategy giving priority to local entrepreneurs rather than to large outside monopolies climaxed in 1958–9 in the brief alliance between the SOFIS and the Milazzo government (a short-lived alliance of the Right and the Communists with dissident Christian Democrats to form a regional government without the DC). The return of the DC to power in 1959 sealed the fate of the "autonomist" illusions of Milazzo and opened the way to the intensive penetration of the Sicilian economy by the northern monopolies.

19 *IRFIS Vent'anni, 1954–1973 (Noriziario IRFIS,* no. 34, April 1974), pp. 56–67.

20 Interview with Franco Amoroso, president of API-Sicilia (Associazione Piccola e Media Industria), November 29, 1976; *L'Ora* (March 11, 1973).

21 The critical role of the commercial banks in furthering the careers of certain well-placed building contractors in Palermo will be discussed in Chapter 6.

22 The parts of this section that deal specifically with the traditional middle classes in Palermo are based on information from the following sources: for the shopkeepers, interviews with the provincial secretaries of the two leading associations – the Federazione Provinciale dei Commercianti (Confcommercio), close to the DC (December 17, 1976), and the Confesercenti, allied with the Left (November 30, 1976) – as well as with Pietro Lorello, municipal assessor of commerce (December 23, 1976; for the artisans, interviews with the provincial secretaries of two of the three local associations – the Federazione Unitaria degli Artigiani (C.N.A.), allied with the Left (December 15, 1976), and the Unione Provinciale dell'Artigianato, formally nonallied but rumored to be close to the faction of Lima (January 10, 1977).

23 Carmelo Miceli, president of the Confcommercio (personal interview, December 17, 1976).

24 For further discussion of measures to favor small shopkeepers, see Suzanne Berger and Michael Piore, *Dualism and Discontinuity in Industrial Societies* (1980), Chapter 4; Roberto Ariotti, "Pretese corporativistiche ed esigenze di sviluppo nella programmazione del commercio," *Il Mulino,* no. 216 (July–August 1971): 611–36; Tiberio Torrato, "Valvassori e Valvassini: Comuni e bottegai," *Il Mulino,* no. 207 (January–February 1970): 114–16.

25 Torrato (1970), p. 116.

26 Lorello and Miceli interviews.

27 Cited in Giuseppe Sottile, "Ecco come un vigile può essere trasformato in grande elettore," *L'Ora* (November 13, 1972).

28 Ibid.

29 Interview with Salvatore Genovesi, president of the Federazione Unitaria degli Artigiani (December 15, 1976).

Chapter 6. The mafia as entrepreneur

1 ISTAT, *9° Censimento generale della popolazione* (1951).

2 *L'Ora* (June 23, 1961).

3 Franco Pitisi, president of SUNIA (left-wing tenants' organization), cited in *L'Ora* (June 7, 1973).

4 *L'Ora* (June 21, 1973).

5 *L'Ora* (January 25, 1963).

6 The information concerning the PRG has been taken primarily from the following sources: "Inchiesta sul sacco di Palermo," *L'Ora* (June 23, 27, 30, 1961); "Cronaca della speculazione edilizia," *L'Ora* (June 7, 13, 21, 1973); *Relazione Bevivino* (report to the president of the Region by the *commissione per l'ispezione straordinaria presso il Comune di Palermo,* February 13, 1964 [mimeograph]), pp. 3–7.

7 Senato della Repubblica, *Commissione parlamentare d'inchiesta sul fenomeno della mafia in Sicilia, Relazione conclusiva* (February 4, 1976), p. 217. Hereafter referred to as *Antimafia Commission* (1976).

8 *L'Ora* (June 27, 1961).

9 *L'Ora* (June 13, 1973).

10 For a list of the most prominent figures involved, see *L'Ora* (July 24 and 25, 1962).

11 The information on the career of Vassallo was taken from the following sources: *Mafia e potere politico* (1976), pp. 62–72; Marcello Cimino, "L'impero Vassallo" (article based on the unpublished dossier of the first Antimafia Commission), *L'Ora* (September 30, 1969).

12 Cimino, "L'impero Vassallo" (1969), citation from the dossier of the Antimafia Commission.

13 *Relazione Bevivino* (1964), pp. 31–6, 43–4, 51–3.

14 *Testo integrale della relazione della commissione parlamentare d'inchiesta sul fenomeno della mafia,* Vol. 2 (1972), hereafter referred to as *Antimafia Commission* (1972), pp. 1921–2; this volume of the report of the Antimafia Commission devotes an entire chapter to the issue of school construction, pp. 1857–941.

15 *Antimafia Commission,* Vol. 2 (1972), p. 1920.

16 Ibid., p. 1918.

17 *Il Domani* (Palermo), August 1962.

18 "He who is deaf, blind, and keeps his mouth shut will live a hundred years in peace."

19 Napoleone Colajanni, *Nel regno della mafia* (Palermo: Renzo Mazzone, 1971), p. 110.

20 For a self-description by a powerful mafia boss, see "Portrait of a 'Capo-Mafia,'" in Danilo Dolci, *Waste* (New York: Monthly Review Press, 1964), pp. 109–22.

21 The above analysis of the nature of the mafia is taken from Henner Hess, *Mafia* (Bari: Laterza, 1973). Illustrative of the image of the mafioso as *galantuomo* is the epigraph of a powerful mafia boss who died in 1961: "Enemy of all injustice, he demonstrated by his words and his works that his mafia was not delinquency but respect for the laws of honor." (Gaia Servadio, *Mafioso* [New York: Dell, 1976], p. 166).

22 For a listing of the victims of mafia violence against the peasant movement, see Pantaleone, *The Mafia and Politics* (1966), pp. 207–11.

23 *L'Ora* (October 20, 1958).

24 *Antimafia Commission,* Vol. 1 (1972), p. 146.

25 Ibid., p. 147.

26 For the results of the inquiry of the Antimafia Commission on the wholesale markets of the city of Palermo, see *Antimafia Commission,* Vol. 2 (1972), pp. 1761–864.

27 It is a well-known fact in Palermo that Don Paolino Bontà, one of the most prominent *capi-mafia* of the Conca d'Oro and a *grande elettore* first for the Monarchists and subsequently for the DC, virtually controlled the Sit-Siemens, the most modern industrial firm in Palermo, serving as an intermediary to obtain water rights and land for expansion, as well as personally "suggesting" the names of the workers to be hired. See *Mafia e potere politico* (1976), pp. 222–3.

28 *Relazione Bevivino* (1964), pp. 10–14.

29 Michele Pantaleone, *Antimafia: Occasione mancata* (Turin: Einaudi, 1969), p. 19. The word "friends" in Sicilian signifies the mafia.

30 *Relazione Bevivino* (1964), p. 13.

31 *L'Ora* (June 21, 1973).

32 For a detailed description of the war between the Grecos and the La Barberas, see *Antimafia Commission*, Vol. 1 (1972), pp. 469–520.

33 Ibid., p. 475.

34 The *lupara* is the traditional type of shotgun used in the Sicilian countryside. When loaded with a special type of shell, it constituted the preferred weapon of the agrarian mafia for use in vendettas.

35 For a listing of the victims, see Pantaleone (1969), p. 159.

36 *Antimafia Commission*, Vol. 1 (1972), pp. 878–9.

37 *Antimafia Commission* (1976), p. 221.

38 The information on Ciancimino was taken primarily from the following sources: *Antimafia Commission* (1976), pp. 221–37; Orazio Barrese, *I complici: Gli anni dell'Antimafia* (Milan: Feltrinelli, 1973), pp. 222–47; Giulia Sala, "Vita di un cittadino che non è al di sopra di ogni sospetto," *L'Ora* (January 23, 1971).

39 *L'Ora* (January 23, 1971).

40 As of the end of 1976, one-fifth to one-quarter of the party members in the city of Palermo belonged to party sections controlled by Ciancimino (data from membership figures of the DC, Comitato Provinciale di Palermo).

41 Cited in Barrese (1973), p. 231.

42 Asked how he would explain the rapid disintegration of Gioia's "empire" in Palermo in 1976, Ciancimino replied, without batting an eyelash: "He lost the support of Ciancimino." (Personal interview, August 2, 1978.)

43 Ciancimino himself estimated that at least 95% of entrepreneurs in Palermo vote for the DC. He added, "I personally do not know a single entrepreneur who doesn't vote for the DC." (Personal interview, August 2, 1978.)

44 *Antimafia Commission* (1976), pp. 236–7.

45 Michele Reina, Lima's right-hand man and provincial secretary of the DC from January 1976 until his death in March 1979, was deeply involved, both as ex-president of the Province and as provincial secretary of the DC, in the allocation of highly lucrative public-works contracts. Although, as usual, the inquiries into his death have failed to produce any conclusive evidence, the most widely held hypothesis is that he ran up against mafia interests in one of these dealings. The case of Piersanti Mattarella, head of the Moro faction in Sicily and spokesman for an "historic compromise" with the Communists at the regional level, is more complex. The first hypothesis was that, like Moro, he had been killed by left-wing terrorists in order to prevent the consummation of the DC–PCI alliance in Sicily. Subsequently, however, the theory of a mafia execution gained increasing credibility. Unlike Reina, no one suspects Mattarella of collusion with the mafia; on the contrary, during his two years as president of the Region, Mattarella had initiated a series of top-level investigations into both the regional and city governments, investigations which, it is surmised, may have threatened vital mafia interests. Whoever committed the crime, one basic objective was achieved: the reform both of his own party and of local government that Mattarella championed has become a nonissue since his death.

46 Franco Amoroso, president of API-Sicilia, estimated that in 1976 only 5% of current residential construction was constituted by public housing (interview, November 29, 1976). Data from a 1974 study by the Centro Ricerche Economiche, Sociologiche e di Mercato nell'Edilizia (CRESME) indicated that, after Rome, Palermo was the Italian city with the highest percentage of luxury apartments, but in second-to-last place for low-income housing (*L'Ora*, June 21, 1974).

47 Data on construction workers from *L'Ora* (February 13, 1975).

48 A summary of the legislative provisions regarding *risanamento* was prepared by the Faculty of Architecture of the University of Palermo, "Materiali per il dibattito sul risanamento del centro storico di Palermo" (mimeograph, 1976). The text of the agreement between the city government and the REP, as well as the subsequent resolutions of the City Council, can be found in *Quaderni Siciliani* (March–April 1974): 53–6.

49 *Quaderni Siciliani* (March–April 1974): 56.

50 Only in October 1980 did the City Council finally approve the plan for the first project, the reconstruction of a neighborhood near the port, which has remained bombed-out since 1943. Approval of the project by the regional government is still necessary, however, and in Sicily the wheels of bureaucracy move very slowly.

51 Estimate by the chief engineer of the Ripartizione Urbanistica of the City of Palermo (internal memorandum, 1976).

Chapter 7. The urban poor: poverty and political control

1 Estimate of the chief engineer of the Ripartizione Urbanistica of the City of Palermo (internal memorandum, 1976).

2 Dolci, *Report from Palermo* (1970), p. xxi.

3 Survey by students of the Faculty of Medicine of the University of Palermo (1975–6 academic year).

4 Interview with social worker of the Missione Palermo (February 9, 1976).

5 Karl Marx, "Class Struggles in France," in Lewis S. Feuer, ed., *Marx and Engels: Basic Writings on Politics and Philosophy* (New York: Doubleday, Anchor Books, 1959), p. 298.

6 Friedrich Engels, "Preface to *The Peasant War in Germany*," in Marx and Engels, *Selected Works* (New York: International Publishers, 1968), p. 243.

7 Karl Marx and Friedrich Engels, "Manifesto of the Communist Party," in Marx and Engels, *Selected Works* (1968), p. 44.

8 The declining political influence of the Church is also in part a result of a more general process of secularization of Italian society over the past decade. This phenomenon is most evident in the results of the referenda on divorce and abortion. 59.1% of Italians (56.3% in Palermo) voted in favor of divorce in 1974, and 67.9% of Italians (66.3% in Palermo) voted in favor of abortion in 1981.

9 Cited in *L'Ora* (April 23, 1963).

10 The above paragraph is based on personal conversations with Alessandro Pizzorno.

11 Account of a DC organizer, reported in *L'Ora* (July 1, (1975).

12 Giuseppe Sottile, "Un dittatore chiamato capo-zona," *L'Ora* (February 22, 1974).

13 *L'Ora* (July 1, 1975).

14 *L'Ora* (July 5, 1975).

15 Dolci, *Chi gioca solo* (1967), p. 271.

16 Ibid., p. 273.

17 *L'Ora* (July 1, 1975).

18 Letter reproduced in *L'Ora* (March 14, 1961).

19 For a detailed description of the "electoral beneficence" practiced by the regional Assessorato agli Enti Locali, see *L'Ora* (March 14, 1961, and March 10, 1972).

20 *L'Ora* (October 23, 1967).

21 The episode of the "tax fraud" was recounted in *L'Ora* (May 28, 1971).

22 On the role of the *vigile*, see Giuseppe Sottile, "Ecco come un vigile può essere trasformato in grande elettore," *L'Ora* (November 13, 1972).

23 *L'Ora* (July 9, 1975).

24 Hess, *Mafia* (1973), p. 49.

25 Cited in Dolci, *Waste* (1964), p. 122.

26 Personal interview (February 21, 1976).

Chapter 8. The urban poor: three neighborhood studies

1 The information in the three neighborhood studies comes from personal interviews with party activists, trade-union leaders, priests, social workers, and local residents in each of the neighborhoods considered. These interviews were supplemented by participant observation of political activity at the neighborhood level, including meetings of PCI sections and of the *Comitati di Quartiere*, electoral meetings of the PCI and the DC prior to the June 1976 elections, and the *movimento per la casa*, from the perspective of both the PCI and the extraparliamentary Left.

2 A resident of the *centro storico* and PCI activist (cited in Dolci, *Chi gioca solo* [1967], p. 133).

3 The information on the *movimento per la casa* comes from participant observation, from interviews with both leaders of the movement and participants, and from local press accounts.

4 *Giornale di Sicilia* (March 25, 1976).

5 Document of the "Coordinamento per le case pericolanti" (representing Avanguardia Operaia, PDUP, and the Movimento Studentesco), November 1975.

6 Cited in Dolci, *Chi gioca solo* (1967), p. 135.

7 Michael Lipsky, *Protest in City Politics* (Chicago: Rand McNally, 1970).

8 *L'Ora* (April 23, 1968).

9 *L'Ora* (May 25, 1973).

10 P. Ignazio Vitale, "Un caso di sottosviluppo: L'analfabeta della porta accanto," *Notiziario IRFIS*, no. 31 (April 1972). This study shows rates of scholastic evasion of 42% and illiteracy of 37%.

11 Cited in Dolci, *Chi gioca solo* (1967), p. 133.

12 *L'Ora* (November 6, 1972).

13 Survey conducted by Padre I. Vitale and Padre G. Russo in the *quartiere* CEP; results reported in *L'Unità* (June 1, 1974).

14 Document published in *L'Autonomia: Quindicinale siciliano di politica e cultura*, Supplement to no. 1 (early 1960s, exact date unknown).

15 Interview with Alberto Morandi, director of the Provincial Federation of the Coltivatori Diretti and president of the Cassa Mutua Coltivatori (October 19, 1976).

16 Interview with Salvatore Curatolo, provincial secretary of the Federbraccianti-CGIL (April 8, 1976).

17 Interview with Salvatore Bronte, DC city councillor and delegate of the mayor to the *borgata* of Villagrazia, and visit to the *delegazione* (January 5, 1977).

Chapter 9. Why does clientelism survive?

1 Mancur Olson, *The Logic of Collective Action* (New York: Schocken, 1968), p. 51.

2 Ibid., p. 165.

3 This argument was made most recently in Caciagli et al. (1977).

4 *L'Ora* (July 22, 1978).

5 The one case in which an eventual restriction in public spending could have a negative impact on the bases of DC support is that of public employees. Well organized in defense of corporative privileges, they could represent a serious threat to political stability if an attempt were made to limit or to eliminate those privileges. Precisely because of their political clout, however, it is unlikely that such an attempt would be made. The tremendous leverage exerted by public employees is one of the major obstacles in the way of rationalization of the Italian state.

Chapter 10. Naples under the Left

1 For a detailed description of the Lauro period, see Allum (1973), pp. 274–89.

2 Good in-depth accounts of the Gava machine can be found in Allum (1973), pp. 289–324, and Massimo Caprara, *I Gava* (Milan: Feltrinelli, 1975).

3 The career of Antonio Gava, as well as his continuing hold over key centers of power in Naples, are described in two recent articles in *L'Espresso*. See "In nome di Gava" (November 8, 1977), pp. 46–9, and "Tutto Gava miliardo per miliardo" (November 23, 1980), pp. 275–80.

4 This is contrary to the general pattern in the South, where Communist strength has tended to be concentrated in the countryside and weakest in urban centers.

5 For an in-depth analysis of the 1975 and 1976 votes in Italy, see Arturo Parisi and Gianfranco Pasquino, eds., *Continuità e mutamento elettorale in Italia* (Bologna: Il Mulino, 1977).

6 In 1970 Naples registered 23.6/1,000 still births and 58.9/1,000 deaths in the first year of life, in contrast to national averages of 15.3/1,000 and 29.2/1,000 respectively; in the same year infectious diseases reached a level of 33.8/1,000 in contrast to a national average of 8.3/1,000. ISTAT, *11° Censimento generale della popolazione* (1971).

7 Interview with Andrea Geremicca, PCI assessor of economic planning in the city government and former secretary of the Neapolitan Federation of the PCI (June 26, 1978).

8 For a detailed account of the movement of the "organized unemployed," based on first-hand accounts by participants, see Fabrizia Ramondino, ed., *Napoli: I disoccupati organizzati* (Milan: Feltrinelli, 1977).

9 Caprara (1975), p. 124.

10 "Napoli che si rinnova, Dossier 2" (Naples: Partito Comunista Italiano, 1980).

11 Beginning with protest demonstrations against the city and regional governments, the unemployed turned to blockades of major arteries and occupations, first of the state employment office and subsequently of the local offices of the major political parties, including the PCI. Such an unprecedented move demonstrates the extent to which the unemployed no longer distinguish between the Communist Party and the state in their protest.

12 The most recent demonstration of the insensitivity of the national government to the seriousness of the Neapolitan situation came in the wake of the 1980 earthquake. After a series of increasingly violent demonstrations by the unemployed, whose numbers had been further augmented as a result of the damage inflicted on the local economy by the quake, the minister of labor met at the beginning of March 1981 with representatives of the unemployed and promised 10,000 jobs by June. In exchange for the promise of jobs and of a reform of hiring practices, the unemployed agreed to form a single list at the unemployment office (with over 108,000 signees by the beginning of June). As the deadline approached, however, the minister was obliged to admit that he had "made a mistake" and that there were in fact only a handful of jobs available.

13 Special legislation to promote youth employment was passed with the support of the PCI in 1976. Of the 28,000 jobs created in all of Italy on the basis of this legislation, 6,668 were in the city government of Naples.

14 In 1977 the PCI lost control of two medium-sized cities in the Neapolitan area, Castellammare and Capua, to the DC. The loss of Castellammare was particularly painful for the PCI, which had won 42% of the vote in the previous election, because this is the home base of the Gavas; the result was widely interpreted as a warning of a possible Gava comeback in Naples itself. In those towns and cities that voted in May 1978, the PCI lost 9% with respect to 1976, while the DC gained 3.6%.

15 A prominent Italian political scientist has calculated that 1,000,000-1,500,000 of the PCI's 1976 voters went against the party's orders in the June 1978 referendum. See Giorgio Galli, "Analisi del voto," *La Repubblica* (June 14, 1978).

16 While the DC lost votes in every region of the North in 1979, it gained in seven out of nine southern regions.

17 Antonio Bassolino, "Per capire torniamo al 20 giugno," *Rinascita* (June 22, 1979: 12–13.

18 The pro-repeal vote in June 1978 was strongest in many of the same neighborhoods that had swung the elections for the PCI in 1975 and 1976 (i.e., the middle-class neighborhoods and the old city), while the anti-repeal forces prevailed in the party's traditional strongholds. In 1979, on the contrary, PCI losses were heavy throughout the city, but were concentrated most heavily in the low-income neighborhoods, both working-class and *sottoproletariato*, while the middle-class vote, relatively speaking, remained more loyal.

19 Although the PCI withdrew its support for the government in January 1979, the "historic compromise" continued as the official party line until the beginning of 1980.

20 The objective of the DC was, in a phrase attributed to ex-mayor Bruno Milanesi, "to cook the PCI over a slow fire."

21 Andrea Geremicca, *Dentro la città: Napoli angoscia e speranza* (Naples: Guida Editori, 1977), pp. 142–3.

22 Andrea Geremicca (cited by Franco Giustolisi in "Napoli non è in provincia di Castellammare," *L'Espresso* [May 1, 1977], p. 24).

23 Interview with Andrea Geremicca (June 26, 1978).

24 Data on unemployment and *lavoro nero* from "Economia delle macerie," *Panorama* (December 22, 1980): 56.

25 Maurizio Valenzi, *Sindaco a Napoli* (Rome: Editori Riuniti, 1978), p. 141.

26 According to Ugo Grippo, leader of the DC Left in Naples and head of the DC delegation to the regional assembly, of 88 positions of economic power in Naples, all continued to be held by the DC in 1977, and 65% were concentrated in the hands of the *dorotei*, the faction of the Gavas (cited in Valenzi [1978], p. 141). One of these agencies, the Port Authority, with 11,000 employees, is the second largest employer in Naples, after the city government. The only major source of economic power outside DC control is the Cassa per il Mezzogiorno, claimed by the Socialists when they entered the government in April 1980.

27 For detailed documentation of the economic crisis on the South, see SVIMEZ, *Rapporto sul Mezzogiorno, 1977*.

28 Valenzi (1978), p. 166.

29 Geremicca (1977), p. 144.

30 Rosellina Balbi, "Dove soffia il vento del Sud," *La Repubblica* (June 22, 1977).

31 During the electoral campaign some of the concrete though less visible achievements of the left-wing administration were made public for the first time (for example, reduction of the infant mortality rate by one-half between 1975 and 1980 and construction of 333 kindergarten classrooms in five years as opposed to 210 constructed during the previous thirty years).

32 Campaign speech (June 4, 1980).

33 Valenzi received over 92,000 preference votes, while Almirante, whose party won almost 10% fewer votes than the PCI, received 115,000 preference votes.

34 On April 27, 1981, the Red Brigades kidnapped Ciro Cirillo, the DC regional assessor for urban planning, demanding as the price for his release the requisition of private apartments to house the earthquake victims and the payment of unemployment compensation to all the unemployed. Shortly thereafter the Communist munici-

pal assessor for urban planning was kidnapped, "tried," and knee-capped. Since the quake the terrorists have mounted a major propaganda effort in the temporary camper villages set up for the homeless.

Conclusion

1 The South itself has become increasingly differentiated over the past decade. A recent study by ISVEIMER, "Rapporto 1981 sullo sviluppo economico del Mezzogiorno" reports that since 1976 a process of development has been underway in 12 out of the 34 southern provinces, which in 1980 attained levels of GNP equal to 80% of that of the nonsouthern provinces bordering on the Mezzogiorno. These oases of development, however, do not alter the fact that 10 of the remaining southern provinces have regressed since 1976, while the others have stagnated. (*La Repubblica*, July 26, 1981.)

2 The "assisted" character of southern society is demonstrated by the incidence of pensions which, together with salaries from the public administration and the flow of investment funds and subsidies from the Cassa per il Mezzogiorno, constitute a principal source of income in the South. Although the total value of pensions is lower in the South than in the North (because of the lower rate of labor force participation and the higher levels of *lavoro nero*), the relative weight of pensions is much higher in the South. In 1975 the South, with 34% of the Italian population, received 31% of pensions; because of the factors mentioned above, this was twice the amount the South should have received on the basis of contributions paid into the system. (Raimondo Catanzaro, "Le cinque Sicilie: Disarticolazione sociale e struttura di classe di un'economia dipendente," *Rassegna Italiana di Sociologia* [January–March 1979], pp. 21–2.) This is because of the much greater incidence in the South of *pensioni di invalidità* and *pensioni sociali* (the latter a minimum pension paid to those who reach retirement age without having paid sufficient social-security contributions to receive a regular pension). The following table compares the rates of labor force participation and the levels of *pensioni di invalidità* in one northern industrial region and two southern regions in 1975.

	Rate of labor force participation (in %)	*Pensioni di invalidatà* (as % of total pensions)
Piedmont	40.2	27.1
Calabria	31.1	59.6
Sicily	29.6	54.3
All Italy	35.7	38.0

Source: CENSIS, "Un discorso su Palermo" (Mimeograph: Rome, 1978).

3 In 1965 the gross product of Calabria was 649.0 billion lire, while total consumption was 741.9 billion. This is in contrast to a northern region like Lombardy, where the gross product was 7,793.9 billion and consumption 5,018.0 billion. (Ada Collidà, "Aspetti clientelari," in Marelli, ed., *Sviluppo e sottosviluppo nel Mezzogiorno d'Italia dal 1945 agli anni '70* [1972], p. 208.) A more recent source indicates a gap of almost

1,000 billion lire between gross income and total personal consumption in Sicily (*La Repubblica*, July 29, 1981).

4 Laura Guasti makes a similar argument about the perceived importance of patron–client bonds among low-income Peruvians, even in the absence of any evidence of concrete benefits ("Peru: Clientelism in Decline," in Eisenstadt and Lemarchand, eds., *Political Clientelism, Patronage and Development* [1981]). This argument applies not only to the Christian Democrats but to their coalition partners as well. Thus, both during the period of the Center-Left (1962–72) and since their reentry into the national government majority in 1980, the Socialists have benefited in the South from their association with national power, and their propensity to use that power in much the same way that the Christian Democrats have.

5 The difference in the use of the personal preference vote in the North and the South emerges clearly from the following data. Although since 1968 there has been a decline throughout the country in the use of the preference vote, in 1976 in the Center-North only 26.4% of all possible preference votes were expressed, as opposed to 46.0% in the South. (Richard S. Katz and Luciano Bardi, "Voti di preferenza e ricambio del personale parlamentare in Italia (1963–1976)," *Rivista Italiana di Scienza Politica*, Vol. 9, no. 1 [April 1979]: 76.) These figures support the argument of Parisi and Pasquino, who posit an inverse relationship between the level of political consciousness and the use of the preference vote (*Continuità e mutamento elettorale in Italia* [1977], pp. 215–49).

6 *La Repubblica* (June 19, 1980).

7 *La Repubblica* (June 17, 1980).

8 See Scott, "Corruption, Machine Politics and Political Change" (1969); and Merton (1957), pp. 70–82.

9 F. Vianello, "La DC e lo sviluppo capitalistico in Italia dal dopoguerra a oggi," in F. Vianello et al., *Tutto il potere della DC* (Rome: Coines Edizioni, 1975), p. 43.

Selected bibliography

Books, articles, and papers in English

Allum, Percy (1973). *Politics and Society in Post-War Naples.* Cambridge University Press.

Bachrach, Peter, and Baratz, Morton (1970). *Power and Poverty: Theory and Practice.* New York: Oxford University Press.

Bamberger, Michael (1968). "A Problem of Political Integration in Latin America: The Barrios of Latin America." *International Affairs* (London), 44 (4): 709–19.

Banfield, Edward C. (1961). *Political Influence.* New York: Free Press.

Banfield, Edward C., and Wilson, James Q. (1963). *City Politics.* New York: Vintage Books.

Belmonte, Thomas (1980). *The Broken Fountain.* New York: Columbia University Press.

Berger, Suzanne, and Piore, Michael (1980). *Dualism and Discontinuity in Industrial Societies.* Cambridge University Press.

Blau, Peter (1964). *Exchange and Power in Social Life.* New York: Wiley.

Blok, Anton (1969). "South Italian Agro-Towns." *Comparative Studies in Society and History,* 11: 121–35.

(1975). *The Mafia of a Sicilian Village, 1860–1960.* New York: Harper & Row.

Braudel, Fernand (1972). *The Mediterranean and the Mediterranean World in the Age of Philip II,* 2 vols. New York: Harper & Row.

Chubb, Judith (1975). "The Functions of Economic Marginality: The Case of Italian Industry." Unpublished paper presented at M.I.T.

Cornelius, Wayne A. (1975). *Politics and the Migrant Poor in Mexico City.* Stanford University Press.

Dahl, Robert (1961). *Who Governs?* New Haven: Yale University Press.

Dolci, Danilo (1964). *Waste.* New York: Monthly Review Press.

(1970). *Report from Palermo.* New York: Viking Press.

Eisenstadt, S. N., and Lemarchand, R., eds. (1981). *Political Clientelism, Patronage and Development.* Beverly Hills: Sage.

Epstein, David G. (1973). *Brasilia: Plan and Reality.* Berkeley: University of California Press.

Frankel, Francine R. (1969). "Democracy and Political Development: Perspectives from India." *World Politics,* 21 (3): 448–68.

Graziano, Luigi (1973). "Patron–Client Relationships in Southern Italy." *European Journal of Political Research,* 1 (1): 3–34.

285

(1976). "A Conceptual Framework for the Study of Clientelism." *European Journal of Political Research*, 4 (2): 149–174.

(1978). "Center-Periphery Relations and the Italian Crisis: The Problem of Clientelism." In Sidney Tarrow et al., eds., *Territorial Politics in Industrial Nations*, pp. 290–326. New York: Praeger.

Hilowitz, Jane (1976). *Economic Development and Social Change in Sicily*. Cambridge, Mass.: Schenkman Publishing Co.

Hobsbawm, Eric (1959). *Primitive Rebels*. New York: Norton.

Hunter, Floyd (1953). *Community Power Structure*. Chapel Hill: University of North Carolina Press.

Katznelson, Ira (1973). *Black Men, White Cities*. London: Oxford University Press.

Lampedusa, Giuseppe Tomasi di (1960). *The Leopard*. New York: Pantheon.

Lange, Peter, and Tarrow, Sidney, eds. (1980). *Italy in Transition: Conflict and Consensus*. London: Frank Cass.

La Palombara, Joseph (1964). *Interest Groups in Italian Politics*. Princeton University Press.

Leeds, Anthony, and Leeds, Elizabeth (1976). "Accounting for Behavioral Differences: Three Political Systems and the Responses of Squatters in Brazil, Peru and Chile." In John Walton and Louis H. Masotti, eds., *The City in Comparative Perspective*, pp. 193–247. Beverly Hills: Sage.

Leeds, Elizabeth (1972). "Forms of 'Squatment' Political Organization: The Politics of Control in Brazil." M.A. Thesis. University of Texas.

Lewis, Oscar (1961). *The Children of Sanchez*. New York: Random House.

(1965). *La Vida*. New York: Random House.

Lipsky, Michael (1970). *Protest in City Politics*. Chicago: Rand McNally.

Lyttelton, Adrian (1973). *The Seizure of Power: Fascism in Italy, 1919–1929*. London: Weidenfeld and Nicolson.

McGee, T. G. (1974). "The Persistence of the Proto-Proletariat." Comparative Urbanization Studies, University of California at Los Angeles (April).

Merton, Robert K. (1957). *Social Theory and Social Structure*. New York: Free Press.

Mills, C. Wright (1956). *The Power Elite*. New York: Oxford University Press.

Nelson, Joan M. (1979). *Access to Power: Politics and the Urban Poor in Developing Nations*. Princeton University Press.

Olson, Mancur (1968). *The Logic of Collective Action*. New York: Schocken Books.

Pantaleone, Michele (1966). *The Mafia and Politics*. London: Chatto and Windus.

Peattie, Lisa (1975). "Tertiarization and Urban Poverty in Latin America." In W. A. Cornelius and F. M. Trueblood, eds., *Urbanization and Inequality: The Political Economy of Urban and Rural Development in Latin America*, pp. 109–24. Beverly Hills: Sage.

Perlman, Janice E. (1976). *The Myth of Marginality: Urban Poverty and Politics in Rio de Janeiro*. Berkeley: University of California Press.

Podbielski, Gisele (1978). *Twenty-Five Years of Special Action for the Development of Southern Italy*. Milan: Giuffrè Editore.

Purcell, John F. H., and Purcell, Susan Kaufman (1976). "Machine Politics and Socio-Economic Change in Mexico." In James W. Wilkie et al., eds., *Contemporary Mexico*, pp. 348–66. Berkeley: University of California Press.

Rosenbaum, Allan (1973). "Machine Politics, Class Interest and the Urban Poor." Paper presented to the Annual Meeting of the American Political Science Association (New Orleans, September 4–8).

Schmidt, Steffen W., et al., eds. (1977). *Friends, Followers and Factions: A Reader in Political Clientelism*. Berkeley: University of California Press.

Scott, James C. (1969). "Corruption, Machine Politics and Political Change." *American Political Science Review*, 63 (4): 1142–58.

(1972). "Patron–Client Politics and Political Change in Southeast Asia." *American Political Science Review*, 66 (1): 91–113.

Servadio, Gaia (1976). *Mafioso*. New York: Dell.

Shefter, Martin (1972). "The Electoral Foundations of the Political Machine." Unpublished paper presented at Cornell University.

(1976). "The Emergence of the Political Machine: An Alternative View." In Willis D. Hawley et al., *Theoretical Perspectives on Urban Politics*, pp. 14–44. Englewood Cliffs, N.J.: Prentice-Hall.

Smith, Dennis Mack (1959). *Italy: A Modern History*. Ann Arbor: University of Michigan Press.

(1968). *A History of Sicily*, 2 vols. London: Chatto and Windus.

Tannenbaum, Edward R. (1972). *The Fascist Experience: Italian Society and Culture, 1922–1945*. New York: Basic Books.

Tarrow, Sidney (1967). *Peasant Communism in Southern Italy*. New Haven: Yale University Press.

(1977). *Between Center and Periphery: Grassroots Politicians in Italy and France*. New Haven: Yale University Press.

Weiner, Myron (1967). *Party-Building in a New Nation: The Indian National Congress*. University of Chicago Press.

Wolfinger, Raymond E. (1972). "Why Political Machines Have Not Faded Away and Other Revisionist Thoughts." *Journal of Politics*, 34 (2): 365–98.

Zuckerman, Alan S. (1979). *The Politics of Faction: Christian Democratic Rule in Italy*. New Haven: Yale University Press.

Books and articles in Italian and French

Ancisi, Alvaro (1976). *La cattura del voto: Sociologia del voto di preferenza*. Milan: Franco Angeli.

Ariotti, Roberto (1971). "Pretese corporativistiche ed esigenze di sviluppo nella programmazione del commercio." *Il Mulino*, no. 216 (July–August): 611–36.

Arlacchi, Pino (1980). "Mafia e tipi di società." *Rassegna Italiana di Sociologia* (January–March): 3–49.

Barrese, Orazio (1973). *I complici: Gli anni dell'Antimafia*. Milan: Feltrinelli.

Bassolino, Antonio (1979). "Per capire torniamo al 20 giugno." *Rinascita* (June 22): 12–13.

Bonazzi, S., Bagnasco, A., and Casillo, S. (1972). *Industria e potere in una provincia meridionale*. Turin: L'Impresa Edizioni.

Caciagli, Mario et al. (1977). *Democrazia Cristiana e potere nel Mezzogiorno*. Florence: Guaraldi.

Cafiero, Salvatore (1976). *Sviluppo industriale e questione urbana nel Mezzogiorno*. Milan: Giuffrè Editore.

Caizzi, Bruno, ed. (1975). *Nuova antologia della questione meridionale*. Milan: Edizioni di Comunità.

Capecelatro, E., and Carlo, A. (1972). *Contro la questione meridionale*. Rome: Samonà e Savelli.

Caprara, Massimo (1975). *I Gava*. Milan: Feltrinelli.

Carocci, Giampiero (1971). *Giolitti e l'età giolittiana*. Turin: Einaudi.

Cassano, Franco (1979). *Il teorema democristiano*. Bari: De Donato.

Catanzaro, Raimondo (1975). "Potere e politica locale in Italia." *Quaderni di Sociologia*, 24 (October–December), pp. 273–322.

(1979). "Le cinque Sicilie: Disarticolazione sociale e struttura di classe in un'economia dipendente." *Rassegna Italiana di Sociologia* (January–March): 7–35.

Catanzaro, Raimondo, et al. (1979). *L'Imprenditore assistito*. Bologna: Il Mulino.

Colajanni, Napoleone (1971). *Nel regno della mafia*. Palermo: Renzo Mazzone.

Collidà, Ada (1972). "Aspetti clientelari dell'intervento straordinario nel Mezzogiorno." In Luigi Marelli, ed., *Sviluppo e sottosviluppo nel Mezzogiorno d'Italia dal 1945 agli anni '70*, pp. 182–7. Naples: Morano Editore.

Dolci, Danilo (1967) *Chi gioca solo*. Turin: Einaudi.

Donolo, Carlo (1972). "Sviluppo ineguale e disgregazione sociale: Note per l'analisi delle classi nel meridione." *Quaderni Piacentini*, no. 47 (July): 101–28.

Dorso, Guido (1969). *La rivoluzione meridionale*. Turin: Mondadori.

Esposito, Gennaro (1973). *Anche il colera: Gli untori di Napoli*. Milan: Feltrinelli.

Franchetti, Leopoldo, and Sonnino, Sidney (1974). *Inchiesta in Sicilia*, 2 vols. Florence: Vallecchi.

Galasso, Giuseppe (1978). *Intervista sulla storia di Napoli*. Bari: Laterza.

Geremicca, Andrea (1977). *Dentro la città: Napoli angoscia e speranza*. Naples: Guida Editori.

Gorrieri, Ermanno (1972). *La giungla retributiva*. Bologna: Il Mulino.

Grammatico, Dino (1974). *Processo alla Regione Siciliana*. Milan: Edizioni del Borghese.

Gramsci, Antonio (1966). "Alcuni temi della quistione meridionale." In *La questione meridionale*, pp. 131–60. Rome: Editori Riuniti.

Graziano, Luigi (1975). "Partito di regime e clientelismo di massa." *Rinascita* (August 8): 14–15.

   (1980). *Clientelismo e sistema politico: Il caso dell'Italia*. Milan: Franco Angeli.

Grosso, Claudio (1973). "Per una storia della Cassa per il Mezzogiorno." *Quaderni Siciliani* (October): 41–63.

Hess, Henner (1973). *Mafia*. Bari: Laterza.

Hytten, E., and Marchioni, M. (1970). *L'industrializzazione senza sviluppo: Gela, una storia meridionale*. Milan: Franco Angeli.

La Malfa, Giorgio, and Vinci, Salvatore (1972). "Disoccupazione palese e disoccupazione nascosta." In A. Graziani, ed., *L'economia italiana, 1945–1970*, pp. 331–6. Bologna: Il Mulino.

Mazzacane, Lello, ed. (1978). *I "bassi" a Napoli*. Naples: Guida Editori.

Menapace, Lidia (1975). *La Democrazia Cristiana: Natura, struttura e organizzazione*. Milan: Gabriele Mazzotta Editore.

Molfese, Franco (1964). *Storia del brigantaggio dopo l'unità*. Milan: Feltrinelli.

Orfei, Ruggero (1976). *L'occupazione del potere: I democristiani '45/'75*. Milan: Longanesi.

Paci, Massimo (1973). *Mercato del lavoro e classi sociali in Italia*. Bologna: Il Mulino.

Pantaleone, Michele (1969). *Antimafia: Occasione mancata*. Turin: Einaudi.

Parisi, Arturo, ed. (1979). *I democristiani*. Bologna: Il Mulino.

Parisi, Arturo, and Pasquino, Gianfranco, eds. (1977). *Continuità e mutamento elettorale in Italia*. Bologna: Il Mulino.

Pizzorno, Alessandro (1974). "I ceti medi nei meccanismi del consenso." In Fabio Luca Cavazza and Stephen Graubard, eds., *Il caso italiano*, pp. 315–38. Milan: Garzanti.

Pumilia, P., and Buscemi, M. (1971). *Il volto di una classe dirigente: Uomini e responsabilità nella realtà ESPI*. Palermo: Centro Regionale Studi CISL.

Ramondino, Fabrizia, ed. (1977). *Napoli: I disoccupati organizzati*. Milan: Feltrinelli.

Rochefort, Renée (1958). "Les bas-fonds de Palerme." *Annales, Economies, Sociétés, Civilisations* (April–June), pp. 349–58.

   (1961). *Le travail en Sicile*. Paris: Presses Universitaires de France.

Rossi-Doria, Manlio (1948). *Riforma agraria e azione meridionalistica*. Bologna: Edizioni Agricole.

Saladino, Giuliana (1972). *De Mauro: Una cronaca palermitana*. Milan: Feltrinelli.
Salomone, W. A. (1949). *L'età giolittiana*. Turin: De Silva.
Sylos-Labini, Paolo (1975). *Saggio sulle classi sociali*. Bari: Laterza.
Torrato, Tiberio (1970). "Valvassori e Valvassini: Comuni e bottegai." *Il Mulino*, no. 207 (January–February): 114–16.
Valenzi, Maurizio (1978). *Sindaco a Napoli*. Rome: Editori Riuniti.
Vianello, F., et al. (1975). *Tutto il potere della DC*. Rome: Coines Edizioni.
Villari, Rosario, ed. (1972). *Il Sud nella storia d'Italia*, 2 vols. Bari: Laterza.
Vinci, Salvatore, ed. (1974). *Il mercato del lavoro in Italia*. Milan: Franco Angeli.
Vitale, P. Ignazio (1972). "Un caso di sottosviluppo: L'analfabeta della porta accanto." *Notiziario IRFIS*, no. 31 (April).

Primary sources in Italian

CENSIS (1978). "Un discorso su Palermo." Rome: mimeograph.
Comitato Provinciale INPS Palermo (1974). *Annotazioni sulla situazione socio-economica della Provincia di Palermo*. Palermo: Author.
Comune di Napoli. *Bollettino di Statistica* (annual statistical bulletin). Naples: Author.
Comune di Palermo. *Panormus* (annual statistical bulletin). Palermo: Author.
IRFIS (1974). "IRFIS vent'anni, 1954–1973." *Notiziario IRFIS*, no. 34 (April).
ISTAT (1951). 3° Censimento dell'industria e del commercio. Rome: Author.
  (1961). 4° Censimento dell'industria e del commercio. Rome: Author.
  (1971). 5° Censimento dell'industria e del commercio. Rome: Author.
  (1951). 9° Censimento generale della popolazione. Rome: Author.
  (1961). 10° Censimento generale della popolazione. Rome: Author.
  (1971). 11° Censimento generale della popolazione. Rome: Author.
Mafia e potere politico: Relazione di minoranza e proposte unitarie della commissione parlamentare d'inchiesta sulla mafia (1976). Rome: Editori Riuniti.
Partito Comunista Italiano (1980). *Napoli che si rinnova: Dossier 2*. Naples: Sezione Stampa e Propaganda.
Relazione Bevivino (report to the president of the Region by the *commissione per l'ispezione straordinaria presso il Comune di Palermo*), February 13, 1964. Palermo: Mimeograph.
Senato della Repubblica (1974). *Commissione parlamentare d'inchiesta sul fenomeno della mafia in Sicilia, Relazione Conclusiva* (February 4). Rome: Author.
SVIMEZ (Associazione per lo sviluppo dell'industria nel Mezzogiorno). *Rapporto sul Mezzogiorno* (annual publication). Rome: Author.
Testo integrale della relazione della commissione parlamentare d'inchiesta sul fenomeno della mafia, 3 vols. (1973). Rome: Cooperativa Scrittori.

Newspapers and newsweeklies

Corriere della sera (Milan)
Giornale di Sicilia (Palermo)
La Repubblica (Rome)
L'Espresso
L'Ora (Palermo)
Panorama

Index

Allum, Percy, 77
Almirante, Giorgio, 240, 242, 283n33
Antimafia Commission, 143–4, 146–7
artisans, see traditional middle classes

bourgeoisie, southern, see middle class
bureaucracy: inefficiency of, 100–1, 174–5; politicization of, 90–1, 174–5; techniques of patronage hiring and promotion, 95–9; and the urban poor, 174–5, 207; see also public employees; regional government

Cassa per il Mezzogiorno, 77, 139, 266n1; economic impact of, 28–9; expenditure of, 266n2; investment strategy of, 30–1; and political patronage 32–3, 74; see also development, failure of
CGIL, 106, 107, 108; see also unions
child labor, 52–4
Christian Democratic Party (DC): and the banking system, 120, 275n16; and the Cassa per il Mezzogiorno, 32–3; and the construction industry, see construction industry; factional struggle, 66, 146–9, 215; and the mafia, 57–8, 139–42, 143–51; membership, 65; in Naples, 219–20, 234–5, 238, 240, 242, 282n26; organizational structure, 64–6, 73, 164; political strategy vis-à-vis middle class, 84–5, 87–8, 108–9; relationship with Catholic Church, 56, 61, 166; and right-wing political movements, 57–61, 68–9; and secondary associations, 73–4, 166–7, 206–7; and traditional clienteles, 57–9; and the urban poor, see urban poor
Church, Catholic: and Fascist regime, 56; political role of, 61, 165–6; referendum on divorce, 223

Ciancimino, Vito, 133, 144–50
CISL, 70, 73, 106, 107, 108, 207; see also unions
city, southern Italian: historical development, 34–6; industrial structure, 40–5; labor market, 37–9, 266n3, 267n20; postwar urbanization, 36–7; see also tertiary sector
clientelism: and dependency, 246–7, 283n2; and economic crisis, 214, 239–40, 247–8; incentive structure, 211–12; links to national power, 214–15, 238, 250; nature of bond, 167, 214; resource base, 212–14; and underdevelopment, 215–16, 246, 251–2
Coltivatori Diretti, 73, 206–7
Communist Party (PCI): causes of electoral victory in Naples, 221–5; electoral results, 1977–1980, 230–3, 240–2, 282n18; "historic compromise," 188, 234–5; and middle class, 223–4, 233; and "organized unemployed" in Naples, 227–9; policies of left-wing administration in Naples, 225–9; and public employees, 99, 105–6; reasons for weakness in southern Italy, 248–9; relationship with mass base in Naples, 235–6; and urban decentralization, 236–7; and the urban poor, 164–5, 209, 224–5, 227–9, 233, 236; see also protest movements
construction industry: and the mafia, 140–50; structure of, 43–45; ties to DC, 68, 129–38, 156–8
Crispi, Francesco, 20

De Gasperi, Alcide, 61, 62
Democrazia Cristiana (DC), see Christian Democratic Party
De Pretis, Agostino, 19
development, failure of, 28–33, 111–12, 115–16, 119, 215–16, 246–7, 251,

as patronage resource, 172–3, 194; political behavior of inhabitants, 199–202; and speculation, 131–2, 193

questione meridionale, see Southern Question

regional government, 36, 61, 69, 213; and job patronage, 94–5, 100, 273n18; privileged treatment of employees, 103–4; subsidies and credit to private enterprise, 117–19, 121
Restivo, Franco, 61, 63–4, 100, 130
Right, *see* Monarchists; MSI; Uomo Qualunque
risanamento, see urban renewal
Risorgimento, *see* unification, Italian
Ruffini, Cardinal Ernesto, 130, 132, 166

Salvemini, Gaetano, 20
Scaduto, Francesco, 130, 132
Scaglione, Pietro, 150
Separtism, Sicilian, 57
shopkeepers, *see* traditional middle classes
Sicilian Region, *see* regional government
sottoproletariato, see urban poor
Southern Question: economic basis of, 15–18, 24, 264–5n2; political basis of, 19–24
speculation, real estate, *see* construction industry; mafia; urban expansion
state intervention in the South, *see* Cassa per il Mezzogiorno
Sturzo, Luigi, 56

Tarrow, Sidney, 17, 73, 77
tertiary sector; functions of, 47–8; structure of 46–7
traditional middle classes: and DC, 123–7, 173; stabilization function of, 85–6,

112, 122–3; trade associations, 125–7; see also middle class
trasformismo, 19–21, 25, 27; and local government in southern Italy, 22–4

unemployment: and left-wing administration in Naples, *see* "organized unemployed"; *see also* city, southern Italian, labor market
unification, Italian, 15–16, 19, 22; impact on southern economy, 16–17, 264–5n2; political basis of, 16
unions: and "organized unemployed" in Naples, 228; and public employees, 96–7, 106–8; *see also* CGIL; CISL
Uomo Qualunque, 57, 58, 84, 273n3
urban expansion: and building speculation, 128–38; and DC power, 149, 156–8; and the mafia, *see* mafia
urban poor: attitude toward the state, 165; and the Catholic Church, 165–6, 205; conditions of life, 49–54, 159–64, 178–9, 196–9, 203–5; and the Left, 164–5, 188, 199–202, 209; links to local political power, 167–77, 206–7; and the mafia, *see* mafia; in the pre-industrial city, 35–6; support for the Left in Naples, 224–5; and urban struggles, 180–93, 194–5, 200–2, 208–9; *see also* "organized unemployed"
urban renewal, 152–6, 182, 185, 189–190, 193
urban social movements, *see* protest movements

Valenzi, Maurizio, 238, 239–40, 282n33
Vassallo, Francesco, 135–8

working class: characteristics of in southern Italy, 40–5; political role in Naples, 43, 221, 224

For EU product safety concerns, contact us at Calle de José Abascal, 56–1°,
28003 Madrid, Spain or eugpsr@cambridge.org.

www.ingramcontent.com/pod-product-compliance
Ingram Content Group UK Ltd.
Pitfield, Milton Keynes, MK11 3LW, UK
UKHW042154130625

459647UK00011B/1327